ISHMAEL

HARPER TORCHBOOKS / The Cloister Library

(continued on next page)

HARPER TORCHBOOKS / The Science Library

Arthur Eddington	SPACE, TIME AND GRAVITATION : *An Outline of the General Relativity Theory* TB/510
Alexander Findlay	CHEMISTRY IN THE SERVICE OF MAN. Illus. TB/524
D. E. Littlewood	THE SKELETON KEY OF MATHEMATICS TB/525
J. R. Partington	A SHORT HISTORY OF CHEMISTRY. Illus. TB/522
H. T. Pledge	SCIENCE SINCE 1500 : *A Short History of Mathematics, Physics, Chemistry, and Biology.* Illus. TB/506
John Read	A DIRECT ENTRY TO ORGANIC CHEMISTRY. Illus. TB/523
George Sarton	ANCIENT SCIENCE AND MODERN CIVILIZATION TB/501
Paul A. Schilpp, *ed.*	ALBERT EINSTEIN : *Philosopher-Scientist : Vol. I,* TB/502 ; *Vol. II,* TB/503
O. G. Sutton	MATHEMATICS IN ACTION. Foreword by James R. Newman. Illus. TB/518
Stephen Toulmin	THE PHILOSOPHY OF SCIENCE : *An Introduction* TB/513
A. G. Van Melsen	FROM ATOMOS TO ATOM : *The History of the Concept* Atom TB/517
Friedrich Waismann	INTRODUCTION TO MATHEMATICAL THINKING TB/511
W. H. Watson	ON UNDERSTANDING PHYSICS : *An Analysis of the Philosophy of Physics.* Intro. by Ernest Nagel TB/507
G. J. Whitrow	THE STRUCTURE AND EVOLUTION OF THE UNIVERSE : *An Introduction to Cosmology.* Illus. TB/504
A. Wolf	A HISTORY OF SCIENCE, TECHNOLOGY AND PHILOSOPHY IN THE 16TH AND 17TH CENTURIES. Illus. *Vol. I,* TB/508 ; *Vol. II,* TB/509

HARPER TORCHBOOKS / The Academy Library

James Baird	ISHMAEL : *A Study of the Symbolic Mode in Primitivism* TB/1023
Henri Bergson	TIME AND FREE WILL : *An Essay on the Immediate Data of Consciousness* TB/1021
H. J. Blackham	SIX EXISTENTIALIST THINKERS : *Kierkegaard, Jaspers, Nietzsche, Marcel, Heidegger, Sartre* TB/1002
Walter Bromberg	THE MIND OF MAN : *A History of Psychotherapy and Psychoanalysis* TB/1003
G. G. Coulton	MEDIEVAL VILLAGE, MANOR, AND MONASTERY TB/1020
Editors of *Fortune*	AMERICA IN THE SIXTIES : *The Economy and the Society* TB/1015
G. P. Gooch	ENGLISH DEMOCRATIC IDEAS IN THE SEVENTEENTH CENTURY TB/1006
Francis J. Grund	ARISTOCRACY IN AMERICA : *A Study of Jacksonian Democracy* TB/1001
W. K. C. Guthrie	THE GREEK PHILOSOPHERS : *From Thales to Aristotle.* TB/1008
Henry James	THE PRINCESS CASAMASSIMA : A Novel TB/1005
Henry James	RODERICK HUDSON : A Novel. Intro. by Leon Edel TB/1016
Henry James	THE TRAGIC MUSE : A Novel. Intro. by Leon Edel TB/1017
Arnold Kettle	AN INTRODUCTION TO THE ENGLISH NOVEL : *Vol. I, Defoe to George Eliot,* TB/1011 ; *Vol. II, Henry James to the Present,* TB/1012
L. S. B. Leakey	ADAM'S ANCESTORS : *The Evolution of Man and His Culture.* Illus. TB/1019
Arthur O. Lovejoy	THE GREAT CHAIN OF BEING : *A Study of the History of an Idea* TB/1009
J. P. Mayer	ALEXIS DE TOCQUEVILLE : *A Biographical Study in Political Science* TB/1014
John U. Nef	CULTURAL FOUNDATIONS OF INDUSTRIAL CIVILIZATION TB/1024
Samuel Pepys	THE DIARY OF SAMUEL PEPYS : Selections, ed. by O. F. Morshead ; illus. by Ernest H. Shepard TB/1007
Georges Poulet	STUDIES IN HUMAN TIME TB/1004
Priscilla Robertson	REVOLUTIONS OF 1848 : *A Social History* TB/1025
Ferdinand Schevill	THE MEDICI. Illus. TB/1010
Bruno Snell	THE DISCOVERY OF THE MIND : *The Greek Origins of European Thought* TB/1018
W. H. Walsh	PHILOSOPHY OF HISTORY : *An Introduction* TB/1020
W. Lloyd Warner	SOCIAL CLASS IN AMERICA : *The Evaluation of Status* TB/1013

ISHMAEL

A Study of the Symbolic Mode in Primitivism

JAMES BAIRD

HARPER TORCHBOOKS / The Academy Library

HARPER & BROTHERS   NEW YORK

HARPER TORCHBOOKS / *The Academy Library*
Advisory Editor in the Humanities and Social Sciences: Benjamin Nelson

ISHMAEL: A Study of the Symbolic Mode in Primitivism

Copyright © 1956, The Johns Hopkins Press

Printed in the United States of America

First published in 1956 by The Johns Hopkins Press, Baltimore, and reprinted by arrangement.

First HARPER TORCHBOOK edition published 1960

Library of Congress catalog card number: 56-8064

TO N. J. B.

AND IN MEMORY OF

C. O'C. B.

We have let the house that our fathers
built fall to pieces, and now we try to
break into Oriental palaces that our
fathers never knew.

Carl Gustav Jung

Contents

Introduction

Apologists for the practice of criticism during the last two or three decades of American literary history have variously spoken of the age as distinguished by great critical literature. It may be so. But the superlatives cannot very much matter. At its highest reach criticism can never be more than secondary art. It is the indentured servitor; and its justifiable claim to distinction may rest only in its maximum of service. In the severe estimation of the master, the number of the ways of criticism into the problems of literary art and the thoroughness of its performance alone count, not its measurement of its own inherent greatness. This would seem to be immutable truth regarding the nature of criticism.

Thus, it is a most curious circumstance that T. S. Eliot, upon whom much of recent criticism has waxed to greatness, should have proposed an extension of critical service in the twentieth century which has been minimized. Eliot had in mind the question of " allegiances " in the creating artist. His proposal was advanced in " The Function of Criticism " in 1923:

> I thought of literature then, as I think of it now, of the literature of the world, of the literature of Europe, of the literature of a single country, not as a collection of the writings of individuals, but as " organic wholes," *as systems in relation to which, and only in relation to which, individual works of literary art, and the works of individual artists, have their significance.* There is accordingly something outside of the artist to which he owes his allegiance, a devotion to which he must surrender and sacrifice himself in order to earn and obtain his unique position. A common inheritance and a common cause unite artists consciously or unconsciously: it must be admitted that the union is mostly unconscious. Between the true artists of any time there is, I believe, an unconscious community. [Italics mine.]

Comparison and analysis, he continued, are the tools of the critic; and one fact produced about a work is more valuable than nine-tenths of "the most pretentious critical journalism." It follows, in the nature of Eliot's view, that the investigation of organic wholes in literary history is a vital function of criticism.

I take it that an organic whole, in Eliot's sense, may be defined as *a multiple system of literature demonstrating through forms of symbolic expression, which are singularly developed, a uniform allegiance to a subject idea.** Symbols exist invariably within larger symbols. The system to which the symbol belongs is an aggregate of symbolic parts. Criticism must deal in relevance, both in the interdependences of subject ideas in the individual work and in the relationships of separate works encompassed by the organic whole. The subject of this book is the nature of modern primitivism. Literary history may describe the outer nature of this system of literature appearing through the last century of Western civilization; it may do so by the disciplines of biography, or those of bibliography and historiography. But it cannot describe elements of form without critical methodology, since criticism is alone appropriate to the analysis of symbols as the forms of art.

This introduction intends to set into clear relief the premises of the study at hand. It is not designed as comment upon schools of criticism. But one must be considerably dismayed by the expenditure of so much energy on the part of recent critics to deny the intention of the artist and to disavow the authority of the unconscious community in which he was involved. For these conditions and the particularity of his own sentient being formed the matrix of his art. Criticism alone can describe the artistic nature of this community because, unlike the discipline of literary history, it may properly concern itself with one of the supreme functions of studious (as differentiated from creative) art: the direction of comparison among the texts of literature, the arrangement of literature in such a pattern of juxtaposition that the greatest of all criticism may appear, the comment of art

---

* The Graeco-Roman symbolic reference of French and English poetry in the late Renaissance may be thought of here as an organic whole.

upon art. The organic wholes of literature, the systems to which Eliot refers, may be defined only through the critical act of freeing the critical power inherent in literature.

The range of this power may be suggested in two statements of fact apparent in the nature of literature: *literature in its very continuity interprets its own past; literature, arranged comparatively, constantly criticizes literature.* In illustration of the first fact, I propose here that Joseph Conrad's *Heart of Darkness* will speak more authoritatively upon the meaning of primitivism in the novels of Herman Melville than the most adroit critical interpretation of these novels; in explanation of the second, I submit that if one seeks to grasp the essential meaning of existence on the island of Anopopei in Norman Mailer's *The Naked and the Dead*, the fictions of Jean-Paul Sartre, read in relation to Mailer's subject ideas, will provide more " insight " than professional criticism is able to provide.

Criticism is forever humanistic rather than scientific. It is emotively informed and temperamentally conditioned. History shows us that works of art are essentially impervious to stain, no matter how frequently they are washed in the dyes of sequent sensibilities. Perhaps the only logical reason we have for talking endlessly of " masterpieces " is simply that the masterpiece is the work of art possessing whiteness, the all-inclusive property in which every color is contained. It will match itself to the hue of any sensibility; and it shows again and again in the history of readings from criticism that its meaning exists absolutely only in terms of the sensibility in which it was approached. The more pure the property of white, the more claim to the immortality of the work. Criticism cannot aspire to absolute authority because it cannot escape the sensibility of the individual critic. In its choice of works for study and in its final judgments of the value of these works, it has to content itself with aesthetic relativism. It can, however, answer one requirement which is usually thought to apply only to literary history, textual emendation, and semantics; it may add constantly, if it pleases, to the known facts of both genesis and form. For this undertaking criticism must extend itself to encompass any and

all means of study at its disposal. Within the limits of its service
to literature, it must get on with the job of collecting the facts
of the sensibilities which produced the systems, the unconscious
communities where the allegiances of artistic makers and doers
(not critical interpreters) eternally rest.

The way toward an extension of fact to serve the reading of
organic wholes in literature lies in the analysis and comparison
of symbolic forms. A group of representative symbols, each
singularly developed or cast by the individual artist, describes
the system to which each artist involved owes his allegiance.
Several groups or clusters of symbols express what has been
" going on " or what " goes on " in literature. They force into
terms the material of art hinted at by the schools of literary
history, hints such as those of the old Prussian *Zeitgeist*, or *le
moment* in the sense of Taine, or the even less specific " intellectual climate." In these the authority of literary history col-
lapses and criticism must take over.

A *Zeitgeist* is an amorphous body of systems, each of which,
particularly in the literature of the last one hundred years with
its conscious projection of the " symbolic " style, requires critical analysis. The function of criticism begins where that of
literary history ends: its obligation at this point is a relentless
sounding of the material from which symbols are formed; from
the soundings and samplings it may proceed to describe the
structure of the system toward which the symbols are oriented.
Thus the processes of criticism in the analysis of symbols become rather more complex than the acts of literary history in
defining the supremacy of taste, as, for example, in its brilliant
forays through the phenomena of neoclassicism. The complexity of the task has, of course, nothing whatever to do with
the value of the result. Very probably the achievement of criticism in the precarious business of reading symbols as emblems
of universal systems lags in value at least a century behind the
attainment of literary history.

Much of the difficulty attendant upon justifying studies of the
literary symbol stems from some inherent hostility in critical
theory toward accepting *modulations* in the idiom of literature.

It is clear that shifts in sensibility determine shifts in taste. But the history of taste, which is properly subject to the study of the literary or aesthetic historian, is the record of modes of social behavior and the reflections of these modes in artistic form. It may preserve, for example, a great many memorials to taste demonstrated in the experimental use of metrics, as we say that Samuel Daniel's essay on rhyme investigates certain properties of Elizabethan English in relation to current theories of prosody. It may propose, as it does in the criticism of Coleridge, that the great problem of the poet is one of surmounting the seeming inadequacies of language itself (for the inclination of both Wordsworth and Coleridge as theorists is a preponderant doubt of what language can represent in poetic usage). But this history of taste does not concern itself with symbolistic representation; for a symbol in art is a structure of the imagination which rises to supplant language itself in describing a feeling which language cannot describe. The symbol obviously depends upon the medium of the artist for its form. What it accomplishes, however, is an extension of meaning emotively far richer than any representational pattern which taste can provide. Even as the words which contain it are symbols, so it shapes from these words a structure transcending the nature of language itself.

Strictly speaking, in genuine symbolism there is no such thing as a " taste for symbols." Susanne K. Langer, in *Feeling and Form* (1953), defines a symbol as " any device whereby we are enabled to make an abstraction." But she also declares that " the artistic symbol, *qua* artistic, negotiates insight, not reference; it does not rest upon convention, but motivates and dictates conventions." Two examples from the plays of Ibsen may be useful here: General Gabler's pistols, and the white horse in *Rosmersholm*. Both are referential and conventional, even though they are capable of abstraction. They are bound to convention, in this case the aggregate values of the society investigated by the dramatist. They rest finally upon taste and are actually representational dramatic devices rather than symbols. They are not instances of a modulation in idiom since they

depend upon the conventions, the customs of society from which
the entire range of Ibsen's dramaturgy is constructed.

*A modulation in idiom occurs only when art is confronted
with an inheritance of exhausted symbols which can no longer
describe the belief or feeling antecedent to the forms of art.*
In the history of literature there can have been only a few such
modulations. The meaning of existence is dimly heard in a
new tonality. The symbols which formerly established and
perpetuated the conventions to which taste constantly refers are
found to have spent their energy. The modulation begins at the
moment when new symbols, to supplant the old, begin to take
form.

Mrs. Langer noted in her introduction to a study of the
symbolic mode in philosophy (1942) that "as every shift of
tonality gives a new sense to previous passages [i. e., in music],
so the reorientation of philosophy which is taking place in our
age bestows new aspects on the ideas and arguments of the
past." In the study of primitivism which I have undertaken in
this book, I have extended her description of the "new key"
to suggest that modulations in the symbolic structure of literature, as new symbols are substituted for old, initially compel
regression to primordial, as opposed to "civilized," forms. The
material for the symbol of the new key is taken from a state of
human existence which is prototypic, unsophisticated, and, in
some respects, universal for man. The act of forming the new
symbol gets back to the *need for symbolization*, the symbol-
making function which, in Mrs. Langer's view, is one of man's
primary activities, "like eating, looking, or moving about."
It gets back to what she calls the most characteristic mental
trait of the human being, the power of understanding symbols,
i. e., "of regarding everything about a sense-datum as irrelevant
except a certain *form* that it embodies." This power issues in
the unconscious, spontaneous process of *abstraction*. The refine-
ment of this reasoning upon the origins of symbols emerges in
her recent *Feeling and Form* as her definition of art: "the
creation of forms symbolic of human feeling." All the forms of
art are abstracted forms. They present semblances and pure

appearances freed from the context " of real circumstance and anxious interest." The only addition which I need to make, for my own purposes, to these indispensable readings of the new key is a simple one: since man, in this case represented by the literary artist, will make new symbols for abstracting the meaning of existence when old symbols will no longer serve him —will do so even as he breathes and eats because he must—the description of the material which he compels into these new symbols must be undertaken by criticism.

It has already been said that symbols exist within symbols. The title of this book is the name of the symbol of modern authentic primitivism: Ishmael, the aggregate of the symbols representing this system in the recent literature of the Western world. That Herman Melville should appear in these chapters as the chief redactor of the system is a circumstance which is certainly more inevitable than " American." As far as our knowledge of organic wholes in recent art is concerned, *Moby-Dick* might as well be Norwegian. Because of the nature of my study, I am more particularly concerned with Melville's relation to the modulation of idiom which engendered the literature of primitivism than I am with his place in the canon of American letters. Melville, the artist, is a supreme example of the artistic creator engaged in the act of making new symbols to replace the " lost " symbols of Protestant Christianity. Here, in preference to attempting yet another study of this man in exclusive relation to the ideas which his work contains—a method which, at this juncture in American criticism, seems to have been exhausted of nearly all its possibilities—I have chosen to set him among the authors of primitivism who were his contemporaries and successors, with whom he belongs in a community of allegiance to a system. It was his peculiar fate to have to write in a new key. In using Melville as the chief exemplar of the system, I have in mind the following premises which I take to be fact: of American poets and novelists of the last one hundred years he is the most religiously impelled; among his contemporaries, both English and European, who are subsumed in the community of mind of which modern primitivism was born, he is of supreme importance; and of all writers encompassed in the form of modern primitivism, he is the most useful for a study of symbolism and the Protestant mind. To hope that a study of him in recognition of these facts will also serve the critical estimate of his position as an American author is to suggest a second purpose for this book.

Much has already been written, much more will be written of Melville's real contribution to American myth, and of his reflection of myth already existing when he began to write. But I cannot see that American myth, new or inherited, will ever be sufficient for a critical examination of formal elements in Melville's symbols. The White Whale owes his origin, in part, to Owen Chase's renowned account of the fate of the *Essex,* sunk in the mid-Pacific in 1820 by a vindictive sperm whale, and to the American myth of Mocha Dick following upon that disaster. But in his symbolic elements Moby Dick is related to an international group of symbols, principally Occidental rather than American. Melville's art merges with the imagistic character of Leconte de Lisle's poetry rather than with any American mythos, whether crude in the whaleman's legend of Mocha Dick, or refined and " literary " in the American legends of Cooper, Simms, Whittier, or Longfellow; with the symbolic elements of Gauguin's art rather than with the representational matter of William Sidney Mount's paintings of the American frontier. These are symbolistic directions from the depths of Melville. I do not intend to deny the correspondence of his art with other American forms in the upper, more familiar waters.

There is a second approach to the nature of Melville's symbolism which has already been used with distinguished critical talent and impressive success by Charles Feidelson in his recent *Symbolism and American Literature* (1953). Feidelson's method is concerned with American semantics. In this study he examines the philosophical processes toward American symbolism as these originate in the collapse of Puritan simplistic logic applied to the meaning of language, particularly the language of Biblical texts. The Puritan theologian who passed his life in speculation upon the meaning of words gives place to Emerson and Thoreau who develop an American philosophy of linguistic symbolism and a language which is multiple in meaning, as opposed to an impossible Puritan insistence upon uniformity. Both philosophy and language, as these appear in American transcendentalism, are therefore nascent within " the sense of paradox," and appropriate to a world of " opposite and discordant " qualities in which the literary symbolist appears as " a writer for whom the world, theoretically, is indeterminate." Both Emerson and Thoreau, liberated from the authority of words as absolutely fixed terms, evolved a compensatory American theory of multiplicity, which resulted in linguistic media intended to delineate realities elusive of concrete linguistic definition. I do not wish to oversimplify Feidelson's thesis in summarizing Melville's relation to Emersonian philosophy. But it argues substantially that Melville's idiom derives from the system of Emerson and Thoreau, that Melville, the artist, exemplifies the theory in practice, that *the theory of the symbol* contributed very largely to the possibilities of Melville as a symbolist.

Feidelson's analysis of Emerson and Thoreau as semanticists is very probably the most authoritative one yet written. There can be no question of Emerson's system of universal multiplicity as a purposive and profoundly reasoned act. The system is refined and strengthened by Thoreau. But it is well to bear in mind that both Emerson and Thoreau were master scholars clearly aware of every American theory of language which had preceded them. I cannot see, despite Feidelson's excellent account of Melville, that Melville was an inheritor of Emerson during the major period of his productivity. Unless one confines his estimate to the last two decades of this man's life, he cannot, I think, justifiably call him a scholar or a philosopher. Melville's symbolism proceeds from feeling. Its elements are emotive and intuitive rather than reasoned (or better, intellectualized). Now there can be no question that he profits from the liberation of American literary idiom effected by Emerson and Thoreau. But I think it better to regard the genesis of his symbolic form as doubly conditioned: he is related to the

American tradition of Emerson and Thoreau in the freedom of linguistic form which he displays; he depends upon his own unique experience, all of it profoundly emotional, all of it very unlike any experience which Concord provided, all of it *felt* in areas comprehensible to Emerson and Thoreau, yet considerably removed from what they actually saw and touched. Feidelson's study achieves an indispensable description of the first condition for the symbols of Melville, that of American transcendental philosophy. The second condition is one of the concerns of my study: the unique elements of these symbols as they relate to the system of primitivism.

The genuine symbol of feeling is formed in the grasp of the imagination. It was never before seen in exactly the same shape which it exhibits. It is a newly struck medal from a unique alloy, cast of material which lay potential to art in the consciousness of the artist, which in both its personal and extrapersonal origins was singularly his; tempered in the sensibility, the particular emotional condition through which he saw human existence. Once cast, it contains and radiates the energy of feeling in which it was conceived. The presence of the genuine symbol in art commands the attention of the spectator with sovereign power. In direct relation to his imaginative complement fit to match the significance of the symbol, he is aware of his presence before an abstraction which dominates him through its mysterious power of multiplicity, its demonstration of its origins from various materials brilliantly and flamingly fused. Consider, for instance, the final stanza of Milton's hymn, " On the Morning of Christ's Nativity ":

But see the Virgin blest,
Hath laid her Babe to rest.
   Time is our tedious Song should here have ending,
Heav'ns youngest teemed Star,
Hath fixt her polisht Car.
   Her sleeping Lord with Handmaid Lamp attending.
And all about the Courtly Stable,
Bright-harnest Angels sit in order serviceable.

The power of this great symbol of Christ as Light derives from the fusion of materials gathered into the grasp of the poet. Christian legend is apparent in the setting of the stable; this is succeeded by reference to the inadequacy of poetry as a descriptive medium, and followed at once by a star image deriving from three sources, in which cosmic origin appears in " youngest teemed," Hellenic myth in " polisht Car," and allusion to the parable of the New Testament in " Handmaid Lamp "; the fusion is completed in the concluding couplet with the " Courtly Stable " itself made one with the " polisht Car " and the cosmic star, as the supernatural of Christian dogma appears in the figure of Angels " bright-harnest " to pull the car through unending time. The inner variety of this symbol, a complex of intersecting planes, as in a crystal, forms the strange compulsion which it exerts as a unit in a work of art. Integration constitutes its beauty, the beauty of the poetic mind firing multiple materials, whether these be scholastically " learned " or experientially derived, into a symbolic unit, flashing in all directions at once.

Such symbols illuminate where no uniform description can shine even with the dullest measurable lustre. And if they are symbols attendant upon a modulation in the idiom of literature, which, indeed, Milton's symbol is not, they will compel order from chaos, whether this order be in any respect comparable to that of the old, preceding symbols. The student of literature sees them as a splendor of art, a human treasure incontestably revealing the beauty which proceeds from man's ability to make abstractions of his experience.

Scarcely anyone who studies art in the mid-twentieth century will contend that beauty has any essential business with what we regard as normal or charming or sensuously pleasing. As soon as we have comprehended the expressiveness of a work of art, it may become beautiful to us, whether comprehension came by way of intuition or analysis. Elements of the work which, in isolation, appear hideous will serve the interests of beauty. We respond to power in expressiveness, and to commanding form. In illustration of this principle one needs to recall, for instance, such appearances of beauty as expressiveness in Salome's address to the head of Jochanaän in Strauss's opera, or the progress of Addie Bundren's corpse in Faulkner's *As I Lay Dying*. In relation to the anxious interest attendant upon real experience they are hideous; as artistic abstractions freed of our concern for the real they are beautiful. These definitions are valuable as one approaches the symbols of primitivism. For there is a kind of hideousness in many of them if they are regarded as signs outside the realm of artistic abstraction. They are " abnormal " forms pointing away from the Western origins of their makers, toward the Orient. If to denounce and to desert the culture of the West is to be hideous, then those students ill disposed to accepting primitivism as a valid manifestation of art will find little beauty in the expressiveness of these symbols. In my own view, the exploration of cultures alien to the Western tradition for materials to inform a new religious symbolism is one of the beautiful acts of recent and contemporary art.

One last premise, and I have finished with these prefatory remarks. In order to simplify my task, I have proceeded upon the assumption that the literature to be examined may be regarded as poetry, in the sense of *poesis*. This means, of course, that I am not to be concerned with the technical form of any of the works here considered. My purpose is to isolate and to examine the symbols of each which belong to the system of primitivism. With gratitude I depend upon Mrs. Langer again in her approach to the distinctions between poetry and prose:

> In reality . . . prose is a literary use of language, and therefore, in a broad but perfectly legitimate sense (considering the meaning of " poesis "), a *poetic form*. It is derived from poetry in the stricter sense, not from conversation; its function is creative. This holds not only for prose fiction (the very term, " fiction," bespeaks its artistic nature), but even for the essay and for genuine historical writing. [*Feeling and Form*]

Were it not for the justice which I see in this contention, I should be unable to deal with the forms of Melville's art as predominantly those of the novel in contradistinction to poetry.

Feidelson and many others have called attention to Melville's contempt for form. This observation is indisputable. *Moby-Dick* and *Mardi* and *Pierre* are no more novels in the traditional sense of that term than are the " chants " of Whitman in *Leaves of Grass* poems in the light of " prosody." One of the distinguishing phenomena of this last century of practice in Western literary art is a constant diminution of the line which was once sharply drawn between poetry and prose. Here is more evidence for the collapse of tradition in the authority of *form*. With the mutations proceeding from this collapse I have had no concern. *Poesis* sufficiently defines the art of literature in its function of providing symbols for abstractions. Poetry and prose are equally capable of arriving at the presentation of symbols expressive of the same type of abstraction.

These, in brief, are the premises at hand. I assume that certain critics who deny that a work of art is relevant to the conditions of its origin would condemn this study as an inadmissible combination of objectives and methods. Then I anticipate the possibility of such judgment by suggesting that Parts I, II, and V of this book may be read as social history and biography and that Parts III and IV are at least aspiring criticism. But the pragmatist in the study of literature cannot be very much taken to task by others who share his view. They will agree with him that the means he used to arrive at the facts of sensibilities involved in symbols are in themselves of no critical value. The fact demonstrated is all that can essentially matter, since the nature of art and the nature of criticism do not permit logically the imposition of a code of critical law. I have intended in this book to suggest a method for defining the system of modern primitivism, the system regarded in the sense of Eliot's " organic whole," as an adjunct to the recent history of Protestant thought; and I have wished to show that this system may be described in terms of the dominant symbolism which projects its form. I can make no pretense to having shown the whole of the system. Most of this study must be regarded as exploratory. But I believe that there is an essential beauty of human expressiveness subject to criticism in its ultimate function: so to interpret and to arrange the symbols of the great systems, the organic wholes of art, that art may comment definitely upon its own nature.

NEW LONDON   *James Baird*
JANUARY, 1956

Acknowledgments

The central idea of this book, although I should like to claim it, is not originally mine. It was shaped in the humanism of two friends. As I have proceeded with my definition of the idea and its significance in art, I have been aware that the purpose of these men as defenders of humanism is constantly represented in my objective, whether in their estimations the credit to them be for good or ill. For the genesis of the idea I am grateful to Stanley T. Williams, of Yale University, who proposed to me a study of the material from which this book has had its beginning, and who directed my first analysis of primitivism in the art of Melville; and to George Boas, of The Johns Hopkins University, whose authority in the history of primitivism is perhaps no more valuable to me than the examples of integrity in judgment which his friendship unceasingly provides.

I am indebted to Norman Holmes Pearson of Yale University for his constructive comments upon my first study of Melville; and to colleagues, teachers, and critics who have contributed multifariously, and perhaps unwittingly, to the shape of this study: Richard Beale Davis, John C. Hodges, Clarence P. Lee, Roscoe E. Parker, and Alwin Thaler, of the University of Tennessee; A. Grove Day and Carl Stroven, authorities on the literature of the Pacific area, of the University of Hawaii; and my colleagues in Connecticut College. For recent assistance I am particularly indebted to my associates in the Department of English of Connecticut College, Rosemond Tuve and Robert E. L. Strider, both of whom have criticized portions of the manuscript; to Hazel Johnson, Librarian of Connecticut College, and to the staff of the Palmer Library for many kindnesses; and to Dr. Bertram Schaffner, of New York City, who made useful suggestions for the terminology of chapter headings. I wish to thank Lawrence S. Willson, of Santa Barbara College in the University of California, and Andrew R. Hilen, of the University of Washington, for several approaches to the study of American literature which are implicit here.

To Susanne K. Langer of Connecticut College I am indebted for careful advice toward an appropriate use of her theory of the symbol of feeling. Although I am aware that several conclusions appearing here will be found to disagree with her ultimate definitions of nondiscursive form, I must acknowledge the indispensability of this theory, certainly in any quarter of the modern world one of the major contributions to the philosophy of art. My description of primitive feeling in recent literature could scarcely have been written without it.

The following persons have contributed variously to this book, and it is my hope that each will recognize the nature of the gratitude which I owe him: Dr. and Mrs. George B. Germann, Norwalk, Connecticut; Edwin Wigglesworth, New York University; George H. Kerr, Stanford University; Yasuhiko Kosa, Yuichiro Munakata, and Yukio Ogata, my students in Japan; and Dr. Georg Hans Doll, of Eppingen, Germany, distinguished Japanologist and my former colleague in the Daigō Kōtō Gakkō, Kumamōtō, Kyūshū; William H. Ittel and Bernard McKenna, Pittsburgh, Pennsylvania; Dudley R. Johnson, Dean of Washington and Jefferson College; Evanita S. Morse; Thomas E. Ratcliffe, Jr., Reference Librarian of the University of Illinois; Elizabeth and William Huntsberry, of the University of Hawaii; Richard D. Olson, Chicago, Illinois; Charles B. Gilbert and Charles Rain, New York City; and Donald R. Currier, of Yale University. For the hospitality of one province of Oceania at the close of the Second World War I am grateful to King John of Kusaie, East Caroline Islands, who, if he still lives, is of all my friends whose influence appears here the one least accessible to me.

I wish also to acknowledge the material aid extended to me by the Rockefeller Foundation in a Post War Fellowship for Research in the Humanities during 1948 and 1949. This grant enabled me to study French literature of the nineteenth century at the University of Paris and to conduct research in the Orientalism of French romanticism. I am grateful for assistance toward an understanding of the comparative method in literary criticism which this fellowship provided.

The progress of the study toward completion has subsequently been supported by a grant in aid from Connecticut College, whose president and other administrative officers I wish to thank for their good will and confidence.

I wish finally to thank Betty Harper Fussell, former Assistant in Instruction in the Department of English of Connecticut College, and Paul Fussell, of Rutgers University, for their generous contribution of time and patience in proofreading; and Simone Brangier Boas, who contributed her skill by transferring from the art of Marquesan iconography decorative motifs for section and chapter headings.

For permission to quote from manuscript sources and from copyrighted materials I am indebted to the following administrators:

Harcourt, Brace and Company, Incorporated, New York, for use of excerpts from T. S. Eliot's *After Strange Gods*, Copyright 1934 by Harcourt, Brace and Company, Incorporated.

The Houghton Library of the Library of Harvard University, and Mrs. Eleanor M. Metcalf, Cambridge, Massachusetts, for use of manuscripts in the Melville collection of Harvard.

Houghton Mifflin Company, Boston, for use of Amy Lowell's " Moon Haze," in *Pictures of the Floating World*, Copyright 1919 by The Macmillan Company.

Alfred A. Knopf, Incorporated, Publisher, New York, for use of " This Solitude of Cataracts " from the *Collected Poems* of Wallace Stevens, Copyright 1950, 1954 by Wallace Stevens.

Liveright Publishing Corporation, New York, for use of lines from " Voyages II " and " The Broken Tower " of Hart Crane, from the *Collected Poems*, Copyright 1933 by Liveright Publishing Corporation.

A Note

On Documentation and Translation

Unless otherwise specified in footnotes, all references to the text of Herman Melville are to the *Collected Works*, edited by Raymond Weaver (London, Constable and Co., 1922). These references appear often in titles of volumes from this edition used at particular points in the discussion.

Some discrepancy will be discovered among methods of reference to the texts of Melville. Wherever, in my estimation, a passage quoted or referred to in the text of the study should be examined by the reader in relation to the full chapter or section of Melville's work in which it appears, I have referred by parenthetical comment in the text to the chapter in which it is to be found: e. g., Ishmael has the dimensions of the whale's skeleton in a valley of the Arsacides tattooed upon his arm (*Moby-Dick*, Ch. cii). Wherever the reference to Melville's text, in either direct or indirect quotation or general comment, does not, in my opinion, recommend attention to interrelationships with other aspects of the passage in which it appears, I have cited volume and page numbers in footnotes. In general, references to chapter (or section) numbers of Melville's text are parenthetically contained in the course of my discussion through Part III, concerned with Melville's symbols; references to specific passages which do not require study in their particular contexts in the original appear in footnotes to the chapters of Parts IV and V, concerned primarily with Melville's imagery. Otherwise, there are no irregularities in documentation. Apart from citations to Melville by title only of volumes in the Constable edition, I have not made use of short titles.

Except for a few uses of established translations from the

original French and German texts of primitivists related to this study, I have consistently used my translations of texts from foreign sources. In translations of the texts of Émile Verhaeren and Leconte de Lisle, particularly, I have been more concerned with literal readings than with matters of poetic style related to metrical adaptation.

PART ONE

THE NATURE OF
RECENT PRIMITIVISM

I

Primitivism
and Cultural Failure

Authentic primitivism is a mode of sentience, a creed springing inevitably from a state of cultural failure. It represents one attempt of Western man to restore the symbolism of human existence. It is a willful exit from crisis and from the chambers of the dead and the dying, *as these manifestations of failure are interpreted in the moral view of the primitivist.* The definition of primitivism which this book undertakes is conducted from the aesthetic and the moral positions of the primitivist. It does not intend to speak of the beliefs of artists, theologians, or laymen who have no relationship whatsoever to

3

the system. Nor is it in any sense to be regarded as apologetic or polemical. I take it that the personality of a student of the arts may not logically be confused with the individualities and the beliefs of the artists whom he studies. The method and the judgments of the following discussions are directly concerned with the genetic facts of primitivism, a system appearing in the art of the Western world during the last century, as measured from approximately 1850 to the present.

If a paradox seems to exist in the genesis of restoration from decay, the explanation lies in the fact that the imagination of man is perpetually inventive and self-fortifying. In the view of the primitivist, society may cease to possess a common agreement upon the meanings and the purposes of existence; it may experience moral death; it may ultimately accept nihilism as its destiny. In the tradition of the Western world, the symbols of Christianity may exhibit the pallor of inertia. They may represent what Melville saw as a " palsied universe." But the inventiveness of the individual endures. There is no end to the possibility of new prophets and new messiahs; nor is there any limit to be placed upon the importation and extension of old symbols into new and unaccustomed parts of the world. Neo-Hellenism may be preached in the Orient; neo-Buddhism may dominate the civilization of Europe; or a religion never before seen may make impossible the reappearance of these ancient systems in unfamiliar lands. These are imponderables. But the resourcefulness of the individual imagination in religious symbolism is everlastingly certain and potential.

To speculate upon the nature of God, whether this speculation take place in the smallest compass of imaginative vigor, as in the mind of the primitive Maori, or in the highest reaches of professional theology, and to originate symbols for the deity are but to exert the distinguishing power of symbolization in the human mind. Modern primitivism is significant not in terms of its success in supplanting old symbols with new but rather in the brilliant imaginative thrusts which its literature preserves.

1 *Academic Primitivism and the Symbol of Primitive Feeling*

Whoever deals with any of the large *isms* in the parlance of literary studies is confronted with such an accretion of meanings and critical intent that he must question his own integrity in employing his term. Every generation of critics needs to reëxamine the connotations of each *ism* in the total inheritance. A growing body of comment upon the presence of these "ideas" in the arts is essentially one of the coarsest structures in intellectual history. Nobody really knows exactly what any one of these structures means unless his critic has told him through analysis and illustration. A. O. Lovejoy's famous essay of 1924 on the discrimination of romanticisms is but one brave attempt to disentangle the hopelessly matted and intertwined impurity that the term *romanticism* really is; [1] and since the time of Lovejoy's writing, three decades of usage have further complicated the meaning which he attempted to resolve.

These isms of literature—platonism, naturalism, or what one pleases—are all like the nests of the osprey, tangles of sticks and stones, the picked spines of fish, glitter, and much dross. At his business of fishing, his pure act, the osprey is a conqueror. At home, among the trophies of the nest, he is a dunce king of an impure hoard; and the nest goes on growing as a monument to his ingenuity for making a consistently impure structure. There is nothing at all rational about it except its shape. So it is with the generations of those who study the ideas of art. Their fishing is a pure act in itself; but the extending commentary to which they contribute is really a nesting criticism. They could not meet together and agree to build with only thus and so. Each member of each generation flies home with what he supposes appropriate; thus the nest goes on growing and swaying in the sea wind with its full burden of assorted plunder.

Primitivism, as a category used variously in criticism, is only one of several nests. Whoever would sit there, if he is annoyed

---

[1] "On the Discrimination of Romanticisms," *PMLA*, vol. 39 (1924), pp. 229–53.

by the conglomeration about him, must first try to purify his place by throwing out as much of the material as he dares without removing the framework of the structure as well. It could not be otherwise. The word he uses to establish his reference has already been employed to describe so many acts or " movements " in the histories of art and philosophy that he is confounded by the burden of accumulated meanings: Montaigne's reflections upon cannibals; the taste of nineteenth-century poetry for Scandinavian legend; Tolstoy's celebration of simple goodness among the Cossacks and his comfortable denunciation of sophisticated art from his palace in Russia; Picasso's African " period " and his recent experiments in the " primitive plasticity " of ceramics; Hemingway's or Elliot Paul's preferences for elemental Spain; Faulkner's Negroes as the true inheritors of the South; Steinbeck's Mexican peasants or Californian sardine fishermen as " primitive " honest men. These are random selections from a list the limits of which no one has ever proposed. Perhaps the critic supposes that he may speak of neo-primitivism; but his hope for discrimination is idle. Even as he writes with his new term, someone else is using the same word in a different meaning. He has established nothing which is really his own.

The clearing of the nest of primitivism must begin with getting rid of everything that is nonessential to the purpose at hand an act which can be accomplished only by imposing strict limits upon what the critic will accept as authentic evidence of the system. *In this study, the mode of feeling which exchanges for traditional Christian symbols a new symbolic idiom referring to Oriental cultures of both Oceania and Asia is admitted as genuine primitivism, with the even closer qualifications that most of the authors involved, certainly the major ones, should have traveled in the Orient and that they should have derived from direct physical experience a medium of feeling to inform the symbols which their art presents.*

But it is not enough to announce such a deliberate intention. There must be a logical excuse for excluding other kinds of primitivistic expression. The major difficulty in presenting a clear profile of the symbolism of primitive feeling is that of disassociating it from the systems of Rousseauism and exoticism, each of which is distinguished by a mode concerned with symbolic expression of *nostalgia for the primitive*.

Mircea Eliade, in a recent study of archetypes in myth and ritual, asserts that in " primitive " ontological conception " an object or an act becomes real only insofar as it imitates or repeats an archetype." [2] For example, the archetype of sacrifice belongs to what this critic regards as the " symbolism of the Center ": thus every sacrifice repeats the initial sacrifice " revealed by a god *ab origine*, at the beginning of time." [3] The center, or the beginning, is " sacred " or mythical time, and the individual's (i. e., the symbolist's) projection into this center establishes for him the reality of existence. All else, all time flowing from this center outward, is " profane," and, in the process of " becoming " which it actually measures, a time without meaning. " Just as profane space is abolished by the symbolism of the Center . . . so any meaningful act performed by archaic man, any real act, i. e., any repetition of an archetypal gesture, suspends duration, abolishes profane time, and participates in mythical time." [4] The conclusion of Eliade's remarkable discussion proposes that Christian man has lost " the paradise of archetypes and repetition," [5] the archaic center which once redeemed him from the " terror of history " (or the unreality, as we may understand it, of profane time) .

An elaboration of these concepts would require a certain intricacy which I wish at this point to avoid. Their central issue may be simply put: modern man is not, in time, a separate creature; archaic man, whether vestigial or dominant, is preserved in him. To follow Eliade, we must assume that there is a vital time at the center, and a phantom time apart from it. And to understand modern primitivism, we must agree that art can and does create symbols of feeling which imitate archaic

[2] *The Myth of the Eternal Return*, trans. Willard Trask, Bollingen Series XLVI (New York, 1954), p. 34.
[3] *Ibid.*, p. 35.
[4] *Ibid.*, p. 36.
[5] *Ibid.*, p. 162.

myth and ritual in a restoration of archetypes. Hence we must see the distinctions between the artist of nostalgic reference, the symbolist of externalities which are apparent in the flow of profane time; and the artist of primitive feeling, the restorer of the sacred center, the maker of life symbols reconstituting an archetypal reality. We must admit, finally, to a phenomenon of contemporary art: modern man, for reasons which will presently be discussed here, recaptures in at least some provinces of his creativity as artist the sentience of archaic man.

Initially, and through the courses of this chapter, it may then be understood that the symbolism of nostalgic reference to the primitive, the symbolistic presentation of *instances* of the archaic, or distant, or " remotely good " is a contrived or " assembled " and hence *academic* primitivism. The symbolism of the center, the restoration of sacred time through the *life symbol* of an archetypal reality, is to be isolated from this form, and so established as the form of primitivism admissible to the method and the analyses of this book. The *symbol of primitive feeling* repeats a feeling *ab origine*, at the center. Its signification lies not in the exoticist's reverie upon distant cultures but in the deeper artistic act of the true primitivist who shapes reality from the archetypes of primitive feeling. This life symbol does exactly what Eliade has proposed as the accomplishment of any meaningful act performed by archaic man: it repeats archetypal reality as it abolishes profane time and participates in mythical time. These definitions will be refined and simplified as the following discussions take form. They are offered here as descriptions of premises.

2 *Rousseauistic Primitivism*

Thus emerges the requirement for new evaluations, first of Rousseauism, which has been generally accepted, since the beginning of the nineteenth century, as synonymous with primitivism. Rousseau appears in his distinctive " primitive " character in the *Discours sur l'Origine et les Fondemens de l'Inégalité parmi les Hommes*, dedicated to the Republic of Geneva in 1754.

O man, of whatever country you are, whatever your opinions may be, listen . . . . The times I shall speak of are indeed remote: how you have changed from what you were . . . [from] the life of your kind that I shall describe according to the qualities you have received, [the life] that your education and your customs have been able to deprave, but could not destroy. . . . Unhappy in your present state through reasons which announce to your unhappy posterity even greater unhappiness, perhaps you will wish to go backward; and this feeling must induce praise of your first ancestors, criticism of your contemporaries, and terror for those who will have the misfortune of living after you.[6]

It must be assumed here that every student of ideas is familiar with the extensions of this sentiment. The basic theory takes form upon the assumption that the God-intended *égalité* of man is preserved only among savages, who live with divine *pitié* toward their fellow creatures. The restoration of man to equality reinstates him as natural man, good, free, intelligent, religious, happy. This principle is extended variously through the whole of the theory: in *Émile* where the child instructed " naturally " grows into the free and loving being equal to its fellows; in the *Nouvelle Héloïse* where Julie reëstablishes the family, the most ancient of societies, the first model for political institutions, the " natural " family of equal individuals; in the *Contrat social* where men reclaim liberty and equality by submitting individual desire to the will of the community. Society in all its known forms, being contrary to the principle, sins against God.

If one assumes that the capacity of man to exist in a state of pure equality is innate and subject to recall, he has, as Rousseau indicates in his direction toward revolution and anarchy, two methods of demonstrating the capacity: he may conduct an orthodox reading of Scripture in which he sees man as naturally good at the moment when he was given divine law, and he may frame the hypothesis that the " uncivilized " state of man on this planet still perpetuates an original God-intended good-

[6] *Oeuvres Complètes de J. J. Rousseau* (Paris, Armand-Aubrée, 1829), vol. 1, p. 176.

ness. Rousseau does both. In the second method he devises a group of instances which refer to imagined states of primitive existence. He is the first of a long line of modern thinkers who fabricate a theory of return to " natural " states and then proceed to search the ranges of geography and the literature of travel for illustrations of the theory. An analogy from a less sublime context would be some theory arguing that the phases of the moon control productivity in women, with the conception of Javanese mothers or the superior performance of European female musicians in the benevolent period of the waxing moon as " cases " for illustration. Such is the capability of the human mind to fortify whatever it chooses to theorize. Rousseau established a technique of reference in the literature of primitivism; and the character of Rousseauistic reverie and nostalgia is so impressive as to have made " Rousseauism " of every manifestation of subsequent Western thought in which the institutions of civilization are condemned. The fact is that Rousseau is quite alien to the makers of recent primitivism, the artists of the life symbol. In the business of purifying the idea of primitivism as a system. Rousseauism must be the first of useless materials to be discarded.

G. A. Borgese's definition of primitivism in the *Encyclopedia of the Social Sciences* reads: " [T]he cult and proposed imitation of the past . . . the glorification of an earlier stage in the history of a culture—a period either beyond recall or partially restorable or present in some contemporary form as in the case of childhood or the folk mind or savage innocence . . . supposed, in contrast to the sophistication and weakness of later ages and periods, to have preserved or still to preserve the secret of an uncorrupted, vigorous, genuine expression of life." [7] A. O. Lovejoy and George Boas, both philosophers and authoritative historians of primitivism, distinguish between the forms of the idea as *chronological* and *cultural*. Chronological primitivism is historiographic.[8] It refers endlessly to earlier stages in human

---

[7] Vol. 12, p. 398.

[8] For a full discussion of the forms of primitivism by these authorities, see the initial chapter of *Primitivism and Related Ideas in Antiquity: A Documentary History of Primitivism and Related Ideas*, ed. Arthur O. Lovejoy, Gilbert

history as "better" or wholly good, as though one were unrolling a long coil of existence. At the beginning of the process man stood free, perfect, uncorrupted; at the end of the unrolling he will be totally evil. The duration of the coil is the duration of man, the history of his acts, and so the history of human culture. By pulling back what has been unrolled, the points of better times and of the Golden Age itself may be identified. The sense must be rather that of a motion picture being run off backward. Cultural primitivism concentrates on the imagined goodness of existing states of man.

The two forms, as Lovejoy and Boas point out, may be combined. Since all the literature encompassed in this study of symbols in primitivism is related to the second of these types, the chronological form will have only incidental notice in the chapters to follow. These definitions are irrefutable for all primitivism established upon instances of the good life. In essence, they suggest the total history of intellectual man in his acts of calling attention to some state of existence which he supposes better than the civilized state of his own being.

The case of Chateaubriand establishes in practice the theory of Rousseau. In his voyage westward he is Rousseau's man of action, even as Thoreau is Emerson's prospector sifting the streams for gold. Chateaubriand sailed for America in May, 1791.[9] During the five months of this celebrated tour he "visited" the Indian tribes of Canada and of the regions of Kentucky, Tennessee, Alabama, and Mississippi. Three works were to come of this Rousseauistic venture to live "with simple Indian swains". the *Voyage en Amérique*, *Atala*, and the *Génie du Christianisme* (the last, of course, by indirection). At the outset, one would suppose that the nostalgia of Rousseau is now to be exchanged for the symbol of primitive feeling, the

Chinard, George Boas, and Ronald S. Crane (Baltimore, Johns Hopkins, 1935). See also Edith A. Runge's *Primitivism and Related Ideas in Sturm und Drang Literature* (Baltimore, Johns Hopkins, 1946), p. 264. "There is perhaps in many cases little difference between ideas expressing cultural primitivism, and those which harbor a pessimistic view of culture, civilization and its various manifestations."

[9] Le Vicomte de Chateaubriand, *Oeuvres Complètes* (Paris, Pourrat Frères, 1836), vol. 12, *Voyage en Amérique*, p. 11.

religiously inspired emblem deriving from both the impoverishment of Christian symbols in the native European *milieu* and
the new sensuous experience among savages to which the voyager submits his whole being. But such is not the case.

From his observations of the southern Indians Chateaubriand
has little to offer beyond cursory descriptions of village life and
savage dances.[10] In Canada he is almost exclusively concerned
with the religious health of the natives.

> Religious traditions have become a great deal more confused;
> the instruction undertaken by the missionaries of Canada
> has mixed foreign ideas with the native and the indigenous.
> One perceives today, despite reports to the contrary, the dis-
> figurement of Christian beliefs. The majority of the savages
> carry crosses for ornaments, and Protestant traitors sell them
> what [i. e., religious emblems] the Catholic missionaries give
> them. Let us say, to the honor of our country and to the
> glory of our religion, that the Indians are strongly attached
> to the French . . . and that a black robe [a missionary] is yet
> venerated in the American forests.[11]

In this token passage the French Catholic mind of Chateaubriand advances into the North American wilderness as strongly
inspired by Christian symbolism as the mind of the most de-
voutly dedicated missionary. His observation actually centers
upon evidence for the progress of Christian missions in Canada;
his real complaint is not raised against the loss of primitive
excellence through the institutions of European civilization but
toward an imperfect assimilation of Christianity into Indian
culture, with an accompanying reflection upon the chicanery of
Protestants. The record of five months among the Indians becomes, among its romantic effusions on American landscape,
an exotic description of adventure.

With the publication, in 1801, of *Atala*, the first " primitive "
novel of the nineteenth century, Chateaubriand manifests the
inherent quality of a mind firmly grounded in the authority of
Christian civilization. The theme of this book is Christian

[10] *Ibid.*, pp. 148-49.
[11] *Ibid.*, p. 268.

fortitude in the wilderness. To Atala, the Indian heroine, the beautiful, " natural " soul saved for the kingdom of God, the old missionary bears the example of Christian fortitude in affliction. " My daughter, replied the priest with a sweet smile, what is this compared to what my divine Master endured? If the idolatrous Indians have afflicted me, they are the poor blind whom God will one day enlighten." [12] With this example Atala dies beseeching Chactas, another Indian, to embrace the Christian faith and so prepare for their reunion in heaven.[13] These scenes are not in any sense symbols related to primitive feeling. They are abstractions from a nostalgic sentiment, instances of a Christian symbol in an alien setting.

As the first sentimental primitivist of modern times who lived among " savages," Chateaubriand is also the first of recent exoticists who affect the " primitive " pose. He is no worse than any others of them, and probably better than most. In the objectivity of this present study, a judgment upon Chateaubriand's integrity is not pertinent. All that matters is the evidence of his primitivism as a technique of reference. The " savagery " of Rousseauism on the one hand and of Chateaubriand's Atala on the other bears about as much relation to genuine primitivism as does the exoticist's dream of Cathay to the actualities of China.

In point of time, the five months of Chateaubriand's sojourn in America are roughly comparable to the months of Herman Melville's travel, on ship and on shore, in Polynesia. Furthermore, Chateaubriand's voyage westward is the counterpart of the voyage to the Orient, as Melville's voyage becomes the authentic symbol for the journey *away from* the Occident. The descriptions of these journeys of 1791 and 1842/1843, some fifty years apart, present some most informative differences when they are compared. The fact that Melville knew nothing of Rousseau as he approached the Marquesas Islands is of no importance. The best of all critical judgments on the real content of *Typee*, its burden of unique feeling, will be surpassed in

[12] *Ibid.*, vol. 18, *Atala*, p. 50.
[13] *Ibid.*, p. 78.

authority by a comparative reading of this novel beside *Atala*.
If Chateaubriand's American experience results in a celebration of Catholic missions and in the image of the Christian
cross revealed in the gloomy recesses of the Canadian forest,
how is it that Melville's descent into the umbrageous wilds of
Typee Valley appears in description which vituperates against
the forms of missionary endeavor and the emblems of Christian
culture reminding him of the world beyond the Marquesas?
It is very wrong indeed to regard *Typee* as picaresque fiction
and nothing more. The book is vitally involved in the total
process of Melville's symbolistic idiom. The descent into Typee
Valley is the first act in making Moby Dick. An answer to this
question lies in the nature of that unconscious allegiance which
each of these men bears to his parent culture. In clear terms,
it amounts to the degree of magnetism which accustomed and
anciently installed (and revered) symbols in this parent culture
exert upon the individual. A succeeding question follows: Is
this magnetism sufficient to restrain the individual from the
construction of new symbols to oppose it?

Granted that all sorts of differences in native aptitude, temperament, and intelligence separate Chateaubriand and Melville, the fact still remains that the first is commanded back to
allegiance by his cultural inheritance of symbols, the second
defies and rejects the allegiance in the act of making his own
symbols of deity. Chateaubriand comes to write of the genius
of Christianity, to celebrate, however superficially, the ineluctable power of its symbols over the mind of Western man
(for we do not discover in his work the sense of symbolic loss
until the account of his journey to the Holy Sepulchre some
years later) ; Melville comes to write *Clarel*, in which the symbol of the cross recedes like the waning light of a constellation
descending into the nether heaven.

It may be proposed that the Christian tradition of Europe
has an authority greater than the Protestant heritage of Melville possessed. And it may as well be said at this point as at
any other that in a strictly professing Catholic mind primitivism, in the sense of this study, is an absolute impossibility.

Paul Claudel offers a case in point. Possessed of an incalculable knowledge of the Orient, he not only preserved his allegiance to accustomed symbols; he also carried on at great remove the voluminous correspondence and argument of the counsellor by which he won Francis Jammes to the same allegiance, and reasoned with André Gide until his death.

There are, of course, varying degrees of allegiance to Catholic orthodoxy. The important fact here is that, in the half-century between the American journey of Chateaubriand and Melville's voyage, the drift of the Western world toward cultural failure, both moral and symbolic, had become considerably accelerated. The Protestant inheritance of Melville is the native, the indigenous circumstance of his origin as a maker of symbols; its complement is the sensed experience accumulated during the voyage. It follows that such a sensed experience is endowed with awareness which widens in exact proportion to the need to compensate for the loss in the native social endowment.

Rousseauism, manifested by Rousseau himself and by Chateaubriand, and primitivism displayed in the work of Melville and other authors selected for study here are, respectively, primitivism *as an idea* (as art, referential to exterior states of the primitive) and primitivism *as sentient expression of religious emotion conceptualized* (as art, symbolic of primitive feeling). That they are united in the same term is a misfortune which cannot be overcome save by an entirely new terminology. An attempt to supply that will not be made here. Rousseauistic instances of the good life have less in common with symbols of primitive feeling as literature continues to write its own history. All that can be done here is to isolate the genuine form by the term *existential primitivism*.

This act leaves Rousseauism and exoticism joined in an unjust proximity. But the distinction between these must be effected elsewhere. Both these dominant forms of primitivism, academic and existential, possess however two common characteristics: a continuing and clearly measurable survival through the nineteenth century and as much of the twentieth as has yet passed, and a uniform projection upon the conditions of cultural failure in the Western heritage, the collapse of tradition and the constant display of an anarchic individualism.

3   Cultural Failure

Cultural failure accelerates primitivism, whatever the type. *In this discussion cultural failure means the loss of a regnant and commanding authority in religious symbolism, since religion is here understood as the ultimately effective symbolic authority in the total culture of a race.* There is abundant evidence before every thinking person of the twentieth century that the decline of religious authority is a condition absolutely requisite to shifts in the structures of national conventions. The symbol of the state as the magnetic force supplants the system of Christian symbols and commands allegiance which was formerly directed to the humanistic individualism of Christian orthodoxy. There are no political demagogues more subtle or cunning than those who know that a nation seized in a state of symbolic inertia will support nearly any collective symbol designed to revitalize allegiance. The new nationalistic symbol or symbolic system will have a compulsive force as inevitable as that of armaments and battle standards.

When the relation of cultural failure to the health of religious symbols is understood, there can be nothing very strange in the Oriental inclination of existential primitivism. The return to the Orient is the imagined return to the source of religion. Considerable attention will be directed later to the veracity of this Orient as observed and understood by recent primitivists. For the present, it is enough to say that the act of the return countermands the dogma of established Christian tradition and overleaps the old symbols without consideration of means for restoring them. It is a primitivism which affords the expenditure of enormous energy in constructing a symbolic system near the Orient, if it has not the requisite knowledge to place itself actually there.

Rosemond Tuve, in her recent analysis of George Herbert's " The Sacrifice," calls attention to the symbols of *love* and *blood* as they " mingle in a single image when a poet is using symbols and not merely the private creations of his own wit." [14] One understands, as he proceeds through Miss Tuve's sensitive study, that Herbert was perfectly sustained by the authority of traditional symbols from the mediaeval church. He leaves Herbert's poem in this reading with the reflection that no poem comparable to " The Sacrifice " has come from a Protestant mind of the last century. Moreover, if he is aware of the course and the promise of existential primitivism, he sees that none is forthcoming. Among the makers of this recent art, at any rate, these ancient Christian symbols have lost their power to evoke artistic statements in which they are subsumed in a valid religious emotion and become supreme abstractions of feeling. The devotional allegiance of Herbert's symbols strikes through the integument of mere ritual; it is reverential allegiance transcending the states of form and exerting an astringent power over the emotive life. Like a priest, this poet breaks and pours the tokens of the corporate body of man. Genuine religious symbols such as these are incarnations, even when they are considered aesthetically, outside the realm of Christian theology.

In existential primitivism the journey to the Orient is the quest for the material of new symbols to serve the need of the Protestant mind. The purpose at hand is to study the nature of these new symbols, not to measure them against the devotional subscription of Herbert, or another poet of equal power. If it be permissible to compare Melville, granting his ineptitude as a traditional poet, with Herbert, then it appears that *Clarel* is one of the important poems in the English language on the subject of the sacrifice. The symbols of *love* and *blood* are present, but they have lost the power to command allegiance. To Melville's particular sentience, as to that of every authentic primitivist considered in relation to him, nineteen hundred years of Christianity do not prove that the implications of these symbols are susceptible of human realization. Furthermore, to this same primitivistic mind, the meaning of

[14] *A Reading of George Herbert* (London, 1952), p. 60.

the original Christ has been obliterated by constant accretions of symbolisms. If love and blood will not redeem man from error, then as symbols they become eventually meaningless. The typical Protestant mind must have, at all costs, the emblems of progress. It cannot submit to an evidence of stasis in morality; it cannot entertain the probability that man gets neither better nor worse from age to age. To the primitivist originating in the confusion of these Protestant requirements, the unknown Orient is a last resort. As an artist, he sets about a reading of human existence through symbols abstracting both his experience in the Orient and his feeling toward it.

It has been said earlier that the content of primitivistic symbols depends upon the religious condition of a cultural inheritance and upon the specific derivation from a *sensed* physical and emotive experience which is the unique, as opposed to the commonly shared, property of the artist. These observations are too general for subsequent reference in this study. They will now be exchanged for specific terms. The symbolist's awareness of cultural failure becomes *atavism*, reversion, thoroughly dependent upon feeling, to the past in a search for a prototypic culture. This atavism is commonly shared among a group of artists, and it permits the use of archetypal concepts in the making of new and " personal " religious symbols. Physical and emotive experience, as uniquely possessed by the artist, reaches expression in form by way of *a facsimile of singular experience*, which will be hereafter referred to as the *autotype*. This autotype is selected by the artist from his remembered experience and employed in his act of making an artistic abstraction in answer to the demands of feeling. The autotype is fused with some archetypal emblem from atavistic reversion, and thus determines the primary elements of a symbol.

In the linguistic arts, the expression which the symbol displays, specifically the words and the patterns of words which are used to describe formal elements, will depend upon conditions of logic and semantic theory.[15] But atavism is quite

---

[15] Cf. Charles Feidelson, *Symbolism and American Literature* (Chicago, 1953), discussed in the introduction to this study, particularly pp. 86–91.

another matter. It signifies that particular awareness of cultural failure which was shared by makers of symbols in Western literature, irrespective of national boundaries. Whatever the form it eventually employed, it was experienced by these makers apart from the problems of linguistic expression. In the case of primitivistic expression, *atavism arises from the artist's awareness of his impoverishment in Christian symbolism.* The following discussion is intended to review acknowledgments of this impoverishment by some representative philosophers and theologians. They describe the conditions in which traditional symbols lose their authority in the realm of religious feeling and new symbols must and will be made.

The recent observations of Albert Schweitzer on the crisis of Western civilization are actually pertinent to a complex of conditions emerging through the last one hundred years, roughly from about the time Herman Melville began shaping, " hewing out," with certain of his contemporaries, a new symbolistic literature. Writing in 1931, Schweitzer spoke from Lambaréné of two perceptions which cast their shadows over contemporary existence: " One consists in my realization that the world is inexplicably mysterious and full of suffering; the other in the fact that I have been born into a period of spiritual decadence in mankind." [16] He found his age " filled with disdain for thinking." The " spiritual decadence " and the fear of thought named here are extensions of his thesis of 1923, in which the nature of war itself is interpreted as symptomatic of a universal Occidental condition. " We are living to-day under the sign of the collapse of civilization. The situation has not been produced by the war; the latter is only a manifestation of it." [17] Philosophy has degenerated into pedantry, the scholasticism of degenerates, destined only to play an empty role in schools and universities; it has lost its moral import.[18] Schweitzer does not specify the loss of symbolic authority in this moral context; but

---

[16] *Out of My Life and Thought* (New York, 1933), p. 254.
[17] *The Decay and the Restoration of Civilization* in *The Philosophy of Civilization*, Part I, trans. C. T. Campion (London, 1923), p. 1.
[18] *Ibid.*, p. 10.

he would seem to imply it when he speaks (again in 1931) of our spiritual life " rotten throughout because it is permeated through and through with scepticism, and we live in consequence in a world which in every respect is full of falsehood." [19]

These are the judgments of a theologian, and the reference to rottenness through scepticism strikes into the factual condition of contemporary Protestantism. The first of these relates to precisely that scepticism antithetical to belief which is displayed by Ernest Renan, his *reasoning out* of Christianity as he leaves Catholicism and St. Sulpice: " One of the worst kinds of intellectual dishonesty is to play upon words, to represent Christianity as imposing scarcely any sacrifice upon reason, and in this way to inveigle people into it without letting them know to what they have committed themselves." [20] Loss of allegiance to an established symbolism is indirectly posed by Renan's confession, as an example of scepticism appearing in spiritual decadence, in the sophism that reason cannot permit a blind subscription to Christianity. The act of submitting oneself to Christian dogma is the submission of the individual will to an unreasoning custom of popular acceptance; it is not the allegiance of the individual acquiescing even as he retains his entity as a reasoning being. This is the sense of Renan's apostasy.

The mistake which we commit in our endless reference to the eighteenth century as the " age of reason," primarily because we see that Deism makes the power of human reasoning synonymous with God, is revealed in our improper measurement of this scepticism. For conditions urging the appearance of primitivism, at any rate, the last one hundred years of man's existence in the Western world mark the true age of reason (rationalization). The summary and prophetic observation of Paul Bourget, in 1886, on the manifestations of European " melancholia " suggests the outcome of rationalization in a " free thinking " civilization.

It seems to me more reasonable to regard melancholia as the inevitable product of a disparity between our need of civil-

[19] *Out of My Life and Thought*, p. 259.
[20] *Recollections of My Youth* (Boston, 1929), p. 261.

ized [institutions] and the reality of exterior causes;—whereby, from one end to the other of Europe, contemporary society presents the same symptoms, the subtleties according with racial backgrounds, of that melancholia and discord. A universal nausea before the insufficiencies of this world seizes the spirit of the Slavs, the Germans and the Latins, and manifests itself among the first by nihilism, among the second in pessimism, and among us in solitary and bizarre neuroses. The murderous rage of the conspirators of Saint Petersburg, the books of Schopenhauer, the furious arson of the Commune and the fleshly misanthropy of the naturalistic novelists,—I choose with intention the most disparate examples,—reveal the same spirit of negation of life which, each day, obscures effectually the civilization of the Occident. We are near, without doubt, to the suicide of the planet, the supreme desire of the theorists of evil.[21]

This is the senescence of vigor. The negation of life in the import of Bourget is the expression of an insufficiency in the reading of existence, a universal incapacity to grasp significance from the facts of *being*. It is, as well, the symptom of the nausea of Sartre, the root of the existential mood, whereby we get the realization, according to a recent essay by Margaret Walker, that " existence itself, whatever its form or symbolization, must nauseate because of its very contingency." The very quality of the viscous matter that promotes growth throughout nature evokes disgust; for Sartre it becomes entirely obscene. " Fertility in all its forms is revolting because it *is* life, because it perpetuates existence for which there is no reason." [22] This existential position would seem to be the terminal point of Bourget's projection. In the clear understanding that to the existentialist life must be nauseous no matter what symbolization of existence may be made, this critic touches the vital center of a contemporary doctrine. Miss Walker shows us the philosophy of Sartre as the sickness of over-reason. Lest it be thought that the expression of a collective awareness of symbolic impoverishment is nothing more than a series of jeremiads,

---

[21] *Essais de Psychologie Contemporaine* (Paris, 1886), fourth edition, p. 15.
[22] " The Nausea of Sartre," *The Yale Review*, vol. 42 (1953), pp. 253–54. Readers of this essay will wish to study further Sartre's renowned " novel," *La Nausée* (1947).

the evidence of what has gone on in symbol-making shows that Schweitzer, Renan, Bourget, and Sartre heterogeneously demonstrate the same condition. The spiritual essence of man's existence must be represented not through reason *qua* reason but through the authority of vital symbols commanding the subservience of the individual, existentially sceptical will.

The most impressive of all recognitions pointing toward the genesis of nihilism in symbolic impoverishment comes from Oswald Spengler. In the first volume of *The Decline of the West* he found the state of post-Rousseauistic European culture a condition of annihilation by discussion (here regarded as " reason "), a supreme decimation of symbolic authority.

[Rousseau] . . . *stands, like Socrates and Buddha, as the representative spokesman of a great civilization.* Rousseau's rejection of all great Culture-forms and all significant conventions, his famous " Return to the state of Nature," his practical rationalism, are unmistakable evidences. Each of the three buried a millenium of spiritual depth. Each proclaimed his gospel to mankind, but it was to the mankind of the city intelligentsia, which was tired of the town and the Late Culture, and whose " pure " (i. e., soulless) reason longed to be free from them and their authoritative form and their hardness, from the symbolism with which it was no longer in living communion and which therefore it detested. The culture was annihilated by discussion. If we pass in review the great 19th-century names with which we associate the march of this great drama—Schopenhauer, Hebbel, Wagner, Nietzsche, Ibsen, Strindberg—we comprehend in a glance that which Nietzsche, in a fragmentary preface to his incomplete master-work, deliberately and correctly called the *Coming of Nihilism.* Every one of the great cultures knows it, for it is of deep necessity inherent in the finale of these mighty organisms. Socrates was a nihilist, and Buddha. There is an Egyptian or an Arabian or a Chinese de-souling of the human being, just as there is a Western. This is a matter not of mere political and economic, nor even of religious and artistic, transformations, nor of any tangible or factual change whatsoever, but of the condition of a soul after it has actualized its possibilities in full.[23]

[23] Trans. Charles F. Atkinson (London, 1926), vol. 1, *Form and Actuality*, p. 352.

In immediate contrast to this condition of the soul—and here the description is entirely appropriate to the obsolescence of symbolic authority—Spengler cites Gothic and Doric man, Ionic and Baroque man as human beings fully possessed of their ability to carry and to actualize the whole symbolic structure of existence without " knowing " it. " They had over the symbolism of the Culture that unrestrained mastery that Mozart possessed in music. . . . The feeling of strangeness in these forms, the idea that they are a burden from which creative freedom requires to be relieved, the impulse to overhaul the stock in order by the light of reason to turn it to better account, the fatal imposition of thought upon the inscrutable quality of creativeness, are all symptoms of a soul that is beginning to tire." [24]

In the dispassionate calculations of Spengler this fatal imposition of thought is the emblematic act of a *reason-doomed* culture. As Spengler's theory of decline shows indubitably a most profound grasp of causation in the waning of symbolic authority, so it advances a philosophy of acquiescence. The emergence of new symbols in the arts is not assumed as a corollary. At least, Spengler's definition of the tiring soul does not show that symbolization as a human act is constantly sustained. This omission is fallacious. Even though the universal symbol declines as reason plays upon it, there are no real interludes of total suspension in the act of making symbols. The life of art, like the life of religious feeling in man, is constant. When formulated religion loses its sovereignty in a total culture, the manifestations of religious intent still continue to appear in art, no matter how antithetical and anarchic its abstractions may be.

The means of offsetting the destructive force of reason are not real concerns of primitivism. But the expedients of Nietzsche serve as well as the defeatism of Spengler to illustrate the extremes of this failure of a culture. Nietzsche argued for a revaluation of morals sufficient to reinstate the unconscious sources of the individual will to power. The life of reason, of

[24] *Ibid.*, p. 353.

superintellectuality leads to decadence.[25] He found nihilism incipient in Europe " not because the sorrows of existence are
greater than they were formerly, but because, in a general way,
people have grown suspicious of the ' meaning ' which might be
given to evil and even to existence." [26] The restoration of belief
in meaning is possible only through triumph over the vitiating
influence of Christianity. For Nietzsche, although he is dealing
with the evidence of cultural failure in nihilism, is actually
describing the effect of Christian symbolism when the symbols
have lost the authority to absorb and to render inconsequential
the individual's consciousness of himself.

Nietzsche is the first of modern thinkers to call attention to
personality and excessive self-awareness as eventualities in the
constantly dispersing systems of Protestant thought. He seems
to strike at the whole history of Christianity; but his attack is
more specifically directed to the extensions of Protestantism, as
these have been recently noted by both T. S. Eliot and Paul
Tillich in their analyses of the human personality substituted
for God. In answer to the question " What is it we combat in
Christianity? " Nietzsche replies that Christianity " knows how
to poison the noblest instincts and to infect them with disease,
until their strength, their will to power, turns inward, against
themselves—until the strong perish through their excessive
self-contempt and self-immolation." [27]

This self-contempt is the product of a characteristic Protestant equation, personality as God. Some notice of this anomaly
will follow later in this discussion. Paul Tillich explains
Nietzsche as an existentialist in terms of the courage " to look
into the abyss of nonbeing in the complete loneliness of him
who accepts the message that ' God is dead.' " The definition
of this courage Tillich finds in *Zarathustra* (IV, 73, sec. 4) :
" ' He hath heart who knoweth fear but *vanquisheth* it; who
seeth the abyss, but with *pride*. He who seeth the abyss but

[25] See Frederick J. Hoffman, *Freudianism and the Literary Mind* (Baton
Rouge, 1945), pp. 316–17.
[26] *The Will to Power*, trans. Anthony M. Ludovici, Vol. 14 in *The Complete
Works of Friedrich Nietzsche*, ed. Oscar Levy (New York, 1924), p. 27.
[27] *Ibid.*, p. 209.

with eagle's eyes,—he who with eagle's talons *graspeth* the abyss: he hath courage.' " [28] Tillich's definition of existentialism ensues in the same discussion, as a creative expression of decay: " It is the expression of the anxiety of meaninglessness and of the attempt to take this anxiety into the courage to be as oneself." [29] All this Nietzsche exemplifies in the famous doctrine of the will to power. One does not acquiesce; one fights at the edge of the abyss of meaninglessness without symbols for meaning, supreme only in the will to exert one's entity, to extract meaning from the defiance of nothingness. Theologically, the argument, even as that of modern existentialism, must seem inconclusive since it does not attribute to a superior origin outside the individual the strength to defy the meaninglessness of existence. The theological answer to existentialism must become ultimately the question, Whence comes the will to power?

The significance of the Orient does not appear in the Nietzschean system except in the sociological observation that Europe hangs upon the brink of nihilism. Yet, oddly enough, Nietzsche's subscription to *paganism* is exactly the same as that of modern primitivism in its quest for symbols from the Orient. " *Paganism*," he writes in *The Will to Power*, " is that which says yea to all that is natural, it is innocence in being natural, ' naturalness.' *Christianity* is that which says no to all that is natural, it is a certain lack of dignity in being natural; hostility to Nature." [30] This distinction adumbrates the morality of D. H. Lawrence to the effect that man's disposition has been warped by an ideal Christian love, his blood thinned out with false principles of conduct, utterly opposed to the true principles of being and becoming evident in the ways of primitive societies.[31] Lawrence was not a symbolic primitivist unless one is willing to accept him as such in his invocation of the " dark gods " of primitive societies, the gods that enter man not above,

[28] *The Courage to Be* (New Haven, 1952), p. 30.
[29] *Ibid.*, pp. 139–40.
[30] *Complete Works*, vol. 14, p. 127.
[31] See the introductory essay by Diana Trilling in *The Portable D. H. Lawrence* (New York, 1947), p. 23.

in the head, but below. He does not make genuine religious symbols to compensate for the lost authority of Christian tradition. As for Lawrence in the Orient, his letters from Ceylon, particularly, show no preference for the East as the source of religion.[32] Yet he is a twentieth-century embodiment of Nietzschean theory in his contention against nihilism, which, if not an expression of existential philosophy, is a symbolic return to paganism accomplished through his celebration of elemental, thick-blooded passions and the power of sexual expression.

As a philosopher, Nietzsche defines the atavism essential to the life symbols of primitivism. The autotype or facsimile of feeling from experience is absent. Autotypes work upon atavistic paganism as dies cut into metal and impress it; through the symbolist's awareness of cultural failure they compel a new paganism into symbolic form. But this coinage is not the business or the aptitude of philosophy. The symbols of art are made from universals by the imposition of feeling; philosophy in its pure state dispassionately defines universals.

Paul Bourget had much to say of the " cellular " breaking up of modern society. The social organism is a " federation " of lesser organisms. The individual is the social cell. " For the total organism to function with energy, the composing organisms must function with energy, but with a subordinate energy; and for the lesser organisms themselves to function with energy, their composing cells must function with energy subordinated. If the energy of the cells becomes independent, the organisms composing the total organism cease equally to subordinate their energy to the total energy, and the anarchy which comes into being constitutes the decadence of the whole." [33] In this examination Bourget has suggested the most important single Protestant condition in the genesis of symbolic primitivism: the I-You relationship, in which the I is the individual and the You, God. The practical (not the theoretical) history of Protestantism, as far as the authority of symbols is concerned, is the essential history of the cellular breaking up of a corporate

---

[32] See the *Letters*, ed. Aldous Huxley (New York, 1932).
[33] *Essais de Psychologie Contemporaine*, pp. 24–25.

allegiance to Christian symbolism, the dispersion of total energy resulting in a condition of symbolistic anarchy. Tillich, as a Protestant theologian, advances the heroism of fighting Protestantism since the Reformation and attends closely to the Protestant meaning of this heroism: "When the Reformation removed the mediation [i. e., the church] and opened up a direct, total, and personal approach to God, a new nonmystical courage to be was possible." [34] Examined through the psychology of personality, this same condition is interpreted by Carl Gustav Jung in these terms:

> As the Christian vow of worldly poverty turned the senses from the good things of the world, so spiritual poverty seeks to renounce the false riches of the spirit. It wishes to retreat not only from the sorry remnants of a great past that call themselves today the Protestant Church, but also from all the allurements of exotic reputation, in order to dwell with itself where, in the cold light of consciousness, the barrenness of the world extends even to the stars.[35]

How much of this human state Tillich is able to regard as heroism entails a subjective answer in which this book cannot indulge. But it is indeed a most arresting phenomenon of Protestantism that a theologian of Tillich's stature should have found it necessary to write a doctrine of "Courage to Be" at the midpoint of the twentieth century. The meaning of the doctrine is discovered in the mystical union of the individual with what Tillich speaks of as "the God beyond God." What necessity for the making of new symbols of this God beyond theism to obviate the barrenness of Jung's Protestant world, or the "cellular" dissolution of Bourget's, may be recognized by Tillich is here solely a matter for conjecture.

The range of Jung's observations on the *aloneness* of the Protestant individual and the relation of this man to outworn symbols demands full notice at this point. For it was Jung who first perceived the reasons for the journey toward the Orient,

---

[34] *The Courage to Be*, p. 162.
[35] *The Integration of the Personality*, trans. Stanley M. Dell (New York, 1939), p. 64.

and who first suggested a method of accounting for " Oriental-ism " in the literature of the Western world.

It is not surprising that the religious need, the believing mind, and the philosophical speculation of the cultured European feel themselves attracted to the symbols of the East—the grandiose conceptions of divinity in India and the abysms of Taoistic philosophy of China—just as once before the heart and mind of the Graeco-Roman were gripped by Christian ideas. There are many Europeans who surrendered so completely to the influence of the Christian symbol that they were enmeshed in the neurosis of a Kierkegaard; and others, again, whose relation to God, owing to a progressive impoverishment of symbolism, developed into an unbearably refined I-You relation. It is not surprising that such persons later succumbed to the magic of the fresh strangeness of Eastern symbols. This surrender is no defeat, but rather bears witness to the receptiveness and vitality of the religious sense. We can observe the same thing in the Oriental man of education, who not seldom feels himself drawn in the same way to the Christian symbol, and even develops an enviable understanding of it.

That people succumb to these eternal images is an en-tirely normal matter. It is for this very purpose that the images came into being. They are intended to attract, to convince, fascinate, and overpower. They are created out of the primal stuff of revelation, and portray the first-hand experience of divinity that every revelation contains. Thus they always lead men to premonition while defending them against experience. For these images do not stand isolated like volcanoes, but, thanks to a labour of the human spirit often centuries long, have been moulded into a comprehen-sive system of thought ascribing an order to the world, into an ethical regulation of human actions, and into a mighty, far-spread and ancient institution called church or religion.[36]

As Spengler's picture of the soul " after it has actualized its possibilities in full " suggests the total condition of modern morality, so this description of Jung presents a demonstrated course of egress from the barrenness of I-You. If the symbols inherited will not fascinate and overpower, if they will not

[36] *Ibid.*, pp. 57–58.

command, and get, allegiance, the "fresh strangeness" of Eastern symbols offers a possibility of escape. This condition of I-You, of course, might as well prompt the search for expedients in the Congo. It can be said only that it is the nature of primitivism to seek out what it supposes to be the richest and the least exhaustible alien cultures. Almost instinctively, it tends to fix its allegiance upon a symbolic potential which appears unsusceptible to exhaustion. In the practice of cultural primitivism (as earlier defined), evidence points to the fact that Oceania and Asia, taken collectively as the Orient, provide the greatest store of symbolistic material and the superior possibility of infinite and sustained variation.

The primitivist who flees from I-You as an intolerable condition of his feeling is invariably the Protestant man who overvalues himself,[37] who in the barrenness of his world has made personality synonymous with God. T. S. Eliot, speaking at the University of Virginia in 1933, asserted that "when morals cease to be a matter of tradition and orthodoxy—that is, of the habits of the community formulated, corrected, and elevated by the continuous thought and direction of the Church—and when each man is to elaborate his own, the *personality* becomes a thing of alarming importance." [38] Tillich, accounting for the disintegration of the God-symbol in the ascription of human attributes to God, remarks that personality is "the most emphasized ideal of modern religious and secular humanism." When God (in the habit of Protestant thought) ceased to be the transcending center, i. e., God apart from God identified with human perfections, men were left alone, centered in themselves, in a situation of monadic loneliness. "When God became *a* person, man's personality was driven into neurotic disintegration." [39] Cultural disintegration produced loneliness, the loss of the remnants of a common world.[40] When this happened, the individual was driven in upon himself. Tillich's

---

[37] On the Christian compulsion of the individual toward overvaluation of the self see Nietzsche, *The Will to Power, Complete Works*, vol. 14, p. 25.

[38] *After Strange Gods: A Primer of Modern Heresy* (New York, 1934), p. 58.

[39] *The Protestant Era* (Chicago, 1948), pp. 62–63.

[40] *Ibid.*, p. 246.

analysis shows that this subsequent elaboration of personality, the Nietzschean overvaluation of the self, was not counteracted by the God-symbol which itself had been lost in the act of making God a person.

Such confessions of egocentricity in modern man, wherever they appear in contemporary thought and religious feeling from Nietzsche to Tillich, and by way of the new orthodoxy of Eliot, all attest to the fact that in recent Protestantism communion-in-symbol has been lost. The irrelevance of orthodox and devout Roman Catholic practice to this condition is obvious. It is rather better to turn to the Protestant Anglo-Catholicism of Dom Gregory Dix, monk of Nashdom Abbey, for a theory of the Eucharist as the supremely regnant symbol. The ortho-doxy of this view both emphasizes what Protestantism, in its less characteristic areas, still offers to its communicants, and warns, as perhaps no other statement could, against the loss of an essential symbol, a loss which delivers the unorthodox indi-vidual up to a God-as-personality.

> The Body of Christ, the church, offers itself to *become* the sacrificed Body of Christ, the Sacrament, in order that thereby the church itself may become within time what in eternal reality it is before God—the " fulness " or " fulfilment " of Christ; and each of the redeemed may " become " what he has been made by baptism and confirmation, a living member of Christ's Body.[41]

> The more we can learn to think of our own worship at the eucharist . . . in terms of " pan-human " fulfilment of the Messianic sacrifice, the nearer we shall be to entering into the mind of the apostolic church about the eucharist and the further from most of our present controversies.[42]

These are definitions of the utmost clarity. The obverse of the symbolic authority which they describe is human personality contending alone with God. The universe is made of I and You, and the towering egoism of the individual becomes the nexus of both the existentialism of Nietzsche and Sartre and

[41] *The Shape of the Liturgy* (Westminster, 1952), p. 247.
[42] *Ibid.*, p. 752.

the symbolic primitivism of modern literature. The existentialist wills to endure it, to grasp the abyss alone; the primitivist, even though he will not share the human corporateness of the Eucharist as the central Christian symbol, aspires, at least, toward escape through new symbols to explain the nature of You (God), and to restore the ideality of corporateness lost in the Protestant condition of symbolic inanition.

Civilization has been defined by Schweitzer as " progress, material and spiritual progress, on the part of individuals as a mass." [43] In the light of this reading directed upon the conditions which have just been considered, it must appear that civilization has reached the state of decay revealed by Schweitzer's description. The moral progress of individuals as a mass, save the " progress " of totalitarian states where collectivism is decreed at the peril of life itself, diminishes. And if a mass subscription to the authority of traditional symbols be regarded as one condition requisite to progress, then it may be concluded that symbolic impoverishment is one clear proof of decay.

The deepest symbols of artistic expression, especially when they proceed from genuine religious compulsion, are endowed with sacramental properties. (A thorough defense of this statement will follow.) It is difficult to see how Tillich's contemporary Protestant " can become aware of the God above the God of theism in the anxiety of guilt and condemnation when the traditional symbols that enable man to withstand the anxiety of guilt and condemnation have lost their power . . . when . . . what was once the power in those symbols can still be present and create the courage to be." [44] As I have already noted, the act of symbolization is a vital function of the human being. This is the view I shall follow, without deviation, throughout this study. Tillich's words of courage to the Protestant appear, then, as not very much more than an exhortation to accept the loss of the symbol and to transfer the power which once animated it to himself. In this interpretation, the impoverished Protestant must relinquish his allegiance to all symbols which

[43] *The Decay and the Restoration of Civilization*, p. 35.
[44] *The Courage to Be*, p. 189.

no longer mean anything to him, and grasp the feeling which was once contained in allegiance for a simple " redirection " to a new courage to be and to believe in a meaning of existence without symbols. I cannot judge the theological subtlety of this process. But it clearly denies that the process of symbolization must and will go on. Tillich's contention may be answered in the meaning of symbols from recent primitivism and other systems of contemporary art.

Poetry and religion, the indivisible ones, can subsist without traditional symbols; but without symbols of any sort, old or new, they cease to exist. The poetic display of dead symbols, beginning with Eliot's earlier study of fragments totally dead and forms expiring (in " The Waste Land ") , goes on into the living reality of the present. Consider, for instance, the façade of the dead in Dylan Thomas's concluding stanzas of his lyric beginning " It is the sinners' dust-tongued bell claps me to churches."

> Forever it is a white child in the dark-skinned summer
> Out of the font of bone and plants at that stone tocsin
> Scales the blue wall of spirits;
> From blank and leaking winter sails the child in colour,
> Shakes, in crabbed burial shawl, by sorcerer's insect woken,
> Ding dong from the mute turrets.

> I mean by time the cast and curfew rascal of our marriage,
> At nightbreak born in the fat side, from an animal bed
> In a holy room in a wave;
> And all love's sinners in sweet cloth kneel to a hyleg image,
> Nutmeg, civet, and sea-parsley serve the plagued groom and
>   bride
> Who have brought forth the urchin grief.[45]

If one wishes to understand what has happened to these symbols, he will do well to resort to comparison and lay this palimpsest of the Resurrection and the Birth of God the Son beside Milton's hymn " On the Morning of Christ's Nativity." In Tillich's sense the symbols " that enable man to withstand the

[45] No. 15 in Dylan Thomas, *Selected Writings*, ed. J. L. Sweeney (New York, New Directions, 1946).

anxiety of guilt and condemnation " have become powerless. But no one will contend, if he is a student of either Eliot or Thomas, that man goes on in the " courage to be " without symbols. Eliot goes back to tradition in his allegiance to Anglo-Catholicism; Thomas moves into a new area where symbols of sexual impulse supplant the expiring forms of Christian theism.

It may be argued that Tillich writes of the layman, of the man who may be called " average," rather than of the artist. But since Tillich has chosen to speak of modern art as " not propaganda but revelation," of the creators of modern art as those who have been able to see the meaninglessness of our existence,[46] he has advanced the symbol-maker as the supreme percipient. For this maker, this doer reveals more than meaninglessness. Through the abstractions of art he creates order and meaning. With him the authentic primitivist takes his place. It will be well to summarize here the character which we may expect to recognize in him. He will be the man familiar with the I-You relationship. He will be the egoist-romanticist, as Santayana has described him, the man who " disowns all authority save that mysteriously exercised over him by his deep faith in himself," the man who would be " heir to all civilization, and, nevertheless . . . take life arrogantly and egoistically, as if it were an absolute personal experiment." [47] As an extreme individualist, he may return at the end of his quest for a new symbolism to an established collective, even as Friedrich von Schlegel and many other individualists in the last one hundred years became Roman Catholics.[48] But as long as he remains the primitivist, he will entertain the idea of God in every form. He will say with Pierre Loti in search of the wisdom of Benares: " For there are no false gods, and the wisdom of sages who profess that theirs is the true God, and that they alone know his name, is but childish folly." [49] Finally, in the solitariness of the I-You from which he proceeds, he will have acquired the dis-

[46] *The Courage to Be*, p. 147.
[47] *Works*, Triton Edition (New York, 1936), vol. 6 (" Three Philosophical Poets "), p. 96.
[48] Cf. Tillich, *The Courage to Be*, p. 117.
[49] *India*, trans. A. F. Inman (London [1906?]), p. 54.

tinguishing habit of the primitivist, the custom of making symbols for the meaning of his own existence before a God whose nature he sees as inscrutable. Thus Isidore Ducasse, Comte de Lautréamont, in the satanic mysteries of the *Chants de Maldoror*, speaks of the smile of puissant hate which the deity casts upon him; [50] Arthur Rimbaud, "slave of his own baptism," flees Christianity into "reality," [51] Christianity to which he will return to die at Marseilles; Gauguin at Tahiti, in 1897, praises Ernest Renan for fighting the church in the cause of man " who knows its iniquity and its lies," Renan who, taking Jesus as a model, became dangerous to the church.[52]

But long before these Herman Melville had written with more quiet and less mephistophelian intent: " Our own hearts are our best prayer-rooms, and the chaplains who can help us most are ourselves." [53] This is the locus of origin for the symbols of primitivism. For unlike the Deistic calm of Paine and Jefferson, to whose confessions it bears so striking a resemblance, Melville's Protestant aloneness before the inscrutable nature of God makes possible the symbols of his art and explicates the conditions which engender primitivism through a century to come. Life was, indeed, an absolute personal experiment for him; so it became for the makers of symbols who follow.

4   Exoticism and Professional Orientalism

Beside the gaunt extremities of an emaciated culture which these notices have traced, the academic form of primitivism, particularly of exoticism, must appear in a kind of flaccid obesity. Some reference has already been made to the dual and opposing manifestations of primitivism as an idea in the nineteenth century. The conditions producing existential symbol-

[50] *Oeuvres complètes*, ed. P. Soupault (Paris, 1946), p. 58.
[51] *Baudelaire, Rimbaud, Verlaine* [Selections], ed. J. M. Bernstein (New York, 1947), p. xxi.
[52] *Lettres de Gauguin à Sa Femme et à Ses Amis*, ed. M. Malingue (Paris, 1946), pp. 280–81. This judgment appears in a letter addressed to Charles Morice.
[53] *White-Jacket*, p. 197.

ism in primitivistic art are collectively a universal atavism seized by autotypic individualized experience and the artist's necessity of fashioning from these organic elements the forms of his creation. But there is, of course, no special claim of the symbolist of primitive feeling upon this atavism. The technique of exoticism referential to the Orient is impelled by cultural failure, specifically by the impoverishment of religious symbolism, as well.

Exoticism shares in a universal awareness of cultural failure through its exhibited fondness for distant and unknown cultures. It demonstrates satiety with the near and familiar backgrounds, be they as actual as the profile of London from Westminster Bridge or the architectural panoply of the Tuileries and the Louvre, the back-drops localizing the thought and action of Western man. Whistler's famous " Japanese " study of Battersea Bridge, Bizet's *Les pêcheurs de perles*, the " Chinese " poetic ruminations of Judith Gautier or the comparable preciosities of Amy Lowell—all these are emblems of a system. They belong to the history of primitivism—these and hundreds of other pieces of their kind from as many different *ateliers*— through one common bond: a capricious appetite for exotic flavor, most frequently for the strangeness of " primitive " Oriental grace and color. This is technical (and secondary) primitivism. By some anaesthesia, which would have to be defined in terms of psychology, its member creators are able to escape the moral vortex where the true primitivist is made. Their legacy to the Western world is a symbolism of nostalgic themes pointing to exotic distance.

Some recognition of this primitivism of nostalgic reference is necessary in defining the character of existential primitivism. The difference between symbolic instances in a representational and " recreating " art and, on the other hand, central life-symbols must be made entirely clear. The impressive fact of all exotic primitivism is that it attempts to " recreate " what it supposes to be the mood of an alien culture. In the ensuing chapter this study will propose that existential primitivism does not itself reveal absolute fact as this exists in the foreign culture employed. But the distinction between this province of art and the domain of exoticism must already have been defined: the maker of life-symbols has grasped the implications of cultural failure and has acquired an autotype of personal experience sufficient to create a symbolic compensation for this failure; the typical exoticist has neither full sensitivity to cultural impoverishment nor uniqueness of emotive experience actually located at great distance from his environment. In these terms, whether or not the true primitivist has conveyed absolute fact from the Orient cannot matter. His fact is his symbol. Many intelligent persons experience an extreme distaste in looking at or reading or hearing examples of, for instance, *chinoiserie*. They are sure of their dislike; they suspect the work, in some intuitive way, of being fraudulent. The explanation of this spontaneous judgment gets into the vitals of what makes artistic authority. Primary art escapes from nothing, nor does it recreate anything. It casts the spell of authority by its sense of mastery. Its living process is an act of grappling, where there is no room for aping anything or for devising means of " escape." In this context art wills to cast from all the materials of one individual's existence a meaning of life in deliberately chosen forms of expression. It has nothing to do with exotic instances and techniques as the supreme gestures of the creative act.

Not the slightest claim can be made here for an inclusive description of the recent history of exoticism. Certain problems which appear in a study of exotic art should, however, be considered. There is, first, the aesthetic question of artistic " effect," as we say that a bigness of effect is achieved in the score of Gustav Mahler's *Das Lied von der Erde* with its libretto of texts from Li T'ai Po adapted by Hans Bethge. Judged purely as exotic music, the score is artistically successful. It invokes a " mood " which gives the overwrought intellectual an excuse for escape. W. Somerset Maugham has somewhere remarked cynically that music outside the practice of the professional musician is the opiate of twentieth-century man. Works of art that busy themselves with creating effects are membranous devices through which feeling passes by a kind of soporific osmosis into reverie. A criticism intent upon judging works of art in terms of *affective* meaning (outside the work itself) should be properly concerned with the works of exoticism. It must relate inevitably to the dogma that art exists purely for the sake of pleasure, however this may be ultimately achieved and whatever form it may take. In this study literature which devotes itself to this form of artistic existence is not accepted as primary art. Exotic primitivism is artistically inferior because it contents itself with references or cues intended to achieve " artistic effects " as stimulants for the spectator's imagination. It permits and even encourages a whimsical straying from both artistic content and artistic form; the more far-ranging the reverie, the more successful the technique. No matter what its reference to the new and the strange or how wide the panorama it represents, the exotic work avoids the making of the primary art symbol which alone commands the labor of attention *to itself for what it says*.

A second question refers ultimately to the shaping-power of taste and intellectual fashion upon the directions of reference in exoticism. The technical symbol of the exoticist, his instances of the distant and the strange, are directly influenced by popular longing for the unknown. His symbols suit the traumatic nature of all international expositions. They induce a form of excitement—to speak further of artistic effects—not unlike that attending the public spectacles of balloon ascensions and fireworks. They complement a fairly constant public taste for exotic voyaging. There is no difficulty here in genetics. Exotic symbols come not of the artist's quest for reality, but of his impulse toward escape from the commonplace. They are abstractions of *Ferneweh*, the longing for distance.[54]

[54] This longing for distance will be contiguous to, but not within, pure exoticism when it receives an additional element of the philosophy of will, or of socio-political purpose. Thus the exoticism of Jack London and that of Bruno Traven are clearly apparent. But the Oceanic narratives of London, particularly the *South Sea Tales* (1909) and the " Polynesian " novel, *A Son of the Sun* (1912), are minor allegories of Nietzschean will in defiance of adversity and have, actually, little if any relation to a realm of feeling toward Oceania and the Orient. Of Traven's political novels, *The Rebellion of the Hanged* (1936) and *The*

Within the scope of recent primitivism here considered, the longing of the exoticist has usually taken form in his taste for the Orient. Technical Orientalism in art is the only major form of primitivism opposed to the primary art of the symbolist who accepts the Orient as the center of existential meaning. This exotic technique may be called " Oriental " academicism. The Orientalism of this tradition is almost entirely the allegiance of intellectuals to a notion of the Orient suggested by academic scholarship. Under its sign the total array of Oriental reference in art is customarily impounded; and it would seem to be the clear obligation of criticism to define authoritatively what amounts to life symbolism here and what should be understood as the deliberately elected " Oriental pose."

The lack of proper critical distinctions is obvious in recent published literary history. The late Arthur E. Christy, for instance, proposed that reference to the Orient in literature gave evidence of what he called " the Asian legacy " to the Occident.[55] It would seem admissible that the literary historian, on the grounds of recurrence in reference, may speak generally of an " Asian legacy." Christy's study is discriminating in its recognitions of a various " Oriental " usage. But it is inadequate for criticism because it declines to distinguish between the kinds of art deriving from Oriental material.

Art does not partition itself into categories of universals on the ground of common reference to cultures and geographical locations. Gautier does not belong with Leconte de Lisle because both created symbols referring to the Orient; nor does Byron belong with Melville in respect to literature in English, despite the fact that Byron " thought about " Oceania in " The

Bridge in the Jungle (1938), it may be said that propagandistic intent in favor of the doctrines of world communism outweighs the exotic qualities of these " primitive " works. Through the mitigations of exotic appeal we are given two sentimentally conceived parables of capitalistic evil victimizing the simple peons of Central America. But if one ignores the purposes of both London and Traven, it will be obvious, I think, that Traven has at least some claim upon art. (On the identity of Traven, now living in Mexico, see _Time_, vol. 59, no. 16, [April 21, 1952], p. 114.)

[55] " The Sense of the Past," in _The Asian Legacy_, ed. A. E. Christy (New York, 1942), p. 39.

Island." Asia bequeathed nothing to the Occident. One of the striking attitudes of the Oriental mind is its usual indifference to the dissemination of "Asian" culture abroad. It has shown little concern, even in its long experience with hordes of Western missionaries and entrepreneurs, with the propagation of its morality and its art among a group of intended Occidental proselytes. What one gets in the "Asian legacy" is simply reference to the Orient, be it either well or ill informed, in terms of symbolic instances (academicism and then academic primitivism) or life-symbols (existential primitivism). One logically proceeds to a definition of Orientalism from a position of measuring what is attained, by reference to the Orient, in terms of primary symbolistic art.

At this point, some attention must be directed to Emerson, Thoreau, and Whitman as contemporaries of Melville. For all these belong to this history of Oriental reference, to this "Asian" legacy; and it should appear strange, particularly, that the author of "Brahma" and the man who wrote that the waters of Walden Pond were mixed with those of the Ganges do not belong to the history of primitivism. Romain Rolland, writing of Emerson and Thoreau, in *Prophets of the New India*, thought that "it would be a matter of deep interest to know exactly how far the American spirit had been impregnated, directly or indirectly, by the infiltration of Hindu thought during the xixth century; for there can be no doubt that it has contributed to the strange moral and religious mentality of the modern United States which Europe has so much difficulty in understanding,—with its astonishing mixture of Anglo-Saxon Puritanism, Yankee optimism of action, pragmatism, 'scientism,' and pseudo-Vedantism." [56] Rolland was impressed that Thoreau had proposed "a joint Bible" of Asiatic scriptures and formulated the motto, *Ex Oriente Lux.* H. Maitra, an Indian scholar studying at Harvard, had some years before Rolland praised Emerson's essay "Circles" for its attainment of the "eternal" through Oriental discipline, and the poem "Brahma" for its masterly interpretation of a line

[56] Trans. E. F. Malcolm-Smith (New York, 1930), p. 329.

from the *Katha-Upanishad* reproduced in the *Bhagavad Gita*. In his summary estimate of " Brahma," Maitra returned to a judgment of the great Harvard Sanskritist, Lanman: nowhere, neither in Sanskrit nor in English, had this truth of the *Gita* been presented " with more vigor, truthfulness, and beauty of form than by Emerson." [57]

Within recent years the leavening force of Oriental scriptures among the community of the Concord Transcendentalists has been definitively described by both Frederic I. Carpenter (*Emerson and Asia*, 1930) and Arthur E. Christy (*The Orient in American Transcendentalism*, 1932). There can be no question of the reading of Emerson and Thoreau; they read every translation of Hindu scripture available to Concord. It is their eclecticism that reappears in the feeling of Whitman and produces " Chanting the Square Deific " and " Passage to India," to say nothing of incidental reference to the Orient throughout *Leaves of Grass*. What is to be done with these bodies of American Orientalism in the history of primitivism? The answer lies in Thoreau's simple confession: " Like some other preachers, I have added my texts—derived from the Chinese and Hindoo scriptures—long after my discourse was written." [58] It is pseudo-Vedantism, indeed, and the character of the practice is even more clear in the token ascriptions which Whitman makes to the Orient.

Nothing could be more ill-placed than an argument that these three American makers of modern literature belong to the company of the exoticists. But it is self-evident that the fascinating power of the Orient *as idea*—in oversimplified terms the idea that good and evil are relative and hence resistant to absolute definition—presides over the thought of these men even as " Oriental " nostalgia persists in the realm of exotic art. The two, both idea and exoticism, are contemporaneous, and they contribute simultaneously to the nature of Oriental-

[57] " Emerson from an Indian Point of View," *Harvard Theological Review*, vol. 4 (1911), pp. 405, 411.

[58] *The Writings of Henry David Thoreau*, ed. Bradford Torrey (Boston and New York, 1906), vol. 8 (*Journal*, 2), p. 192.

ism. Yet, despite the fact that " primitivism " has been found in the concepts of nature advanced by Thoreau and Whitman, particularly, the attribution is flagrant. The structure of cosmic optimism in which these artists lived and moved and had their beings gives no quarter to authentic primitivism, even in Whitman's extraordinary whim to live with the animals. One must return here to the conditions of universal atavism and of the singular autotype, as earlier defined. Certainly Emerson, Thoreau, and Whitman are great American originators of the genuine symbol in art. But their symbolism lies outside the concerns of this study. It is not informed by the Orient, in the true sense, the reasons being that these artists do not admit to cultural failure as the distinguishing condition of the century, and that the autotype, as experience actualized in the Oriental journey, is absent.

Every great symbol of primitivism proceeds from both atavism and an autotypic rendering of experience. Its content, as has been said before, is the fusion of a universal sensibility with the particular, individualized feeling arising from singular emotive experience. The sensibility of Emerson, Thoreau, and Whitman will reveal, when it is examined, the reverse of sensibilities recognizing cultural failure. These artists are all dedicated to romantic organicism and the idea of progress in Western civilization. The autotypes of symbolic form in the art of each man describe the sovereignty of his indigenous American experience: Concord, with its industry and Yankee sagacity, as Emerson's microcosm; the Maine woods, the Merrimack, Cape Cod, and Walden Pond as Thoreau's proving grounds where Nature is handmaiden and man shows how he becomes the " lesser savage "; Paumanok, grass, Brooklyn Ferry, lilac, star, and bird as Whitman's symbols of the interdependence of all existence. No more should be said than that they are contemporary with exoticism and that coincidentally they meet with it in the Orient where they delight, with their parent Emerson, in the " immense goddery " of the Hindus. They seek cosmically to embrace the universe and to exalt the profusion of life.

Technical Orientalism has been shaped by professional exoticists in quest of the novelties and sensations of *tourisme*. Regarded from the domain of primary art, these excursionists appear to have a symbolic relation to the Orient about equal to that of theosophists in the style of Mme. Blavatsky, or of " Oriental seers " among the Hollywood Hindus of California. They depend, of course, upon the true skill of the Sanskritist, the Sinologue, the Japanologist, and the Pacific ethnologist for the series of instances which they employ. Moreover, these exoticists know better than any other patrons of the arts how to enshrine the tokens of the Orient which both scholarship and the exhibits of international expositions afford them. They are the lineal successors of Georgian Londoners who were enchanted by Omai from Tahiti, or of Parisians who " felt the spell " of Hokusai and Hiroshige in the Japanese pavilions at the expositions of 1867 and 1878. The great Oriental scholars, represented by Sir William Jones and Sir Charles Wilkins at the end of the eighteenth century, and by Max Müller, Léon de Rosny, and the Marquis d'Hervey-Saint-Denys in the nineteenth, extended a kind of aural influence over the proclivities of a taste which was in turn strengthened in the spectacles of exhibitions from the mysterious East. This influence makes possible, for instance, the London following of the Hindu " poetess " Toru Dutt (1856–1877) who wrote from her father's garden in Baugmaree, Calcutta, some "sheaves" for her English friends and won the critical sympathies of none other than Sir Edmund Gosse at her death.[59] It permits the enormous popularity of Arnold's *Light of Asia* and FitzGerald's *Rubaiyat*. In France it tempers the " Oriental " dispositions of Théophile Gautier and the Goncourt brothers.

In America, to the unique credit of our national art, it emerges in the Oriental illustrations of a new symbolistic literature from Emerson, Thoreau, and Whitman and in the genuine Oriental symbols of Melville.[60] Orientalism in "serious"

[59] *Ancient Ballads and Legends of Hindustan*, with an introductory memoir by Sir Edmund Gosse (London, 1888).
[60] For several excellent observations on the uniqueness of American literature

American art actually defers its appearance as exoticism until the twentieth century and the debut of the so-called Imagist school of poets.

The scholar made possible the Orient of the Imagists; and he must look upon the by-products of his industry with considerable dismay. These are the gauds of the expositions, the souvenirs of " progress," the *babioles* of those bizarre neuroses held up to view by Paul Bourget. Collectively, they make in the history of the fine arts an indescribable *mélange* of moon gates, pagodas, samurai armor, flower arrangements, tea ceremonies, ivory carvings, and Nirvana. Wherever the climate is warm, particularly in certain areas of the United States, they will be matched by as many pseudo-religious exotic sects, so far removed from the Reformation and systematic theology that they are no longer discernibly Protestant. They all adorn exoticism. The display of Oriental trinkets, however, has been more particularly French than English or American; and with a few exemplary notices of these an end must be made of this discussion. They are all emblematic of exotic Orientalism; they suggest as well how this tradition passes into American literature by way of the Imagist poets, most of whom were thoroughly Gallicized.

So begins the course of French professional Orientalism. The salon of the Comte Robert de Montesquiou in Paris, crowded with Eastern treasures purchased in a " Japanese fit " brought on by the Exposition of 1878, was a *musée extraordinaire*. There Huysmans found the inspiration of *A Rebours*; and there the Parisian temple of " le Japonisme " was raised.[61] The epidemic of this Oriental fit wrought so great an effect on the artistic health of Europe that the preciosity of the condition extended far into the twentieth century. It received sustenance again in 1900 from another great exposition when musicians were enchanted by the strange instruments of the Indochinese

in the symbolistic mode during the nineteenth century see Feidelson's *Symbolism and American Literature*.

[61] Cf. William L. Schwartz, *The Imaginative Interpretation of the Far East in Modern French Literature, 1800–1925* (Paris, 1927), p. 92. Here, as elsewhere, I am indebted to this excellent bibliographical study.

and Siamese pavilions and by the witcheries of the pentatonic scale. In the *atelier* of the painter the evanescent beauties of Chinese and Japanese calligraphy and brush drawing taught a new ideal of charm based upon the principles of irregularity and a new sensitiveness to perceive the " fugitive " aspects of Nature.[62] The refinements of such fugitive aspects are really incalculable. All these large and yet so finely spun effects of exoticism are embodied, of course, in the encomiums poured upon Oriental art by the Goncourt brothers; but for the purposes of this study they may be summarily disposed of to best advantage in a notice of Théophile Gautier and his Chinese-bewitched daughter, Judith.

W. L. Schwartz has called Gautier the first imaginative writer of the nineteenth century to discover the possibilities of Far Eastern literature as stimulus.[63] This judgment, as it stands, is open to question. But it is obvious that Gautier is a supreme example of the European who knew how to live the big effect of Orientalism. His experience, all of it dreamed out upon the substance of Oriental scholars and translators, is exoticism scholastically conditioned; yet he satisfied his longing for China, at least, by keeping a Chinese in his household in Paris as a dinner companion when he entertained Flaubert, Bouilhet, and the Goncourts. China to him was what he supposed the Near East to have been to Gérard de Nerval. In a preface to Nerval's *Voyage en Orient*, he found that this traveler, " his spirit more and more detached from practical life and lost in the infinite of dreams," appealed because of his " displacement at the end of existence," his nature " winged, flying " above reality.[64] This adoration of Nerval is Gautier's projection of his own ego. In the history of primitivism there is no better example of complete egocentricity. Nor is there better witness to the search for escape from Europe. The pages of Gautier's own *L'Orient* are filled with the symbols of exoticism. His " Souvenirs de l'Exposition Universelle de Londres " are his dreams of China, the

[62] *Ibid.*, p. 111.   [63] *Ibid.*, p. 24.

[64] Gérard de Nerval, *Voyage en Orient*, augmentée d'une Préface nouvelle par Théophile Gautier (Paris, 1889), vol. 1, pp. xxxiv-xxxv.

unknown, " civilized when the rest of the world was barbarous, barbarous when this world is civilized "; of Constantinople, proposed again, in the manner of the mad Rousseauist Fourier, as the admirable capital of the world, the " Omniarchat "; of polygamous " Oriental " societies preferable to the European world full of the adulteries and disorders too frequent in monogamy.[65] This London Exposition of 1862 was a mine of exotic treasure.

Judith Gautier, the true daughter of her father, was seized with transporting enthusiasm by the Japanese and Chinese exhibitions in London.[66] It would seem, as well, that she must have been awakened by the scholarship of the Marquis d'Hervey-Saint-Denys, whose masterly *Poésies de l'époque de Thang, avec une étude sur l'art poétique en Chine* appeared in the same year. On returning to Paris, she took up the study of Chinese with her father's exotic companion, Ting-Tun-Ling, and marvelously confessed: " I am Chinese, I am even the reincarnation of a Chinese princess." [67] Exactly how far this reincarnation of Judith became evident or how much Chinese she may have mastered are of no matter. The publication in 1867 of her *Livre de Jade,* a sheaf of translations, admitted her to the elect company of Parisian intellectuals; and in 1885 she gave evidence of her versatility in reincarnations with a " Japanese " volume, the *Poèmes de la Libellule.*[68] Through her long life which ended in 1917, at the very threshold of Imagist poetry and the emergence of Oriental exoticism unabashed in England and America, she influenced the *japonisme* and *chinoiserie* of a whole school of taste. Heredia studied her and came to write poetic ascriptions to the daimyōs of ancient Japan; Verlaine, Cros, and Renaud were turned to Oriental subjects through her influence.[69] She left, beyond her translations and adaptations, *Le Dragon Impérial,* a prose work of 1868, *Les Peuples*

[65] Paris, Charpentier, 1877, vol. 1, pp. 235–36, 80–81.

[66] Cf. M. Dita Camacho, *Judith Gautier, Sa Vie et Son Oeuvre* (Paris, 1939), p. 28.

[67] *Ibid.,* pp. 30–31.

[68] *Ibid.,* pp. 46–47, *et passim.*

[69] Cf. Schwartz, pp. 41–46.

Étranges of 1879, and a drama of 1904/1905 undertaken with Pierre Loti, *La Fille du Ciel.* Finally, in 1914 she went " East " to Morocco to visit the Prince of Annam.[70] The *Livre de Jade* had already realized its most triumphant eventuality in Gustav Mahler's exotic masterpiece, the gigantic *Das Lied von der Erde*; for it was from Judith Gautier that Hans Bethge derived the Chinese texts used by Mahler. Bethge's *Die Chinesische Flöte*, published in 1907, is 'a Germanic off-shoot of French Orientalism.[71]

But the most striking fact about Judith Gautier is her adoration of Richard Wagner, whom she revered, by her own confession, above Homer, Aeschylus, Dante, Goethe, Beethoven, and Shakespeare.[72] In 1868 she began a long correspondence with Wagner.[73] It is probable that the letters which passed between these two, evaluated as documents in the history of primitivism, would describe very well the essential nature of exoticism. There could not have been a more apt confluence of tributary and stream. It is, in fact, hard to say which is the more exotic, the message from Peiping or the message from Valhalla.

The case of Miss Amy Lowell represents in American letters a kind of transposition and transubstantiation of Judith Gautier. Miss Lowell had been busy with *Six French Poets* (1915) for some years; and without offense to her reputation as a critic, it may be assumed that she had made herself thoroughly familiar with Oriental exoticism in France, even though she does not deal with the subject in these essays. The year 1919 is her *annus mirabilis*; for it was then that she gave up her full burden of Oriental treasure in the " Japanese " *Pictures of the Floating World* and in *Fir-Flower Tablets*, " Poems from the Chinese " undertaken with the assistance of her friend, the translator then living in China, Florence Ayscough. These volumes are windfalls of the Imagist school. But they were not, of course, fashioned single-handed by Miss Lowell. In the first section

---

[70] Camacho, pp. 82 ff.
[71] See Bethge's commentary in the Inselverlag edition (Leipzig, 1907), p. 104.
[72] Camacho, p. 82.
[73] *Ibid.*, p. 79.

of the Japanese collection, which she called "Lacquer Prints," she fancied that she was following the spirit of the old Japanese *hokku* (as devised by the poet Bashō in the late seventeenth century), a form remarkable indeed for its utmost compression and terseness, and its subtlety. Thus we have a piece entitled "Moon Haze" which reads in its entirety: "Because the moon-light deceives / Therefore I love it." [74] Miss Lowell esoterically selects her title from the Japanese terminology of the art of caricature in the eighteenth century: *ukiyo-e*, "passing world pictures" from contemporary plebeian life, represented particularly in the art of the print-maker. These imitations of a Japanese form express nostalgia; they are exotic instances of a "recreating" art.

Miss Lowell's priestly duties in spreading the Oriental gospel are manifestations of her Yankee determination to "get at" the evanescence of object qualities by an authority of art as image. The rigor of her cause is well known, and it is all of a piece with her generous willingness to advance the new ideal. But she really originated very little. John Gould Fletcher taught her to seek the image alone; he almost certainly taught her how to be "Oriental." For Fletcher goes back to Hans Bethge and so to Judith Gautier, by his own confession. Bethge, he wrote, confirmed the method of the "Blue Symphony" (1914) and influenced the form of all the "symphonies." [75] How Oriental, indeed, was this mood? "While I was writing the series of 'Symphonies,' during 1914 and 1915, I was content to abide by the Chinese influences that had been absorbed in the translations I had found accessible." [76] The "Chinese influences" give us, then, these lines from "Irradiations":

[74] See the author's preface (p. vii) and Section I of *Pictures of the Floating World* (New York, Macmillan Co., 1919). The only thorough study of Miss Lowell's "adaptations" from Oriental texts is that of W. L. Schwartz in his evaluation, "A Study of Amy Lowell's Far Eastern Verse," *Modern Language Notes*, vol. 43 (1928), pp. 145–52. Schwartz reaches the conclusion that these experiments are quite distant from Oriental poetry.

[75] See Fletcher's essay, "The Orient and Contemporary Poetry," in *The Asian Legacy*, ed. Christy, pp. 157–58.

[76] *Ibid.*, p. 159.

" Winds from the mountains of cinnabar, / Lacquered mandarin moments . . ."; or these from the " Blue Symphony ":

Sombre wrecks—autumnal leaves;
Shadowy roofs
In the blue mist,
And a willow-branch that is broken.

Oh, old pagodas of my soul, how you glittered across green
    trees! [77]

The question might be proposed: in a country of old pagodas of the soul is it Chinese to combine green trees with blue mist if one is writing a blue symphony?

The Orientalism of Ezra Pound cannot be appropriately evaluated here, since Pound's deliberate obscurity, his obtuse mature idiom after he passes from the aegis of Imagism, does not readily show what partial allegiance he bears to exotic primitivism. H. G. Porteus in a recent essay on Pound's " Chinese " character praises the method of *Cathay* in its adaptation of Li T'ai Po; [78] he chooses to compare him with the greatest Sinologue and translator of the twentieth century, Arthur Waley. Thus Pound's translations, even when they fumble, " contrive to capture the spirit of the originals." [79] The worth of this statement would have to be confirmed by a Chinese who had mastered the English of Pound's translations. If it be granted that the purpose of Pound's *Cantos* is to describe poetically the vitiating force of usury in Western civilization, and that as a philosopher this poet is concerned not with systems of thought and the classifications of ideas but with entering our minds perceptually rather than dogmatically,[80] then his fondness for the Chinese ideogram may be explained: he wishes to renovate poetry by finding a linguistic equivalent in a " reconstructed " English idiom. Harold H. Watts, a recent critic, calls

[77] John Gould Fletcher, *Selected Poems* (New York, Farrar and Rinehart, Inc., 1938), pp. 4, 15.
[78] " Ezra Pound and his Chinese Character: a Radical Examination," in *Ezra Pound: A Collection of Essays*, ed. Peter Russell (London, 1950), p. 204.
[79] *Ibid.*, p. 205.
[80] Cf. Brien Soper, " Ezra Pound: Some Notes on His Philosophy," in Russell's *Ezra Pound*, p. 229.

attention to Pound's hope for such an idiom which exploits the
essence of the ideogram " by associating particular objects . . .
that have not been put together before—objects that, juxtaposed
in their unaltered simplicity, create . . . a totality of appre-
hension that takes in far more than what, in the poem, is
stated." [81] This may all very well be; and if it be true, Pound's
allegiance to the ideogram cannot mean much more than
Eliot's devotion to the objective correlative. There comes to
be, then, nothing " Oriental " about it all, even though it
should be clearly understood that this emphasis upon the Chinese language, as a medium of expression, stems from the
earlier years of Pound when he was temporarily encompassed by
exotic " Orientalism."

Watts notes that Pound is impatient with all concepts of
God, including the doctrine of Buddha's incarnation and the
" waftiness of Taoist mysticism." [82] This would seem pretty
clear, even with the benefit only of partial and inexpert reading
of the *Cantos*. Awareness of cultural failure, the incipient idea
of Western civilization as synonymous with malevolence—in
Pound's case the malevolence of capitalist-democracies—is there,
without possible doubt. It is less evident that Pound is anywhere concerned, even in his unclear relation to primitivism,
with the construction of compensatory religious symbols. Standing as he does at the latest point of Orientalism, emerging
through his career into a literature of full renascence in which
he becomes a dictator of poetic convention, he illustrates at
least one fact of art antithetical to the whole nature of exoticism. This fact was simply stated by Ferdinand Brunetière in
1888, in an essay on European decadence: " *Ce n'est pas enfin
l'homme qui est fait pour l'art, c'est l'art qui est fait pour
l'homme.*" [83]

---

[81] *Ezra Pound and the Cantos* (London, 1951), p. 38.

[82] *Ibid.,* p. 34.

[83] " Symbolistes et Décadents," *Revue des deux Mondes,* vol. 90 (3ᵉ période,
1888), p. 226.

The uses of art as the distinctive property of the human being are as various as the kinds of symbols which the making of art produces. Man as the secondary artist is man who is servile to art; man as the primary artist is man who commands art to incarnate what had not before attained form. The ranges of this discussion of primitivism related to the Orient have one excuse for being: they are deemed essential if one is to know what the content and the form of life-symbols in this system of recent Western culture really mean. For all these things go on as Ishmael, a symbol of symbols, begins his perilous and chartless voyage. He seeks the distant and the strange, even as the exoticist. But he is the actor and the doer, playing his part as an artist among a mixed company of fugitives to the Orient. He alone is the artist who dares to make new symbols to describe the relationship of man to his God. His symbols are made to fortify him against ruin; for even as he works, the great fissures of his culture widen into abysses for some men and thrust up, with unknown vulcanism, the saving islands of others.

There is a certain island in the ocean called Perdita, which is by far the most outstanding in its delightfulness and the general fertility of all its lands. Once found by accident, it was thereafter never found when sought, and is therefore called Perdita. To this island Brendan is said to have come.

Honoré d'Autun
(trans. George Boas, *Primitivism and Related Ideas in the Middle Ages,* from Migne's *Patrologia Latina*)

II

Perdita:
The Volcanic Center

In the preceding chapter the structure of primitivism was traced with the objective of suggesting criteria for aesthetic judgment. The act of purifying the terminology of primitivism by isolating the forms which it displays led to the assertion that the symbols of existential primitivism come into being through the imposition of an autotype, a facsimile of actual sensed experience, upon atavistic feeling in which the contemporaneous allegiances of a group of artists are related. Opposed to these primary (life) symbols were the instances and references of Rousseauism and exoticism, wherein either awareness of cultural failure specifically demonstrated in the impoverishment of Protestant symbolism, or an autotype derived from physical proximity to the point of reference, or both were absent. It was also said that the value of these manifestations as primary art may be determined by examining the character of the forms produced through use of material which, in this limited study, is essential to both: the culture of the Orient. It is assumed that sufficient analysis has been made to permit rejection of further concern with academic primitivism. Henceforth, the term *existential primitivism* will be dropped, with the understanding that *primitivism* refers to the art of the life-symbol admissible to this study.

Atavism, the reversion of the creating mind to an earlier state of man's cultural (religious) history, is determined by the awareness of cultural failure which has been described. In recent primitivism, atavism discards the symbolic structures of Christian tradition and permits, as has already been suggested, the reëmergence of archetypes. This amounts to saying that the I-You relationship of the Protestant condition eludes the authority of traditional dogma perpetuated in Christian symbols and reverts to archetypal patterns which were always there in the unconscious, but earlier "controlled" or "obscured" by traditional symbols. Thus atavism is expressed by archetypes; and the symbol which is the artistic result of atavism contains both archetype and the unique autotype of the individual artist. Before the Oceanic and Oriental symbols of primitivism can be studied effectively, two additional analyses are necessary: an investigation of the nature of archetypes, and an inquiry into the materials of autotypes possessed by artists who are the makers of true symbols. The purpose of this chapter is to examine the archetypal condition of primitivism. The chapters of the following section will seek to define the nature of autotypes as symbolistic potentials in the experience of primitivists related to the Oriental journey.

1 *Archetype and Sacrament*

" What is actually happening in the world," wrote Jung, " is due not merely to ' dim remnants of formerly conscious activities,' but to volcanic outbursts from the very bottom of things." [1] To paraphrase, what has happened, and what does happen in the world of art, bursts upward in vulcanism from the bottom. Perdita is any one of a festoon of islands—figuratively like the great festooned chains of the Pacific from Hawaii to the Philippines and Japan, all rising from the vulcanism of submerged mountains. On each one was a solitary maker of symbols, lending, in the sense of Eliot's description noted in the preface to this study, his allegiance to an unconscious community. Unlike the Perdita of Brendan, it will be seen again; but what is to be made there will not be exactly like what was made before. It will be generically related to other symbols of its system only because the material of its island origin is very much like that of all the other islands. Even now a new Perdita is rising somewhere from the volcanic bottom, just as in the realm of good solid matter a new island is boiling up in a mass of basaltic rock somewhere north of the Philippines and south of the Ryukyus. Perdita is each man's Orient, the " lost " island of each Ishmael, who, like Brendan, must see it as " by far the most outstanding in its delightfulness and the general fertility of all its lands." That its generic relation to the *actual* Orient is unlike and even does violence often to what the scholar knows in fact is a condition which cannot very much disturb the artist. Nor should it disturb criticism. The business at hand is to show how Perdita relates to what the artist says.

There is no law which requires the study of literature to take all or nothing of psychology. It may take what it pleases. For it so happens that much of what Jung said of archetypes is more common sense than particularized psychological theory for the specialist. On the other hand, Freudian psychoanalysis is not the means of critical entrance into the elemental domain of a work of art. The difference between the two doctrines (as

[1] *The Integration of the Personality* (trans. Dell), p. 12.

critically interpreted) will appear in the specific readings which
Freudians may direct toward the incidence of the *ruined tower*
in three chronologically disparate poets, Melville, Verhaeren,
and Dylan Thomas,[2] and the interpretation which followers of
Jung may make of the same motif. It is assumed here that there
is common knowledge of both schools sufficient to suggest what
the possibilities in both readings would be. In general Freud
and Jung differ with respect to the question of sexual authority
in the symbolic use of a given device. To followers of Freud,
the tower will appear as a symbol of sexual power, adversely
rendered impotent. Thus Richard Chase applies Freud to
Melville. "The tower and the bell are common sexual symbols. But in the dreamlike conclusion of Melville's story the
imagery is more startling. It is a dream of castration."[3] Followers of Jung will read the same symbol as a manifestation
of archetypal awareness. The ruined tower as archetype is revealed through a commonly shared body of evidence that suggests the idea: man's Christian estate is impotent. This archetype transcends and ignores Freud's blood consciousness and
his sexual configuration of all human impulse. Certainly
"dream content" is dictatorial in both readings. But in justice
to both Freud and Jung it should be remembered that neither
is concerned solely with the processes or the objectives of art
criticism. It is their critical followers who have established
criteria, and methods of analysis.

The interpretation and the judgment of art must rest finally
upon individuated form, that form which is singularly achieved
by the artist who shapes his symbol from multiple feeling. It
is critically dishonest to read symbols through Freud unless the
artist by his own confession intended to project the Freudian
method; it is critically dishonest to read symbols through the
archetypes of Jung, *without concern for any other genetic factor*.
To reduce art to evidence for psychology is to deny the author-

[2] Compare Melville's story *The Bell-Tower*, Verhaeren's "Le Sonneur" from
the poetic sequence *La Revolté*, and the poem of Dylan Thomas already cited,
"It is the sinners' dust-tongued bell claps me to churches" (with the symbol
of "mute turrets").

[3] *Herman Melville* (New York, 1949), p. 124.

ity of the artist as creator. The authority of individuated form
is potentially within the grasp of the artist through the particular autotype which gives both locus and singularity to feeling.
Thus Melville's savages aboard the *Pequod* are singular symbolic forms. As autotypically wrought symbols, they are exclusively his. They were not made of " dream content " alone.
Yet the fact that they all refer to an archetype defines a misfortune in the vocabulary of criticism. It happens that no one
other than Jung has yet offered a terminology of the collective
unconscious, and in its use of Jung's language, criticism may
find itself misread as psychoanalysis. Let some critic devise a
new terminology, and the study of literature may be freed from
professional psychology as a source of vocabulary. The bases
of feeling antecedent to the shaping of a symbol are archetypes
for want of another term. They are the " drives " in the sentience of the primitivist which elicit individuated forms and
authorize the purpose of genuine artistic construction. The
allegiances of an artist discover the substructure of his symbols.
It is of the greatest importance for the ends of this study that
the *partial* dependence upon Jung's terminology evident here
should be understood for what it is. With the dream content of
Freud's theory, as sexual authority manifest in the trauma and
" infantile amnesia " of the " neurotic " artist, this study has no
concern whatsoever.

Much has already been said initially of cultural failure manifest in the impoverishment of Protestant symbolism. It is this
impoverishment which uncovers feeling at the volcanic base
of primitivism. The feeling is first expressed through archetypes. It now follows that the great faulting in sensibility which
thrusts primitivism into the light and air of art is an upheaval
in the religious and emotive consciousness.

*The symbols of primitivism are formed in answer to the basic
human need for sacrament, when previously authoritative forms
of sacrament have become powerless.* The history of Protestantism is, in one of its provinces, a history of the limitation of
sacrament, the tempered orthodoxy of Lutherans and Anglicans
notwithstanding. It is understood that the Roman Catholic

and the Eastern churches recognize seven sacraments, viz.,
baptism, confirmation, the Eucharist, penance, extreme unction,
holy orders, and matrimony; the larger number of Protestant
churches (those usually referred to in " Low Churchism "),
only baptism and the Lord's Supper. This is not to say, of
course, that the human being requires seven doctrinaire forms
of sacrament. The point is simply that Protestantism shows a
willful and consistent process of discarding sacramental forms,
when sacramentalism itself is a distinguishing property of the
human imagination in its symbol-making power, from the most
primitive rite of segregating adolescent boys in a tribal house of
puberty to the most sophisticated theological doctrine of baptism. Sacrament is essentially an archetype appearing in universal religious custom which informs the concept that *through
corporateness the individual is made one with his fellows in
communion with the deity*, the mystery of man-in-God (Christianity) or man-in-Nature (primitive totemism and animism).
The need for sacrament will out, even as man's need for food
and shelter and for symbols to represent his existence will out.
A religion that proceeds intellectually to discard sacrament
dooms itself. The refinements of Buddhism show this cardinal
fact, if one wishes to reserve judgment on Protestantism for the
moment. The farther the sophistication of Buddhism moved
from the old legend of the Buddha baring his breast in the
forest to feed a starving tigress and her cubs, the more it broke
into the refinements of dogma, the more sectarian it became, the
more " thoughtful " and arid, until it accomplished in the end
the "de-souling" of the human being noted by Spengler.

The analysis of man's instinct for sacrament is the business
of anthropology, ethnology, and psychology. Exactly why sacrament appears in Oceania as a corporate celebration of puberty
and oncoming sexual power and fecundity and why it takes to
itself the symbol in the Christian world of God who died for all
men are questions which primitivism does not suggest. Its sole
concern is with the impelling, unceasing need in the human
being for sacramental form. Some reference has already been
made to Santayana's view of the romantic egoist as the man for

whom all existence is an absolute personal experiment. This man is indeed Ishmael, the primitivist. But as egoist he is dedicated to finding a new sacrament. He is the antithesis of the solitary tragic hero, whom Santayana has somewhere else called absurd. The tragic hero is the man who turns his back on all sacrament, who denies his own nature as a human being. His folly is the supreme absurdity of Captain Ahab's contempt, as he baptizes the harpoons in the name of the devil; it is the folly of every Nietzschean hero grasping the abyss with the eagle's talons, alone.

In Jung's view—and here close attention is invited to his theological reasoning cast in the frame of psychological reference—the history of Protestantism is the history of chronic iconoclasm.[4] Paul Tillich agrees with Jung, with this qualification, that "the Protestant protest has rightly destroyed the magical elements in Catholic sacramentalism but has wrongly brought to the verge of disappearance the sacramental foundation of Christianity and with it the religious foundation of the protest itself." He continues: "Protestants often confuse essential symbols with accidental signs. They are often unaware of the numinous power inherent in genuine symbols, words, acts, persons, things. They have replaced the great wealth of symbols appearing in the Christian tradition by rational concepts, moral laws, and subjective emotions."[5] Tillich does not demonstrate the line which he draws between the magical elements of Catholic sacramentalism and the sacramental foundation. Presumably he is talking about "primitive" as opposed to ritualistic Christianity, e. g., the Sermon on the Mount as opposed to the communion of the saints in hagiology.

It was inevitable, of course, that Christianity in development should take unto itself an elaborate sacramentalism; for the extension of sacramental form is an essential act of the human being, no matter what his religious subscriptions. Sacraments extend their symbols constantly by accretion. The recent Roman Catholic pontificated dogma of the Corporeal Assumption

---

[4] *The Integration of the Personality*, p. 61.
[5] *The Protestant Era*, p. xxiii.

of the Virgin is only one instance of an extending sacramental pattern, the sacrament of penance; and another canonization will extend it further. That is why Protestantism with its disdain for an accreting sacrament proliferates into all sorts of substitutions for orthodox sacrament as religious symbol; that is why it breeds, with its infinite sectarianism, vast new systems of sacramental symbols each year. H. Richard Niebuhr sees denominationalism as " the moral failure of Christianity ": the denominations are " emblems, therefore, of the victory of the world over the church, of the secularization of Christianity, of the church's sanction of that divisiveness which the church's gospel condemns." [6]

In the realm of art, something has been going on in the last century which is wholly unlike any other development in the aesthetic history of the Christian era. Artistic expression originating in the Protestant or " Protestantly " derived mind has been laboring with the construction of symbols to compensate for a lost sacramentalism. In this act, art has become, in the strictest possible sense, religion. T. S. Eliot contended in 1933 that " the chief clue to the understanding of most contemporary Anglo-Saxon literature is to be found in the decay of Protestantism "; the rejection of Protestant Christianity being the rule rather than the exception, " individual writers can be understood and classified according to the type of Protestantism which surrounded their infancy, and the precise state of decay which it had reached." [7] (It is interesting to note that if Eliot, the chief mentor of the early " new " critics, does not here corroborate the essentiality of relevance between a work of art and the intent of its maker, no one else ever has!)

Maud Bodkin, who subscribes to Jung with considerably more scrupulousness than my study will allow, believes that " when the development of individuality, and of sincerity in thought and feeling, has made impossible the acceptance of a dogmatic religion, while still a temperamental subjection to tidal changes of feeling enforces the need to find some stay in

---

[6] *The Social Sources of Denominationalism* (New York, 1929), p. 25.
[7] *After Strange Gods*, p. 41.

symbols of a collective tradition and suprapersonal life, the function of poetry may be realized in its highest value." [8] She is entirely right in her view of poetry as in its highest value *in crisis*, the crisis which has been earlier represented here by the term *modulation*.[8a] But when she talks of finding a stay in symbols " of a collective tradition," she is using Jung to the letter. The symbols of primitivism do not belong to a collective *tradition* at all. They are the unique symbols of the artists who created them. Jung would contend, of course, that the total array of symbols in this system is a collective since each one reveals the " dream content " of an archetype common to all. Although it is indeed true that primitivistic symbols are bound together through a community of feeling antecedent to form, Miss Bodkin's view of a " tradition " must be rejected. So must her judgment that " a form of control outgrown and become oppressive is replaced by a control objectified under a different symbol, *transcending still* the individual, but deeply akin to him, sustaining and renewing within him the values which he most intimately accepts." [9]

The archetype in the form of symbolic structures, in primitivism at any rate, does not *transcend* the individual. It impels the symbol into being; and therefore it fortifies the artist, in this case the man who seeks a new sacrament. The singular intuition of the artist and his mastery of his material in bringing form into being make the work of art; the progenitor is not the dream-motif of the archetype. But Miss Bodkin is eminently correct when she calls attention to Whitman's symbol of the star in the great elegy on the death of Lincoln. Although she does not name it as such, this is a sacramental symbol compensating for the " lost " symbols of Whitman's Protestant heritage. From the " black mirk " and " harsh surrounding cloud " in which the poem begins, Whitman " gropes individually for symbols of deliverance and finds the star." [10] Eliot's pro-

---

[8] *Archetypal Patterns in Poetry* (London, 1934), p. 88.
[8a] See the Introduction.
[9] *Ibid.*, p. 329. Italics mine.
[10] *Ibid.*, p. 131.

posed measurement for understanding contemporary Anglo-Saxon literature may be applied here.

A question immediately arises: if sacrament is symbol representing corporateness in which the individual is subsumed, why do not these new compensatory symbols transcend the artist in the collective of the archetype which Miss Bodkin envisions? For on this point must depend the authority of the artist as opposed to the sovereignty of the archetype, and art must stand for what it is, or fall to the ignominious position of a mere record of " dreams." The answer is discovered in the ideality of the symbolist. The abstraction of his created form as sacrament singularly envisions the corporateness of men in a religious act. To extend, in this sense, the description of Perdita and its solitary symbol-maker, each man worships alone on his island. The sacrament which he creates invokes for his comfort and his " salvation " a world of the ideal where what he remembers of lost symbols is mixed with what his heretical allegiance to non-Christian (Oriental) custom supplies. Whether this custom, displayed to him through the aperture of his Oriental journey as experience, was mastered or merely " sampled " cannot very much matter. His symbol suggests the possibility of a new sacramental corporateness. As a maker of sacramentalism he belongs to an unconscious artistic community of his age because, as artist, he is like other workers who find art a better means of affirmation than existential courage. He has cast off convention and traditional theology, and in his act of creating, he descends to the true primitivity of religiousness: he returns to the authority of primitive feeling and the emotive life.

Richard Niebuhr observes that where " the power of abstract thought has not been highly developed and where inhibitions on emotional expression have not been set up by a system of polite conventions, religion must and will express itself in emotional terms." Energy of expression rather than conformity to a creed is regarded as the test for religious genuineness. " Hence also the formality of ritual is displaced in such groups by an informality which gives opportunity for the expression of emotional faith and for a simple, often crude, symbolism." [11] The fact of this statement may be illustrated by an example from the dead extremities of Protestantism which has not been widely noted: the custom of snake-handling Protestant revivalists in the southern United States. These preachers of a new salvation " demonstrate " the power of God by exposing bare arms and chests to the fangs of a rattlesnake displayed before the frenzied congregation. If the rattlesnake does not bite, or if it bites without killing, the favor of God is with his children. From the practices of new Protestant sects there is no illustration superior to this. Here is the pure emergence of a sacramental symbol from a sovereign archetype. The snake is one of a kind with the Marquesan lizard or the anaconda of the Amazon jungle, as objects of sacramental worship. It is a perfect example of the crude symbolism noted by Niebuhr; and the worship which attends it is orgiastic emotion. It is, furthermore, a superior manifestation of " dream content " in symbolic form, whether one follows the Freudian possibility of reading snake-handling as phallicism or a possibility from Jung that the snake is an atavistic symbol of man's psychic totality, wherein he carries the whole history of the race and through which he can return to the religion of primitive animism.

All this makes the emergence of an archetype *minus art*. Now it is perfectly clear that genuine art could be made of the archetypal material just described. But it would have to present, as it might very well in the hands of Faulkner, for instance, the art symbol as an abstraction of crude themes in the initial material. The snake as sacrament, whether one felt that it was artistically presented with the objectivity of a Conrad or the emotional subjectivity of a Melville, would then become *at least* a device of beauty or *at most* a beautiful artistic device substituted by the artist for his own lost sacraments.

The archetype revealed by this snake-handling is admitted to religious ritual through the failure of existing Christian symbols. The contemporary religious sensibility here represented is to primitivistic art what the new space-time concepts are to

[11] *The Social Sources of Denominationalism*, p. 30.

the nonobjective painter of our century, from Marcel Duchamp's famous nude descending a staircase to the most recent abstraction of Mondrian. That primitivism utilizes archetypes in its unswerving tendency toward sacramental form is the distinguishing condition of its identity. In that it abstracts these forms from both the remnants of Protestant sacramentalism and the " gain " of Oriental emblems, it is set apart forever from the crude, inartistic symbolism of the pure archetype, with its dream content and common motif. It will not submit to any reading of art as mere psychoanalysis. For art alone can seize the crudity of the snake, with its endless symbolic fluidity, and capture it in the deliberate, artistically purposive abstraction of individuated form. This something that has been happening in modern art as an heretical process of making sacrament is more easily identified in the system of primitivism than elsewhere. It is assumed that every apostate creator in the realm of the fine arts is potentially an originator of sacramental form, if he is emotively impelled toward religious expression. As apostate, of course, he is the disbelieving Protestant.

The decadence of Protestantism, as Jung saw it, enables man to " rediscover the gods as psychic factors." [12] This proposal leads now to some account of the psychic factor in sacramental symbolism. Specifically, it introduces archetypes in their true forms, *the contents of the collective unconscious*,[13] and more particularly the archetypes of primitivism as the contents of *a* collective unconscious state. To rediscover the gods as psychic factors is simply to be stripped of allegiances to existing symbols for God and to proceed to make new symbols in agreement with one's psychic condition. Roman Catholic dogma, of course, advises us not to have an unconscious. Jung has noted this.[14] For certainly Catholic dogma of any sort must block, in its own justification for being, any return to a " free floating " psychic state. In that original condition of the religious mind the first symbols for the gods were made and given to some primitive and forgotten tribe. Ernest Renan was entirely wrong

[12] *The Integration of the Personality*, p. 72.
[13] *Ibid.*, p. 53.   [14] *Ibid.*, p. 60.

when he concluded that, since ancient religions had nothing which could be called dogma, humanity did not originally create symbols.[15] Humanity has always created symbols, whether dogma accompanied them or not. It is not the special province of civilized man to act as symbol-maker; primitive man is equally adroit and equally inventive in this function. Furthermore, the psychic factor to which the primitivist returns does not lead the artist to some marvellous state of aesthetic or poetic imagination.

As Charles Baudouin insisted in his study of Verhaeren, there are no kinds of artistic imagination, there is only imagination.[16] The artist has neither more nor less imagination than he would have possessed had he continued to follow old symbols and to work in established modes of expression. In the free psychic state which he reaches, he does not acquire a new and hence " primitive " imagination. He has no more actual knowledge of the mind of the Maori as an imagining creator of symbols than has the " traditional " nonprimitivistic artist knowledge of the same primitive man. What he finds himself living with when he has repudiated his old symbols is simply what he knows of what he has lived, of what he has inherited. He is going to employ his imagination with the material which he can never discard because it is a part of him.

Thus Gauguin gets down to rediscovering the gods as psychic factors as he paints the *Ia Orana Maria*.[17] This canvas displays the dominant psychic quality of all true primitivistic symbols. It shows an imaginative recollection of Christian tradition, and allegiance to the culture of the artist's " new " community. As R. J. Goldwater observes, this picture is simply a transplantation of the Adoration to the South Seas. So, too, is the drawing *Adam and Eve*, in which Adam appears as a Polynesian fisherman and Eve as a Tahitian woman in a loose cotton gown.[18]

---

[15] " Religions of Antiquity " in *Studies in Religious History*, trans. W. M. Thompson (London, 1893), p. 19.

[16] *Psychoanalysis and Aesthetics*, trans. Eden and Cedar Paul (London, 1924), p. 27.

[17] Now the property of the Metropolitan Museum of Art, New York City.

[18] *Primitivism in Modern Painting* (New York, 1938), pp. 65–66.

These pictures are symbols of a very clear double reference, just as nearly all the great symbols of Melville are endowed with both Christian and primitive elements. They derive from the great store of Christian iconography; they assimilate the new material of Polynesia. Yet they are genuine sacramental symbols. The first picture rejects the essential prefiguration of the Redemption in the Christian symbol of the Nativity, the fate of the Son of Man to suffer and to die for the sins of the civilized world; it substitutes in place of this prefiguration the striking concept that the Son of Man is born among a people of innocent goodness and supreme happiness. The traditional Christian symbol is a sacrament of sorrow related to the larger symbol of the Atonement; the new symbol is a sacrament of innocence and "naturalness." That an archetype, as the content of a collective unconscious, is present here would seem unquestionable. Only a few years earlier, and quite without any knowledge of the aspirations of Gauguin, who did not reach Tahiti until 1891, Melville had spoken in *Clarel* (Part IV, Sec. xviii) of Tahiti as the only fit place on earth for the advent of Christ. At this level of feeling Melville, even as Gauguin, was rediscovering the gods as psychic factors.

It has just been asserted that primitive man makes symbols quite as well as civilized man. But if we could be given primitive man again in his original state, before the first act of symbolization establishes tradition, we should find that he is the only potential maker of the *pure* symbol. This might be, for instance, a charm carved on a canoe paddle to ward off carnivorous fish. As soon as tradition has been established, it begins to accrete; and thereafter the possibility of the pure symbol disappears. The device on the paddle originates as a simple representation. It will be duplicated endlessly in other simple forms designed to dispel danger. At this point it is all dream content. At this stage and at no other it is a form suited to analysis posited solely upon the methods of Freud or Jung. But as soon as this device begins to be mixed with other devices, as soon as a form emerges which contains a beginning complex of feeling, it becomes impure; and, more important, as a form in art it becomes singular, distinctive as an emblem of its one creator and no other. In aesthetic method an ineluctable principle must then be asserted: *the creator of genuine art forms his symbol by the act of fusing an aggregate of symbolic materials.* The pure primitive symbol is simplex; the symbol from the mind of art, multiplex. When a primitive society produces an art of multiplex symbolic form, as in the case of ritualistic masks designed by certain African tribes, it has ceased to be " primitive " in the judgment of informed criticism. That it remains so in the eyes of some laymen indicates inability to read the symbolic structure which the work presents.

The question of the appeal or the effect of a work of art is a concern of aesthetic history, as it studies reputation. For the purposes of this study, it may be noted that the validity of reading together the subject of a symbol and the universal acceptance of this subject among an audience, as double evidence of the archetype, must disappear as one passes from primitive " dream " form to individuated form.

When this qualification is applied to the extensions of Jung's theory into the psychology of dreams, it becomes clear that the genuine art symbol asserts the significant power and originality of its maker. Thus the distance of criticism from Jung's elaborate description of a patient who made a traumatic usage of quicksilver and, in so doing, " descended " to an archetype in which the dream was related to Taoist alchemy in China and to the " Quicksilver Systems " of India.[19] This woman who dreamed of quicksilver was not an artist; she was a dreamer helplessly dominated by an archetype. It is assumed here that Jung's contentions for archetypes which appear " when all supports and crutches are broken," [20] " when no obstruction is offered to the happening in the unconscious," and when the " ego-consciousness " enters the image [21] are entirely appropriate to a psychoanalysis of dreams. Nor can any objection be raised

[19] *The Integration of the Personality*, p. 50.
[20] *Ibid.*, p. 82.
[21] *Ibid.*, p. 90.

to his concepts of *anima* (the archetype of woman in man) and *animus* (the archetype of man in woman).[22] It may be very true that these are the primordial figures of the unconscious, that they have given rise to the mythological gods and goddesses, that they function in the " phylogenetic substructures of the modern mind," that " they bring into our ephemeral consciousness an unknown psychic life belonging to a remote past " in which we think and feel in the psychic life of our ancient ancestors.[23] It is also probable, as Jung has contended elsewhere, that " just as the human body connects us with the mammals and displays numerous relics of earlier evolutionary stages, so the human psyche is likewise a product of evolution which, when followed up to its origins, shows countless archaic traits." [24] By the same token, it is possible to believe that the enormous range of water imagery in the art of the nineteenth and the twentieth centuries shows the way of the Protestant soul to its lost father, its return to the unconscious [25] where it may rediscover the gods as psychic factors. Or, if one considers the sea as the universal womb of all creatures, he may be able to capture some primordial feeling through the knowledge that the salt in his blood is one with the salt of fish, serpent, and bird, and of calcined mammoth bones from the Jurassic era. But all these conditions apply to *man*, collectively. If they be accepted as fact, then every human being carries them. They do not make art. A work of art is not an assortment of vestigial organs and archaic impulses. What is common to every man is only primordial mud to the hand of the artist. He owns it as well as the next man. But, as artist, he alone can shape it into singular form.

2 *The Voyage to Perdita*

The Orient of primitivism is a country of the mind. It lies westward of Occidental culture, for the true maker of the sym-

---

[22] *Ibid.*, p. 19.   [23] *Ibid.*, pp. 23–25.

[24] *Modern Man in Search of a Soul*, trans. W. S. Dell and Cary F. Baynes (New York [1933]), p. 144.

[25] *The Integration of the Personality*, pp. 65–68.

bol of feeling, westward of Protestantism in the Christian faith. It lies eastward of the true East, with its realities of famine and disease, poverty and squalor, and its nihilistic philosophies. This Orient of primitivism is Perdita, the volcanic center of the symbol-maker, the new island of a new archipelago lying somewhere in the sea near Oceania, and Asia. Even as the real charts of the cartographer show the great festoons of the Pacific islands swinging sickle-like toward this parent East, so these islands of the imagination swing ever westward, away from the failing inheritance of their solitary inhabitants and eastward toward the vision of man's original center, where the meaning of human existence is expressed in God-consciousness. Perdita rises from a major faulting of the ocean floor. In its origins it is fact. But what the symbol-maker, the new sacramentalist made upon it may be less fact than fiction. As the voyaging Ishmael, he came there circuitously, bearing with him the memory of his " lost " symbols and the sense of indistinct " new " forms, as though seen in a mist, rising from the memory of his journey over chartless seas. He had known shipwreck and storm. He had foundered, and descended into the great deep shrouding the hulls and ribs of a forgotten argosy of symbols. Like Pip of *Moby-Dick*, he had " seen," in his mind's eye amidst the night of those waters, " God's foot upon the treadle of the loom " (Ch. xciii). Like Pip, crazed with fright, he rose miraculously; and as Ishmael he sailed toward Perdita. Walking at last on a new earth, he made his new sacrament and salvation, and worshipped, like every Ishmael, alone. His terrible descent confirmed his artistry. It left him in possession of a sovereign power, the skill of making the multiplex symbol, the fusion of his " old " sacramental tradition and of the " new " sacrament of the mythical East. As maker, he exalted his talent of abstracting from these two sources the unique form of his own ideality.

Midway in these primitive waters, Ishmael turned toward the feeling of archaic man. So is archaic feeling crisis; and from crisis the symbolist of primitivism emerges. The descent and the voyage accomplish the rediscovery of ancient archetypal realities. Ishmael becomes the artist of isolation. His estate becomes two-fold: he retreats in history, bearing with him the memory of all histories and spans of time which were his legacy; he approaches the original character of man's religious being, the frame of theism at the center, *mysterium tremendum* veiled in time passing by the spinning webs of historical progression, as the wrack and spume of sea-surfaces conceal the depths. This is metaphor to suggest the voyage of feeling. Archaic man in his totality is, of course, endlessly elusive. No image may represent Ishmael's arrival at the center. But now he moves in the shadow of the ancient past: he reassumes man's first necessity to describe his identity and his human circumstance through symbols. And in his symbols of existence he comes to do what primitive man could never do with his original pure symbol and learned only with the extension of his experience in the world: he commands art to incarnation. For in this voyager to Perdita history and origin must become one in a new reality. In him the mind of art is to accomplish the synthesis of which art alone is capable.

3   *Emotive Compulsion toward the Orient*

The impossibility of becoming " Oriental " (unless one becomes a Chinese princess at will after the fashion of Judith Gautier) would seem to rest partially in the condition admitted to by Schweitzer: there are no new, gifted peoples forthcoming to save us with a new wisdom, simply because we already know all the peoples of earth. The fact is that the Orient has come to take such a part in our civilization that its spiritual fate is determined by our own.[26] This condition was not, of course, true for the nineteenth century; it is a developmental phenomenon of the twentieth. But at the same point, Schweitzer measures the state of Western decay by acknowledging the failure of Europe to oppose " the pessimistic conception " of Eastern religions with its own theory affirming the world and life.[27] It was earlier stated in this study that primitivism is not

---

[26] *The Decay and the Restoration of Civilization*, pp. 63–64.
[27] *Ibid.*, p. 99.

vitally concerned with Eastern philosophies. This is true. The symbolists of this system, as the description of Perdita suggests, are not interested in mastering the content of Oriental theories. Yet, in one respect every primitivist shows the sharpening of the moral conflict of good and evil in Protestantism. The escape from these opposites, e. g., in the nirvana of the *Upanishads*, becomes, as Jung notes, an escape which presumes their equivalence and hence contradicts Christian truth.[28] Something of this interpretation is implicit in Schweitzer's pessimistic conclusion. But primitivism interpreted as sacramentalism is not to be illuminated in its true nature by so simple a statement as that it seeks out good as opposed to the evil of civilization, or that it escapes into mere equivalence. The criticism of art cannot afford to say that the issue is only this. To do so is only to assert that the forms which it studies here are wholly unrelated to the artists who created them.

Presumably every one of us recognizes that evil opposes good; and some of us may dream that a tropical island is good as opposed to the evil of a city. But in this dream there is no act of art as sacrament or symbol. We are merely the dreamers of the dream like Lavinia and Orin in Eugene O'Neill's *Mourning Becomes Electra*. They are surfeited with incest and death, and they dream of the "blessed isles." They go there and see good and come home again to evil; and that is all they do. Carpenter, in his study of Emerson, asserts that O'Neill became "Oriental" because of his actual visit to Asia, where "he absorbed the spirit of the East at first hand." [29] Not at all, if one is talking of sacramental symbols. O'Neill's characters in the *Electra* trilogy live among symbols, even as the characters in *The Emperor Jones, Desire under the Elms, Dynamo*. But these are the symbols of either Nietzschean self-assertion or European nihilism transplanted to an American setting. Probably they show as well as any other poetically conceived figures of the drama in the twentieth century a related primitivism of good and evil; they certainly illustrate Schweitzer's description of a

[28] *The Integration of the Personality*, pp. 86–87.
[29] *Emerson and Asia*, p. 252.

society with no theory affirming the world and life. Neither
O'Neill nor any one of his characters reveals hope of a new
wisdom available to us from unknown gifted peoples. They
are aware only that good and evil are irreconcilable. Even
though the sacramental element is often potential in O'Neill's
symbols, it differs from that of primitivism: it lacks symbolic
multiplicity. Artistically it is less comprehensive, less inclusive.
In the dynamo, for example, with the meaning of a relationship
of this machine to cultural pessimism (expressed by Henry
Adams through the same device) we get a less complex, a less
authoritative symbol. The dynamo expresses the insensate age
of the machine. It is not concerned with corporateness; it is
not religiously posited; it compensates for none of the loss of
spiritual authority in Protestantism. Here the artist does not
" become " any other, " Oriental " or what not. He merely
describes emblematically what he sees of his culture. Certainly
he is a maker of symbols as abstractions. But his success in
abstraction, even when Oceania and the Orient appear, does not
make him the primitivist.

It must be admitted that " becoming Oriental " is a process
in the artist which cannot be absolutely defined. Its nature may
be only suggested by the description of criticism. The reason
for the elusiveness lies in the fact that " Orientalism " in this
sense is emotive and personally felt. This feeling signifies more
than the academic view of William Butler Yeats, who wrote in
his introduction to the translation of plays from the Japanese Nō
undertaken by Ernest Fenollosa and Ezra Pound: " Europe is
very old and has seen many arts run through the circle and has
learned the fruit of every flower and known what this fruit
sends up, and it is now time to copy the East and live deliberately." [30] It cannot be said that copying the East to " live deliberately " is " becoming Oriental " in the manner of the primitivist. Yeats's judgment here is most strange. The Japanese Nō
which his preface introduces is one of the most highly sophisti-

[30] *Certain Noble Plays of Japan*, ed. Ezra Pound, from the manuscripts of
Ernest Fenollosa, with introduction by W. B. Yeats (Churchtown, Dundrum,
1916), p. ix.

cated abstractions from Buddhistic discipline in existence. But one does not go to this poetic drama, if he is the European primitivist emotionally conditioned, or the American, to " live deliberately." He will go to it rather with the emotive compulsion of a man seeking respite from himself. Every fruit of Europe was not known when Yeats wrote in 1916. There is no end to the variety of symbols for existential meaning which Europe can produce. The primitivist would have gone, as he still goes, to the Nō for a discipline which is release to his unquiet Western being. This Fenollosa knew. There is some question whether Pound and Yeats did.

In primitivism emotive compulsion outweighs every intellectual concern for the Orient. The journey to Asia and to Oceania is like attendance at a performance of the Nō. It is a way out of an endlessly intolerable self-consciousness in the I-You relationship described in the preceding chapter. To the Western observer the Nō with its devotion to economy in gesture, its ancient ritual, its hypnotic intoning declamation, and its dramatic power of divesting the spectator altogether of his consciousness of self may become a symbolic spectacle with the authority of the Roman Catholic Mass. As one of the great arts of Buddhism, it is actually one of the great sacramental symbols of the East. It exalts and dramatizes nature at the expense of the human ego, and total surrender to it invariably means that the spectator loses altogether the ego-sickness of self. As it assimilates this ego, so it becomes a symbol of corporateness. Among Japanese savants its performance constitutes an act of worship. So it may become worship as well to the Western traveler, even though he is no more than dimly aware of what is happening to him. He is not the exoticist in quest of the strange for the sake of strangeness. He is making a genuine substitution for his lost sacrament. In the presence of Japanese symbols this was the act of Ernest Fenollosa as it was that of Lafcadio Hearn. If, theoretically, we have an artist who would make of this drama his own sacramental representation, we are sure to see the act of symbolic fusion once more accomplished. Part of the Nō will be there, part of what is remembered of the

" lost " Christian rite. That this hypothetical symbol, as well as every existing symbol of " Oriental " primitivism, faces two ways and gathers material from both old and new is proof that it is emotively rather than intellectually compelled.

Thus an intellectualizing of the Orient on Perdita never really takes place. T. S. Eliot, who left the refuge of the Orient not long ago to return to orthodox Christian sacrament, knew the futility of the attempt to remake one's spiritual being into Oriental mind. If one is to go about confronting the poverty of Protestant symbolism by mastering and then substituting the intellect of the Orient, he lives apart from the symbol-maker, and his solutions must proceed from reason. Eliot's explanation of his retreat from Oriental studies is as convincing as that of any other artist; certainly it is distinctively explicit. Twenty years ago he published his conclusion after almost as many years of thinking and study. A portion of this statement invites quotation.

Two years spent in the study of Sanskrit under Charles Lanman, and a year in the mazes of Patanjali's metaphysics under the guidance of James Woods, left me in a state of enlightened mystification. A good half of the effort of understanding what the Indian philosophers were after—and their subtleties make most of the great European philosophers look like school boys—lay in trying to erase from my mind all the categories and kinds of distinction common to European philosophy from the time of the Greeks. My previous and concomitant study of European philosophy was hardly better than an obstacle. And I came to the conclusion—seeing also that the " influence " of Brahmin and Buddhist thought upon Europe, as in Schopenhauer, Hartmann, and Deussen, had largely been through romantic misunderstanding—that my only hope of really penetrating to the heart of that mystery would lie in forgetting how to think and feel as an American or a European: which, for practical as well as sentimental reasons, I did not wish to do. And I should imagine that the same choice would hold good for Chinese thought: though I believe that the Chinese mind is very much nearer to the Anglo-Saxon than is the Indian. . . . But Confucius has become the philosopher of the rebellious Protestant. And I cannot but feel that in some respects Irving Babbitt, with the noblest intentions, has merely made matters worse instead of better.[31]

The rejection of the Orient on these grounds, since, indeed, no artist and no scholar will ever be able to cast off the " obstacles " of his Western heritage, was characteristic of the poet we know in Eliot. It was the act of a poet to whom the whole art of poesis has been an art of reason. But the tenets of Eliot as poet and philosopher are too well known to require further comment. His withdrawal from Oriental studies shows very clearly that when the professional and dispassionate interests of the scholar are not the sole motives, and when we have a poet whose art is informed more by erudition and the abstractions of learning than by emotion, the Oriental symbol of primitivism is rendered impossible. Whether Eliot's poetry as art suffers from the aridity of its content is a question which will not be labored here. Enough critical argument has already taken place in this area. But it is interesting to note that this man who would seem already to have given his name to his age, this poet who has encountered and emerged from most of the dilemmas of Protestantism, occupies an American position toward the Orient quite apart from that of Melville and other recent symbolists in primitivism. Beyond this, it is still more interesting to see that he knows much more of the Orient in its religious and philosophical dogma than is usually guessed at by primitivists. A judgment upon which poetic legacy, Eliot's or the primitivist's, has the richer symbolism must be left to posterity.

4 *The Eminence of Melville*

So much has been made here of the primitivist in relation to Perdita that to some readers these initial chapters will seem to argue for the art of Melville, and that of every symbolist in this related island community, as totally primitivistic. But this book does not intend to project such a judgment. It has already been noted that Melville could and did ally himself with an

[31] *After Strange Gods*, pp. 43–44. See Babbitt's appendix to *Rousseau and Romanticism* (Boston and New York, 1919).

American mythos of the frontier, where he becomes accessible
to analysis through such an art as that of Cooper, Simms, or
Dana. He becomes as well, in his protean nature, the political
satirist in the Vivenza section of *Mardi*; the sociologist in
certain portions of *Redburn, White-Jacket, Pierre,* and *Israel
Potter*; the convivial *raconteur* in several stories; the tourist in
parts of *The Encantadas* and even of *Clarel*. Furthermore, he
frequently reveals an adroit comic sense. In the same way,
nearly all primitivists will display a comparable versatility. It
is, indeed, the particular contention of this study that if criticism wishes to grasp the deep symbols of these artists, it must
agree that primitivism provides the means of descent. On the
other hand, I do not intend to deny other manifestations of
the artistic personalities called to the processes of this analysis.
For all artistic personality is manifold. It is like every one of
its genuine symbols, containing within itself a structure of interrelationships. With the utmost willingness to allow Melville to
be all that he was as artist, we may regard him as the chief
redactor of primitivism because his work supplies the clearest
poetic structure we have of interdepending symbols referring
to Protestant neo-sacramentalism. This symbolic structure
shows what has happened in a new religious art. Recent primitivism presents an achievement of a most complex artistic act, a
new reformation of belief, artistically described. In the demonstration of these facts from recent art it must become apparent
that Melville is one of the great symbolistic originators of history. The artistic validity of his symbolism defines his stature
among his Western contemporaries, and he may be seen outside the rather narrow, if critically legitimate, limits of his
national literature.

There is a distinctive attribute of Melville which is intensely
compulsive in the creation of symbols. It is secondary only to
the religious drive of his consciousness as artist. This is his
native poetic sensitivity to expressive forms; and this alone will
account for his unusual retentiveness of memory as it furnishes
again and again, in the most unexpected places, the imagistic
framework in which the great symbol of the Pacific are

mounted. Melville was an artist who had not only the power to abstract into the symbol but also the talent to supply a poetically visualized background for the abstraction. No one will contend that he is a superior technician in poetry. He had an extremely bad ear, for one thing; for another, he was as contemptuous of form in poetry as in prose. *Clarel*, particularly, is lacerated with some of the worst aberrations of versification in the English language. But these technical matters are of no concern in symbolism. In the sense of poesis as symbolic form, no matter what the linguistic frame may be, the total range of Melville's art shows a striking poetic sensitivity. Susanne Langer makes clear in discussing this faculty a condition for the symbol which may be called grasping the essence of the object.

> A mind to which the stern character of an armchair is more immediately apparent than its use or its position in the room, is over-sensitive to expressive forms. It grasps analogies that a riper experience would reject as absurd. It fuses sensa that practical thinking must keep apart. Yet it is just this crazy play of associations, this uncritical fusion of impressions, that exercises the powers of symbolic transformation.[32]

In the same work she recognizes the relation between the form of the symbol and the physical process which shaped it. "No matter what heights the human mind may attain, it can work only with the organs it has and the functions peculiar to them. Eyes that did not see forms could never furnish it with *images*. . . . A mind that works primarily with meanings must have organs that supply it primarily with forms."[33]

The truth of these assertions applied to one poem already mentioned must mean that George Herbert could not have written "The Sacrifice" without the visual power of the Eucharist and the iconography of the mediaeval church to supply forms. Here one arrives at the function of the autotype in the making of the art symbol. Somewhere in the abstraction conveyed by the symbol the facsimile of objects actually seen is to

---

[32] *Philosophy in a New Key* (Cambridge, 1942), pp. 123–24.
[33] *Ibid.*, p. 90.

appear. More recently Mrs. Langer notes that "where the symbolic process is highly developed it practically takes over the domain of perception and memory, and puts its stamp on all mental functions."[34] In exactly this condition the mind of Herman Melville is one of the most arresting in the history of art. Actually, we see in him a mind bound to autotypes (from the Pacific journey) in such degree that the "stamp" of the symbolic process deriving from them is felt upon materials far from the symbol itself. Even in the narrative opening of *Clarel* (Part i, Sec. i), separated by several decades from his experience in a Pacific lagoon, Melville thought of his student hero with "those under-formings in the mind / Banked corals which ascend from far . . . ." The survival of Polynesia is made possible by poetic sensitivity to expressive form plus the symbolic custom of a mind in taking over the whole domain of perception and memory.

How much of this thralldom to symbolization Melville himself acknowledged is not known. But it is highly probable that he speaks of this alone as he launches into the metaphysical prose of the famous chapter "Dreams" in *Mardi* (Ch. cxix). With all its rhetorical bombast, it confesses to a very interesting awareness. "My cheek blanches white while I write; I start at the scratch of my pen; my own mad brood of eagles devour me; fain would I unsay this audacity; but an iron-mailed hand clenches mine in a vice, and prints down every letter in my spite. . . . The fever runs through me like lava; my hot brain burns like a coal . . . ." Seen from one angle, this passage looks like the romantic egoist as Byronic author; from another, the iron-mailed hand is the master grasp of the symbol-maker in the artist, the grasp of an authority which shapes all experience into symbolic form.

" Religion," writes Tillich, " is the substance of culture, culture is the expression of religion."[35] As early as *Mardi*, Melville, taking off on the quest for symbols, had observed, " The

[34] *Feeling and Form* (New York, Scribners, 1953), p. 128.
[35] *The Protestant Era*, p. xvii.

world revolves upon an I; and we upon ourselves; for we are our own worlds."[36] Only a few years later, in 1851, the year of *Moby-Dick*, he confessed in a letter to Hawthorne: " I shall at last be worn out and perish, like an old nutmeg-grater, grated to pieces by the constant attrition of the wood, that is, the nutmeg. What I feel most moved to write, that is banned,—and it will not pay. Yet, altogether, write the *other* way I cannot. So the product is a final hash, and all my books are botches."[37] If religion is the substance of culture, Melville, having felt the condition of his Protestant society, was already aware in *Mardi* that matters with God stood strictly within the relationship of I-You. And if culture is the expression of religion, then his demonstration of his culture brought him at the conclusion of *Moby-Dick* to the full awareness that in his society his symbols would never be understood. It is one thing to pose as a prophet, and another to be a prophet of art rejected. The journal of 1857 from the tour to the Holy Land, where the whole panoply of Christendom struck him as a consistent mockery of Christ, shows him alone beside the Dead Sea: ". . . foam on beach [and] pebbles like slaver of mad dog—smarting bitter of the water,—carried the bitter in my mouth all day—bitterness of life —thought of all bitter things—Bitter it is to be poor [and] bitter to be reviled . . . ."[38] In attributing the act of rejection to his audience, he paid an unjust compliment to his contemporaries. All they were guilty of was the sin of ignorance in not knowing what had happened to them as well. A timely symbolist is never understood by an untimely audience. One cannot really call across the ocean to the coasts where the world vaguely lives, making the best of things, and getting through the whole business as painlessly as possible. Tolstoy's manufacture of a creed of art for the " common man " is an aesthetic blunder of the nineteenth century. As soon as man begins to need art and to attend to its symbols, he ceases to be " common."

Melville's church-going can have nothing to do with his re-

[36] Vol. 2, p. 279.

[37] Printed by Julian Hawthorne, in *Nathaniel Hawthorne and His Wife* (Boston, 1885), vol. 1, p. 402.

[38] *Journal up the Straits*, ed. Raymond Weaver (New York, 1935), p. 73.

ligion, of course. No student will contend that it has relevance. In the story *The Two Temples* he uses the symbol of " a gorgeous dungeon " for the whole of the church.[39] Frances Melville Thomas, his daughter, asserted some years ago that she knew him to attend services only twice, at All Souls' Unitarian in New York.[40] By the time he undertook the writing of *Mardi*, he had begun to reflect seriously upon the state of his Christian inheritance. The satiric description of the Pope in *Mardi* is only one early view of the collapse of sacrament in the orthodox structure of Christianity (to say nothing of the near-disappearance of sacrament in Protestantism) : " the priest-king of Vatikanna, his chest marked over with antique tattooings; his crown, a cowl; his rusted sceptre swaying over falling towers, and crumbling mounds; full of the superstitious past; askance, eyeing the suspicious time to come." [41]

That all this time, and through the remaining years of his life, he was reading the Bible assiduously is known fact. The influence of the Bible on Melville's style and symbolism has been thoroughly demonstrated in the critical canon, notably and authoritatively by Nathalia Wright.[42] For an explanation of this interest in relation to Melville's heretical symbols, it should be said here that he read the Bible as literature in the Old Testament, and as a record of a " lost " and profaned idealism in the New. (I shall defend my assertion here in the chapters to follow.) In his devotion to the Bible Melville illustrates better than any other primitivist the essential paradox upon which Tillich has placed the whole of a new salvation for the Protestant.

[39] *Billy Budd and Other Prose Pieces*, p. 175.
[40] In manuscript, Houghton Library, Harvard, Metcalf Collection MS Am 188, Folders 4 and 5. This statement appears as annotation on a letter of Eleanor M. Metcalf, Melville's granddaughter, to Frances M. Thomas, her mother, of Sept. 28, 1919. Mrs. Metcalf, writing in the interests of the biography by Raymond Weaver, asks in the letter: " Did he ever show an interest in ' conventional Christianity '—that is, did he go to church at all at any period of his life? If so, to what church? " On this letter Mrs. Thomas wrote in reply: " I never knew him to go to church but twice that I can remember—All Souls' Unitarian."
[41] Vol. 2, p. 168.
[42] *Melville's Use of the Bible* (Durham, 1949).

So the paradox got hold of me that he who seriously denies God, affirms him. . . . Being religious is being uncondition- ally concerned, whether this concern expresses itself in secular or (in the narrow sense) religious forms. . . . You cannot reach God by the work of right thinking or by the sacrifice of the intellect or by a submission to strange authorities, such as the doctrines of the church and the Bible. . . . Neither works of piety nor works of morality nor works of the intel- lect establish unity with God. They follow from this unity, but they do not make it. . . . [I]f . . . you are desperate about the meaning of life, the seriousness of your despair is the expression of the meaning in which you are still living.[43]

There is enough evidence from Melville's refusal to accept without question the authority of Christian dogma to say here that this paradox might have been written expressly for him. It has already been asserted that in the depths of his symbol- making he is constantly concerned with the problem of God. Tillich's paradox seems to overlook one fact, and that a demand- ing and inescapable one: he who despairs, and so affirms in despair the meaning which he seeks, cannot, even in this affirma- tion, reach the feeling of unity without sacrament, without any emblem of corporateness. The questioner of God, contrary to what Lawrance Thompson supposes in his recent analysis of Melville's quarrel,[44] happens not to be emotionally equipped to avoid believing in some form of sacrament, orthodox or not. Even the " common man " without the creativity of art cannot hate God without revealing and demonstrating the paradox. All this, paradox and the final resolution in art, Herman Mel- ville knew.

In turning to the Orient, Melville used what he remembered of the Marquesas and Tahiti and what he had read. Here he identified the first of three elements to be fused in his total structure of symbols: primitive human innocence, in *tayo*, the fraternal love of innocent and uncorrupted men. Beyond this, he used what he remembered and what he had read of tropic

[43] *The Protestant Era*, pp. xiv–xv.
[44] *Melville's Quarrel with God* (Princeton, 1952).

islands and the sea and its creatures; and here he appropriated
a second element, primitive and fecund nature, in the artist's
return to primitive animism. The third he already had at
hand: the element of his threadbare Protestant sacrament.
These three, all fortified by his awareness of cultural failure,
he commanded into the symbols of his art. That he had little
knowledge of the far Orient is of no consequence. In the frag-
ment " Rammon the Enviable Isles " he wrote of Rammon
thinking of the Buddha: " If Budd[h]a['s] estimate of this present life confirms, and more than confirms Solomon my wise
father's view, so much the more then should a son of his attend
to what Buddha reveals or alleges touching an unescapable life
indefinitely continuous after death." [45] It does not matter very
much that Melville sets Rammon thinking of Buddha five centuries before the birth of the prophet. Nor is it an important
fact that the little poem called " Buddha," written in 1891, is
actually a most awkward comment on the nature of nirvana.[46]
All that matters is the nature of Melville's symbols, as these are
inclined toward the Orient. It has already been agreed that
these were made in the island-domain of Melville's feeling, not,
by a miraculous act of rebirth, in some Oriental community.
Archetypal sacrament which relates all these symbols, which
indeed orders them into one single structure, has been defined.
An examination of the Oriental journey as the source of autotypes remains. To proceed first to Melville, the objective is to
examine his recorded observations of primitive man and primitive nature as these provide the first two elements of his symbols. This examination will be followed by a discussion of
Melville's successors in the Pacific.

[45] In manuscript, Houghton Library, Harvard, Metcalf Collection, MS Am 188,
Folders 6 and 7.
[46] Published with *Timoleon* in the *Collected Works*.

PART TWO

ISHMAEL:
THE WESTWARD
MARINER

III

Melville's Pacific Voyages: An Evaluation

The iron-mailed hand that gripped Melville as he wrote of dreams in *Mardi* is the same hand that points Taji's craft to sea as the book closes: " ' Now, I am my own soul's emperor; and my first act is abdication! Hail! realm of shades!—and turning my prow into the racing tide, which seized me like a hand omnipotent, I darted through.' " This is the symbol-making power of his art, but more tyrant than liberator. It is the power of the autotype in the mind of the artist, the rigid facsimile of experience, or the pattern made of experience fragmented, ordering symbolic uniformity where only disparity among sensa had existed.

Melville's inner feeling as artist when he wrote to Hawthorne of the old nutmeg grater must be related to the " scratching pen " and the " burning brain," to the Ishmael-navigator locked in that omnipotent and redoubtable clasp. But with Melville it was not simply the tyranny of art over its captive; it was something more, in the nature of what this art dictated. It was the mandate of an art which no longer recognized in its symbols the old boundaries between the " sacred " and the " secular," for the reason that what had once been authoritatively " sacred " could no longer be so without admixtures of material which it had never before contained. Melville's confession to Hawthorne (November, 1851) at the end of writing *Moby-Dick* is well-known: " I have written a wicked book, and feel spotless as the lamb." The volcanic processes which here impelled the construction of new symbols have already been described. The premise is now offered that Melville felt wicked because he had been audacious: he had dared to make one symbolic structure where two had existed, to compress into one area of meaning both sacred and secular. The " wickedness " is really foretold in the chaotic throes of *Mardi* (in this sense one of the most important documents in the history of American art) when Melville, newly confirmed to symbolism, assumes the role of Taji and takes to the primitive waters of ocean. The shadow of the hand that impelled him seaward has been over him from the first days in the Marquesas and the first pages of *Typee*. But now it closes about him, and, having reached the end of land and his brief literary journey as adventurer and saunterer, he becomes a religious artist. Everything seen, everything sensed rushes now to the impress of the hand; and so every new thing seen and remembered will be drawn to that inexorable center. The whole world becomes a symbolistic possibility, and the mind captured by the hand becomes at once an instrument impressing experience into synthesis. Everywhere the feeling of the artist becomes a consciousness flood-swept. The symbol becomes all, the conventions of established literary form, nothing. There are no conventions to channel the waters; and a new symbolic idiom-as-form emerges.

1 *Sources of Melville's Autotypes*

The eye has furnished the mind with the stuff which formulates new shaping patterns. In the processes of Melville's art there are two such patterns imposing form. The first of these is made of images from his American environment—New York, the Hudson, Albany, Pittsfield, Illinois, and the Mississippi (where an early journey took him) —and from his voyage across the Atlantic to England, the Continent, and the Mediterranean and Palestine. The images and symbols formed from these facsimiles constitute what may be called here the indigenous group. They all confirm, in some way, Melville's profound scepticism toward the values of Western civilization and his rejection of Christian tradition and orthodoxy. They convey meanings of stoniness, violence, indigence, greed, weariness, senility, and death. (It should be noted here that in symbolizing the stoniness and senility of Western civilization Melville makes one exception: he returns to the Pacific in reference to the wasteland of the Galapagos Islands.)

The second of the master patterns is made of images from the Pacific voyages, most of them considerably strengthened and "reseen" through his reading in the literature of the Pacific navigators and in encyclopaedic material referring to the Orient. The symbols formed from the Pacific experience are here identified as the Pacific group. In these Melville takes his place as the first modern maker of religious art displaying an allegiance to Oceania and the Orient in a deliberate and knowing violation of Christian convention. To a comparable extent, autotypes as patterns in the symbols of primitivists to be discussed here in relation to Melville show the same dichotomy; and the Pacific group peculiar to each of these reveals the same investiture of Oceania and the Orient with religious meaning opposite to meaninglessness in the Protestant inheritance and in the "progress" of Western materialism. All these point, with the symbols of Melville, in the same direction: westward, out of the West. All these speak, as one community, with Melville in *Mardi* (Ch. CLXVIII): "West! West!" Toward this

westward-lying East " point Hope and prophet-fingers "; toward
this at sunset " kneel all worshippers of fire," and " great whales
in mid-ocean turn to die "; and there lie Heaven and Hell.
" Eternal goal! . . . Unattainable forever; but forever leading
to great things this side thyself."

It then becomes the purpose of this chapter to examine the
Pacific voyages in respect to their imagistic significance. Every
biography of Melville has, in some way, added to the knowledge of these voyages as actual circumstance; and Jay Leyda's
monumental *Melville Log* seems to have left unrecorded nothing that was or ever will be potential fact for this record. The
problem here is entirely one of evaluating Melville's recorded
observations in the light of what they may become as facsimiles
of experience appearing in symbols. But for the sake of easy
reference it will be useful to summarize initially the courses
of Melville's trans-ocean journeys, including the Atlantic voyages, since these must be considered in the closing chapters of
this study. For the material of the following outline I am indebted to *The Melville Log*, with the happy realization that
every student of primitivism must henceforth be immeasurably
obligated to Leyda's enormous labor.

ATLANTIC

1. June 5, 1839 (aet. 19), sailed as a common seaman aboard
the packet ship, *St. Lawrence*, from New York for Liverpool;
October 1, 1839, reached Manhattan in the *St. Lawrence* and
returned home to Lansingburgh, New York. (The incidents
of this voyage appear as fictionalized biography in *Redburn*,
with Wellingborough Redburn as the youth and the *Highlander* as the ship.) [1]

PACIFIC

2. January 2, 1841 (aet. 21), sailed as a common seaman
aboard the American whaler, *Acushnet*, from New Bedford
(Fairhaven) for the Pacific, via Rio de Janeiro, Cape Horn,
the Galapagos Islands, Chatham's Island, Tombez, and whaling grounds variously noted in the log of the *Acushnet*; June

[1] For an account of this voyage and of the novel relating it, see the definitive
study by W. H. Gilman, *Melville's Early Life and* Redburn (New York, 1951).

23, 1842 (aet. 22), reached Nukuhiva, Marquesas Islands. (This voyage, without its end in the Marquesas, serves in part the narrative of *Moby-Dick* with the *Pequod* as the ship and Melville's representation of himself as Ishmael.)

3. July 9, 1842, jumped ship with Richard T. Greene, a shipmate; July 14, 1842, reached the valley of the Taipis with Greene; August 9, 1842 (aet. 23), shipped as an able seaman on the British barque, *Lucy Ann*. (These events are represented in *Typee*, with the *Acushnet* appearing as the *Dolly*, Greene as Toby, Melville as Tom, the *Lucy Ann* as the *Julia*, and the actual " visit " of twenty-six days described in the novel as " more than four months.") [2]

4. August 20 [?], 1842, sailed in the *Lucy Ann* for Tahiti, arriving at Papeete on September 20; September 26, imprisoned with certain of his shipmates at Papeete for refusal of duty aboard ship; mid-October, released by native authorities, wandered over the island in the company of a shipmate, John B. Troy; late October, 1842 (after two weeks of happy wandering in the company of Troy) signed as an able seaman aboard the Nantucket whaler, *Charles and Henry*. (These events supply the narrative of *Omoo*, with the *Lucy Ann* again as the *Julia*, Melville as Paul, Troy as Doctor Long Ghost, and the Nantucket whaler as the *Leviathan*.)

5. November 3 or 4, 1842, sailed in the *Charles and Henry* " for the coast of Japan " (*Omoo*), or for the " Bay of Kamschatska " (*Mardi*), the ship yet being unfilled with oil; April 27, 1843 (having sailed presumably over a considerable quarter of the North Pacific to various whaling grounds), discharged from the *Charles and Henry* by his own request at Lahaina, Maui, Hawaiian (Sandwich) Islands. (Materials from this voyage appear in both *Mardi* and *Moby-Dick*.)

6. May 18, 1843, sent by authorities at Lahaina to Honolulu; June 1, employed as a clerk by a ship's chandler, Isaac Montgomery; August 17, 1843 (aet. 24) enlisted in the United States Navy as a seaman aboard the frigate, *United States*. (Melville's observations at Honolulu appear in the appendix to *Typee*.)

7. August 19, 1843, sailed in the *United States* for Boston, via Nukuhiva (again), Tahiti, Masafuera, Valparaiso, Callao,

---

[2] See Charles R. Anderson's biographical study, *Melville in the South Seas* (New York, 1939).

Lima, Mazatlan, Cape Horn, Rio de Janeiro (with no visits ashore in Polynesia) ; October 14, 1844 (aet. 25) , discharged from the Navy on arrival of the *United States* at Boston.[3] (The events of this voyage appear in *White-Jacket*, with Melville as White-Jacket and the ship as the *Neversink*. The captain of the main-top in the *United States*, the Englishman Jack Chase, is recalled in *Billy Budd*, in both the dedication and the character of Billy. Melville's knowledge of life aboard a man-of-war reappears in *The Life and Adventures of Israel R. Potter*, and in *Billy Budd*.)

SUMMARY: Of the three years and nine and one-half months of the Pacific journey, about six months were available to Melville for observations ashore, among native communities of Oceania. Excluding the period of some three and one-half months passed among the " corrupted " native society of the Hawaiian Islands, and the period of his " imprisonment " at Papeete, no more than forty days could have passed among " uncorrupted " communities of Polynesia. The remaining thirty-nine or forty months were passed at sea.

ATLANTIC

8. October 11, 1849 (aet. 30) , sailed in the English liner, *Southampton*, for London; November 5, reached England and remained in London until departure for Paris where he arrived on November 27; after ten days in Paris, traveled to Brussels, Cologne, Coblenz, for about one day in each city; returned to London December 13 and sailed on December 25 in the packet ship, *Independence*, for New York; February 1, 1850, at New York.[4] (The observations from this voyage appear principally in *Israel Potter*, and in the short pieces, *The Paradise of Bachelors* and the second of *The Two Temples*.)

ATLANTIC-MEDITERRANEAN

9. October 11, 1856 (aet. 37) , sailed in the steamer, *Glasgow*, from New York for Glasgow; October 26, at Glasgow; October 26–November 7, visited various points of interest in Scotland and northern England; November 8, arrived in Liver-

---

[3] See Charles R. Anderson's edition of the official record of the ship's voyage, *Journal of a Cruise to the Pacific Ocean, 1842–1844*, in the Frigate United States (Durham, 1937).

[4] See Eleanor M. Metcalf's edition of Melville's *Journal of a Visit to London and the Continent, 1849–1850* (Cambridge, 1948).

pool to visit Hawthorne; November 18, sailed from Liverpool in the *Egyptian* for Constantinople; December 2-8, in the Aegean and ashore at Syra and Salonica; December 12-18, in Constantinople; December 18, sailed from Constantinople in the *Acadia* for Alexandria; January 4-6, 1857, Jaffa; January 8-24, in Jerusalem and environs; January 24, sailed in the *Acquile Imperiale* for Beirut; January 25-31, Beirut; February 1, sailed in the *Smirne* for Smyrna and the Aegean; February 9-11, Athens; February 11, sailed in the *Cydnus* for Messina; thence to Italy, with visits in Naples and environs, February 16-23; Rome and environs, February 25–March 21; Florence and environs, March 24-29; Bologna, Padua, Venice, Milan, Turin, Genoa, March 29–April 12; thence to Switzerland, April 14-19; continued to Strasbourg, Heidelberg, Frankfort, Cologne, Amsterdam, and Rotterdam, for one day in each, April 20-25; arrived London April 26; remained in London until May 1, and then visited Bath, Oxford, Stratford and Birmingham, reaching Liverpool on May 4 for a visit with Hawthorne; May 5, 1857, sailed from Liverpool in the steamship *City of Manchester*; May 20, 1857, at New York.[5] (Melville's observations from his tour in the Mediterranean and in the Holy Land appear as literature in *Clarel*; material from the Italian journey was used in his public lectures on Roman sculpture.)

ATLANTIC-PACIFIC

10.   May 30, 1860 (aet. 40) , sailed from Boston in the American clipper ship, *Meteor,* with his brother Thomas Melville as captain (expected itinerary, San Francisco-Manila) ; August 7 (aet. 41) , passed Cape Horn; October 12, arrived San Francisco (134 days from Boston) ; October 20, 1860, sailed from San Francisco for Panama (the rest of the voyage abandoned by Melville because of prolongation beyond the length anticipated, or because of his own ill health) ; arrived aboard the *Cortes* at Panama, November 4; crossed isthmus to Aspinwall, New Granada, and boarded steamship *North Star* for New York; November 5, sailed from Aspinwall; November 12, 1860, arrived at New York.[6] (This voyage is represented in various poems, notably in " The Haglets.")

---

[5] See Raymond Weaver's edition of Melville's *Journal up the Straits.*
[6] See Melville's fragmentary " Journal of the *Meteor*," printed in *The New England Quarterly*, vol. 2, No. 1 (1929), pp. 120–25.

Every student of Melville knows the nature of his dependence, as artist, upon these voyages. The parenthetical notes serve only to suggest how thoroughly informed his art is with the material of his travel. It is not too much to say that everything he saw and felt is somewhere transposed to the framework of symbolic-artistic reference. Experience was not of itself experience; it was all emblematic to this mind, the token substance of a world which was itself protean, endlessly multiplex. That is why Melville, with forty days among the Polynesians and no more, could sustain the token experience of these days. From 1842 to 1891 they proliferate in meaning; as imperishable images they render more and more symbols, and they lead this artist, who was neither ethnologist nor scholar, beyond Oceania to the Orient. This is the way of a symbolist, as opposed to that of an allegorist who, even though he substitutes the ideal for the actual, must still depend upon mastery of the actual, in all its facts, to embody meaning.

The truism that every artist represents the world as he sees it is scarcely worth repeating. But the intense subjectivity of symbolists in primitivism is quite another matter. It is highly probable that we get from these artists a most approximate replica of a world itself teeming with a multiplicity of meaning, big with a chaos of contradictions. This is the world of the eye and the senses, not the world of the selective logician. As a traveler, the primitivist saw and *felt* more widely than his contemporaries in art. He possessed the larger supply of images for symbols. But his really distinguishing condition is only this: the symbol as synthesis expresses the multiplicity of an appearing world just as this multiplicity impressed him in the duration of the real experience. He does not "make up" multiplicity as he achieves individuated form. He is subjectively autobiographical. The symbol says, in effect: this stands for the multiple nature of existence as I saw and felt it; and because it stands in art, it is the only absolute which I can offer from an experience which is, in every respect, a chaos of fractured absolutes.

It is small wonder that in primitivism form deserts tradition.

Thus it may be assumed that students who are disturbed by the appearance of nontraditional form in primitivism will be equally disturbed by the unique content of feeling in its symbols. Because of the authority of feeling, the burden of multiplicity in these symbols is, beyond question, enormous. To illustrate: let a comparison be made between the representation of English landscape in the canvases of Constable, and Gauguin's treatment of the mountains and waters of Tahiti, or a relative examination of Scott's or Cooper's descriptions of " glens " and valleys with those of Melville (in *Typee, Omoo, Mardi,* or *Pierre*). Constable, Scott, and Cooper all display valid symbolic abstractions; they make art. Indubitably each is telling what he saw of the world, even as Gauguin and Melville tell the same. The point is simply that the first three project an experienced singularity as opposed to multiplicity in the experience of their nontraditional successors. Their symbols are both less replete and less various. For them it was not necessary that art should carry the whole symbolic weight of existential meaning. They were all secure in symbolic allegiances outside their provinces as artists. In this reasoning, one arrives at the principle that *the farther an artist moves from the singularity of symbolic tradition in his society, the more complex, the larger with multiplicity his unique art symbols become.* The reference here is entirely to the symbolic elements of feeling. It is obvious that in an artist of Milton's stature, where the elements of erudition are equal, or even superior to those of emotion, we encounter an equally multiplex form, but of a different sort.

2 *Ishmael, the Overseer*

Writing of Melville's experience among Polynesians, Newton Arvin has noted that the duration of his " visit " really does not matter: " His days in the island valley were long with a length no calendar could measure, and they left a permanent stamp upon his spirit." [7] The permanent stamp was, indeed,

---

[7] *Herman Melville* (New York, 1950), p. 55.

imposed with such weight that it ordered the character of a new artistic personality. Nor should this impression be seen only in its Polynesian outline. The time should be extended to include the whole three years and nine months of the Pacific voyages, as these have been summarized. This was the shaping time of Melville as artist. All that happened after the Pacific journey becomes a kind of exfoliation of youthful perception. Readers of Melville will recall how he dwells upon this idea of exfoliation in himself as artist. He once remarked that he had come down almost " to the inmost leaf of the bulb." This confession appears in the famous letter, earlier cited, with its metaphor of the old nutmeg grater (to Hawthorne in June, 1851). Here he speaks of youth as artistic potentiality. " I am like one of those seeds taken out of the Egyptian Pyramids, which, after being three thousand years a seed and nothing but a seed, being planted in English soil, it developed itself, grew to greenness, and then fell to mould. So I. Until I was twenty-five, I had no development at all. From my twenty-fifth year I date my life." [8] The seed was the voyage of youth, the development the telling of the voyage. For it is upon the experience of this youth, the images which the eye recorded, that the symbols of sacrament take form. The idealized portrait of the outcast was not, of course, new when Melville fashioned Tom of *Typee*. Byron had earlier represented himself as the Ishmael-wanderer in *Lara*. But Melville created the emblem of a new artistic role: he gave the mysterious voyage its end.

At this point in the history of criticism directed to Melville, it must be common knowledge that Ishmael is the overseer of

[8] Printed by Julian Hawthorne in *Nathaniel Hawthorne and His Wife*, vol. 2, p. 405. Obviously Melville " dates his life " from the end of the Pacific journey in October, 1844, and the beginning of his career in the following winter, as he undertakes the writing of *Typee*. The curious reference to the Egyptian seed is explained in an account of Charles L. James, son of the novelist, G. P. R. James, on the growth of some Egyptian wheat at Stockbridge. The James family were neighbors of the Melvilles at Arrowhead, Pittsfield. The account of Charles L. James runs as follows: " At Stockbridge I remember something very curious. We had received and planted some Egyptian wheat taken from the inside of a mummy case. It came up, and I saw it growing; but it did not seed ' worth a continental.' " (S. M. Ellis, *The Solitary Horseman* [Kensington, Cayme Press, 1927], p. 164.)

every major work in his literary record. When he is not the protagonist, he is at least the attendant genius, as the narrator in *Moby-Dick.* He is Tom in *Typee*; Paul in *Omoo*; Taji in *Mardi*; the young sailor-heroes of *Redburn* and *White-Jacket*; the Ishmael of *Moby-Dick*; the tragic hero of *Pierre* in his early life; the veteran fugitive Israel R. Potter; the narrator of *The Confidence Man*; the youth of *Clarel*; the handsome sailor of *Billy Budd.* He is Ishmael, the outcast, condemned to wander, raised above the literal meaning of the Biblical text: " And *he* will be a wild man; his hand *will be* against every man, and every man's hand against him; and he shall dwell in the presence of all his brethren " (*Genesis* 16: 12). In at least four instances Melville himself identifies the character as Ishmael: in *Redburn*, when Wellingborough finds himself " a sort of Ishmael in the ship "; [9] in the opening sentence of *Moby-Dick*; in *Pierre*, when the youth, rebelling against his mother's " immense pride " and feeling himself " driven out an infant Ishmael into the desert, with no maternal Hagar to accompany and comfort him," cries out " Oh heartless, proud, ice-gilded world, how I hate thee "; [10] in *Israel Potter*, when the child, prophetically named Israel by his Puritan parents, is destined to wander for more than forty years " in the wild wilderness of the world's extremest hardships and ills." [11]

Melville defines the meaning of Ishmael in a fifth instance, which has not, I think, been earlier noted. The year before the publication of *Israel Potter* (1855) he submitted to Charles F. Briggs, the editor of *Putnam's Monthly* in which *Potter* had just appeared serially, a manuscript entitled " The Two Temples." Briggs rejected it politely, with the comment that the story " would sway against us the whole power of the pulpit . . . and the congregation of Grace Church." [12] In this sketch a youth makes his way on foot from the Battery to the fashionable Grace Church, Episcopal, in New York. " Politely bowed out

---

[9] *Redburn*, p. 79.
[10] *Pierre*, pp. 125–26.
[11] *Israel Potter*, p. 5.
[12] The letter is printed by Weaver in the Constable edition, prefacing the story in *Billy Budd and Other Prose Pieces*, p. 173.

of the nave " because of his poor dress, he takes refuge in the
belfry tower where he finds a stained glass window facing into
the nave. He scratches a small opening in a " great purple star "
of the window and looks down, as through goggles, on the
service. He hears the *Venite*. Then he ascends farther and
stands before another opening in the stone. He hears the invocation, " Govern them and *lift* them up forever," and the
text of the sermon, " Ye are the salt of the earth." The service
ends, and before he can descend to the belfry door, he is locked
in by the beadle. Subsequently he rings the bell for his freedom, and pays a fine in court " for having humbly indulged
myself in the luxury of public worship." But first he mounts
the stairs again and gazes down into the empty church, its stony
recesses lit by rays of sunlight streaming from colored glass.
" A Puseyitish painting of a Madonna and Child, adorning a
lower window, seemed showing to me the sole tenants of this
painted wilderness—the true Hagar and her Ishmael." [13] The
symbol of Ishmael in this " gorgeous dungeon," this " painted
wilderness," is of the highest importance in what it reveals of
the meaning of Ishmael everywhere else. The dungeon and
the wilderness are full of the dead, of symbols without meaning.
Here Melville, as the young impostor in the belfry, admits to
the chief act of his art as symbolist: he substitutes Ishmael and
the symbols of which Ishmael is the originator and the maker for
the impoverished symbols of Christian convention. Ishmael is
exchanged for the iconographic emblem of the Nativity. We
are to understand that each man's Ishmael becomes his redeemer in a world lost irretrievably to Christian love.

As in the orthodox confirmation service of the church the rite
administered signifies the individual's acceptance of duty to a
traditional symbolism, a system of abstractions through which
the meaning of Christian life is represented, so in the Pacific
journey Melville was confirmed not in hatred, as some may
suppose, but in the art of constructing symbols toward the
restoration of belief. The vagrant courses of a whaling ship
and the pilgrimages ashore become the ways of egress from this

[13] *Ibid.*, p. 180.

man's dungeon. This is the ulterior meaning of " Marquesan Melville," and this we see with perfect objectivity in the mid-twentieth century. We have had a good deal of experience, even the most orthodox of us, with man, as Jung saw him in the title of his book, in search of a soul. That Melville's age refused to see him as other than " Marquesan Melville " is fact for biographers. As his star declines with *Moby-Dick* and passes altogether from sight with the appearance of *Pierre*, he becomes willing to acquiesce in what the world would have him be in reputation: a curiosity, the man who lived among cannibals.

But it is improbable that the portrait of " Marquesan Melville " had any relation whatsoever to Melville's view of himself as artist. Reputation may influence the art of lesser men. In his case, much as the passing of fame may have been lamented, it had no bearing upon the artist's obedience to the iron-mailed hand. The record of his renown as a Pacific voyager and an adventurer among " cannibals " yields only one significant fact: " traveling " the Pacific again as both writer and lecturer, Melville betrayed his indissoluble unity with the images of the journey. For, apart from a substantial number of the poems in *Battle Pieces* and a few of the short stories, there came from this mind no work which does not display his allegiance to the Pacific and the westward-lying East, and, still more strikingly, to a small group of islanders encountered during forty days ashore in Polynesia. Other artists will experiment with unaccustomed material; they will try, at least, to write the novel of manners when the metaphysical narrative fails to be understood. Melville persists as Ishmael because he cannot escape the power of an original experience. He cannot dispel the images which order the structures of symbols from autotypes.

This particular condition of his mind is nowhere better illustrated than in a comment from one of his public lectures in 1857. He was speaking in Cambridge of the Venere de' Medici in the Vatican Museum. The figure, he said (and not very profoundly), seems to blend the actual and the ideal. " He had authority for the assertion, as one day from his mat in the Typee Valley he saw a maiden surprised in the bath re-

treating with the grace of nature to a friendly covert. These
beautiful figures he contended showed that the violence of the
Romans as a conquering race did not engross them wholly.
When he stood in the Colliseum [sic] its mountain hights [sic]
of ruins [and] waving foliage girdling him around as some vast
green hollow in the Appenine [sic] range, the solitude was that
of savage nature, but restoring its shattered terraces and arches
he repeopled them with the statues from the Vatican and in the
arenas [sic] turfy glen he fancy free confronted the fighting
Gladiator from the Louvre with the dying one from the Capi-
tol." [14] Through the jargon of this account, written by Henry
Sanford Gansevoort, Melville's cousin, one encounters the sovereignty of Ishmael, and he must look with amazement at the
unrelenting control exerted over the artist's feeling. These facts
appear. First, even the Venus must be made one with Fayaway
of Typee Valley, or one of her island sisters; and Melville goes
on to describe not a hollow in the Apennines, but yet again a
Polynesian valley, be it of Nukuhiva in *Typee* or of Tahiti in
Omoo. "Mountain heights," "waving foliage," "turfy glen,"
"savage nature" are emblems of Polynesian landscape, even in
1857, when the same valley has already been used at the very
crest (1851) of symbolic power: in *Moby-Dick,* "A Bower of
the Arsacides" (Ch. cii). Second, either Melville saw the
Colosseum with both Roman and Polynesian vision, or,
in retrospect, the image drifted into a Polynesian framework,
making a double image representing antiquity. This example
illustrates the power of the autotype in the sort of association
which appeals to the psychologist. It demonstrates an omni-
presence of image which must be acknowledged when the process of the genuine primitivistic symbol is brought to account.
The Polynesian Valley is reseen wherever this artist travels. As
an obverse setting, it accompanies certain emblems of landscape
from the Western world.

The following discussion intends to isolate some basic auto-

---

[14] Printed by Victor H. Paltsits in "Family Correspondence of Herman Melville," *Bulletin of the New York Public Library,* vol. 33 (July, 1929), p. 519. The
lecture attended by Gansevoort was delivered in Boston on December 2, 1857.

types or imagistic patterns which Melville acquired in the Pacific. It will seek to evaluate certain experiences from the voyages which become symbolistically authoritative—experiences which belong to the dominion of Ishmael.

3 *Melville's Sensuous Experience in Polynesia*

In the year of Melville's birth (1819) the brig *Thaddeus* sailed from Boston for the Sandwich Islands, bearing westward a devoted company of missionaries from the Congregational Fellowship under the direction of the Reverend Messrs. Hiram Bingham and Asa Thurston.[15] The venture was the American equivalent of the English mission which had set forth for Tahiti and the Marquesas in 1796 aboard the *Duff* from Gravesend, on the tide of the hymn, " Jesu, at thy command we launch into the deep." [16] News of success in Tahiti must have reached Boston; for only a few months after the *Duff* arrived at Papeete, King Pomare had been persuaded to relinquish his family idols, among which was the image of Teriiapotuura, the son of the great Oro, god and protector of Polynesia.[17] The extension of salvation to Papeete offered a challenge to Americans. The Reverend Heman Humphrey, pastor of the Congregational Church in Pittsfield, Massachusetts, had exhorted Bingham and Thurston with the stern words, " Your mission is to *a land of darkness, as darkness itself.*" [18] His farewell sermon had sent the mission aboard the *Thaddeus* with a text from *Joshua: And there remaineth yet very much land to be possessed.* " As the land of Canaan belonged to Israel, in virtue of a divine grant, so does the world belong to the church." The islands of the Pacific and most of Asia remained yet to be subdued. There

---

[15] Heman Humphrey, *The Promised Land:* A Sermon, delivered at Goshen, Conn. at the Ordination of the Rev. Messrs. Hiram Bingham . . . [and] Asa Thurston . . . as Missionaries to the Sandwich Islands—Sept. 29, 1819 (Boston, 1819), p. 3 [Harvard College Library].

[16] *The South Sea Islander; Containing Many Interesting Facts Relative to . . . the Island of Otaheite: with some Remarks on the Best Mode of Civilizing the Heathen* (New York, 1820), pp. 117–18.

[17] *Ibid.*, Appendix, p. 138.

[18] *The Promised Land*, p. iv.

the powers of darkness reigned. The exhortation ended with a statement of objectives to be pursued among the Sandwich Islanders: "To obtain an adequate knowledge of the language of the people; to make them acquainted with letters; to give them the Bible, with skill to read it; to turn them from their barbarous courses and habits; to introduce, and get into extended operation and influence among them, the arts and institutions of civilized life and society;—and above all, to convert them from their idolatries, superstitions and vices, to the living and redeeming God." [19]

In the year of Melville's return from Palestine and his journey to the shrines of Jerusalem (1857), the son of the Reverend Mr. Bingham set forth from Honolulu in the mission ship *Morning Star* for the islands of Micronesia. Passing near Mentchikoff Island (Kwajalein in the Marshalls) en route to Strong's Island (Kusaie, East Carolines), he sent ashore the following letter:

> *To the Inhabitants of Mentchikoff Island:*
>
> Glad tidings! "Glory to God in the highest; peace on earth; good-will toward men." "God so loved the world that He gave His only-begotten Son, that whosoever believeth in Him, might not perish, but have everlasting life." We hope soon to bring you the Gospel of Jesus Christ, and some of His missionaries to teach you.
>
> Very truly yours,
>
> *Hiram Bingham, Jr.*
>
> P. S. We left Honolulu August 7th, and are bound for Strong's Island.[20]

To imagine the dismay greeting this letter, even if it were translated accurately, is only to speculate upon the efficacy of techniques in converting the heathen. The thing to note here is the business of dispensing Christian symbols, as though some currency were being offered at face value. The history of missions to Oceania and the Orient has no real bearing upon primi-

---

[19] *Ibid.*, p. x.
[20] Rev. Hiram Bingham, Jr., *Story of the Morning Stars, the Children's Missionary Vessels* (Boston, Congregational House, 1907), p. 32.

tivism, save that its record of both empathy and technique displays something of the rhetoric which Melville and his successors suspected of all Christian preaching, missionary or domestic. To them the achievement of persuading an agreeable people (those of Tahiti, for example) to give up a traditional symbolism in answer to vague mumblings of peace, where peace and good will were already known, was an act of sacrilege, suspect in itself of " civilized " evil. This feat of persuasion was a virtual token of the symbolic impoverishment in which the zeal of missions originated.

Nothing dramatizes the experience of Melville in the Pacific more forcefully than a comparison of his observations with the contemporary view of Christian civilization toward Oceania and Asia as *the regions of darkness*. The preceding notices of missionary ventures offer a suggestion toward defining the antithesis of Melville's intent and sympathy as he leaves the Pacific. For him these areas are to become the only regions of light. Thus Melville, voyaging westward, and later reflecting upon the voyage, displays a " non-Christian " sympathy sharply opposed to every attitude carried into the Pacific by the Christians of the *Thaddeus* and the *Morning Star*. Given the problem of describing the difference, Melville might conceivably have proposed this: the cargo of mission ships was a store of counterfeit; the cargo of the symbolic *Pequod*, " freighted with savages," was the burden of art, heretical, proud, purposively divine. Christian poverty to the wealth of a " neo-savage " art! For if one discounts Melville's just observation that no affront to primitive man exceeds the missionary's intent to strip him of his native symbolism and leave him naked in the world, save for the ill-fitting habiliments of a misunderstood Christianity, one gets to the moral residue of his feeling: Christianity *as devised, tempered, fitted, and imposed by the church as Christian convention* is not worth carrying anywhere.

If Melville yields at all in this view, he subscribes unconsciously to the Roman Catholic rather than the Protestant theory of missions. Father Murphy of *Omoo* (Ch. XXXVII), " thoroughly disliked throughout all the Protestant missionary settlements in Polynesia " for his humanity, is really the only firm Christian recalled from the Pacific voyages. He is a man more interested in doing " good works " than in praying and hymn-singing. His character suggests the humanity which Stevenson admired in Father Damien and the Catholic missionaries to the lepers of Molokai. It may be supposed that had Melville seen more of Catholic wisdom toward the established conventions of primitive societies, he might have come to admire, if he could not accept, Catholic tolerance toward a mixed religious symbolism. Throughout Oceania, and certain primitive regions of Central and South America, one finds in Catholic communities the evidence of this tolerance: indigenous custom and superstition mixed with the elements of Christian feasts.

Charles R. Anderson, in his biographical study of Melville in Polynesia, observes that the young voyager was rather indifferent to the religious state of his pagan companions. " Although Melville, just on the point of freeing himself from the religious tyranny of an overstrict Calvinism, indulges in none of the missionary's evangelical dreams of reclaiming a ' back-slidden generation ' of heathens—and even treats their ' religious sloth ' with levity, if not actual rejoicing—he certainly makes full use of Stewart's impressions that the Marquesan religion was in a state of decay. Melville, indeed, never treats the pure paganism of the Marquesans forthrightly and in sober earnest." [21] This is all true. Melville's agreement with C. S. Stewart, chaplain in the United States Navy,[22] as he gathered the material for *Typee*, has been noticed by nearly every biographer and critic. The Marquesan religion was, indeed, in a state of decay. But it was precisely this liberation from religious convention, the collapse of the mouldering gods, and the transcendent position of each Marquesan as his own priest that appealed to him.

The more Melville thought of this spectacle of decay, the more he thought of himself as a savage, the maker of his own

---

[21] *Melville in the South Seas*, p. 175.
[22] *A Visit to the South Seas, in the United States' Ship* Vincennes, *during the years 1829 and 1830* (London, 1832), 2vv.

symbols for his god. So Ishmael speaks in *Moby-Dick* (Ch. LVII) :

> I myself am a savage, owning no allegiance but to the King of Cannibals; and ready at any moment to rebel against him. Now, one of the peculiar characteristics of the savage in his domestic hours, is his wonderful patience of industry. An ancient Hawaiian war-club or spear-paddle, in its full multiplicity and elaboration of carving, is as great a trophy of human perseverance as a Latin lexicon. For, with but a bit of broken sea-shell or a shark's tooth, that miraculous intricacy of wooden network has been achieved; and it has cost steady years of steady application.

Ishmael is describing the custom of sailors in their hours of "ocean leisure." They amuse themselves by carving out little images of the whale in wood and bone. It cannot matter very much that the Hawaiian of 1843 was probably less interested in the ancient art of paddle-carving than in various embroilments with his imperialistic oppressors. The spear-paddle remembered by Ishmael, with its *full multiplicity* and elaboration of design, is Marquesan and Tahitian as well as Hawaiian. It stands for the Oceanic custom of making art symbols on paddles; and its meaning as symbol may be beautifully extended by considering its relation to the sea and to the canoe in which the voyager is carried. The striking significance of what Ishmael is talking about appears in his remarks following upon this passage. He goes on to say, in this same unveiling chapter, that these seamen, the "white sailor-savages," work even as the Pacific savage, and even as the "Greek savage" carving Achilles' shield, and the "old Dutch savage," Albert Durer [sic], engaged in making a print "full of barbaric spirit and suggestiveness." The sailors are all making the same thing; they are making images of the whale, each in his own way and according to his own idea. You can see the whale, Ishmael says, in "bony, ribby regions of the earth," too. You can see him in the profiles of undulating ridges; and you can trace him out in the starry heavens. But you must be a thorough whaleman to see these sights. It follows, from what Ishmael says, that when you are a thorough whaleman, you are a savage, with no allegiances to idols (and, therefore, symbols). You make your own. You carve away, with the art of the spear fisherman; you represent there, in that cabalistic device, all that you want to put there, all the multiplicity of God, as you saw him. And no one is to gainsay you.

A " back-slidden " generation of heathens is a race of men liberated from the authority of simplex symbols. The only sacrament to which the savage is bound is the symbolic act of paddle-making. The shape of the paddle contains the design, multiplex and uniquely his own, just as the paddle, as object, propels each of a hundred village fishermen over dangerous waters. Something was said earlier of judging the devices of art as shaped of dream content described in Freudian terms. It is obvious that when the design on the paddle has become multiplex, " primitive " man has ceased to be primitive. He has become an artist making his own representation of God. It was in this superior human form as artist liberated from religious convention, free to make the complexity of his own religious art from the skills of tattooing or of paddle carving, that Melville saw and remembered the Polynesian. That is why Melville holds with unyielding tenacity to his concept of himself as a savage. It may be, as Anderson says, that he was freeing himself from an overstrict Calvinism. But the tyranny was less tyrannous than most people suppose. As Ishmael, he was nearly destitute, threadbare, and " liberated " when he reached Nukuhiva. The real meaning of Melville's rejoicing in the " religious sloth " of the Orient lies in his own awareness of being liberated to art and the religion which he was to make of art. Where it did not seem vicious, the affrontery of Christian missions was only ridiculous. For as a carver of whales and spear-paddles, Melville saw himself, with his Polynesian fellow savages, as more civilized than the most erudite messenger of the Gospel. Whoever would grasp Melville's concept of himself as symbol-maker and artist must begin with this chapter of *Moby-Dick*, " Of Whales in Paint; in Teeth; in Wood; in Sheet-Iron; in Stone; in Mountains; in Stars." From this he must retrace the development of Ishmael, the savage, to Nukuhiva and to Tahiti. For the savage in Melville is the symbolist.

As autotype, the image of the solitary Polynesian artisan, be he the paddle-maker and carver or the tattooer or the tapa-maker, was the strongest single impression which Melville as Ishmael brought away from his forty days in the wilderness. To this image the form of his personality as artist came to be bound, limb by limb. Thus the "accident" of a youthful journey from Lansingburgh, New York, to the Marquesas and the Society Islands eventuated in a kind of modern miracle. It was Melville's good fortune to have seen and felt these experiences, as well as to have lived them, in his twenty-third year. It was equal good fortune that he saw the last authentic manifestations of Polynesian culture. No one need set forth for the Marquesas or Tahiti today with the hope that a similar miracle might happen to him, unless he believes that landscape and nothing else will suffice. A recent traveler to Nukuhiva reports that the last survivors of a decimated population wander disconsolately on the beaches, waiting for a ship to take them to civilization. When he asked two youths of the nearly-forgotten Taipis to provide him with a calabash as a souvenir, he found them, a few hours later, poring over the plates in an ethnological volume from the library of the French administration, in a vain effort to find out how to make one.[23] But this is common knowledge, perhaps, all of it agreeing with the knowledge universally possessed that the Western world has finally persuaded most of the Orient to emerge from "darkness" to the light of Western "conveniences." The autotype of the symbol-maker still lies potentially to his hand in any quarter of this Orient. But the symbol which he makes is very probably not to be religious. Schweitzer is evidently correct when he reminds us that no new cultures are forthcoming to give us new beliefs. We not only know them all; we have also removed most of the unknown from them and substituted envy toward us.

Stewart wrote (and undoubtedly Melville copied him as he

---

[23] I am indebted to Mr. Ernest Simmerer, yachtsman of Honolulu, T. H., for this information.

began *Typee*) : " . . . the images are literally crumbling into dust and ashes . . . . My heart sighed for the beginning of missionary instruction among them." [24] The first observation Melville confirms; the second, for reasons implicit in the preceding discussion of the seaman-artist, he rejects. In *Typee* Tom's companion Kory-Kory beats a decayed idol of the sacred groves when it topples upon him. Tom reflects: " The woodrot malady is spreading among the idols—the fruit upon their altars is becoming offensive—the temples themselves need rethatching—the tattooed clergy are altogether too light-hearted and lazy—and their flocks are going astray." [25] What Melville saw here was an exhausted religious symbolism. His observation is supported by another student, more informed than Stewart. Shortly after Tom's visit to Typee Valley, Max Radiguet, an officer of the newly-installed French administration, was even more explicit concerning Marquesan irreverence toward the *tikis* (images) . " Seated one day near the dais of the high priest, where the two statues of which we had spoken were situated, we asked the islanders with the aid of an interpreter for information concerning the measure of respect commonly paid by them to these exterior emblems of the cult. The irreverence of their responses, the small seriousness which they seemed to show toward the neighboring idols, at the feet of which one saw, nevertheless, a recent offering of fruit, bread, and coconuts, agreed ill with the rigid observance of the law which had been imposed in the name of religion." [26] Certainly, it is remarkable that Melville, with about three weeks among the Taipis, should have reached an intuitive conclusion no less authentic than the studious one of Radiguet. Having seen a superior people (for indeed Queequeg of *Moby-Dick*, as transposed Marquesan, is the superior human being of that book) free of religious authority and happy with this freedom, he came to suppose that the Oriental, whether he be Polynesian or Asiatic, had found his religious destiny in release from disci-

[24] *A Visit to the South Seas*, vol. I, pp. 268–69, 271.

[25] *Typee*, p. 241.

[26] *Les Derniers Sauvages: Souvenirs de l'Occupation Française aux Iles Marquises, 1842–1859* (Paris, Hachette [1860]), p. 54.

pline and dogma. Hence, the imposition of a legislating Christianity upon the Orient was a supreme folly of civilization. In 1857, as he traveled to Jaffa, he wrote in his journal: " It is against the will of God that the East should be Christianized." [27]

All this Melville advanced even in view of Marquesan cannibalism. Whether he knew very much of human sacrifice as well is not certain. Radiguet reported from Nukuhiva that human sacrifice was practiced at the death of a high chieftain; [28] and Sir James Frazer has confirmed this with a notice of the Marquesan practice of appeasing ancient men of the tribe, who were deified to the power of inflicting disease or death, with sacrificial victims.[29] This second practice seems to be reflected in *Mardi* (Chs. xxxix and xliii) as Taji boards the double ceremonial canoe, slays the old priest, and enters the tent where Yillah is retained as the sacrificial victim. Enough is said of cannibalism throughout Melville's art to indicate, however, that this practice was habitually associated in his mind with Polynesian savagery.

Ralph Linton, in his scientific report on the Marquesans, asserts that there can be no question of their cannibalism. From his talks with the old men who had indulged in the practice, he became convinced that " while there was ceremonial cannibalism, there was also eating of human flesh because they found it good." Here, too, women and children, as well as men, were admitted to cannibal feasts.[30] Readers of *Typee* (Ch. xxxii) are familiar with Tom's description of his visit to the " taboo groves " and his discovery of a covered vessel " in the shape of a small canoe " containing bones of a human skeleton still fresh with moisture and with particles of flesh clinging to them. Elsewhere the narrator defends the Marquesans by asserting that they practiced the rite of cannibalism only on the bodies

[27] *Journal up the Straits*, ed. Weaver, p. 69. In the same year he proposed in the bitter pages of *The Confidence Man* that missions should be quickened with the Wall Street spirit, and all China converted *en masse* with an army of ten thousand missionaries (Constable ed., pp. 53–54).

[28] *Les Derniers Sauvages*, pp. 169–70.

[29] *The Golden Bough*, Abridged ed. (New York, 1930), p. 96.

[30] Abram Kardiner, *The Individual and His Society* (New York, 1939); Ch. 5, " Marquesan Culture," by Ralph Linton, pp. 142, 181.

of slain enemies; at its worst it could not very far exceed
in barbarity the old English practice of lopping off the head
of a convicted traitor, " perhaps a man found guilty of honesty,
patriotism and such like heinous crimes," and exposing it on a
pike.[31] Cannibalism, as an obstacle to accepting the morality of
Polynesians, had very little to do with Melville's allegiance.
After *Typee*, except for references to cannibals in the ancestry
of Queequeg in *Moby-Dick*, it is dismissed.

The first of Melville's Polynesian autotypes, the image of
the solitary artisan, has been defined. The second may now be
isolated. This is the autotype of the savage in relation to the
missionary, with Melville's speculation upon the savage's superior humanity (when the practices of cannibalism and sacrifice have been discounted). It was Frazer's opinion that
Melville, since he did not learn the native language, was not
able to throw much light " on the inner life of the people, and
in particular on their religious ideas." [32] The supposition may
be ventured that he observed nearly all there was to observe
of " religious ideas." What he did not understand was the
great body of native lore and the intricate system of Polynesian
tabu. This could scarcely have been touched in three weeks of
living among the Taipis. The mind of Oceania is really dis-
coverable only through *tabu*, and the nature of this phenomenon can be learned only after several years of proximity, and
investigation through the native language, if, indeed, it is ever
learned at all. Associated with *tabu* is the whole range of
Polynesian legend and epic, of which we have as yet very slight
knowledge. The oral traditions of Polynesia were inaccessible
to Melville, although there is good evidence, as will be presently noted, that he made limited use of legend available to him
through English transcriptions or the accounts of chance ac-
quaintances of his own race. It becomes more and more
apparent, as one proceeds in examining the Pacific voyages for
autotypes, that we have only Melville's undirected, highly sen-

---

[31] *Typee*, p. 166 (and p. 277).
[32] *The Belief in Immortality and The Worship of the Dead* (London, 1922),
vol. 2 (*The Belief among the Polynesians*), p. 373.

sitive eye. No one had told him what to look for. He saw what emotion impelled him to see.

The solitary artisan and the savage superior to the missionary from the Christian world are the primary images from Melville's experience which order, first, the evolution of his symbolistic art and, second, his representation of primitive Polynesians as ideal human types. The other images, all of them important as facsimiles in the making of symbols, are considerably easier to define. If the two which have already been discussed show attributes of profound reflection, the remaining ones are almost wholly impressionistic, fully received in pure sensuousness. At the risk of sentimentalizing Melville's arrival in the bay of Nukuhiva aboard the *Acushnet*, it must be said that something akin to a geniune mystical experience seized him. The first of these " secondary " images fell upon him with immeasurable power and engraved the inner vision of the youth with so deep an outline that thereafter it governed in his art like a master signature, tracing its duplicates again and again in the outlines of symbols and the devices of metaphor. Every traveler to Polynesia has known this vision. The bay is green to blue to violet; the reef and the beach are indistinguishable in the splintering and powdering flashes of light on sand and surf; above the water rise the- walls of volcanic peaks waving and dripping with the green of creation; and these together seem to drift endlessly under clouds scudding before the trade winds. All this vividness burns incomprehensibly through the eye into the life of feeling. It will exist prodigiously in the being of the least communicative mariner; and if it confronts the eye of the artist, it will grip him relentlessly, though he travel to an opposite hemisphere. Every reader of Melville must " see " for himself the vision from the *Acushnet* on June 23, 1842; every student of Loti, of Stevenson, of Charles Warren Stoddard, every beholder of the canvases of Gauguin must speculate upon the meaning of this vision elsewhere in the Pacific. One may almost be persuaded that the human being does, indeed, bear the history of creation in himself and that in the moment of his first encounter with Polynesia he senses his coming to a new earth.

Melville's description of the bay of Nukuhiva through which he begins his Polynesian observation presents it as a vast natural amphitheater, overgrown with vines, marked with the furrows of deep glens like enormous fissures caused by the ravages of time.[33] Thereafter in *Typee*, where he gives first proof of his bad ear in his failure to transcribe Nukuhivan dialect accurately, he reveals, on the other hand, one of the most striking senses of color in the history of American literature. All is green, traversed by slender cascades and upland streams, opened here and there by palmetto-thatched houses, " glistening in the sun that had bleached them to a dazzling whiteness " (Ch. VII) . The landscape is variously treated with the same mastery in the passage through the ravine and the descent into the valley of the Taipis (Chs. IX and X) . In *Omoo* the pattern of waving foliage and flashing streams is further extended, as Paul and Doctor Long Ghost reach the valley of " Martair." This gorge runs inland " terminating . . . in a range of the most grotesque elevations, which seem embattled with turrets and towers, grown over with verdure . . . waving with trees . . . with links of streams flashing through." [34]

Melville's borrowing from Stewart and other authors of the literature of Pacific travel has been ably accounted for by his biographer, Leon Howard. " Stewart's narrative," writes Howard, ". . . became so intimately a part of Melville's mind while he was writing his own book [*Typee*] that his visual remembrance of the Marquesas was adapted to Stewart's descriptions and some of his observations on manners and customs were simply borrowed from it." [35] He further asserts that without the help of William Ellis's *Polynesian Researches* Melville would scarcely have finished *Omoo*.[36] This conjecture seems reasonable enough. There is much evidence that Melville was heavily derivative in his first two volumes; in *Typee*, at least,

---

[33] *Typee*, p. 29.
[34] *Omoo*, p. 239.
[35] *Herman Melville* (Berkeley, 1951), p. 93.
[36] *Ibid.*, p. 101. For a detailed account of Melville's indebtedness to Stewart's record, see Russell Thomas, " Yarn for Melville's *Typee*," *Philological Quarterly*, vol. 15 (1936), pp. 16–29.

he scrupulously acknowledges his sources in the accounts of navigators and missionaries.[37] In *Omoo* he appears, as well, to have made use of various plates representing Polynesian landscape in the published journals of two missionaries to Tahiti.[38] But these derivations have no more relation to the autotypes of the symbolist than have the " cetological " chapters of *Moby-Dick*, with their impressive bibliography, to the real artistic value of the whale. To call them to account here for evaluation suggests that criticism of the material of symbols should be concerned with veracity. No amount of proof that Melville depended upon Stewart or any other voyager can diminish the strength of the impression which was indubitably his, the emotional reaction to the blazing whiteness of beaches and upland cascades, the waving green of towering escarpments. The ethnologist, reading *Typee* and *Omoo*, may agree with Stevenson that Melville had " no ear for languages whatsoever." [39] By the same token, his accuracy in Polynesian dialects has scarcely any relevance to his acquired image of Polynesians as men and women of preëminent physical beauty.

Nearly every traveler to the Marquesas from Captain Cook to the followers of Melville agreed that the inhabitants of these islands were the most beautiful of Oceanic ethnic groups. Captain David Porter, patrolling the Pacific in the United States frigate *Essex* during the War of 1812, had called at Nukuhiva in the interests of an imperialistic " reconnaissance." " The honest naked Nooaheevan," he wrote, showed " every emanation of his pure soul " in his face.[40] " Their faces are remarkably handsome, with keen piercing eyes; their teeth white, and more beautiful than ivory; countenances open and expressive . . . ; limbs which might serve as models for a statuary, and strength

---

[37] E. g., *Typee*, pp. 32, 227, 238, 239, 246, 247, 285.

[38] Cf. various plates appearing in James Montgomery's *Journal of Voyages and Travels by the Rev. Daniel Tyerman and George Bennet, Esq.* (London, 1831), 2vv.

[39] Stevenson in a letter to E. L. Burlingame (February, 1890), *The Letters of Robert Louis Stevenson*, ed. Sidney Colvin (New York, 1911), vol. 3, p. 185.

[40] *Journal of a Cruise Made to the Pacific Ocean . . . in the United States Frigate* Essex, *in the Years 1812, 1813, and 1814*, second edition (New York, 1822), vol. 2, p. 133.

and activity proportioned to their appearance." [41] Porter further noticed that virtue among them, " in the light in which we view it," was unknown. They attached no shame " to a proceeding which they not only considered as natural, but as innocent and harmless amusement, by which no one was injured." [42] Since few Marquesans survive in the twentieth century, it is difficult to verify this extravagant statement. For a reading of Melville, however, it is important to note that the autotype of Polynesian beauty which appears in his symbols is closer to the account of Porter than to that of Stewart, even though the young author of *Typee* presumably took from Stewart his technique of describing women. Stewart supplies the term *mantling*,[43] as Melville recalls the charms of coloring in the complexion of Fayaway and her companions of Typee Valley. But there is something of Frazer's equanimity and detachment in Stewart which will not represent Melville's experience in the image. Frazer stated simply and scientifically: " Observers are generally agreed that from the purely physical point of view the Marquesan islanders are, or used to be, the noblest specimens of the Polynesian race." [44] For Melville this is not enough.

What the sensuous image of Melville reveals approaches voluptuousness: he is celebrating the nakedness of the Polynesian body and the innocence in which it is displayed.[45] It is

[41] *Ibid.*, pp. 58–59.

[42] *Ibid.*, p. 59.

[43] *A Visit to the South Seas*, vol. 1, p. 231.

[44] *The Belief in Immortality and The Worship of the Dead*, p. 331.

[45] The contemporary poet Muriel Rukeyser has included in her recent volume of verse, *The Green Wave* (New York, 1948), nine translations and adaptations of Marquesan " rari," or love chants. Her introductory note states that the original Marquesan texts were the work of Moa Tetua, " the leading poet " of the Marquesas in the nineteenth century. She asserts that Marquesan poetry was suppressed by the missionaries because of its erotic symbolism. Following her acknowledgment of Samuel Elbert as translator, she adds: " These songs are like the songs that Melville heard." The eroticism of the images would not have been apparent to him through the language, of course; but he could certainly have understood some of it through the dance which they were intended to accompany.

Reference should also be made at this point to the account of the Oceanic dance by Robert Dean Frisbie in *The Island of Desire* (New York, 1944). Here he describes the sensuousness of the dance on Danger Island (northeast of Samoa): " The moonlight was an actor in this scene of pagan loveliness, as was

strange, indeed, that Freudian critics have not made more of this simple fact; for it is assumed that, if psychoanalysis of Melville, not aesthetic judgment, be the objective, the most important single *sensed* experience of his life was his encounter with a society ignorant of the pruderies of civilization. His successor in Typee Valley, Lt. Henry Wise, published some gossip of the Navy that Melville left behind him a child by Fayaway (whoever she may have been).[46] True or false, all this is beside the point. In the twentieth century, it makes no difference, one way or the other. Melville's image as autotype acquires significance only as it is related to the sense of liberation from convention, which has already been analyzed with reference to religious custom. That he enjoyed the sight of unabashed nakedness is fact. There is too much evidence from his mature symbols to permit denial of it. Thus in *Typee* " the artless vivacity and unconcealed natural graces of these savage maidens " is set in relief against the affectation of stiffly attired " coronation beauties " in Westminster Abbey.[47] The men with their classic beauty of profile, as in the features of the stranger Marnoo, need nothing of the cunning artifices of the tailor and stand forth as sculptor's models.[48] The same intensity of feeling appears again in *Omoo* as the wanderers enter the valley of Tamai, on " Imeeo," adjacent to Tahiti.[49] At its most undisciplined, as in the lush portrait of Fayaway,[50] it is pure sensuousness conveyed in the manner of an *odalisque*; in its more significant form it is a primitivist's token revolt against what he sees as the artificiality of civilization.

In this province of feeling Melville belongs with every subsequent literary observer of Polynesian nakedness. As the

the wind with its tantalizing smell of hot bodies, of the night breathing of wilted flowers " (p. 30). Elsewhere (in *Mr. Moonlight's Island* [New York, 1939]) Frisbie describes native freedom from the sense of licentiousness, and uninhibited sexual behavior on Danger Island (pp. 229, 289).

[46] [Pseud. Harry Gringo], *Los Gringos* (New York, 1849), pp. 398–99. See a full consideration of this report by Clarence Gohdes, " Gossip about Melville in the South Seas," *The New England Quarterly*, vol. 10 (1937), pp. 526–31.

[47] *Typee*, p. 216.

[48] *Ibid.*, pp. 243, 248.

[49] *Omoo*, pp. 282, 284.

[50] *Typee*, pp. 114–15.

makers of primitivism, these artists discover a race of men opposite to the emaciated and half-alive Christian inhabitants of " enlightened " cities. If one wishes to desert the autotype for notice, momentarily, of the archetype, then it is a thing most curious that Samuel Butler, not one of their number, wrote of the inhabitants of Erewhon (1872) exactly as though he were describing the grace of Polynesians. " The women were vigorous, and had a most majestic gait. . . . Their colour was equal to that of the finest Italian paintings; being of the clearest olive [cf. Fayaway], and yet ruddy with a glow of perfect health. . . . The men were as handsome as the women beautiful . . . a compound of all that is best in Egyptian, Greek, and Italian." [51]

The image of physical beauty as autotype is at least equal to that of primeval nature. But as a potential facsimile in the symbol it is superior since it carries with it the arts and activities related to the physique and the bearing of the Polynesian. From *Typee* it appears that Melville learned something of native crafts. Here he mentions native building practices in the community,[52] the lost art of stone fortifications in a " Polynesian Stonehenge " near the village,[53] the process of making *tapa*,[54] and meat cookery.[55] These are of slight importance after the composition of *Typee*. In another category, there is the art represented by the " Hawaiian " fisherman carving a spear-paddle in the fifty-seventh chapter of *Moby-Dick*. It would seem nearly certain that Melville has in mind here a Marquesan artisan. Linton has reported that by primitive standards the Marquesans were an exceedingly wealthy group in their holdings of various artifacts (weapons, carved bowls, mats, etc.) .[56] These articles remain, in the exhibitions of a few museums, as the finest examples of Oceanic art. Canoes appear in *Typee*, *Omoo*, and *Mardi*; and it is probable that either in the Marquesas or in Tahiti Melville saw a mortuary canoe, the pro-

[51] *Erewhon or, Over the Range* (London, 1923), pp. 45–46.
[52] *Typee*, pp. 108-109.
[53] *Ibid.*, pp. 207–208.
[54] *Ibid.*, pp. 197–98.
[55] *Ibid.*, p. 213.
[56] Kardiner's *The Individual and His Society*, p. 147.

totype of Queequeg's "coffin" to which Ishmael clings for survival at the close of *Moby-Dick*. The great Polynesian double canoe which appears in *Mardi*, bearing the old priest and the captive Yillah, is, however, somewhat less authenticated by Melville's experience. There is little doubt that by the time of his arrival in Polynesia these large sea-going canoes were no longer being made. But these Polynesian crafts are all of considerably less value in a study of symbols than the most impressive visual art which Melville encountered in the Pacific: the art of tattooing.

There are very good reasons for the persistence of tattooing as an autotype in the mind of Melville, the artist. It is the one facsimile of Polynesian experience which he could easily transfer to wider significance through his images of this device as it appeared on the bodies of his shipmates, whether these were men of the *Acushnet* or the *United States*. In the second place, it became as easily related to the permanence of the autotype representing Polynesian "nobility." Porter recorded in his journal that he believed the Marquesans had among them "professional" tattooers and that the wealthy and high-born seemed to be more fully covered than those of inferior station.[57] This statement Melville seems to have taken as his cue. He describes, first, the noble chief Mehevi, in *Typee*. "All imaginable lines and curves and figures were delineated over his whole body, and in their grotesque variety and infinite profusion, I could only compare them to the crowded groupings of quaint patterns we sometimes see in costly pieces of lacework . . . . Two broad stripes of tattooing, diverging from the center of his shaven crown, obliquely crossed both eyes—staining the lids—to a little below either ear, where they united with another stripe, which swept in a straight line along the lips, and formed the base of the triangle."[58] Another among several descriptions appearing in *Typee* will serve as illustration at this point. Kory-Kory's decoration seems to be a prototype for the adornment of Queequeg in *Moby-Dick*: ". . . the entire body of my savage valet,

[57] *Journal of a Cruise*, vol. 2, p. 12.
[58] *Typee*, p. 104.

covered all over with representations of birds and fishes, and a
variety of most unaccountable-looking creatures, suggested to
me the idea of a pictorial museum of natural history, or an
illustrated copy of Goldsmith's *Animated Nature*." [59] The re-
liability of these accounts was first confirmed by the German
traveler in the Pacific, Friedrich Gerstäcker, a few years after
Typee appeared. In the third volume of his *Reisen* he paid
tribute to Melville as an authority on tattooing, with the comment that in Tahiti, at least, the art had been discontinued by
missionary order.[60] Like Porter, Melville believed that he distinguished a difference in the quality of tattooing performed
upon "inferior" members of the community. Willowdean
Handy, after an ethnological study in the Marquesas some years
ago for the Bishop Museum, Honolulu, reported that there was
no evidence for such discrimination.[61] Furthermore, she proved
Melville wrong in his notion that there were orders of tattooing
artists in the Marquesas, as there were "orders" of London
tailors. The Marquesan *tuhuna* (tattooer), Mrs. Handy concluded, tattooed one and all without discrimination.[62]

It may be, too, that no less than the right leg of Queen
Vaekehu of the Marquesas is involved in the autotype of tattooing. This remarkable woman (1827-1901), who died in the
year of Victoria's death and who became in the Pacific as legendary as Victoria, was about fifteen years old when she visited
Melville's frigate, the *United States*, in the late summer of
1843.[63] Melville records in the first chapter of *Typee* that she
came aboard the ship, lying in the bay of Nukuhiva, with her
husband, King "Mowanna," wearing "a gaudy tissue of scarlet
cloth, trimmed with yellow silk, which, descending a little be-

[59] *Ibid.*, p. 111.

[60] *Reisen* (Stuttgart, Tübingen, 1853), vol. 3, *Die Südsee-Inseln*, pp. 397-98.

[61] Willowdean Handy, *Tattooing in the Marquesas*, Bernice P. Bishop Museum
Bulletin no. 1 (Honolulu, 1922), p. 5.

[62] *Ibid.*, p. 9. Mrs. Handy's plates from photographs of tattooed natives in
Polynesia are the best representations to be had. They confirm Melville's
accounts.

[63] Mabel Weaks, "Long Ago and 'Faraway': Traces of Melville in the Marquesas in the Journal of A. G. Jones, 1854-1855," *New York Public Library Bulletin*, vol. 52 (1948), p. 366.

low the knees, exposed to view her bare legs, embellished with spiral tattooing, and somewhat resembling two miniature Trajan's columns." But it seems that this noble queen, known also to Stevenson and to Loti, had only one Trajan's column, not two. Frederick O'Brien, the best informed of recent travelers to the Marquesas, asserts that she was converted to Christianity with but one leg done, and thereafter refused to have the design completed.[64]

There must certainly be wonder in any account of Melville's three weeks in the Marquesas, wonder that he assimilated in so short a time so much to use in the Polynesian romances, and in the great symbolic works which follow them. If one must check into fact, he will certainly discover less and less knowledge after he leaves the subject of tattooing. It will be remembered that Tom in *Typee* enjoys every evening an anointment of fragrant oil, from the yellow root of the "aka," at the hands of "the girls of the house."[65] The description is not far wrong. This is really the *eka* described by Linton, a yellow dye ground from a species of *amomum*, which grew in only one locality, at Muake, in the interior of Nukuhiva.[66] But this is only one detail in a pattern of reference which must have been very largely supplied by the imagination. It is probably enough to know that a few of the characters of *Typee*, apart from Toby, have been authenticated through the discovery of the journal of A. G. Jones, a visitor to the scenes of the book thirteen years after Melville had known the island. His interpreter, Jones said, had lived on Nukuhiva for twenty-five years and remembered Melville, but not Fayaway. "Mr. Jones met the King, Te Moana, and his wife, Queen Vaekehu, who came aboard the *St. Mary's* as they had visited previously the frigate *United States* when Melville was a member of the crew of that ship. He learned that the 'noble Mehevi,' chief of all the Taipis, had been killed by Te Moana; and he obtained evidence that

[64] *Atolls of the Sun* (New York, 1922), p. 343.

[65] *Typee*, p. 148.

[66] Ralph Linton, *The Material Culture of the Marquesas Islands* in *Memoirs of the Bernice Pauahi Bishop Museum*, vol. 8, no. 5 (Honolulu, 1923), p. 421.

such persons as Kory-Kory, Melville's personal attendant; Tinor and the one-eyed chief, Mow-Mow, had once existed; but had passed away. He was convinced that the Taipis were cannibals until a very late period and concluded that Melville had a truthful basis for his book but that his imagination was very largely drawn upon for the attractive features of the same." [67] This is as near as one needs to come to truth. If Jones is in any degree reliable, then it is quite enough to know that Melville represented in *Typee* with imagistic accuracy certain tattooed Marquesans who indelibly marked his art.

These, in brief, are the sovereign autotypes from Polynesia: the savage as artisan; the savage as the superior " man of religion "; tropical landscape; Polynesian physique, with its adornment of tattooing. Melville's use of Polynesian legend does not belong with these. The assertion has already been made that this material was not accessible to him, since he neither knew the languages of Polynesia nor remained in the area long enough to learn from an interpreter very much narrative of oral tradition. It cannot mean very much, for instance, that he refers to the fire goddess of Hawaii, Pele. This deity of the volcano was known to every Pacific mariner of the nineteenth century.

But Melville had somewhere learned enough Maori lore to suggest an Oceanic mythological background for *Mardi*. In describing the origin of Yillah, from Oroolia, the Island of Delights, Melville writes that she was one day snared in the tendrils of a vine. There she was transformed into a flower and hung in a trance, until, regaining her senses, she was about to free herself from her prison. But at this moment, the blossom was snapped from its stem by a wind and borne to sea, where it fell into the opening valve of a shell. The shell, in turn, was cast up on a beach. The old priest Aleema (whom Taji slays for the liberation of Yillah) finds the shell, opens it, and, when Yillah emerges as a goddess from the blossom, keeps her captive in a sacred temple. In a dream the priest has been instructed to offer Yillah to a whirlpool, that she may be restored to her native Oroolia.[68] To this account Melville adds that Yillah is of the race of the Tullas, Polynesian albinos who have a supernatural origin and who are particularly suitable for sacrifice.[69] It is fairly certain that he is using here the old Maori legend of Hina, the bride of a heavenly race, who appears on earth under another name and takes an earthly husband. When she returns to the sky, she instructs the husband to join her by clinging to a tendril which will hang from heaven and root itself upon earth.[70]

So much for Hina in her guise of human flesh. In her true heavenly role, she is Hina untransformed: as this divine spirit she becomes the bride of either Tane, the light (the sun), or of Ma-Rama, moonlight (the moon).[71] Now, since Hina, as legend, belongs to all Polynesians rather than to the Maori alone, it happens that the mythology of Nukuhiva and the neighboring islands of the Marquesas knew the same goddess as well. On Nukuhiva she was called Ina; and " Marama (the moon), who from afar had often admired her, became so enamoured of her charms that one night he descended from his place in the heavens to fetch her to be his wife." [72]

It is impossible to suppose that Melville could have learned the Nukuhivan version of the legend without any knowledge of the language. But there seems little doubt that Yillah of *Mardi* is a somewhat garbled variant of Hina and that the aspiring and pursuing bridegroom, Taji, is a variant of Tane who, in Maori legend, is eligible to be her husband. Taji in *Mardi*, appearing to a king of the Mardians, identifies himself as having arrived from the sun; [73] and thus he recalls the legendary Tane, god of light. The alternate " suitor " for Hina, Marama, who abducts her in the Marquesan legend and carries

---

[68] See *Mardi*, vol. 1, p. 160.

[69] *Ibid.*, vol. 1, p. 178.

[70] E. Tregear, " Hina's Voyage to the Sacred Isle," *Transactions and Proceedings of the New Zealand Institute*, vol. 19 (1886), p. 497. (For another account of Hina see William W. Gill, *Myths and Songs from the South Pacific*, with a preface by Max Müller [London, 1876], pp. 88 ff.).

[71] *Ibid.*, p. 504.

[72] *Ibid.*, p. 496.

[73] *Mardi*, vol. 1, p. 194.

her off to his native element, the moon, lends his name, presumably, to the pages of *Mardi*. But the spelling is altered to Maramma (which, of course, cannot mean very much) and the name designates an island, not the moon at all (which means more). Merrell R. Davis is probably correct in his study of this novel when he suggests that Maramma is really altered from Maremma of Dante's *Inferno* (xxix).[74] This proposal seems more suitable when Melville's reading of Dante in the year of completing *Mardi* (1848) is taken into account. The novel itself is so tangled and chaotic in form that the course of such legends as this one exemplifies may never be charted. It seems quite clear in this instance that Melville was using legend by hearsay or by some inferior transcription. Its dim agreement with the great mythological complex of Hina suggests that, all things being equal, Polynesian legend might be isolated profitably as an additional autotype for consideration in the analysis of Melville's important primitivistic symbols. Since the difficulties which it proposes are insurmountable for this study, it is better to acknowledge the possibility and to follow strictly the autotypes already defined. These are the important imagistic outlines, anyway, which impose the patterns of remembered feeling as the artist goes about the business of fusing the multiple symbol. If one could add to them an autotype of acquired legend, he would eventually confront what he possesses in the multiplicity of Milton's symbols, as these present structures of both feeling and erudition for analysis.

4   Selectivity and the Polynesian Autotype

In conclusion, an old question referring to Melville's attitude toward primitive societies must again appear. Why is it that we have in this artist's feeling a deification of Polynesians and a seeming contradiction of the tendency in his condemnation

[74] *Melville's* Mardi: *A Chartless Voyage* (New Haven, 1952), p. 150, n. 1: "The name suggests Dante's marshy and 'pestilent fen' called 'Maremma' in the *Inferno*, xxix, 46–9, which is also placed in opposition to 'Sienna' (could this be Melville's Serenia?) in the *Purgatorio*, v, 132: 'Sienna gave me life;/ Maremma took it from me.'"

of African Negroes in *Benito Cereno* and of American Indians in *The Confidence Man?* What is the meaning of this inconsistency? If one takes Melville's sympathies in *Benito Cereno* to be those of Captain Delano as he sustains the tortured and weakened Don Benito in defiance of the black Babo, where does he resolve the difficulty, particularly when it is remembered that the Negroes are indentured slaves, deported against their wills from Africa? If he resists the temptation to judge all the substance of *The Confidence Man* as satire, how does he resolve Colonel Moredock's determined vengeance upon this bloodthirsty " gang of Cains," the Indians who owned America, with Melville's hatred of imperialism in Polynesia? Nathalia Wright has provided one way out of the difficulty.

> The Indian-hating interlude in *The Confidence Man*, which is in fact the crux of the book, thus places two of Melville's symbols in curious juxtaposition. Elsewhere in this novel, as in others, Melville used Indian culture to represent primitive innocence, as he also used the culture of the Polynesians, the fable of Eden, and the idealism of the Gospels. And elsewhere this state though immature is idyllic, outgrown but loved and longed for. That it is here a state to be fiercely and implacably warred upon is not, however, a contradiction of thought, but an ironic presentation of precisely the same symbolic value. This is the cruel farewell taken by the tragically committed Pierre of the fair Lucy, by Hamlet of Ophelia.[75]

Miss Wright's analysis is ingenious, but it does not show the selectivity of Melville's symbolistic mind. The solution of the entire difficulty must lie there. For though it is foolish to try to hold an artist to consistency, Melville and all other primitivists happen to be quite consistent in this matter. The state of nature represented by these primitive types was not outgrown. It became the whole exterior authority of a symbolistic process in art.

Thus it follows that only that aspect of primitive existence which was sensuously known and emotively *felt* figures in the creation of primitivistic symbols. In the major provinces of

[75] *Melville's Use of the Bible*, p. 56.

recent primitivism, *the eye has seen the things which are
abstracted into symbols.* The fact that a primitivist in art
makes such symbols from experience cannot mean that he
sympathizes with every state of primitive man or that he advo-
cates the imposition of primitive states of being upon the whole
human family. He is only the maker of art and, as primitivist,
the reëxaminer of God. Who can tell what he might have
been as artist had he lived in a wigwam of the Sioux or hunted
the cape buffalo with a tribe of the Congo? Melville's sentimental condemnation of the African, and the American Indian
thus becomes irrelevant. But the Ishmael in him and in every
westward mariner of primitivism will protect the autotypes
which he gained at incalculable depths of feeling from his
Oriental journey. And in the case of Melville these exclude
totally and reasonably the dangers and hardships of Tom in
Typee Valley, even the threat upon his life as he embarks to go
aboard the *Julia* and sail to the beaches of Papeete. As the symbolist remembering Polynesia, Melville the artist took only
what he needed, and no more.

Who, then, can insist upon the Polynesia that was omitted?
The traveler who has looked into the bay of an Oceanic island
has also looked ashore upon filth and disease, idiocy and
cruelty. He has smelled the stench of burning coconut husks;
he has endured plagues of stinging flies; he has breathed the
fetid heat of the jungle. It must in the end come to what one
looks for and wills to make his own. Chateaubriand had earlier
confessed that he found the *cabane* of the Indian a receptacle of
ordure.[76] Melville's favorite authority for *Typee*, Stewart, was
nauseated by what he saw at a funeral feast in the Marquesas, a
whole hog swarming with flies and vermin before it was torn
to pieces by the mourners in a frenzy of gorging food.[77] William
Ellis reported that on an island near Tahiti he had seen a
hungry child given a piece of her own father's flesh for nourish-
ment.[78] Lt. Wise, following Melville on Nukuhiva, saw the

[76] *Oeuvres Complètes* (Paris, 1836), vol. 12, p. 273 (*Voyage en Amérique*).
[77] *A Visit to the South Seas*, vol. 1, p. 265.
[78] *Polynesian Researches*, vol. 1, p. 358.

chief's brother, drunk with *ava*, coiled upon a bed of filthy mats, "half dead with some loathsome disease." [79] The affliction may very well have been yaws, the ugliest scourge to be found in the whole of Oceania. Its festering lesions have been seen by many primitivists as well. Victor Segalen describes them in his expert novel of Tahiti, the modern equivalent of *Omoo, Les Immémoriaux*. Once again a sick man is the symbol of primitive destitution, an old man lying on a filthy bed, covered with ulcers, drunk with the liquor of *ava*.[80] All these images are, indeed, far from Paradise.

But Melville, the westward mariner, did not agree to encompass the world. He reached the abstraction of art only through what he felt to be promising of human nobility as a reflection of God, the God beyond professional theology. He made his courage to be as Ishmael, the wanderer. The Pacific voyages were the religious confirmation of Ishmael. So, too, they confirmed other Ishmaels who followed him in these waters. For whether they were as devout as he, as poetic, as sensitive, or as purposive, they all belonged to the same communion. The tattooed skin of the Polynesian was to Herman Melville cassock and surplice, dalmatic and stole. If his inheritors were less ardent in this allegiance than he, it may be said only that no endowment of the human being varies more greatly among individuals, even those of one agreement, than the capacity for religious feeling.

[79] *Los Gringos*, pp. 385–86.
[80] Paris, 1921, p. 36.

IV

The Perpetuity of Ishmael

With the conditions of Melville's art which govern the tendency toward the Oceanic and Oriental symbol, this study arrives at the problem of evaluating other artists traveling Ishmael's course to the East. These voyagers contribute to the definition of a Pacific community of mariners. The initial problem of Melville expands now into the requirement of determining what these artists yield in relation to Melville as the religious symbolist. The purposes of this fourth chapter in a history of Ishmael are to extend the approaches of the study to the threshold of critical analysis, and to anticipate a reading of Oceanic and Oriental symbols as art forms containing the multiplicity of feeling already described. The intent of the following chapters will be to retain Melville as the symbolistic center and to interpret the symbols of Ishmael comparatively, first by reading them as unique structures in Melville's art and, second, by evaluating them, wherever possible, through surrounding symbolic cognates or artistic representations of primitive character.

The first of these methods is anticipated through the definitions of the preceding chapter; the second must be approached through a summary account of artists showing a relation of some sort to the master symbol of Ishmael. These are the successors of Melville in the Pacific and the makers of the cognates. Studied collectively as a group of artists, they describe primitivism as a system, an organic whole of literature and, in a wider sense, of the fine arts. That each of these reflects cultural failure in some degree and that each travels the Pacific are in themselves only qualifying conditions. It does not follow that the artist becomes equivalent to Melville; his ways out of the condition of symbolic impoverishment may have been very different. Nothing refutes more impressively a Pacific "category" of artists than the unique character of each man's creativity, even as it is encompassed in the organic whole. The custom of referring generally to a group of Pacific travelers as workers in the same material leads only to confusion. The similarities and the differences between Melville, on the one hand, and Loti, Stevenson, Adams, and Gauguin on the other, have never been defined. They all belong to the Pacific community, but exactly how and to what end?

Before proceeding to this problem, certain exclusions must be made. The criterion becomes one of judgment between the makers of the life-symbol, and narrators. Primitivism encompasses existential symbolists and potential makers of life-symbols. It is not represented in a craft of fiction distinguished only by substance derived from Oriental material. The Oceanic narratives of Jack London, for instance, provide suitable examples of the Pacific voyage without the appearance of primitive feeling. To these should be added the picaresque novels of Captain Marryat and Mayne Reid and the "travels" of Jules Verne, all of immense renown in the nineteenth century, and the vastly better Pacific art of W. Somerset Maugham, Charles Nordhoff, James Norman Hall, and Robert Dean Frisbie in the twentieth. All these, and the novelists of another " primitive " school established upon the good earth of China, were and continue to be devoted to narrative as the preëminent responsibility of art. One must look beyond this condition to the fact of *singular* representation in this literature, as opposed to *multiple* representation in the symbols of primitivism. He must recall *poesis* as his principle, the linguistic representation, whether in formal " poetry " or " prose," of symbolic abstraction from a manifold of feeling into the multiplex form of the fixed symbol.

No argument may be required for *poesis* as the more " personal " art. It is generally recognized that poetry as abstraction of the subjective emotion is symbolistically more authoritative than the nonsubjective art of story-telling. An example of an " Oriental " novel outside the particular character of *poesis* as symbolic form will be useful in getting at the distinctions which must be made here: E. M. Forster's *A Passage to India.* Without disparaging the narrative power of this work, the conclusion may be ventured that the " Oriental " transmutations of Mrs. Moore and Adela Quested are described with extra-personal, objective intent. Forster is not really interested, even in his extended symbol of the caves of Marabar, in a process of rendering a personal (religious) feeling toward the Orient. He is not describing the religious sensibility of Forster; rather he is exposing a state of cultural confusion as the English character of these women disintegrates under the cryptic signs of an alien and terrifying collective Oriental mind. Whatever his sympathies, he leaves us with a deeply exploring narrative of cause and effect. The technique of this novel as genuine art is undeniably superior. It is much richer with erudition, proportion, and genuine humanity than any of the Oceanic and Oriental " narratives " of the nineteenth century; much more contemplative than the objective fiction of recent story-tellers in the Pacific and the Orient (including Maugham's *The Razor's Edge*). Yet with all these advantages, it is no more subjectively symbolic than they are. Too much emphasis cannot be placed upon these distinctions between objectivity and subjectivity, singularity and multiplicity in the processes of description and in the forms of art. For it appears quite clear that traditional form in the novel, for instance, is possible only when objectivity and singularity govern. *As soon as an artist surrenders himself to the necessity of rendering symbolically the subjective and the multiple, as these are determined by affective feeling, he deserts the requirements of traditional form.*

The last page of Leyda's *Melville Log* proposes the following question: " Hudson, Loti, Conrad—they were certainly touched off by a spark of Herman Melville, but when and how, exactly? " There are good reasons for supposing that Loti was so inspired, even though he does not acknowledge any indebtedness; as for Hudson and Conrad, it is recorded fact that both read Melville. Artists may influence their successors through form and subject matter. (Theoretically, *Typee* and *Omoo* may have led every successor of the original Ishmael to the Pacific.) But artists do not influence by making their inheritors symbolistic in expression. The drive toward symbolism in an artist is a native, nontransferable endowment.

No attempt will be made here to examine *Green Mansions*, or *Lord Jim*, or *An Outcast of the Islands* as examples of art deriving initially from Melville. Certainly all three display profound concern with primitive existence. Furthermore, Hudson's novel shows precisely the symbolist's desertion of traditional form which has just been noted. But the South American locus of this work isolates it from the proper concerns of this study, and its symbols are expressly informed with primitive animism rather than with the multiplicity of Christian and pagan elements common to Melville. Of Conrad it is enough to say that his studies of civilization in conflict with savagery or paganism all reach the conclusion that surrender to the primitive becomes the tragic loss of soul. (Maugham, with a lesser art, has dealt with the same theme in his Samoan story, *The Pool*.) Certainly the same abounding and primeval sea dominates the imaginations of Melville and Conrad. But when this element has been acknowledged, and with it the fact that both artists deal with the meeting of civilization and primitiveness at the deepest level of conflict—and so illuminate each other— there is not much room for any other agreement in the realm of symbols. (There is a similarity, as I shall later show, in imagery.) Conrad's objectivity and his profound allegiance to European civilization lead him to an art of narrating human action; and the variety of his characters stands apart, in signal independence, from Melville's smaller range in characterization and larger talent for the representation of feeling through symbols. Conrad affirms the values of established society; these Melville denies, substituting for them the simplicity of primitive existence and the ideal of incorruptible innocence.

These exclusions from this final chapter in an approach to the criticism of symbols are requisite, lest it be supposed that artists selected here for comparison with Melville have been erratically chosen. Some of them are no more symbolistically inclined than, for example, Conrad, Forster, or Maugham: then their reference to both the archetype and the autotype appearing in the symbols of Ishmael is of sufficient importance to invite their presence as examples of artistic differences in the system of primitivism. They support the symbols of Melville through the demonstrations of contrast. Others are like Melville in the nature of the symbolistic imagination, but unlike in the character of the multiple symbol which they create, religiously, in art: then these support Melville by analogy. The nature of the community appears in the definition of both unanimity and disparity, not in the simple fact that all of them traveled the Pacific and lived in Oceania or the Orient. They all yield something toward the description of primitivism as an organic whole.

These successors in the perpetuity of Ishmael are logically divided into two groups: those directly concerned with Polynesia; those concerned with other areas of the Orient, in the wider inclusiveness of that term. It is assumed here that these artists are the important contributors to the literature of primitivism from American, British, and French origins. (The German primitivist, Hermann Hesse, will be considered elsewhere in this study.) I know nothing of possibilities for study in recent Italian, Portuguese, and Spanish literature; but I assume that the art of this realm, springing from a culture deeply rooted in Roman Catholic sentience, will provide few significant examples of primitivism in its religious character. Beyond the areas which I have been able to consider lies the unexplored range of Australian art (excepting that of Louis Becke), where certainly much valid symbolic abstraction from experience with primitive societies must be available to the purposes of comparative criticism. The limitations of the following discussion are ordered both by the necessity of economy and by the impossibility of surveying a larger body of material.

1   Stoddard, Mark Twain

The chronology of the Polynesian group following Melville begins with Charles Warren Stoddard (1843-1909); the poet and journalist of San Francisco. William Dean Howells remarked in 1892 that he considered the Oceanic sketches of this now forgotten American voyager " the freshest things that ever were written about the life of that summer ocean." [1] The less sentimental judgment of R. L. Stevenson reads simply: " There are but two writers who have touched the South Seas with any genius, both Americans: Melville and Charles Warren Stoddard." [2] The traveler in the South Seas must decide for himself upon the value of these opinions, if he can imagine the character of a now lost Polynesian culture apparent in the art of both Stoddard and Melville.

The descriptive power of Stoddard is not his distinguishing attribute. His real importance—and this would certainly seem enough to secure his place in American letters—is his stature as a lesser Melville, a Melville, let us say, abruptly cut off at the point when he advances into the sea of the symbol-maker's art

---

[1] See a letter of Howells to Stoddard (August 11, 1892) in the preface to Stoddard's *South-Sea Idyls* (New York, 1892).
[2] *In the South Seas* (New York, 1897), p. 28.

in *Mardi*. For it happens that Stoddard is one of the first recent artists who choose the orthodox way out of symbolic impover-ishment. He becomes a convert to Catholicism. The real ques-tion, one which could scarcely have occurred to Howells and Stevenson, is just this: to what extent does the autotype of the Pacific journey compensate in the quest of Ishmael, art becoming religion or art being limited by the artist's return to religious convention?

It is in his modern significance, then, as the voyager of re-ligious feeling that Stoddard becomes relative to Melville. His conversion to the symbols of Roman Catholic orthodoxy oc-curred in 1867, following his first journey of 1864 and 1865, when he went to the Hawaiian Islands in search of health. But the original purposes of the journey have really very little rela-tion to the artistic use made of it. (So, too, in the instances of Melville's whaling voyages, or the Oceanic and Oriental itiner-ary of Pierre Loti, as an officer of the French Navy.) After two years in San Francisco as a journalist, Stoddard returned to Oceania, making two journeys between 1868 and 1873 to Hawaii and Tahiti. These, with the first voyage, provided the material for *South-Sea Idyls* (1873). It is this work, more than any other, that establishes his relation to the early Melville. His subsequent travel in Europe and the Near East, in his service as a correspondent for the *San Francisco Chronicle*, extended his literary career with *Mashallah* (1881) and *A Cruise under the Crescent* (1898); but these records show clearly that his artistry depended upon the Pacific for its inspira-tion. It was inevitable that he should return to this setting. A third residence in Hawaii from 1881 to 1884, unproductive as it was of new excursions into Oceanic life, closed with his account of his approach to Catholicism in *A Troubled Heart*. There is a particular appropriateness in the Hawaiian back-ground of this confession. Even though Stoddard lacked the artistic strength of Melville, which resisted every claim of re-ligious convention upon it and made of *Moby-Dick* a testament of a new belief, his Catholicism is at least unique in that it excludes civilization from the structure of faith. What his orthodoxy sets forth is actually a Polynesian Catholicism. His religious conformity and his limitations as an artist render him incapable of the symbolic compensation offered by Melville.

" I know and have always known that, inwardly, I am purple-blooded, and supple-limbed, and invisibly tattooed after the manner of my lost tribe! " [3] Like Ishmael of *Moby-Dick*, Stoddard as the voyaging artist here establishes his " inheritance " from the Polynesian. This is the savage wanderer, Roman Catholic proselyte notwithstanding, who contended, in his account of a conversation with Stevenson in San Francisco: " Truth, when naked, of whatever sex or condition, is sun-browned." Melville's savage artisan, the solitary mariner who shapes the symbol of his God, appears again. A French critic, Thérèse Blanc Bentzon, noted in 1896 after a reading of Stoddard that his heroes were not variant aspects of the artist himself but " restored " Polynesian youths: Kahèle of Hawaii, Kána-Anà of Tahiti, Hua-Manu of the Paumotus.[4] These she regarded as " heroes " of friendship. Her observation is perceptive. As " heroic " figures they are abstractions of experience from the autotype of the noble Polynesian. They take form as symbols from retained images, and they are in every respect comparable to Melville's Marnoo of *Typee*, to Queequeg of *Moby-Dick*, and to the innocent Tahitian as contributor to the ideality of Billy Budd. In Kána-Anà of *South-Sea Idyls* Stoddard presents the symbol of *tayo* (fraternal love) as this is employed by Melville in *Typee* and *Omoo*, and in the relationship of Taji and Jarl in *Mardi*. The origin of this symbol from autotypes of the same sort relates Stoddard to Melville more clearly than any other condition of his art. More than the descriptive power exerted in the representation of Polynesian landscape, more than the measurement of destitution following upon the work of missionaries, this one venture into the making of the life-symbol validates Stevenson's view of Melville and Stoddard as sharers of the same act in " touching the South Seas with genius."

[3] " Taboo—a Fête-Day in Tahiti " in *South-Sea Idyls*, p. 72.
[4] " Un Loti américain: C. W. Stoddard," *Revue des Deux Mondes*, vol. 138 (1896), pp. 621-23.

This review of Stoddard suggests incidental comment on
Mark Twain in the Pacific. Traveling toward Europe and the
Near East as a journalist in 1873, Stoddard was temporarily
employed in London as secretary to the novelist.[5] Although
the two did not share the same attitudes toward Pacific culture,
an exchange of opinion and experience must have taken place
between them during these months. Mark Twain had visited
Hawaii in 1866, two years after Stoddard's first journey, as a
reporter for the Sacramento *Union* on conditions of the island
sugar industry. The incidents of this year are narrated in the
concluding chapters of *Roughing It*, where the nature of his
attitude toward the Oceanic native is made entirely clear. The
tone is one of ridicule and contempt, when it is not humorous,
with the balance heavily in favor of missionary endeavor. Van
Wyck Brooks attaches considerable importance to Mark
Twain's view of the missionaries as the " devoted old Puritan
knights " and to his dislike of the native dance as " strange and
unpleasant." [6] These observations seem to negate the theme of
Huckleberry Finn, that " all civilization is a hateful mistake." [7]
Brooks concludes that this artist possessed a curious ambivalence, both affirming and condemning civilization.[8]

But the provenance of primitivism in Mark Twain is not to
be explained by a recognition of ambivalence. It is governed
by the superiority of autotypes. In his case the Mississippi
River, as the scene of a commanding imagistic experience, over-
comes and invalidates the experience of the Pacific journey.
Thus he emerges in his mature art as the wanderer of another
description. His religious symbols from the recollection of a
boyhood on the Mississippi possess the same sacramental nature
exhibited by Melville's multiple symbolic structure from a
whaling voyage and a sojourn in Polynesia. Actually he is no
more ambivalent as artist than Melville or Stoddard. He is an

---

[5] See Mark Twain's comments on his relationship with Stoddard during this
period in his correspondence from London, ed. Dixon Wecter in " The Love
Letters of Mark Twain," *Atlantic Monthly*, vol. 181, no. 1 (1948), pp. 83–88.

[6] *The Times of Melville and Whitman*, p. 289.

[7] *Ibid.*, p. 460.

[8] *Ibid.*, p. 461.

American primitivist of a different order. For it will, I think, be admitted by every student of Mark Twain that, as soon as he turns his attention to the meaning of Protestant culture in its native American character, he begins a compensatory symbolism which is opposed to the meaning of evangelistic Christianity. It must also be true that he is exactly comparable to both Melville and Stoddard in his awareness of cultural failure. There is no real difficulty in reconciling his symbols in *Huckleberry Finn* with his rejection of Pacific society as a symbolistic locus. Like Melville, he chooses the primitive state of man which will serve his art descriptive of his unique feeling; like Melville in his rejection of the American Indian and the African in favor of the Polynesian, Mark Twain declines to sanctify every state of primitive existence.

The second of Mark Twain's Pacific journeys was undertaken in 1895 and 1896, as he made his way around the world lecturing and writing in an effort to retrieve himself from bankruptcy. By this time his view of civilization had darkened to the measure of Melville's depression through his journey to Palestine in 1857-58. In Australia Mark Twain observed, as he looked at the poverty and " slow murder " visited upon the savage by the white " squatter," that " there are many humorous things in the world; among them the white man's notion that he is less savage than the other savages." [9] This judgment has no reference to primitivism. It suggests only the maximum significance of Mark Twain's Pacific and Oriental travel; so do most of the pages of *Following the Equator*, as these turn to the East, display the same meaning. They are informed with the growing pessimism of the artist who loses in the end the religion of art. Having neither his friend Stoddard's subscription to orthodoxy nor Melville's sustaining power in the religious symbol (which reëmerges in *Billy Budd*) , he ends his days in the shadow of nihilism. Neither civilization nor savagery has anything to say toward meaning. Tillich's definition has already been noted: religion is the substance of culture,

[9] *Following the Equator*, vols. 5 and 6 in Harper Hillcrest Edition (New York, 1904), vol. 5, pp. 215–16.

culture is the expression of religion. When no culture is deemed to have meaningful substance, the construction of the religious symbol is made impossible. It is said that Mark Twain was "saved" by an undiminished humor in his last decade. The nature of this later humor remains to be defined. I take it that the awesome refutation of existential meaning in all human existence, as this reaches us in *The Mysterious Stranger* (posthumously published), is the valedictory of this "humorist."

2 Becke

In the literature of the Pacific the voyager who knew the seas and the islands of Oceania with knowledge unmatched in the last century was George Louis Becke (1848-1913). A native of Port Macquarie, New South Wales, he deserted an early plan for residence in the United States and took to the merchant lanes of the South Seas. From 1870 to 1893 he wandered as trader and supercargo over the breadth of the equatorial Pacific. Thereafter he settled in London and turned to a narrative transcription of this long experience. If Charles Warren Stoddard is nearly forgotten, Becke is altogether absent from the notice of European and American critics. He is read only in a few academic communities where the ethnology of the Pacific is of particular interest. The twenty-three years of his voyages appear in an extensive sequence of tales and sketches which make the Polynesian romances of Melville, Stoddard, and Loti, in comparison, thin and inadequate as representations of native life. As a student of the Oceanic temperament, he is authoritative; as an observer of insular existence he has, more than any of his contemporaries, an accurate knowledge of the native mind, of what happens in it, of the dimensions which set it apart from the mentality of civilization. He is of particular relevance in a discussion of Melville and other primitivists because he provides, unlike any other artist of his experience, the reality of Oceanic culture, as this existed until the First World War and the contemporary extension of mandates and trusteeships over the Pacific area. For a study of primitivism his historical importance in literature is indispensable.

Becke's long career in Oceania isolated him from the major sources of cultural pessimism. The Pacific tales also suggest that he was not inclined to metaphysical readings of existence, as these contribute to the evolution of the religious symbol. But with Melville, Stoddard, and Gauguin, particularly, he is capable of symbolizing the death of a race overcome by the scourge of civilization. From the Micronesian island of Kusaie (Strong's Island) in the East Carolines, where he had known the American pirate William (Bully) Hayes, he derives the symbol of Tasia, a half-caste girl, with eyes in which " one may read the coming fate of all their race, doomed to utter extinction before the inroads of civilization with all its deadly terrors of insidious and unknown disease." [10] She is of yet another community offered salvation by the Christian missionary. It is Becke's distinction that he recognized the same misdirection of the Protestant symbol revealed in the letter of the Reverend Mr. Bingham from the *Morning Star* to the community of Mentchikoff Island. Now the same mission ship reaches Kusaie, and the Reverend Mr. Bawl (Bingham?) comes ashore. Before the voyage, he has converted a native seaman from Kusaie in Honolulu; now he is concerned with the welfare of the other souls of the island. Thus he addresses Togusā, the chieftain of Kusaie: " You are King Togusā; I am the Reverend Gilead Bawl, and I bring you peace beyond price an' a message from the King ev Kings." [11] The chieftain is indifferent, and the missionary continues his argument: " [I]f Togusā would cast away his idols, and keep but one wife, and take the missionaries to his bosom . . . he would not be taken away to the lake of fire with the bad white men, but when he died his soul would be taken in a man-of-war to Honolulu first, and then to Boston, to live with God and President Andrew Jackson." [12] In this grotesque scene the missionary becomes a symbol commensurate with the repre-

[10] " An Island Memory: English Bob," in *Pacific Tales* (London, 1897), p. 8.
[11] " In the Old Beach-Combing Days," in *Pacific Tales*, p. 35.
[12] *Ibid.*, p. 37.

sentations of Melville and Stoddard: the bringer of salvation insults the dignity of the savage.

3 Loti

At some time near the first months of Louis Becke's long voyage as trader, Pierre Loti [Julien Viaud (1850-1923)] arrived in Oceania as a junior officer aboard a French man-of-war. For the purposes of this study he cannot be dispensed with, however frequently he has been excluded as an exotic sentimentalist from the record of serious literary art. Gauguin held him in contempt, "our great, great academician, Pierre Loti . . . an effete and blasé young man." [13] Henry James's estimate of Loti as impressionist is probably as just an appreciation as has yet been extended to him. Writing in his critical preface to Loti's *Impressions*, James recognized his particular gift of *feeling* every element in the strangeness of foreign scenes, all this without vulgarity. "He drinks . . . so deep of impressions that places where he has passed are left dry: there are none . . . we pay him the questionable compliment of wishing to visit after him. We are content to go nowhere—which is a much greater tribute." [14] This opinion is nearly the only critically respectable commendation from Loti's English and American readers. E. M. Forster calls him a self-styled "great French artist" who salutes the Orient, in homage to a "misunderstood people," with tears, cypresses, and coconuts, and who apotheosizes the genius of each country "in an intrigue with one of its female inhabitants." [15] Stuart Pratt Sherman remarks sternly that the crises of Loti's characters "are not crises of the will but crises of the emotions." [16] This last judgment may be entirely correct. No one would sanely argue that Melville's crises of the will are matched by the overwrought sensitivity which Loti constantly dramatizes.

[13] *The Intimate Journals of Paul Gauguin*, ed. Brooks, p. 44.
[14] Pierre Loti, *Impressions*, with an introduction by Henry James (Westminster, 1898), p. 20.
[15] *Abinger Harvest* (New York, 1936), pp. 267–68.
[16] "Pierre Loti and Exotic Love," in *Critical Woodcuts* (New York, 1927), p. 201.

James's estimate, free of prejudice, is serviceable outside this area of indifference or scorn from Oriental travelers. What he says of Loti's talent for extracting the sensuous qualities of Oceanic and Oriental existence is exactly appropriate to a measurement of Loti in relation to *poesis* and the conditions of symbolic form. Loti is Ishmael, not Julien Viaud, the observer. That he does not proceed beyond the crises of the emotions means only that he is not rendering a symbolic description of persons and places in which the crises of "civilized" man occur. One might as well accuse Melville of having neglected the anguish of the will in the Polynesian romances. The contention will not be made that Loti becomes a symbolist of multiplicity in the manner of Melville. But there is too much of genuine *poesis* in this art to justify discarding it as irrelevant exoticism. Furthermore, his representation of the "sailor savage" and the primitivity of the sea in *Pêcheur d'Islande* and the symbolic religious pilgrimage to the Orient in *L'Inde sans les Anglais* bring him very close to the structure of Melville's mature symbols.

Rarahu, ou le Mariage de Loti (1880) is constructed from the same autotypes which render the imagistic form of Melville's *Typee* and *Omoo*. More important, exactly as *Typee* initiates the recurrent description of Melville's mariner-outcast, so this first novel of Julien Viaud introduces Loti as Ishmael. The book is made of a sea-going youth's experiences in Oceania. When it is opened beside *Typee*, it is difficult to suppose that Loti did not carry Melville's book with him, in that same devotion revealed by Charles Warren Stoddard. There is the same notice of the breadfruit tree, recalling Melville's observation of Marquesan children picking food from the tree beside the door, a scene presented in sharp contrast to the suffering of the civilized poor.[17] The landscape of reef and beach, palms and towering green mountains and drifting clouds is the same.[18] Rarahu, the young girl of the "marriage," is a Tahitian rein-

[17] *Le Mariage de Loti: Rarahu* (Paris, 1880), p. 45.
[18] *Ibid.*, pp. 20–21.

carnation of Fayaway.[19] The pure sensuousness of Melville's
first pages is all there, the voluptuous surrender to physical
perfection.[20] Apart from these, *Rarahu* duplicates both *Typee*
and *Omoo* in its notices of evil introduced by the French administration. The inflictions brought upon Polynesia by foolish
colonial policy and the destructive imposition of foreign custom
figure in this study with about the same prominence which they
display in Melville's work.[21] The structure of the book is identified with the episodic character of Melville's early romances to
such a degree that at some points it seems to be only a very
slightly altered copy. But the "influence" of Melville is neither
here nor there. The only condition of importance is that of the
Polynesian autotype.

Loti's failure to project this experience into symbols beyond
the abstractions of feeling appearing in *Rarahu* attends upon
his slow maturity as the religious voyager. Ishmael he is, indeed, as Loti. But the beginnings of his progress toward the religious symbol are not evident until the appearance of *Pêcheur
d'Islande,* in 1886. No Polynesian images appear in this work;
nonetheless, in its symbolistic treatment of the sea and the sea-
farer it bears a more striking similarity to *Moby-Dick* than any
other novel of the century. During the years following the
cruise to Tahiti, Loti had traveled to Japan (where he found
the material for his inferior novel *Madame Chrysanthème*), and
to Senegal and Tonkin. But he turns to an earlier voyage, one
made in 1870 to Norway, for the autotypes of symbols in this
picture of the sea. The facsimile of experience apparent here
suggests the imagistic authority shaping the fictive *Pequod* of
Moby-Dick from the real *Acushnet* of Melville's whaling
voyages.

An evaluation of Loti's symbols in *Pêcheur* with attention to
Melville's marine symbolism will follow in another chapter. At
this point it may be said that the symbolic form of *Pêcheur
d'Islande* is Loti's arrival at a description of Ishmael in a religi-

[19] *Ibid.,* pp. 9, 14–15. Compare Loti's description with that of Melville.
[20] *Ibid.,* p. 17.
[21] *Ibid.,* p. 7.

ous context. His *Jérusalem* (1895) recalls Melville again, in the similarity of its theme to that of *Clarel*. The subsequent *L'Inde sans les Anglais* (1903), with its record of the pilgrimage to Benares, is the testament of an artist in quest of a new symbolism of faith. Loti in India stands at the same place of crossing where Melville had stood as he began the making of a new theology in *Moby-Dick*. That a new theology does not appear in Loti's art after Benares is a condition which must be understood in terms of his minority as a symbolist. The artistic means of renovating the symbols of Christian culture cannot be discovered in Jerusalem, in India, or in any other realm without the superior endowments of heroic imagination. Loti is related to Melville through the religious feeling antecedent to great symbols. That he seeks the reconstitution of sacrament from the time of his journey to Jerusalem onward is fact; but it cannot be said that he achieves the symbols of ultimate meaning created by Melville.

4 *Stevenson*

The last six years of Robert Louis Stevenson bring an artist of an entirely different character to the Oceanic setting of Melville, Stoddard, and Loti. Customary identification of Stevenson with the Pacific has traditionally assumed that his association has about the same meaning in relation to Samoa as that of Melville and Gauguin in relation to the Marquesas and Tahiti. But the art of Stevenson in the Pacific is vastly different: only the autotype of experience is quite similar, as this is presented in the letters and the journalistic account of the voyage, *In the South Seas* (1890), and in such stories as *The Beach of Falesá*. Something has already been said of the distinctive objectivity of Conrad, his representation of human action in terms of individualized personalities. The mark of Conrad is not the multiplex symbol of primitivism. Stevenson, with his knowledge of Polynesia and with his artistic command of the journey for the form of so distinguished a narrative as *The Ebb-Tide*, stands nearer the art of Conrad than that of

Melville. Of the artists here related to the Pacific and the Orient, he is the one least disturbed by his Protestant inheritance. In fact, he is another Ishmael scarcely at all, but a man sensitive to every new experience and remarkably curious about its potentiality *as narrative.* The question must then occur: why does he belong here, if Conrad, sailing in waters even closer to the true Orient, is excluded from this Ishmael generation? The reason is that Stevenson, the artistic observer of primitiveness without the resultant artistic condition of primitivism, illustrates better than any other traveler in Oceania what happens when the compulsion of religious feeling does not order the symbol of " native " innocence and well-being, as opposed to the poverty and wretchedness of Christian civilization. Stevenson, in this particular condition, emphasizes the meaning of Ishmael. He contributes to the interpretation of Melville and primitivists related to Melville not by analogy but through contrast.

Stevenson's first voyage, undertaken in the *Casco* from San Francisco in June, 1888, brought him to the Marquesas and thence to the Paumotus, Tahiti, and Hawaii. In his later narrative *The Wrecker* he tells of his meeting Stoddard before boarding the *Casco* and remarks that he sailed with a copy of Melville's *Omoo* [22] under one arm and " my friend's [Stoddard's] own adventures under the other." [23] From the observations of this voyage to his last comments on Samoa at Vailima, he exerted a detached, nonsentimental power of discrimination among the cultures of Polynesia which give his reports a valid ethnological character. Thus, during a visit of six months in the Hawaiian Islands, beginning early in 1889, he could find the inhabitants of the lee coast of Hawaii superior to any white men of his acquaintance in Honolulu: " God's best—at least God's sweetest works—[were] Polynesians." [24] It was a blessing to live with them, as Charles Warren Stoddard had already said.

---

[22] Stevenson's copy is in the possession of the Harvard College Library.

[23] *The Wrecker* in *The Works of Robert Louis Stevenson* (Vailima Edition, New York, 1922), vol. 17, pp. 193–94.

[24] *Letters*, ed. Colvin, vol. 3, p. 141. Stevenson to Charles Baxter, Honolulu, May, 1889.

But his admiration of island life is expressed more firmly in his patronage of the Catholic missionary leprosarium on Molokai than in the symbols of a new ideality in art.

Stevenson left Honolulu on the trading schooner *Equator* in June, 1889, for twelve weeks in Apemama and Butaritari, in the Gilbert Islands (Kingsmills), and thence for a visit to Sydney by way of Apia, Samoa. His survey of the Gilberts brought him, after Hawaii, several degrees nearer what he came to read as the true nature of primitive society. Thus he chose to describe the spectacle of two Gilbertese women biting each other in a dog fight under the hot sun.

> The return to these primeval weapons, the vision of man's beastliness, of his ferality, shocked in me a deeper sense than that with which we count the cost of battles. There are elements in our state and history which it is a pleasure to forget. . . . [The imagination] instinctively rejects . . . whatever shall call up the image of our race upon its lowest terms, as the partner of beasts, beastly itself, dwelling pell-mell and hugger-mugger, hairy man with hairy woman, in the caves of old. And yet to be just to barbarous islanders we must not forget the slums and dens of our cities: I must not forget that I have passed . . . through Soho and seen that which cured me of my dinner.[25]

Despite the closing reflection upon urban life, this statement comes from a realist dealing in the hard prose of the reporter. Stevenson's imagination obviously is not busy here with a selective reading of Polynesian existence in terms of religious symbolization. As a report from the Pacific, this account stands at the opposite pole from Melville's representation of island life.

Stevenson happened to have believed, like Conrad, in a civilization which Melville could not accept; and it follows that as an artist without very much religious compulsion, he was disinclined to question the authority of established symbols. His admiration of Father Damien and the sisters of Molokai suggests that he would have turned to Catholicism if he had anywhere rebelled against the inadequacies of Scottish Presby-

[25] *In the South Seas*, pp. 257–58.

terianism. How much allegiance he might have continued to bear toward a civilization capable of atomizing Bikini and Eniwetok (which he probably visited when he toured the Marshalls in the summer of 1890) cannot be guessed. In his day it was still possible to see "the image of our race upon its lowest terms" in the Gilbert Islands. Of Melville's possible reaction to recent scientific experimentation in the Pacific there can be little question.[26]

Like Conrad, Stevenson holds to the singularity of action. There is no narrative in the language more direct, more clearly lacking in symbolistic intent, more faithful to narrative form than *The Ebb-Tide*. All of it is made from autotypes of the Pacific journey; and everywhere it is adjacent and yet opposite to the art of Melville. At Papeete, on the beach, Herrick, Davis, and Huish, ill with influenza, lie through a feverish night and take refuge with the day in the " old calaboose," Melville's Calabooza Beretanee of *Omoo*. On the walls about them are the memorials of all the imprisonments of the past. "The crumbling whitewash was all full of them,—Tahitian names, and French, and English, and rude sketches of ships under sail, and men at fisticuffs." [27] There Herrick draws a stave and writes, as his epitaph, the "fate" theme from Beethoven's *Fifth Symphony*. Stevenson's recognition of the crime against Polynesia, the criminal " irregular invasion of adventurers," follows in the narrative, but only in this theme of fatalism. In all the literature of the Pacific there is no scene which quite matches, in

[26] A recent petition (printed by *The New York Times*, May 15, 1954) from the people of the Marshall Islands to the United Nations and the United States Government demands notice here. The petition, dated April 20, 1954, requests that "all experiments with lethal [atomic and hydrogen] weapons within this area [the trust territory of the Marshall Islands] be immediately ceased." The United Nations Assembly and the United States Government are here informed that residents of the atolls of the Marshalls were seriously injured by radioactivity from hydrogen explosions at Eniwetok in March, 1954. No document from the political and social history of the twentieth century could illustrate more clearly the distance between primitive innocence and " Christian " civilization, as this distance was understood by Melville and other travelers in Oceania.

[27] *The Ebb-Tide* in *Works* (Vailima ed.), vol. 18, p. 37. This novel was written in collaboration with Lloyd Osbourne, the novelist's stepson. A comparison of the text with Stevenson's other Pacific narratives suggests that Stevenson wrote most of the work.

what Stoddard called the " haggard realism " of *The Ebb-Tide*,
the " invasion " of the original crew from the *Farallone* on an
island in the Paumotus. The ship's officers, drunk and unaware that smallpox is raging, go ashore and embrace the sick
women who have no energy to repel them.[28] The feverish half-
light which falls here, and the heat and glare of the pearl lagoon
as the *Farallone* is scuttled by her captors in their surrender to
Attwater, attest, as no other statement of Stevenson, to the
nature of his sympathy. This is sovereign art, but of a sort
totally different from the Oceanic symbolism of Melville's
maturity. All this together makes the state of man. In the art
of *The Ebb-Tide* there is no religion. There is only the final
spectacle of the demoralized Herrick, who relinquishes his man-
hood to the chicanery of a " Christian " pearl merchant.

Established finally at Vailima (Apia) among the Samoans,
whom he found the gayest and most pleasure loving, the easiest
and the most merry, if not the most capable and beautiful of
Polynesians,[29] Stevenson worked until his death, in 1894, on
Weir of Hermiston. From his retreat, where he came to live in
baronial splendor with a retinue of Samoan servants, he wrote
in 1892 to J. M. Barrie: " It is a singular thing that I should
live here in the South Seas under conditions so new and so
striking, and yet my imagination so continually inhabits that
cold old huddle of grey hills from which we come." [30] His
longing was for the order and tradition of civilized custom. As
the wanderer he had only made the best of a long exile.

5 *Adams*

The relation of Henry Adams and his friend, John La Farge,
to the Pacific voyage of Ishmael is more difficult to define but,
at the same time, far closer to Melville's symbolism than the art
of Stevenson. The character of Adams's sardonic humor is one
obstacle for definition; a second appears in interpreting the

[28] *Ibid.*, pp. 78–79.
[29] *In the South Seas*, p. 381.
[30] Quoted by David Daiches in his *Robert Louis Stevenson* (Norfolk, Connecticut, 1947), p. 99.

meaning of *Mont-Saint-Michel and Chartres* as a religious symbol, with full recognition of his knowledge of Oceanic and Oriental cultures. There is a strange relationship between the Adams monument (1891) in Rock Creek Cemetery, Washington, executed by Augustus Saint-Gaudens in memory of Mrs. Adams, and the journey to Japan which Adams undertook in 1886 to lessen the pain of his bereavement. His letters from Japan are marked by satiric reflection on the " strangeness " of the Orient and observations of Japanese custom as ridiculous. Yet this great memorial figure, created by the sculptor from the ideas of Adams, is certainly the tangible result of Adams's contact with the East, and must be understood as an embodiment of an Oriental feeling toward the mystery of life and death. Adams named the figure " The Peace of God "; his friend La Farge must have known more of its meaning than Adams would confess when he referred to it as " Kwannon," the Japanese Buddhistic goddess of mercy. At this point the relevance of this figure as Oriental symbol to the symbolistic quest of Adams himself is the matter for definition.

Beneath the humor and irascible temper, the satire and the cynicism of this man, lie the elements of primitivism, beyond question. In the history of recent art he is of the generation of the true Ishmaels; his community is that of Melville, Gauguin, Hearn, and Rimbaud. He belongs with them in his profound awareness of cultural failure and in his search for the symbol to reëstablish existential meaning. Adams's Pacific journeys are the prefaces to *Mont-Saint-Michel and Chartres*; and the great bronze figure over the tomb of Mrs. Adams became in 1891 the emblem of a voyage which ultimately discovers its objective in the stone shrine of the Virgin of Chartres. The final symbol is the quintessence of the historian's art, as he turns back in time, in the true manner of the primitivist. In the twelfth century of Christianity he discovered the last authority of Christian symbolism in Western civilization, and there he made his equivalent of Oceania and the Orient.

The Oceanic voyage of Adams and La Farge began in 1890 and extended in the following year through Fiji, New South

Wales, and Ceylon; the return was made by Suez, the Mediterranean, and Europe. Of the two, La Farge is the more traditional in his observations of " civilized " injustice. He had with him Melville's *Omoo*, Stoddard's *Idyls*, and the *Marriage of Loti*; [31] and during the months in Polynesia he executed a series of illustrations for Melville's *Typee*. With the same insight which Adams reveals, he grasps the condition of Tahiti stripped of its traditional symbols and customs. This he describes as " idleness."

> So here, where, as in all civilizations, religious views, manners, customs, superstitions were woven about every bit of life, the exterminating of anything that might seem pagan involved many habits, and some good ones, which necessarily, from their fundamental antiquity, had been protected by religious rites. Hence we brought on idleness and consequent vice; for idleness is as bad for the savage, whom we innocently suppose to be idle, because we do not understand how he busies himself, as it is for the worker in modern civilization.[32]

All this Adams reads more subjectively as " boredom." Ashore at Papeete in February, 1891, he found every islander hopelessly bored, foreign residents and natives alike; rum was the only amusement; the plantations were neglected and in ruins; disease was undermining the race everywhere. The melancholy of it oppressed him.[33] Within two weeks he was lamenting the loss of the old habits: dancing, kava-drinking, human sacrifice, and " other harmless and simple pagan practices." [34] Within a month he had reached an insupportable state. In desperation he turned to his friend Marau Taaroa, last queen of Tahiti, and amused himself by transcribing the memoirs of this woman, whom he referred to as his " Tahitian sister, Beretania." [35]

[31] John La Farge, *Reminiscences of the South Seas* (New York, 1916), p. 288.
[32] *Ibid.*, p. 312.
[33] *Letters of Henry Adams*, ed. W. C. Ford (Boston, 1930), vol. 1, p. 467. To Elizabeth Cameron, Papeete, February 6, 1891.
[34] *Ibid.*, vol. 1, p. 474. To Elizabeth Cameron, Papeete, February 23, 1891.
[35] Privately printed in Paris in 1893 as *Memoirs of Marau Taaroa, Last Queen of Tahiti*. On January 23, 1894, Adams wrote to Charles Milnes Gaskell: " I

Across the outlying blue water the island of Moorea rose with some promise of another escape. But there life was even sadder in a society which once was " on the whole the most successful the world ever saw, because it rested on the solidest possible foundation of no morals at all." [36] Looking about him before he left Papeete for Fiji, Adams concluded: ". . . the poor creatures have still gone daily to destruction, and only of late years one begins to see the look of sadness which always goes with civilization, and means that a race has opened its eyes to its cares." [37]

A sojourn in Samoa had preceded these boring days in Tahiti. Arriving at Apia from Hawaii in October, 1890, Adams and La Farge had visited Stevenson, then clearing ground for his new home, at Vailima, " a very dirty board cabin, with a still dirtier man and woman in it, in the middle of several hundred burned tree-stumps." [38] Stevenson had told them that the Tahitians were finer men than the Samoans, whom he did not regard as an especially fine race, and that the islands of Tahiti and Nukuhiva were more beautiful.[39] One cannot tell whether Adams was perversely contradicting Stevenson or only indulging in the enthusiasm of a newly arrived traveler. His praise of the Samoan recalls Melville's tribute to the Marquesan, or Stoddard's praise of the Hawaiian.

> As rhetoricians and men of manners, the great Samoan chiefs, and for that matter, the little ones too, make me feel as though I were the son of a camel-driver degraded to the position of stable-boy in Spokane West Centre. Aristocracy can go no further, and any ordinary aristocracy is vulgar by the side of the Samoan. . . . Love marriages are unknown . . . .

have amused myself by printing (ultrissimo—privately) a small volume of South Sea Memoirs, for ' my sister Marau, the Queen of Tahiti,' and it has amused me much more . . . than my dreary American history. . . ." (*Letters*, ed. Ford, vol. 2, p. 35).

[36] *Letters*, ed. Ford, vol. 1, p. 482. To Elizabeth Cameron, Papeete, April 19, 1891.

[37] *Ibid.*, vol. 1, p. 485. To Elizabeth Cameron, Papeete, May 3, 1891.

[38] *Ibid.*, vol. 1, p. 430. To Anne Cabot Mills Lodge, Samoa, October 21, 1890.

[39] *Ibid.*, vol. 1, p. 426.

The consequence is that the chiefs are the handsomest men you can imagine, physically Apollos . . . .[40]

But these are really the impressions of a visitor. Adams is not making any identification of himself with this culture. His approach, like Stevenson's, is objective and essentially dispassionate.

This was the prologue to Tahiti. The epilogue followed in Fiji where he and La Farge found the Fijians "the most ferocious-looking brutes" on earth, but the society itself unlike the rest of Oceania, a culture with some "insides."[41] In Sydney, New South Wales, he concluded that he had been greatly entertained. "The South Seas swarm with laughable satires on everything civilised, and especially every known standard of morality."[42] It is well to relate these heterogeneous reactions to a final statement on insular primitiveness from Adams three years later. This time he is writing of Cuba.

I love the tropics and feel really at ease nowhere else. A good, rotten tropical Spanish island, like Cuba, with no roads and no drainage, but plenty of bananas and brigands, never bores me. . . . Every time I come back to what we are pleased to call civilised life, it bores me more, and seems to me more hopelessly idiotic.[43]

When this sardonic comment is read against the confessions of his boredom in Tahiti, the meaning of "boredom" clears. This to Adams is the token condition of Western civilization. Wherever civilization has been imposed upon a primitive culture, as in Tahiti, "boredom" takes the place of meaning. In the religious sense (religion as the substance of culture), "boredom" stands for the loss of the great life-symbols. Vacuity succeeds to cultural substance. It was this condition in Tahiti, not the strangeness of the culture, which depressed Adams. As a "laughable satire on everything civilised," it was only the mirror of existential meaninglessness which was given

[40] *Ibid.*, vol. 1, pp. 421-22. To Elizabeth Cameron, Apia, October 9, 1890.
[41] *Ibid.*, vol. 1, p. 508. To Elizabeth Cameron, Fiji, June 28, 1891.
[42] *Ibid.*, vol. 1, p. 510. To Henry Cabot Lodge, Sydney, August 4, 1891.
[43] *Ibid.*, vol. 2, p. 46. To Charles Milnes Gaskell, Washington, April 28, 1894.

by the Christian West to Polynesia. This is the true burden of
Adams's thought upon the cultures of the Pacific (and the
Orient as well, where the Japanese had become "laughable"
in a frantic imitation of the West). Adams returned with a
profoundly deepened sense of history. Unlike the Mark Twain
of *Following the Equator*, he turned homeward with the promise of affirmation still before him: he had yet to make his
symbol in answer to the meaninglessness which "boredom"
had everywhere revealed.

The meaning of *Mont-Saint-Michel and Chartres* (1904),
despite its hemispheric distance from the Orient of the primitivist, is still the meaning of the symbol of religion as art in
answer to cultural failure. The cathedral of Chartres, interpreted by Adams as itself a symbol of meaning, invested with
the unifying mastery of meaning over disparate meanings, is to
this art historian what the multiplex symbols of *Moby-Dick* are
to Melville. Melville, in contrast to the historian, has the distinction of having made a new art. The Virgin of Chartres, as
the *idea* of the cathedral, the quintessence of the work as unit,
the emblem of the feeling of its builders in stone, is the master
symbol. To understand her, says Adams, you must go back to
the belief in the Mary of Saint Bernard and Adam de Saint-
Victor; [44] you must do this even though the Latin hymns celebrating her, in whom the whole Trinity was absorbed, sound
now like nursery rhymes.[45] At Chartres you must feel her
presence in every stone they placed and every touch they
chiseled. For she was *unity*. Even in those days, man was as he
is now. "Mankind could not admit an anarchical—a dual or a
multiple universe. The world was there, staring them in the
face, with all its chaotic conditions, and society insisted on its
unity in self-defence." [46] The Gothic cathedral was its symbol
of unity defying the chaos of man's life.

But now, concludes Adams, there is daily evidence of the
increasing complexity of existence. "All experience, human

[44] *Mont-Saint-Michel and Chartres*, with an introduction by Ralph Adams
Cram (Boston, 1913), p. 99.
[45] *Ibid.*, p. 97.
[46] *Ibid.*, p. 371.

and divine, assured man in the thirteenth century that the lines of the universe converged. How was he to know that these lines ran in every conceivable and inconceivable direction, and that at least half of them seemed to diverge from any imaginable centre of unity! " [47] The nineteenth century was not responsible for the loss of the sense of unity. Unity long ago became a reminiscence. Then, in his final long look at the cathedral, Adams makes a curious and wonderful symbolic conclusion: even this structure, built with Faith, the unit mass of stone and the unity of a world of Christendom, was itself but a great symbol of art as existential courage, in which there was the multiplicity of danger and fear, security and confidence.

> . . . Never let us forget that Faith alone supports it, and that, if Faith fails, Heaven is lost. The equilibrium is visibly delicate beyond the line of safety; danger lurks in every stone. The peril of the heavy tower, of the restless vault, of the vagrant buttress; the uncertainty of logic, the inequalities of the syllogism, the irregularities of the mental mirror,—all these haunting nightmares of the Church are expressed as strongly by the Gothic cathedral as though it had been the cry of human suffering, and as no emotion had ever been expressed before or is likely to find expression again. The delight of its aspirations is flung up to the sky. The pathos of its self-distrust and anguish of doubt is buried in the earth as its last secret. You can read out of it whatever else pleases your youth and confidence; to me, this is all. [48]

This is Adams's answer to the " boredom " and the " idiocy " of his world. As a symbol from history, it is art of a familiar form. As a symbol of the past now reshaped as the symbol of feeling for man living in a desymbolized condition of cultural failure, it becomes a new art. As an island in a chaos of contradictions, it has the symbolic value of the symbols of Melville and Gauguin. The one was reshaped from a structure formed, stone by stone, in the evolution of a Christian faith; the others evolved by Melville and Gauguin took shape in a world where form had ceased to exist—took shape suddenly, without prece-

[47] *Ibid.*, p. 381.
[48] *Ibid.*, p. 383.

dent. To Adams this was the all, this symbol of ancient stone, this architecture of feeling; to Melville and Gauguin the all was the Oriental symbol of each man's art. In this end—historically derived, or created outside the sovereignty of Christian convention—is the true end, where the belief of the primitivist finally rests.

6 *Gauguin, Segalen, Middleton, O'Brien*

The character of Gauguin as a symbolist of primitivism has already been suggested. The paintings and the drawings of this artist, from the time of his arrival in Tahiti in 1891, only a few weeks after the departure of Adams, to the day of his death in May, 1903, on Hiva-Oa in the Marquesas, present a symbolic structure which describes the method of Melville's mature symbols. But Gauguin has this particular distinction: he made the voyage of Ishmael in full awareness of what he was to find. Apart from the unpredictable influence of Polynesian light and shadow upon his sense of color, and the peculiarly dramatic forms of landscape and native physique as determinants in the idiom of style, the autotypes of Gauguin which govern his symbolism could very nearly have been foretold as he left Marseilles. They were deliberately there, in the purpose of the voyage, as surely as they were accompanied by the most strongly posited awareness of cultural failure in " accursed Europe " to be found in the history of primitivism.

There are two reasons for this phenomenon. First, Gauguin proceeds to Tahiti already in possession of the image of the tropics from a journey to Martinique (in 1887).[49] Second, his moral view is already formulated by a tradition of his predecessors in Oceania. Thus he begins his relation to the literature of primitivism by attacking the missions as the purveyors of

---

[49] See his correspondence from St. Pierre in *Letters de Gauguin à Sa Femme et à Ses Amis*, ed. Maurice Malingue (Paris, 1946), especially a letter dated June 20, 1887, to Mette, his wife (pp. 109–10): " I cannot tell you my enthusiasm for life in the French colonies; I am sure you would feel the same. Nature is very rich, the climate warm but with intermittent freshness."

hypocrisy almost at the moment of his arrival at Papeete.[50] A
year later he betrays his quest for the *age* of humanity in speaking of Tahitian women, " not beautiful, properly speaking," as
having an indefinable quality " of penetrating the mysteries of
the infinite." [51] It is worth noting that Lafcadio Hearn proceeded from Martinique to his particular quest for the primitive among the Japanese, the distinction here being that, unlike
Gauguin, he chose a land where nearly no precedent for the
quest existed.

This feeling of " preconception " runs through the whole of
Gauguin's Tahitian record; and some of it is purely cynical.
The Maori women were to be possessed nearly for the asking.
" Their skin, of course, is of a golden yellow, which is ugly in
some of them; but is it as ugly as all that in the rest, especially
when it is naked—and when it is to be had for almost nothing? " [52] There is a kind of unequaled ruthlessness in Gauguin
which is wholly foreign to Melville and to every other figure
discussed here. It is very much as though he had grimly determined to compel Tahiti into Paradise. Like Loti (and
Melville before him), he bathes in a fresh pool. Fayaway and
Rarahu are recalled in his mistress Téhura, and Gauguin feels
himself the first man of the earth.[53] He " liberates " himself
from Europe through the ritual of felling a tree and becomes
a savage, " a true Maori "; [54] he is consecrated to Taaroa and the
gods of ancient Tahiti.[55] He seems almost to copy the words of
Melville in *Moby-Dick* (Ch. LXV) as he assails the " cannibalism " of civilization. " Cannibals? " asked Melville, " who is

---

[50] *Ibid.*, p. 219. To Mette Gauguin from Tahiti, July, 1891.

[51] *Ibid.*, p. 227. To Mette Gauguin from Tahiti, June, 1892.

[52] *Intimate Journals*, ed. Brooks, p. 70.

[53] Paul Gauguin and Charles Morice, *Noa Noa*, third edition (Paris, n. d.),
p. 132. Morice, contrary to the opinion of some students, compiled most of
Noa Noa. The text is very largely constructed from Gauguin's letters.

[54] *Ibid.*, p. 89.

[55] *Ibid.*, pp. 177–80. In this time of her husband's " liberation " Mette Gauguin
writes from Copenhagen to Émile Schuffenecker, a family friend, of Paul's
" most monstrously brutal egoism, for me phenomenal, incomprehensible." She
asks: " Do you understand a father who feels nothing, nothing, nothing! I
believe that he would see us all die without being moved in the slightest degree."
(See *Letters*, ed. Malingue, pp. 326–28; September 15, 1893.)

not a cannibal?" So Gauguin: "Civilised! You are proud of
not eating human flesh? On a raft you would eat it . . . before
God, invoking Him even as you trembled. To make up for it
you eat the heart of your neighbor every day." [56]

Preconception toward the art of being "primitive" is only
an adjunct to Gauguin's creative use of themes from primitive
culture. It must occur infrequently to the visitor in the gallery
that he is not looking at Oceanic art or a faithful representation
of Oceania at all. What he sees is exactly what Gauguin wished
to find in the South Seas. R. J. Goldwater notes that "grace-
fulness and simplicity of an almost Pre-Raphaelite sort were an
essential element of Gauguin's conception of the primitive."
He continues: "Neither the decorated canoe prows of the
Maori, the stone statues of Easter Island, nor the angular
designs of the Marquesas have anything to do with grace,
though they are intensive and powerful arts." [57] John Gould
Fletcher intends the same judgment when he says that "Tahiti
had merely given him material out of which his imagination
had evolved pictures." [58] Polynesian art is no more the subject
of Gauguin's symbols, that of the *Ia Orana Maria* (already
noted) as one example, than Marquesan tattooing is the real
subject of Melville's decoration of Queequeg. The "evolution
of the pictures" is exactly like the evolution of the form of
the whale's image in the hands of the "sailor savage."

In 1900, Gauguin, ill at Papeete, "overcome by the misery
and the sickness of an old age altogether premature," determined to leave Tahiti for the Marquesas (Fatu-iva). "I believe that [there], that element entirely savage and that complete solitude will give me before death a last fire of enthusiasm
which will rejuvenate my imagination and will bring my talent
to its conclusion." [59] The following year he departed, observing
that "as his pictures from Brittany were as pure sugar-water
compared to [his] Tahitian canvases, so Tahiti would be

[56] *Intimate Journals*, ed. Brooks, p. 197.
[57] "A Unique Gauguin," *Magazine of Art*, vol. 30 (1937), p. 55.
[58] *Paul Gauguin: His Life and Art* (New York, 1921), p. 132.
[59] *Letters*, ed. Malingue, p. 300. To Emmanuel Bibesco, Tahiti, July, 1900.

cologne-water to the Marquesas." [60] The last two years on Fatu-iva, and Hiva-oa, where he died on May 8, 1903, brought only more intense and studied projection of himself into " savagery." Before he left Fatu-iva for Hiva-oa in April, 1903, he wrote the last letter of his life to his collaborator in *Noa Noa*, Charles Morice. He had been working on his last picture, that curious view of a Brittany village under a heavy snowfall, painted in full view of the Marquesan jungle. How much the self-styled " savage " in him was none other than the symbolist (as this savage was in the art of Melville) must be revealed in these last words to Morice:

> Decidedly the savage is better than we [are]. You made a mistake one day in saying that I was wrong in calling myself a savage. This is nonetheless true: I am a savage. And the civilised perceive it: for in my work there is nothing which excels or shocks if it is not this " unfortunate I, the savage." This is why it is inimitable. The work of a man is the expla-nation of that man. And in the two kinds of beauty, one results from instinct and the other comes from study. [61]

The fact can, of course, be none other than the truth of Mel-ville as " savage." Instinct had nothing to do with it. Every symbol emerged from the recesses of civilized feeling and from the imagination of Christian man.

Victor Segalen (1878-1919) was earlier mentioned as the author of a novel of Tahitian setting, *Les Immémoriaux* (1907) . An archeologist whose residence in the Orient associated him with the eminence of Saint-Denys as a Sinologue, he is not properly identified throughout his career with the history of primitivism. He belongs to the history of professional Oriental-ists and scholars. But a notice of Segalen is particularly ap-propriate with reference to Gauguin. *Les Immémoriaux* was written in 1903, following Segalen's journey to Polynesia as a surgeon in the French Navy. Of all works of art dealing with the native life of Oceania, this study of the meeting of cultures

---

[60] *Künstlerbriefe aus dem neunzehnten Jahrhundert*, ed Bruno Cassirer (Berlin, 1913), p. 660. To Daniel de Montfried, Papeete, June, 1901.
[61] *Lettres*, ed. Malingue, pp. 318–19.

with the appearance of English missionaries in the eighteenth century is the only one possessing the distinction of exact psychological realization. The narrative is related from the mind of the Tahitian, in particular from that of a priest of Oro, Térii. This book is to the literature of primitivism what the art of Gauguin and Melville would be to the same *genre* had they intended to describe Tahitian reality rather than to refer to it with the objectives of the symbolist. Thus Segalen accomplishes an almost unparalleled insight: with accurate knowledge of the Tahitian consciousness, he succeeds in describing the confusion resulting from the loss of an established native religious symbolism. If Loti, in " becoming " Loti as he recounts the story of Rarahu, intended to remake his psychic awareness to equal that of the Polynesian, if Gauguin, felling a tree, signifies his rebirth as a Maori, then Segalen renders these attempts to become " primitive " totally ineffectual. His description of the Tahitian dance, for instance, is established upon the *felt* motion of the dance in the body of the dancer, not upon the impression of the visitor. As a symbol of unabashed native sexuality, this rite, so often condemned as orgiastic and depraved by the missionary, becomes the projection of elemental sexual force. The " sense of sin " has not yet been received, and the cry of the dancer, " *Viens t'enlacer vite à moi*," [62] stands as a commandment of an original Tahitian religion.

A notice of two later visitors to the Marquesas will complete this discussion of the Polynesian group: A. Safroni-Middleton, author of two inferior novels, *Sestrina* and *Sailor and Beachcomber* (1915); and Frederick O'Brien, of the more familiar *White Shadows in the South Seas* (1919) and *Atolls of the Sun* (1922). Middleton's *Sestrina*, despite its ineptitudes in plot and characterization, succeeds in recapturing the charm of Melville's Typee Valley. The setting is Hiva-oa in the Marquesas, and the image of the autotype remains the familiar one encountered in the early work of Melville. Green foliage waves again on the volcanic peaks; the same physical beauty of the Marquesan, recalling Melville's Fayaway, suggests the original

[62] *Les Immémoriaux*, p. 81.

innocence of man.[63] Melville seems to have accompanied yet another Polynesian traveler. At Papoo, in Samoa, where Middleton knew Stevenson,[64] the loss of Polynesian excellence through the imported evils of civilization is again deplored, as the hero of *Sailor and Beachcomber* sees the legacy of the Western world displayed before him.[65]

O'Brien, who has written with greater power and artistry, extends the lament again in his report from the valley of the Taipis. When he visited (in 1918?) this familiar source of Melville's first symbolism, he found a dozen people still living in the valley, all old and wretched. This was the land once " of thousands of men and women whose bodies were as beautiful as the models for the statues the Greeks made, whose hearts were generous, and whose minds were eager to learn all good things." The relation of Christianity to this scene of death is recalled again: " I asked myself what a Christ would think of the havoc wrought by men calling themselves Christians." [66] O'Brien's discussion of the abandonment of *tabu* " under the ridicule and the profanation of the whites " [67] and the loss of all symbolic authority returns, eighty years after Melville's visit, to the first observations of *Typee*. Each man had become old in his religion, free of his idols, free to carve his own intricate design on the spear-paddle, as Melville saw him; but Melville perceived with unusual intuition that *tabu* was the indispensable symbol of mind and life, as well.

O'Brien's account of Gauguin on Fatu-iva is eminently just. At Vaitahu he met Charles Lemoine, a French schoolmaster, who had known the artist in his last year. These remarks describe every primitivist who intended to escape from his parent culture, " the cage formed by heredity, habits, and the thoughts of his countrymen," as O'Brien has called it.

[63] A. Safroni-Middleton, *Sestrina: A Romance of the South Seas* (New York, n. d.), p. 6.
[64] *Sailor and Beachcomber* (London, 1915), p. 62.
[65] *Ibid.*, p. 55.
[66] *White Shadows in the South Seas* (New York, 1919), pp. 308–309. The same observations are continued in *Atolls of the Sun*, pp. 320–25.
[67] *Atolls of the Sun*, p. 284.

Space he had conquered, and in these wilds was hidden from the eyes of civilization, but time he could not blot out, for he was of his age, and even its leader in the evolution of painting. The savage in man [whom] he let take control of himself . . . was spoiled by the inexorable grasp upon him of his forebears and his decades of Europe. He was saturated with the ennui of the West.[68]

The symbol of art, as another generation sees this painter today, was the release from ennui. The year after Gauguin's death, Henry Adams, equally saturated with ennui, found the symbol of release half a world away from Fatu-iva and Hiva-oa, nearly a millennium away in time, in the Virgin of Chartres. Each made his religion in art.

7   Fenollosa, Hearn

These travelers in Polynesia are the sharers in the perpetuity of Ishmael, the makers of the cognates which surround Melville at the symbolistic center of Oceanic reference in modern primitivism. It has been seen that the genetic possibilities for the construction of ultimate symbols from experience with Oceanic cultures are governed by the aptitudes of the individual artist. The nature of the symbol is controlled by the nature and the degree of religious feeling. Thus the feeling of Adams returns to medieval Christian art; the feeling of Stevenson escapes the significance of the great life-symbols; the feeling of Melville and that of Gauguin come to rest in the Polynesian domain, and to order symbolic structures from the emblems of the Oceanic culture encountered. Yet, with the differentiations of symbolistic ends, these four are united by the condition that Polynesia is only an area of transition. Even with Melville and Gauguin the final point of the journey is not the Marquesan valley or the Tahitian harbor. The symbol of the White Whale recalls ultimately the mythology of Hindu India, and Queequeg represents the Oriental source of human innocence and wisdom; the pictures of Gauguin refer more to Oriental prototypes

[68] *Ibid.*, p. 443.

of Tahitian "naturalness" than to the ideal existence of Papeete. The imagistic authority of Polynesia is unquestionable;
but the supreme destiny of Melville and Gauguin lay in the
Far Eastern journey, a destiny which for both was never ful-
filled.

James N. Hall and Charles B. Nordhoff have reported con-
versations with two amateur ethnologists, both primitivists in
the sense of this discussion, whom they met in the Paumotus
in 1920. The one thought of successive migrations from northern India through Indonesia to the Pacific islands, of the Polynesian with Caucasian blood in his veins, "the legacy of
ancestors separated from the parent stock so long ago that mankind had not yet learned the use of iron"; the other, of "scraps
of evidence" of the Polynesian type, traces of a great migration
to Oceania from the western islands off Sumatra, Java, and
Celebes.[69] As these theories signify the primitivist's longing for
origins beyond Polynesia, so the art of Melville and that of
Gauguin refer to the Asiatic source of Polynesian culture.
The imagination producing the symbol extends geography and
deepens time.

Although the true Orient may be the ultimate realm of the
primitivist intent upon the meaning of existence, it does not
follow that he has seen and felt its physical reality. In this
area of great Asia, the Western mind is variously represented
by the Japanologist, the Sinologue, the Sanskritist, the world
traveler, the historian, and the diplomat. These have reported
the facts of Asia; and enough has already been said of their
service to the concerns of exoticism. The primitivist as symbol-
maker in the East is quite another man. He is the fashioner of
an art expressed in the images of an experience directly sensed.
The autotype of the Oriental journey is sovereign in a manner
exactly equal to that of the Oceanic voyage; the symbols which
it compels are derived from the awareness of cultural failure
which is requisite to primitivism. It happens that the locus of
primitivism in the East which supplies valid symbols to the

---

[69] *Faery Lands of the South Seas* (New York, 1920), pp. 70, 83.

system represented by Melville is that of Japanese culture as abstracted by a small group of Americans, notably by Lafcadio Hearn.

The service of Ernest Fenollosa (1853-1908) to American and European knowledge of Japanese art is widely known. Less familiar is the distinction between Fenollosa, as teacher and critic, and Hearn as symbolist. Fenollosa, whose concept of the " Pacific School of Art " [70] and whose symbolic representation of the Japanese (in *Epochs of Chinese and Japanese Art*) will be of later use in an analysis of Melville's symbols, actually establishes a precedent for Hearn. His residence at the Tokyo Imperial University as a professor of political economy and philosophy (1878-86), his long study of Buddhism, his erudition in Oriental art (which he turned to the service of the Boston Museum of Fine Arts) all led to his immersion in " the depth, the wonder and the romance of Japanese thought." [71] He is the first American in the history of primitivism who advances the superiority of Oriental symbolism in art over the symbolism of the West. How intently he had devoted himself to Japan is suggested in the records of Henry Adams and John La Farge touring Japan in 1886. With Fenollosa as instructor and guide, Adams visited the great shrines of Japanese art. Adams was quite aware that what he saw before him was Fenollosa's retreat to an Oriental religion for the symbols of existential meaning. It is scarcely true that Adams's New England conscience was shocked. His reaction to Fenollosa in Japan shows that the direction of his feeling toward the symbol of ultimate meaning was not eventually to point toward the culture of the East. Fenollosa's Buddhistic direction, apparent from his first months in Japan, reached its end in the temples of Nikko and Kyoto.

It is probable that Hearn (1850-1904) turned toward Japan through the example of Fenollosa. There is a record of only one meeting between the two (in Tokyo in 1897).[72] But

---

[70] *Epochs of Chinese and Japanese Art* (London, 1912), vol. 1, p. 4.
[71] *Ibid.*, p. xx (preface by Mary Fenollosa).
[72] Vera McWilliams, *Lafcadio Hearn* (Boston, 1946), p. 386.

Fenollosa had demonstrated, long before Hearn's arrival in Japan, in 1890, the potentialities of Japanese culture as a refuge from Western civilization. Exactly as Gauguin made of Polynesia a liberator from the " cage " of Europe (by way of the reports of Pierre Loti?), so Hearn idealized Japan as the antithesis of captivity in Western civilization. Both Gauguin and Hearn passed toward these final objectives by way of the island of Martinique. Curiously, they were both in St. Pierre in the same year, 1887. In this tropical setting Gauguin made his first encounter with a primitive culture; so did Hearn, who wrote from the island several letters which are so much in the manner of Gauguin that they are nearly indistinguishable. Soon after reaching St. Pierre, Hearn declared: " I am absolutely bewitched, and resolved to settle down somewhere in the West Indies. Martinique is simply heaven on earth. You must imagine a community whose only vices are erotic." [73]

Following his return from Martinique in 1889, he found the cities of the United States intolerable: " This is frightful, nightmarish, devilish! Civilization is a hideous thing. Blessed is savagery! " [74] This denunciation of civilization becomes one of the major themes in Hearn's account of the West Indian journey: the sin of civilized man against nature will be atoned for as the white population declines, the jungle reappears, and the utmost retribution is exacted for " the crimes and follies of three hundred years." [75] Thus Martinique serves Hearn as the first point of reference toward escape from the West. For both Gauguin and Hearn it is comparable to Nukuhiva and to Tahiti in the experience of Melville, the distinction being that Melville's circumstances forbid an extension of the journey. The Oceanic and Oriental autotypes acquired by Gauguin and Hearn from their final destinations displace the autotype of Martinique. So it may be proposed that an extension of Melville's journey into the Far East would have displaced the imagistic authority of Polynesia.

[73] See Herbert S. Gorman, *The Procession of Masks* (Boston, 1923), pp. 131–32.
[74] Elizabeth Bisland, *The Life and Letters of Lafcadio Hearn* (Boston, 1906), vol. 1, pp. 443–44. The letter is addressed to Joseph Tunison.
[75] *Two Years in the French West Indies* (New York, 1890), p. 98.

Hearn's decision to retreat to Japan, whether inspired by Fenollosa or by the reports of Chamberlain and other early Japanologists, was a calculated act. In this he may as well have been Gauguin departing from Marseilles for Papeete. With the Indies as prologue, Hearn sailed for Yokohama in March, 1890, one year before Gauguin's departure, fortified, it would seem, with a stern resolution to discover the opposite of Western savagery. This predisposition toward the Japanese is one with Gauguin's predisposition toward the Tahitians and the Marquesans.

A half-century of reputation has done nothing, unfortunately, to distinguish Hearn from the courses of exoticism. His traditional stature as an *Impressionniste* (with considerable studious attention to his myopia as a determinant in his view of the Japanese!) is adjacent to the figure of Amy Lowell, for example, as an " Oriental " Imagist. Actually, one has in Hearn a striking example of the impoverished Protestant mind in search of compensatory symbols of being. Hearn as Ishmael is as genuinely religious in sensibility as the Ishmael of *Moby-Dick*. If one takes an emblem of Japanese life from any of the essays or stories, it is apparent that the description of the object, in the manner of pure impressionism and imagism, is not the end. A symbolistic destiny lies beyond the object. A useful example here is the representation of the *Bon-odori*, a Japanese dance accompanied by a primitive chant. Feeling *toward* the religious symbol dominates the sense of the observer. " But how explain the emotion evoked by a primitive chant totally unlike anything in Western melody,—impossible even to write in those tones which are the ideographs of our music tongue? And the emotion itself—what is it? . . . something not of only one place or time, but vibrant to all common joy or pain of being, under the universal sun." [76] These terms of universals are inevitable in every emblematic description of Japanese life which Hearn wrote. In this symbol of the *Bon-odori*, with its autotypic form derived from images sensuously received, is contained the idea of the new religion.

[76] *Glimpses of Unfamiliar Japan* (Boston, 1894), vol. 1, p. 138.

Hearn's peculiar " American ' distinction in his symbolistic voyage is the condition of the transcendental mood, or what may be particularized as traumatic cosmology. This mood and its expression are the familiar signs of Whitman's poetry; and they are, of course, perfectly usual in the early work of Melville (e. g., in the chapter " Dreams " of *Mardi* already analyzed). Thus Hearn, approaching Buddhism, writes exactly like Whitman: " I have souls wanting to soar in air, and souls wanting to swim in water (sea-water, I think), and souls wanting to live in woods or on mountain tops. I have souls longing for the tumult of great cities, and souls longing to dwell in tropical solitude . . . souls conservative, delicate, loyal to empire and to feudal tradition, and souls that are Nihilists, deserving Siberia." [77] There is room for " souls mediaeval " as well, loving " the awful solitude of Gothic glooms." But the similarity does not come about from imitation. It is precisely this cosmic amplitude of possibilities, this swirling without symbolic definition and form which precedes the act of symbolization. Whitman performs this final act in the cosmic (but nonetheless tight) symbolism of the ode on Lincoln, of " Passage to India," and of " Chanting the Square Deific." Melville performs it, after the amorphous material of *Mardi*, in the symbols of *Moby-Dick* and *Clarel*. Hearn reaches definitive symbolic form in the chapters of *Gleanings in Buddha-Fields* (1897).

That the continuity of religious symbolism is Hearn's obsessive concern in his approach to Buddhism is perfectly obvious in his examination of Shinshū (a form of Protestant Buddhism in Japan). He has in mind the power of Roman Catholic symbols in the Christian tradition, and the authority of fixed symbols in orthodox Buddhism. " Remembering how strong Roman Catholicism remains to-day, how little it has changed since the days of Luther, how impotent our progressive creeds to satisfy the old spiritual hunger for some visible object of worship . . . it becomes difficult to believe that the iconolatry of the more ancient Buddhist sects will not continue for hun-

---

[77] *Gleanings in Buddha-Fields* and *The Romance of the Milky Way* in *Works*, Koizumi Edition (Boston, 1923), vol. 8, pp. 72–73.

dreds of years to keep a large place in popular affection." [78] The impressive feature of the analogy is its recognition of the Protestant's desire for the object of worship, the abstraction of the values contained in creed. There can be no question of Hearn's new allegiance to iconolatry. Each year in Japan involved him more deeply in the philosophies of Karma and Nirvana. The triumph over the ego and the escape from the false consciousness of sense and desire were substituted for his "Christianized" consciousness of self. In his essay on Nirvana he concluded:

> Demon and angel are but varying manifestations of the same Karma;—hell and heaven mere temporary halting-places upon the journey to eternal peace. For all beings there is but one law—immutable and divine: the law by which the lowest *must* rise to the place of the highest—the law by which the worst *must* become the best—the law by which the vilest *must* become a Buddha. In such a system there is no room for prejudice and hatred. Ignorance alone is the source of wrong and pain; and all ignorance must finally be dissipated in infinite light *through the decomposition of Self*.[79]

It cannot matter that thereafter Hearn vacillated between the iconolatry of Buddhism and the emblems of Shintoism. Kwannon, the goddess of mercy, and the celebration of a national feast in a Shinto temple, whether one or the other is ascendant in this mind, are symbols of equal power. These, and every formal element of Japanese religious ritual, establish the new religion of Lafcadio Hearn, the primitivist. They satisfy the desires of religious feeling; they provide visible objects of worship. Hearn's essays in the spirituality of Japanese ethos then become objects parallel to these in the realm of art.

There can be nothing very unique in Hearn's insistence upon emancipation from the self as he finds his way into Buddhism. Every manifestation of primitivism here subjected to review shows in some way the same direction. Freedom from self-consciousness is an attribute of every Polynesian and every Oriental character represented in the literature of primitivism;

[78] *Ibid.*, p. 128.
[79] *Ibid.*, p. 175.

and so it is that the supreme freedom, the selflessness of Quee-queg in *Moby-Dick* opposes the typically Occidental and su-premely evil egomania of Ahab.

8 *Leconte de Lisle, Ducasse, Rimbaud, Verhaeren*

In the method of this study, the symbol of Ishmael usually requires the directly sensed experience of the journey as this has been outlined through the discussions of Melville and his successors. For the purposes of criticism to follow in the suc-ceeding chapters, it is necessary to make certain exceptions to this requirement. I intend to refer through subsequent com-parative readings to the primitivistic symbols of three French poets—Leconte de Lisle, Isidore Ducasse (" Comte de Lautré-amont "), Rimbaud—and to the Belgian Émile Verhaeren. Each has been earlier related in some context to Melville through the discussion of cultural failure. The brief career of Ducasse ended within Melville's lifetime; Leconte de Lisle and Rimbaud both died in the year of Melville's death; the life of Verhaeren extended beyond that of Melville some three decades. Contemporaneity must in important measure account for the fact of a striking archetypal similarity relating the symbols of these poets to the structures of Melville. Like the voyagers of the Pacific, they provide an indispensable array of symbolic cognates. Each is potentially Ishmael, or Ishmael in fact, without the Oceanic or Oriental journey. The religious den-sity of Verhaeren's symbols is commensurate with the Protes-tant declinations of Melville in the period of the Mediterranean journey described in *Clarel*, even though the autotypes of Ver-haeren are exclusively confined to his European experience. The desertion of traditional poetic form in the *Chants de Maldoror* of Ducasse and his formulation of a symbolism refer-ring to the nature of God are related to the symbolistic defi-nitions of *Moby-Dick*. The structure of Rimbaud's so-called " satanism " complements Melville's description of cultural failure, and the " Oriental " objective of this poet is partially attained in the journey to the Near East. (Here I am quite

aware that Rimbaud's career as a poet ends before he reaches
Abyssinia.) The mythological reference to Polynesia and
Hindu India, and the evocation of primal states of being which
inform the major expression of Leconte de Lisle are more
closely allied to the archaism of Melville than to any other
imagistic idiom of the last century.

The usefulness of Leconte de Lisle and of Ducasse is limited
by the nature of religious feeling described as superior in the
creative force of Melville and Gauguin. The particular strength
of the first is seen in an imagistic display of materials referring
to the Orient rather than in the achievement of multiplex
symbols describing fully the religious intent of Orientalism.
It derives primarily from sources of erudition but is sufficiently
characterized by religious sensibility to invite definition as
existential primitivism. Leconte de Lisle (1818-91) was born
on the Île Bourbon (renamed Île de la Reunion by the French
Revolutionary government). He was sent to Europe to be
educated; and after a period of study in Brittany and at Rennes,
he returned to the island to undertake the practice of law. At
some point in his youth he had broken with the Catholic
heritage of his mother and devoted himself to the " dark view,"
in which he saw the way of the modern world as an essential
perversion of Christianity, and the political evils of France as
derivatives from the corruption and the iniquities of papal
authority in Rome.[80] Repelled by the evils of island life,
especially that of slavery, he abandoned his legal practice, and
in his thirtieth year returned to Paris as a revolutionary.[81] It is
clear that his metamorphosis into the poet came about through
the experiences of an artistic consciousness seeking ways out of
the blind materialism of contemporary society. His direction
toward Hindu thought (translated with particular poetic effectiveness in " La Vision de Brahma ") was suggested by the
translations of the French Sanskritist, Émile Burnouf, just as
the " Japanese studies " of the Goncourt brothers were inspired
by the scholarship of Orientalists and by Oriental art of the

[80] See Irving Brown, *Leconte de Lisle* (New York, 1924), p. 32.
[81] *Ibid.*, p. 40.

Paris expositions. But Leconte de Lisle is preserved from the shallows of exoticism by the feeling which compels his Orientalism. The modern world, in its state of cultural failure, could save itself from total destruction and extinction only by retreat to the " barbarous " and the elemental states of being in the history of the race. The Orient, as projected through the learning of this poet, alone contained this elemental salvation. But it is not in the religious symbol (allowing here for the Brahma of the vision) that Leconte de Lisle most clearly belongs to primitivism. He offers a poetry impressively distinguished by images of primordial states of culture which particularize the area in which his cultural pessimism is represented. Discussions of the Oriental obsession of this artist will follow. At this point it is enough to say that he is like Melville in the " backward drift " of images furnishing the setting for the typical Oriental symbol.

Ducasse (1846-70) was born in Montevideo and educated in France. A critical evaluation of the *Chants de Maldoror*, completed in the year of the poet's death at twenty-five, has no relation to this study. It is obvious that the religious sensibility of this youth does not in any way match the precocious insight of Rimbaud, and that the puerile fixations of his surrealistic art are very far from the mature content of the life-symbol in primitivism. What is of especial advantage here is the archetypal relationship of emerging symbols to the system of symbolism achieved by Melville. The satanic mysteries of Ducasse's Maldoror belong to the same formlessness noted in the presymbolic state of sensibility described by Melville and Hearn. In certain instances to be cited hereafter, the genesis of the symbols of Ducasse is indisputably similar to that shaping the multiple structures of heretical primitivism from Oceanic and Oriental autotypes. What is abundant, if ineptly represented, in the " poetry " of Ducasse is the condition of failure in traditional Christian symbolism; what is lacking is the authority of experience. The South American background does not survive, and only the Atlantic voyage of the youth en route to France, and some knowledge of the streets of Paris appear in the

symbols achieved. At the same time, predisposition toward the
Orient appears, just as it does in the poetry of Rimbaud.

The " Oriental " direction of Arthur Rimbaud (1854-91) has
recently been noted by Wallace Fowlie:

> He had tried to rid himself of the Western symbols: Christi-
> anity and its martyrs, inventions, art, warfare. He had
> secretly been trying to return to the East, to the source of
> eternal wisdom. But that had been a dream. A modern
> Westerner is the man who has harmonized Christ with the
> *bourgeoisie.* . . . What Rimbaud had dreamed of, in his
> revolts and his poetry, had been the purity of Eastern thought,
> the purity of the mind which leads one to the absolute. . . .
> The experiment was doomed to failure.[82]

Obviously, this judgment cannot mean very much unless one
accepts Fowlie's contention for the poet's precocious experience: " Rimbaud was old enough, ironically, in his late adoles-
cence to have lived through most of the dreams of humanity." [83]
This judgment I take to be irrefutable. Rimbaud had, indeed,
lived through most of the dreams when he left poetry, and
Verlaine, at the age of nineteen. But it does not follow that
either the *Saison en Enfer* or *Les Illuminations* achieves the
symbolic definition of " purity of mind " such as Fowlie describes. What one encounters in the poetry of Rimbaud is the
pre-symbolic condition of the European mind in its characteristic act of sloughing off Western symbols. At the same time,
there can be no question of Rimbaud's religious compulsion,
even at the moment of his supreme heresy in Charleville, where
he was born. Again, the paradox of the poet who cannot shake
off his concern with God. In the " Premières Communions "
of the earlier verse Christ (the symbol) becomes " the eternal
thief of energy "; and on the wall of the church of Charleville
the boy writes with open blasphemy, *Mort à Dieu.*[84]

Subsequent journeys to Scandinavia, Egypt (1880), Cyprus,
and then, finally, to Harar, where Rimbaud managed a trading
post and later made a fortune in supplying contraband ammu-

---

[82] *Rimbaud's* Illuminations: *A Study in Angelism* (New York, 1953), pp. 36-37.
[83] *Ibid.,* p. 153.   [84] *Ibid.,* p. 125.

nition to King Menelik of Abyssinia—all these make the voyage which never reaches its ultimate end of desire, the timeless Orient. The cry of Rimbaud, " *Je suis esclave de mon baptême* " (*Une Saison en Enfer*) , voices the apostasy of every Ishmael; it may as well be the lament of Melville's outcast of both *Pierre* and *Clarel*. It reflects for every Ishmael the failure of Christian symbolism to embody meaning. But Melville in the Custom House in New York and Rimbaud in the business of smuggling arms over the Abyssinian desert represent clearly opposed finalities: the one endures and the other deserts. What Rimbaud sought through his season in Hell, and in his journey to Jerusalem (c. 1881) , was the salvation of the symbol of Christian tradition. " Pagan blood returns! The Spirit is near; why doesn't Christ help me by granting my soul nobility and liberty? Alas! The gospel has gone by! The gospel! " [85] Art as poetry could not supply a new gospel; and so art was relinquished. In *Clarel* (Part IV, Sec. xx) Christ has renounced the world. Yet, even in this loss, Melville clings to the religion of art. Rimbaud, after his brief and meteoric youth, recants. He takes a native girl of the Harari tribe. He seeks the fulfilment of his earlier prediction from his season in Hell: " My day is done, I am leaving Europe. . . . . I shall return with limbs of iron, a dark skin, a furious eye; from my countenance I will be known as of a strong race." [86] The life of art is abdicated; the life of satiety in a world of primitive emotions is substituted. Rimbaud becomes by analogy a Gauguin in Tahiti who has ceased to paint.

One biographer of Rimbaud's last years speaks of the " saisons en enfer " of Aden as well. In 1884 he felt himself old

[85] *A Season in Hell*, trans. Louise Varèse (Norfolk, Conn., New Directions, 1945), pp. 11, 13.

[86] See Jean-Marie Carré, " Un Article Inconnu de Rimbaud sur son Voyage en Abyssinie," *Mercure de France* (new series), vol. 200 (1927), p. 573. Carré's account uses an article of Rimbaud written as a letter to the director of the journal *Bosphore Egyptien* and printed in the issues of August 25 and 27, 1887. (See Carré, p. 562.) Rimbaud describes here his traffic for Menelik in *cartouches*. Carré contends that the poet is dead: the adventurer of the real has succeeded to the adventurer of the ideal.

already, at the age of thirty.[87] Since each man is a slave of a miserable fatality—even at Aden, he reasoned—it was better to go to Aden, " where I am unknown, where I am completely forgotten and where I shall have to begin anew." This new beginning brought him a year later to the confession that he was wearing himself out, like a beast of burden, in a country for which he felt an implacable horror.[88] In 1890, a year before his return to Marseilles to die, he came very close to that peculiar despair of Adams in Tahiti: " I have never known anyone more bored than I." [89] The anxiety of meaninglessness is the last condition of his mind: " I am so utterly forsaken that I offer, it matters not to what divine image, flight toward perfection." [90]

The poetry of Émile Verhaeren (1855-1917) may appear to have little relevance at the conclusion of this discussion. If one follows Amy Lowell's " imagistic " judgments in her essay on this poet, that Verhaeren has a Teutonic grandeur " extremely sympathetic to all Anglo-Saxons and Germans," that, opposed to the " coldly analytic " French intellect, " Verhaeren charms by his fiery activity," [91] the comment to follow here may, indeed, seem irrelevant. Miss Lowell, as critic, was interested in finding Gallic examples of her own poetic objectives. If one is less interested in finding " Gallic examples "—Verhaeren's affective power of evoking images of " the red, fat flesh tints of Rubens " (Miss Lowell's enthusiasm) as a colorful instance—if one is more interested in this poet's nonaffective power to symbolize archetypes appearing through cultural failure, he may then read the poetry of Verhaeren as another province of Ishmael. It has already been said that Verhaeren does not belong to the company of voyagers. He is particularly appropriate to this study, however, because the method of his symbolism demonstrates a religious intent precisely related to that of Melville.

---

[87] Marguerite-Yerta Méléra, " Les Voyages d'Arthur Rimbaud," *La Revue Universelle*, vol. 35 (1928), p. 658.

[88] *Ibid.*, p. 670.

[89] *Ibid.*, continued in *La Revue Universelle*, vol. 36 (1929), p. 183.

[90] *Ibid.*, pp. 183–84.

[91] *Six French Poets* (New York, 1915), p. 27.

From his birthplace at Saint-Amand, in East Flanders, he went at the age of fourteen to Ghent, where he entered the Jesuit College of Sainte-Barbe. At twenty-six he graduated in law at Louvain and immediately turned his career toward poetry. In the same year he renounced Catholicism forever. With the appearance of *Les Flamandes,* in 1883, Verhaeren set about the poetic transcription of yet another search for art symbols of existential meaning. *Les Moines* (1886), contrary to Miss Lowell's view of the work as " a book of delicate etchings," [92] marks the descent of Verhaeren into the region of darkness (and formlessness) which the student of Ishmael accepts as the threshold of a new symbolic era. The darkness endures through the intervening record of this art up to and including *Les Villes Tentaculaires* (1895). It is dispelled with *La Multiple Splendeur* in 1906 (if one can read here a final symbolic compensation for Verhaeren's apostasy).

Without distorting the total value of this poetry, it may be proposed that Verhaeren offers the most articulate description of Christian symbols in decay to be found in the last century of literature in French. For it is with this description rather than with the poet's final symbols, which cannot be related to the autotypic kinship in primitivistic Orientalism reviewed here, that succeeding notices of Verhaeren must be concerned. The method of *Les Moines* is particularly close, for instance, to certain aspects of Melville's *Clarel.* The " satanic " content of *Les Débâcles* (1888) and of *Les Flambeaux Noirs* (1890) is allied to the " satanism " of Gauguin and Rimbaud. If Verhaeren does not belong to the system of the Oceanic and Oriental symbol in modern primitivism, then he demonstrates with perfect clarity the method of poetic feeling inexorably required by its own religious sensibility to wrest new symbols of meaning from the modern world. In his awareness of cultural failure through the urbanization of Western man and through this man's loss of sacrament, he stands closer to Melville than to his European contemporaries.

[92] *Ibid.,* p. 13.

Apart from certain artists whose work is in some way useful to the critical discussions to follow, the primitivists reviewed in this chapter provide the symbolic material which will be related to the Oceanic and Oriental symbols of Melville. In the introduction to this study it was proposed that an ultimate objective of criticism should be the arrangement of works of art comparatively, so that art may comment upon art. With the obvious exception of authoritative achievement in the realms of textual and biographical scholarship, it must be asserted here that the voice of art commenting upon art is articulation of fact. If the collections of related symbols may at times appear insufficient for demonstration of the particular organic system under examination, the reason has already been made clear: this study is exploratory and intends to demonstrate method rather than to reach immutable definitions. The following chapters will criticize the major Oceanic and Oriental symbols of Melville and certain symbolic equivalents from related art among which Melville's forms stand as dominant centers.

PART THREE

AVATARS:
SYMBOLS
OF REINCARNATION
FROM THE ORIENT

V

Obsession
with the Primeval East

An *avatar* in the meaning of Oriental theologies is a
descent of the deity into a new incarnation. In the art of
primitivism, the avatar may be regarded as an *archetype of
transformation* [1] rising from the area of inclination toward the
Orient which was traced in the preceding chapters. This archetype, as avatar, replaces the orthodox symbol of Christian sacrament. It becomes an individual symbol at that point in the
creative act when the artist shapes it into unique form through

---

[1] Jung: ". . . typical situations, places, ways, animals, plants, and so forth
that symbolize the kind of change [i. e. change from traditionally established
symbols], whatever it is." (*The Integration of the Personality*, p. 89.)

the autotypes of his own experience. If it be assumed, for purposes of immediate illustration, that the monster of the deep (whale, leviathan, great fish, sea dragon, Loch Ness monster, or giant sea-serpent) is a universal archetype from the collective unconscious, then it appears that this monster becomes a symbol when it is grasped and fashioned by an autotype. (Reference should be made here to the archetype evident in the snake-handling of Southern revivalists as described in the second chapter.) Nonartistic experience with the archetype may be experience with an avatar (as in a primitive Hindu mind the avatars of Vishnu are really archetypes displayed without reflection and without definition, unless they are brought to description through the symbols of art or theology). Artistic experience with the archetype, on the other hand, is destined to define and to impress art from the crude and commonly shared collective unconscious.

The following chapters will analyze six major symbolic forms from the literature of primitivism in which these avatars appear. Considered in relation to the Orient, the symbols to be examined represent six manifestations of God, just as six avatars of Vishnu represent six incarnations of the Hindu Preserver upon the earth. These Hinduistic incarnations, without the sophistication of Hindu theology, are pure archetypes; the Occidental symbol, with its reflection upon cultural failure, with the feeling of Western man's unrest before the inadequacy of his God-symbols and his sacraments, is both archetype and art.

1 *The Sense of Deep Time*

Obsession with the primeval East is a condition of archetypal possibilities in which the symbolistic act is performed. But this obsession is not a condition created by primitivism. It is subtly related to what may be called the sense of deep time characteristic of Western philosophy and art in the last century. The scientific origins of this sense are too obvious to require comment. From the geology and paleontology of Melville and

Whitman to Eliot's " pair of ragged claws / Scuttling across
the floors of silent seas " (" Prufrock ") , the manifestations of
atavism in American poetry, to name only one province of
recent art, have long since received full critical comment. No
more need be said of them. But it is well to remind ourselves
that this characteristic speculation upon origins, this fascination
with archaic physical forms, is the evidence of a universal state
of both mind and feeling which encourages a contemporaneous
speculation upon the Orient. If the breadth and age of endlessly proliferating life engender the organicism of new scientific
thought, then the antiquity of the Orient inspires the dynamic
" Eastward " regression of primitivistic feeling. (I intend here
a clear distinction between intellection and feeling.) Thus the
paradox, that science, in some quarters regarded as the destroyer
of religious symbolism, actually creates the sense of deep time,
the climate in which new religious symbols are brought into
being. Primitivism has been actively concerned, on the other
hand, with the creation of symbols to encompass science in both
its humanity and its inhumanity. In recent primitivism, an
attempt has been made to expand the symbol to contain the
" gyre," the vortex distending and sundering the man-God relationship as Yeats describes the disparities of existence in " The
Second Coming."

The nature of the symbolist's problem is apparent in Rimbaud's confession:

> I see that my disquietudes come from having understood
> too late that we are in the Occident. Occidental swamps! . . .
> [H]ere is my spirit insisting on taking upon itself all the cruel
> developments that the spirit has suffered since the end of the
> Orient . . . .
> To the devil, I said, with martyrs' crowns, the beams of art,
> the pride of inventors, the ardor of plunderers; I returned to
> the Orient and to the first and eternal wisdom . . . .[2]

Recent primitivism has recorded the search for the God in
whom all gods exist, all evil and all good, the limitless encom-
passment of all being. What the artist sought was the beginning

---

[2] *A Season in Hell* (trans. Varèse), p. 71.

of beginnings in the Hindu Brahma (or Bhagavat or Suryâ), and an iconography of this God in his multifarious and endlessly manifested aspects of being. What he dreamed of was the Oriental ideal of escaping self entirely, of getting back into the vitals of Oriental time *where to be was to exist in God-consciousness*. His new sense of time persuaded him to the possibility of losing identity in timelessness. But what it accomplished was a new sacramentalism to express identity in new terms and images. There could, of course, be no escape from self. For the entity of art can be nothing other than the entity of human feeling, the sovereignty of self. Something of what Gauguin was looking for beyond Tahiti, in the realm of his "Oriental" ideality, is suggested in J.-A. Moerenhout's account of a voyage to Oceania. Moerenhout was impressed with the Tahitian concept of deity (Taaroa), the being of all inclusiveness: God, "himself all and in all; in a word, creator and creature, infinite source of all life, of all movement, and of all action; who would ever have supposed the existence of such a dogma among people whom we call savages?"[3] Gauguin was to write at the end of the century: "Oro [a later god of Oceania] appears to be some kind of errant Brahmin, who carried into the Society Islands—when?— . . . the doctrine of Brahma (of whom I have already found some traces in Oceanic religion)."[4]

Melville's concept of Oro in *Mardi* and Gauguin's idea of the same god are expressions of intuitive feeling in which both artists guess at the antiquity of Oceanic religion. And in the instance of Gauguin's theory, as Oro is traced to the prototype of the Hindu Brahma, hypothesis is actually fact. E. S. Craighill Handy, the Pacific ethnologist, has concluded that Tahiti and its neighboring islands were in all probability the center from which Asiatic influences were disseminated throughout Oceania.[5] Thus the culture of all outlying island areas may be traced to Tahiti. As the traits of this "old" culture are fol-

[3] J.-A. Moerenhout, *Voyages aux Îles du Grand Océan* (Paris, 1837), vol. 1, p. 418.

[4] *Noa Noa* (Paris, Éditions de La Plume, n. d.), p. 192.

[5] *The Problem of Polynesian Origins*, Bishop Museum Occasional Papers, vol. 9, no. 8 (Honolulu, Bernice P. Bishop Museum, 1930), p. 4.

lowed beyond Polynesia to the Asiatic mainland, the true prototypes are discovered in Hindu civilization. Handy finds certain
evidence in the following areas of Polynesian cultural inheritance: craft traditions; rites for the first-born and ancestral
cultism; phallic symbolism; *tabu*; the architecture of the walled
temple with the towerlike shrine; the cultism of *tiki* and other
iconographic symbols.[6] (Melville's description of vast terraces
of stone masonry on the island of Nukuhiva and his account of
a rotting idol in the " taboo groves " [*Typee*, Chs. XXI, XXIV],
are tokens of speculation upon an earlier, prototypic culture.
Gauguin's interest in Tahitian artifacts presumably gave him
some iconographic traces of Brahma.) This search for the
prototype in very large measure accounts for the descent into
Oriental time which both Melville and Gauguin make from
their singular points of contact with these Polynesian inheri-
tances. It is probable that Melville was not entirely aware of
what he was doing with phallic worship in that curious chapter
of *Moby-Dick* called " The Cassock." Phallic symbolism he
had certainly seen in Polynesia. But the impressiveness of Melville's symbol and its relationship to the total symbolic weight
of the White Whale, with his full burden of Oriental mysteries,
suggest an imagination concerned with the original phallicism
" behind " the iconography of *tiki* (the symbolism of fertility)
in Polynesian religion. Melville and Gauguin proceeded by
inclination and intuition through an area of history which
anthropology and ethnology in the twentieth century have described through the methods of science.

In the summer of 1855, near that " critical " period of Melville's residence at Arrowhead, Pittsfield, when his family feared
for " the strain on his health," [7] two friends, Maunsell B. Field
and the artist F. O. C. Darley, stopped by to pay a call. Field's

<hr />

[6] *Ibid.*, p. 14.

[7] See Victor von Hagen's preface in his edition of Melville's *The Encantadas*
(Burlingame, California, 1940), p. vi. The phrase is that of Melville's wife,
Elizabeth Shaw Melville, in her notes of her husband's activity from 1851 to 1856.
" We all felt anxious about the strain on his health in spring of 1853." The
anxiety was actually fear that Melville had inherited his father's insanity.
Eleanor M. Metcalf places the visit of Field and Darley to Melville in the summer
of 1855 (*Herman Melville: Cycle and Epicycle* [Cambridge, 1953], p. 152).

record of the visit is very curious, indeed. " We found Melville, whom I had always known as the most silent man of my acquaintance, sitting on the porch in front of his door. He took us to a particular spot on his place to show us some superb trees. He told me that he spent much time there *patting them upon the back.*" After this strange excursion, all three, visitors and host, set off to call upon Oliver Wendell Holmes, who was summering in the neighborhood. Field says that on this second visit of the afternoon he never chanced to hear better talking in his life. "At length, somehow, the conversation drifted to East India religions and mythologies, and soon there arose a discussion between Holmes and Melville, which was conducted with the most amazing skill and brilliancy on both sides. It lasted for hours, and Darley and I had nothing to do but listen." [8]

Of the first of these scenes it may be said that some will find little to wonder at in the anxiety of Melville's family! Yet, without making much of little, it is certainly true that Melville was being perfectly consistent, amazing his guests in that summer grove of trees. The tree, as an antique, living form, appears in one of the avatars of Melville's symbolism to be discussed; and the somewhat " spooky " reverence in which he approaches the symbol cannot be brushed aside, I think, as either the seizure of a mad man or the whimsical joke of a host who is perfectly aware that he is being watched.

The second scene with Dr. Holmes (and the only extant account of Melville as an academic student of Oriental mythologies) supports the conjecture that there was much more heterogeneous knowledge of the Orient in this mind than was ever disclosed in conversation or in correspondence or in the record of Melville's art. William Braswell, a student of Melville's religious thought, grants that, though Melville did not make " a scientifically comparative study of religions, he was familiar at least in a general way with religions other than Christian." [9]

---

[8] Maunsell B. Field, *Memoirs of Many Men and of Some Women* (New York, 1874), pp. 201–202.

[9] *Melville's Religious Thought* (Durham, 1943), p. 18.

This is a properly cautious estimate. There is no way to determine what Melville had read in the literature of comparative religion. His references to Norse and to Egyptian beliefs, to Zoroastrianism and Gnosticism, as examples, are numerous throughout his work. But they are encyclopaedic, exactly as Whitman's references to the *Ramayana* or the *Mahabharata*, to Kronos, Zeus, or whatever other gods, are encyclopaedic. Furthermore, Melville employs them " cosmically," as does Whitman, as imagistic suggestions of antiquity. Readers of *Moby-Dick* will recall Ahab's " Egyptian " chest (anatomical, here) and the " Chaldee brow " of the sperm whale (since Melville intends to suggest prototypes in both Ahab and the whale). One suspects that his reading had depended on encyclopaedias and serial articles for the Oriental terminology of everything he wrote until he left Pittsfield for New York in 1863.

But it is *feeling*, the feeling which informs the symbol, that governs his use of reference to Oriental religion. Consider the Buddhistic image in the following: " An intense copper calm, like a universal yellow lotus, was more and more unfolding its noiseless measureless leaves upon the sea " (*Moby-Dick*, Ch. LXX). The area of " Oriental " timelessness (from the realm of the artist's feeling) suggested by this image is the locus of the symbolic passage which immediately follows: Ahab's address to the black and hooded " Sphynx's " head of a dead whale hoisted along the ship's side. " Speak, thou vast and venerable head . . . and tell us the secret that is in thee. Of all divers, thou hast dived the deepest. That head upon which the upper sun now gleams, has moved amid this world's foundations. . . . O head! thou hast seen enough to split the planets and make an infidel of Abraham, and not one syllable is thine! " Again it is the same feeling which appears in Ahab's invocation of the " dark " (i. e., unknown, undisclosed) Orient: " Oh, thou dark Hindu half of nature, who of drowned bones hast builded thy separate throne somewhere in the heart of these unverdured seas . . ." (Ch. CXVI). The Hindu half, with its drowned bones, knows what the head has seen in its deepest divings. A third example of this " Hindu " mystery appears in the oily smoke from the try-works: " It has an unspeakable, wild, Hindu odour about it, such as may lurk in the vicinity of funereal pyres " (Ch. xcvi) .[10] What image may be more appropriate to feeling? Melville is suggesting again the " Oriental " age of the whale. Even his essence in smoke is as incalculably old as his body and the dark secrets of his head.

These images revealing obsession with the primeval East are all related to the most complex of Melville's symbols. But the sense of deep time which lies beneath them may be as much disposed toward the Orient when no symbol is present. Imagistic reference independent of the symbol appears in the work of Melville in a manner reminiscent of the usage of Emerson and Thoreau, who are both fond of calling in Oriental time when they intend to reach unusual depth in the image. Consider, for example, Thoreau's seemingly off-hand usage in the following remark from " Wednesday " of *A Week on the Concord and Merrimack Rivers*: " The door is opened, perchance, by some Yankee-Hindoo woman, whose small-voiced but sincere hospitality, out of the bottomless depths of a quiet nature, has traveled quite round to the opposite side, and fears only to obtrude its kindness." [11] This good woman had, of course, not one drop of Hindu blood in her body. A Yankee-Hindu woman is simply Thoreau's poetic idea of an ageless type of human being, as the visitor saw her. It is not enough to call her Yankee and old and kind; Thoreau wants the extra depth of time which he feels in his concept of *Hindu*. Melville does exactly the same thing in *Pierre*. He is describing the great estates of early Dutch patroons in the Hudson valley, as he anticipates the wealth of Saddle Meadows, the ancestral seat of the Glendinnings. " Those far-descended Dutch meadows lie steeped in a Hinduish haze; an eastern patriarchalness sways its mild crook over pastures, whose tenant flocks shall there feed. . . . Such

---

[10] Melville is thinking here, undoubtedly, of the Hindu practice of burning the dead on open funeral pyres. Two possible sources are the *Oriental Memoirs* of James Forbes (London, 1834), vol. 1, p. 177, on the immolation of Hindu widows on the funeral pyres of their husbands; and Horace H. Wilson's *Two Lectures on the Religious Practices and Opinions of the Hindus* (Oxford, 1840).

[11] *The Writings of Henry David Thoreau* (Boston, 1893), vol. 1, pp. 256-57.

estates seem to defy Time's tooth, and by conditions which take hold of the indestructible earth seem to cotemporise their fee-simples with eternity" (Book I, Ch. III). How strange all this is and yet how consistent when one relates it to the primitivistic sensibility of all the great symbols of Melville. Wherever this artist wishes to suggest a seeming timelessness, he may return to the same usage of the image. Consider the creation of a timeless background for the cruise of the *Fidèle* on the "Chinese" Mississippi, in the parable of *The Confidence Man*. The ship itself is "bedizened and lacquered within like imperial junks"; the banks of the river, where all varieties of mortals live, show "a Tartar-like picturesqueness; a sort of pagan abandonment and assurance." [12] There is enough here alone to indicate Melville's persistent reach backward into time, and enough, too, for illustration of his tendency to make every scrap of Oriental lore and every Oriental name, in that undifferentiated, semi-factual Orient of the mind of art, synonymous with antiquity, and with freedom from the brief, chronological time of Western man.

The sense of breadth and age, as this appears in literature in the second half of the nineteenth century, does not, of course, begin in every sensibility with the return to the Orient. Conrad discovered his "melancholy" art in the Congo. The American Charles Godfrey Leland studied the gypsies of Belgium and France and Russia and through them retreated into time. But it should be remembered that Conrad's imagination turned eastward from Africa, even though he was not intent upon life-symbols. And Leland, as Brooks notes, was inevitably drawn to the Orient as he listened in the speech of the gypsies to "words one found in the Ramayana and the Mahabharata . . . the spray of the primitive Aryan-Indian ocean." [13] It must be that the Orient remains an ultimate destiny. It must be that the mind turning toward the Orient has an inclination like that of Lafcadio Hearn as he watched some Hindu coolies at George-

---

[12] *The Confidence Man*, pp. 7, 9.
[13] *The Times of Melville and Whitman*, p. 44. See Leland's *The Gypsies* and *The English Gypsies*.

town, Demerara, in the West Indies: " In the mighty swarming
of India these have learned the full meaning and force of life's
law as we Occidentals rarely learn it." [14]

Hearn's collection of translations in his volume *Stray Leaves
from Strange Literature* (1884) is his excursion into Oriental
" amplitude," with its excerpts from the *Anvari-Soheïli, Baitál,
Mahabharata, Pantchatantra, Gulistan, Talmud* (with the Fin-
nish *Kalewala* for good measure). Here, long before his experience in the West Indies, he dedicates himself to the exploration of Oriental time. But the primitivist who exhibits the
purest intent upon breadth and age is Leconte de Lisle. Where
one reaches finally in Hearn's art the Oriental symbol shaped
by his experience in Japan, in Leconte de Lisle one gets pure
reference to the Oriental past which appears as an imagistic
transcription of Oriental texts rather than as a symbolistic
reincarnation.

The range of Leconte de Lisle's interest is prodigious. He
begins his reading for the background of *Poèmes Antiques* and
Poèmes Barbares in the most widely known French translations
of Oriental mythology available to him: the *Bhagavata* of Burnouf (1840), the *Rig-Véda* of Langlois (1848), and the *Ramayana* of Fauché (1854). He seeks the parent god of all gods
below the Hindu trinity, Suryâ, the sun-god worshipped before
the composition of the Vedas by the plainsmen of the Ganges,
two thousand years before Christ.[15] Thereafter, this strangely
" descending " poet tunnels through time like some troglodyte
miner bent upon approaching the original heat of the earth's
core. The following titles make only a small sampling from his
tunnel: the *Maha-Bharata* of Fauché (1865) ; the *Étude sur une
stèle égyptienne* of E. de Rougé (1858) ; Maspéro's *Histoire
ancienne des peuples de l'Orient* (1860?) ; Moerenhout's essay
on Polynesian genesis in his *Voyages aux îles du Grand Océan*
(1837) ; articles on the Polynesian migrations in the *Revue des
Deux Mondes*; Gaussin's studies of the dialects of Tahiti and
the Marquesas Islands (1853) ; Domenech's *Voyage pittoresque*

---

[14] *Two Years in the French West Indies*, p. 77.
[15] Pierre Flottes, *Le Poëte Leconte de Lisle* (Paris, 1929), p. 103.

dans les Grands Déserts du Nouveau Monde (1860?). These translations and studies provide the material for so extensive a display of antiquity as that presented in Leconte de Lisle's " Egyptian " poem of " Néférou-Ra "; in the two Polynesian pieces, " La Genèse Polynésienne " and " Le Dernier des Maourys "; in the curious North American Indian piece, " Le Calumet du Sachem " from " La Prairie." [16]

Beginning with the first of the *Poèmes Barbares* (" experiments " which initially appeared in the journals of Paris from about 1854), the poetic experience of Leconte de Lisle with the heavy age of human culture becomes the obsessive force of his art. Moerenhout's account of the great Taaroa of the Tahitians is obsessive; so is Suryâ; so is Bhagavat; so is the triune Brahma, made multiple in his containment of Vishnu, the Preserver, and Siva, the Destroyer. For obsession here means the dream of original oneness. Vianey's summary statement is definitive: this is the religion of original nature; the poet dreams " that the pantheism of Oceania was apparently adjacent to that of India and to the conceptions of the Greeks, a tradition, extended in space and in time, which authorizes the religions of nature." [17] This is the sense of Leconte de Lisle's " barbarous " poems. Taaroa of Tahiti is but another name for the original god, as these lines from " La Genèse Polynésienne " interpret him: " In the eternal void, interrupting his dream, / The unique [original] being, the great Taaroa rises . . . / All stirs, the sky turns, and, in his great bed, / The inexhaustible sea is poured out . . . / The universe is perfect from summit to base / And after his work the god rests in ecstasy." [18]

Leconte de Lisle's descriptions express the feeling of being *underneath*, in deep time, as this feeling is suggested by the range of the translations at his disposal. The poet wants the ambiguous feeling of relation to the god in whose being all

---

[16] For these explicative references I am indebted to Joseph Vianey's excellent study, *Les Sources de Leconte de Lisle* (Montpellier, 1907), pp. 1, 99, 101, 262, 267, 270, 272 *et passim*.

[17] *Ibid.*, p. 83.

[18] See Vianey's study of the *Poèmes Barbares* (Paris, 1933), pp. 82–83. The date of the poem is 1859.

gods were conceived. Unlike Melville and the makers of life-symbols in primitivism, Leconte de Lisle deliberately seeks an undifferentiated, amorphous concept. God made manifest in sacrament is not his object. He contents himself with the " law " of the Orient, as this is expressed by Édouard Schuré in an exploratory essay on the nature of the *Bhagavad Gita*: " The infinite and space are alone able to comprehend the infinite; God alone is able to understand God." [19] In this consciousness of God without human comprehension he rests; for this is the original unity which the endlessly proliferating sectarianisms and political systems of a new world have destroyed. There are good arguments for concluding that Leconte de Lisle experiences the return of archetypes. But his poetry does not present a description of the avatar at all, for the very clear reason that he is not inclined in the least toward studying the manifestations of God in the immediate, the present world. Primitivist he is, without question. What he lacks conspicuously is the symbol of sacrament.

Yet how close to Melville he is in the Song of Ganga from " Bhagavat " (*Poèmes Antiques*). Compare Melville's whale discernible to the true whaleman, the carver of the whale in the manner of the Hawaiian spear fisherman, the whale in " bony, ribby regions of the earth," in undulating ridges, in stars, and in the clouds (*Moby-Dick*, Ch. LVII). Removing the voluptuous imagery of Leconte de Lisle, one may see the same outline of the original god in these lines of " Bhagavat ":

There, under the thick dome of purple leafage,
Among the koels [cuckoos] and the variegated peacocks,
Lives Bhagavat, whose face illuminates.
His smile is Mâyâ, the divine Illusion;
Upon his belly of azure roll the great waters,
The framework of mountains is made of his bones,
The rivers have sprung up in his veins, and his head
Contains the Védas, his breath is the tempest;
His gait is at once time and action;

[19] " La Légende de Krishna," *Revue des Deux Mondes*, vol. 87 (3e période, 1888), p. 311.

> The eternal glance of his eye is the creation,
> And the vast Universe forms his solid body.

But this picture of the deity, for all its similarity to Melville's outline of a somewhat more " bony " primal god, is not a personal symbol at all. It is a poetic copy of an Oriental text, and its issue is general rather than specific as an exposition of religious feeling.

Reference to Siva, the Hindu god of suffering and death, is a common phenomenon in the poetry of breadth and age. But even in his description of the god, Leconte de Lisle is faithful to the fact of Oriental mythology rather than to the imposition of unique feeling upon the fact. " La Joie de Siva " of the *Derniers Poèmes* is thus only a transcription of myth. American poetry will provide useful comparisons from the poetry of Whitman, for instance. But, to keep the use of analogy close to the milieu of Leconte de Lisle, one may place beside his Siva an appearance of the same god in the " Là-bas " from *Les Débâcles* of Émile Verhaeren:

> And to contemplate, an impassive and tragical witness,
> Flashing, the iron eyes, and the nostrils, distraught,
> Straight before one, over there, the mythological heaven,
> Where the dread Siva ruffles his chariots,
> Along the golden ruts, athwart the clouds:
> Sparklings of axles and thunders of fires.

This poem reaches these concluding lines:

> And before this charred deçoration, curse
> The man, simple and empty, who gorges himself with hope
> When a symbolic and daily martyr
> Bleeds out his life on the cross, at the four corners of the
>   evening.[20]

To the sensibility of Verhaeren, at the time this poem was written, the emblems of the human world are the emblems of Siva's burning. One begins with the poet in the sense of deep

---

[20] Rendered by Eden and Cedar Paul in their translation of Charles Baudouin's *Psychoanalysis and Aesthetics*, p. 144, in the first six lines; my translation in concluding four lines.

time. If he is Leconte de Lisle, he stops with the description. If he is Verhaeren, or any other maker of the great symbols of primitivism, he continues to a point of recall, where the Oriental prototype is forced into conjunction with symbolic material from the "lost" Christian tradition. Thus Verhaeren's Siva is seized here in the grasp of the imagination and compelled into symbolistic union with the "retained" symbol of the daily martyr bleeding out life on the cross "at the four corners of the evening." Siva is Oriental avatar in the mind of the poet. But, more important, Siva becomes the individuated symbol of primitivism when he is introduced as one pole of two in a true symbol of multiple meaning. In this reading Leconte de Lisle, although he expresses the sense of breadth and age with incontestable power for a whole generation of poets, is not the maker of the characteristic symbol of primitivism. Verhaeren's concern with the "charred decoration" of this immediately present world, that is, this world with its burned ruins of symbolic systems once representing the meaning of human existence, *is* Verhaeren's poem as art. It follows that obsession with the primeval East brings about the most characteristic of all the attributes of primitivistic symbols: their Oriental and Occidental polarities. In the work of artists of primitivism, symbols tend to arrange themselves in opposing groups; and so within the individual symbol, the "split" nature of the artist (i. e., his "Oriental" inclination as opposed to his continuing relationship to his own cultural traditions, as this condition was described in the discussion of Perdita) —this "split" nature tends to reveal itself in a condensed structure of opposing values. A definition of this special character of the symbol is the last preface which must precede examination of representative symbols as avatars.

2   *The Tendency toward Symbolistic Polarity*

I shall refer here to the tendency toward symbolistic polarity as the tendency toward inwardly "crossed symbols," as though there were at least two intersecting planes in the symbol. These planes within the structure come about from *experience in the image*. Baudouin, in his study of Verhaeren, contends that the imagination of the symbolist is not free to wander " through its own devices." " It has, indeed, escaped from rational control, but only to enter the service of sensibility. Thus it is that the symbol comes to be the language of sensibility itself." [21] The sensibility of the artist demands the language of the symbol, and, as Baudouin remarks, when this sensibility is in a state of inner conflict between values, the meaning of *obsessive* symbols may be discovered by tracing the images contained in the symbol to their sources.[22] A " crossed symbol " is an art form in which the " interplay " of opposed values is preserved. Baudouin follows T. Ribot's thesis (*Logique des Sentiments*) when he says that a multiplistic symbol is " an imaginative construction, consisting of associations radiating in various directions, but unified by the unconscious selective process of a dominant desire." [23]

My discussion will agree that associations informing the symbol are radial in this sense; but it will deny that the selective process from desire is unconscious. Else we should have to admit that the artistic act of fashioning the symbol is unconscious and hence productive of an art of undifferentiated, and hence fluid expression. The present discussion must be strictly limited to characteristic symbolic structures in the art of primitivism. Thus the dictum of Baudouin is perfectly appropriate here: *the imagination is wholly guided by the affective life*, by the sentiments, the emotions, the instincts that accompany the images.[24] This is another way of saying that the axial (or radial) structure of the full symbol comes about from experience in the image. Through this affective life, the imagination sets up poles around which the images gather and assume unifying symbolic forms. The interplay of opposed values takes place in that area through which the imagination passes in its progress toward the uniquely fixed symbol.

[21] *Psychoanalysis and Aesthetics* (trans. Paul), pp. 296–97.
[22] *Ibid.*, p. 301.
[23] *Ibid.*, p. 19.
[24] *Ibid.*, p. 16.

Baudouin demonstrates two common polarities in his study of Verhaeren's image of the factory, the oil-mill of the poet's childhood and youth in the village of Saint-Amand. This factory belonged to an uncle who wished to persuade the nephew to devote his life to it. After a year of bookkeeping at the mill, the youth left it with an intense dislike for all the mechanistic drudgery which it represented. The factory appears in the poetry as an object of conflict, and freedom from the factory becomes the condition of the individual will. Factory and the world beyond, as opposite poles, thereafter appear in the multiplistic symbols of the poetry.[25] Another set of these polarities appears in symbols deriving from obsessive images of the faces of clocks. In the poem " L'Horloger " (*Toute la Flandre*) " the clock-faces, now lighted and now unlighted, appear to him by turns as golden or as black; now they are burning eyes, and now again the black eye-sockets of a skull." Baudouin points to the full symbolic value of these obsessions from experience in the image when he notes that in Verhaeren's poetry " gold is constantly used as a symbol of the impassioned in its aspects of fertility and love; blackness is a symbol of death; the clash between black . . . and gold is a symbol of the clash between love and death." [26] Baudouin, however, is more particularly concerned with the clustering of symbols at opposite poles of the poet's art than with polarity inside the symbol. The Siva-Christ symbol of Verhaeren's " Là-bas," noted above, is an example of this inner polarity. Baudouin fails to observe that this poem presents not two symbols, actually, but one. The triumph of Siva over the wasteland of modern man depends upon the expiring symbolic force of the Crucifixion and the Redemption. The power of Siva as conqueror derives from the inertia, the weakness of the " inherited " Western symbol; and the weakness of the Christian symbol is described by the imagined strength of the other. So the meaning of the one intersects the meaning of the other, or " plays upon " the other; and the total meaning emerges in one symbolic containment.

---

[25] *Ibid.*, pp. 39–40. Cf. the poem "Liminaire" from *Toute la Flandre*.
[26] *Ibid.*, p. 58.

It is perfectly natural that these polarities in feeling should be most clearly evident in the symbols of primitivism. Whatever the extent of his journey into Oriental time may be, the primitivist carries with him inevitably the remnants of "lost" symbols in his failing culture. In the artist's "Oriental" experience, the autotypes shaping the symbol of primitivism are specifically facsimiles of experience *in the image*. Siva-Christ in Verhaeren's poem is only an approximation of what actually happens; for Verhaeren has no real Oriental autotypes at all, but only the transmitted myth of Siva as this has reached him through popular report. If the polarities of the symbol are discernible here, how much more clear they become when the Oriental value of the symbol arises from *directly sensed* experience in the image. Then the interplay of opposites is even more apparent in analysis. The archetype of the "dark" god arises as an avatar; in the artist's sensibility it usurps the authority of a traditional religious symbol; the artist, guided by the affective life, imposes certain facsimiles of both Oriental and native Occidental experience upon it; and the multiplistic "crossed" symbol comes into being, as fixed, individuated form. In its nature as art, this form is an incarnation. Every fully wrought symbol representing this incarnation in primitivism shows interplay producing an array of opposing values. It could not be otherwise.

Baudouin proposes that condensation (the polarization of images) is a sign of emotional conflict in the soul of the poet.[27] It is, of course. He reaches, through his examination of this "sign," a representation of a resulting symbol which, although it does not show the actual fusion between opposites, does suggest interdependence. The symbol is usable in two ways, like a reversible sheepskin coat: the inside symbolizes the outside, and the outside the inside. At the risk of quibbling here, I must quickly reject the image of the coat as unsuitable. It implies that only one side may be seen or "sensed" at once. One needs here the impossible coat which could exhibit both outside and inside at the same moment. For we see the polari-

[27] *Ibid.*, p. 10.

ties and grasp them together. Baudouin is more acceptable when he concludes that the terms of all the images in each condensation "symbolize the subjacent affective reality." [28] This subjacency is the "lying-under" of that experience which has met the real and the actual and which is antecedent to each image. The principle may be illustrated through a study of the Tahitian and the European images condensing at opposite poles, or intersecting each other, in the full symbol of Gauguin's *Ia Orana Maria*. (Reference to the analysis presented in the second chapter is appropriate here.) The opposing images symbolize in turn the "grace" of Polynesian life and the convention of the Adoration in the Nativity of Christian tradition. The subjacent affective reality is the autotype or facsimile of experience in each special world (Tahitian or European) represented in each imagistic condensation of the picture.

The tendency of Melville toward symbolic polarity is the most impressive attribute of his imagination. Walter Weber, in a recent study of Melville's custom with the symbol, has proposed that there are several symbolic *layers* or strata deposited here. One goes downward in studying Melville. The layers succeed each other in this order: (1) Biblical materials transposed; (2) Greek myth; (3) the twilight of Egyptian history; (4) Hindu legend. The lowest stratum is "the dark origin of our cosmic cycle, the demon Principle [cf. *Pierre*]." [29] The distinction is useful: Weber is quite aware that Melville presents a symbolic description of the descent into time. The materials which are isolated in Weber's discussion are all involved in the process. But this picture of strata is far from fact. We have here not strata but intricately combined tokens of the differentiated material suggested in Weber's system.

Melville himself confesses very early to this fascination with intricacy. Consider, for instance, his habitual fondness for ships freighted, metaphysically, with the human community, in itself so various and so contradictory. Is not the novice already de-

[28] *Ibid.*, p. 30.
[29] "Some Characteristic Symbols in Herman Melville's Works," *English Studies*, vol. 30 (1949), p. 220.

voted to the " polarity " of the ship as he writes, quite simply, in *Omoo* of his adventure aboard an old wreck at Tahiti? Here he stands in view of the green peaks, the beaches, the palm fronds, the surf of a distant island; and here the old wreck lies, a token of civilization like himself. " What were my emotions when I saw upon her stern the name of a small town on the river Hudson! She was from the noble stream on whose banks I was born; in whose waters I had a hundred times bathed. In an instant, palm-trees and elms—canoes and skiffs—church spires and bamboos—all mingled in one vision of the past and the present." [30] Any sailor may be reminded of home by a name; Melville's distinction here is his insistence upon one vision embracing two disparities.

The evolution of Melville's symbolism is the record of a mounting control over the variety of imagistic experience. It is also the record of an increasing concern for the religious meaning which the symbol may be compelled to embody. It is therefore impossible, I think, to study symbolic form in the mature art of Melville without critical examination of the tendency toward polarity in all his work before *Moby-Dick*. As *Typee* suggests Melville's initial fascination with opposites, so *Omoo* stands as a second work much richer in its display of the same fascination. (Melville's symbolism begins to take form as soon as he begins to write, and not, as some students think, midway in the voyage of *Mardi*. It is simply that he pushes off altogether into the symbol-maker's art at this point.) More important, *Omoo* records the first " clusterings " of opposing values, and the first exploration of possibilities for rendering symbolically the polarities of religious experience. The encompassing vision of the old wreck is but a single token of what happens in *Omoo*. Beneath the visible upper parts of this book (an extension of *Typee*) spreads a most impressive store of opposing images.

The nature of this store or hoard is beautifully represented by Melville in his description of the palace of Pomare of Tahiti. Through the good offices of Marbonna, a Marquesan nurse to

[30] *Omoo*, p. 119.

Pomare's royal children, Dr. Long Ghost and the young voyager gain admittance to a most curious audience chamber.

> The whole scene was a strange one; but what most excited our surprise was the incongruous assemblage of the most costly objects from all quarters of the globe. Cheek by jowl, they lay beside the rudest native articles, without the slightest attempt at order. Superb writing-desks of rosewood . . . decanters and goblets of cut-glass; embossed volumes of plates; gilded candelabras . . . laced hats and sumptuous garments of all sorts . . . were strewn about among greasy calabashes . . . rolls of old tappa and matting, paddles and fish-spears.[31]

This fascinating disarray of native and foreign tribute is presented to us through the same sensibility which attempts to reduce the distance between civilization and savagery suggested by the derelict New York whaler. It is very much as though the youth were here proposing the question: what is the form which may unify two conflicting images?

Melville experiments in *Omoo* with some forms to answer this question. He turns to a study of disparities in the Tahitian Protestant mission church, and to a grotesque description of Miss Ideea, a Tahitian " Christian " maiden. Young Paul asks her whether she is a church-goer. Yes, she is a *mickonaree* (missionary) ! But she is only half so. " ' Mickonaree *ena* ' (church member *here*) , exclaimed she, laying her hand upon her mouth, and a strong emphasis on the adverb. In the same way, and with similar exclamations, she touched her eyes and hands. This done, her whole air changed in an instant; and she gave me to understand, by unmistakable gestures, that in certain other respects she was not exactly a ' mickonaree.' " [32] Miss Ideea is, of course, an object of her observer's amusement. So, too, is the Church of the Cocoa-nuts in Papeete to which her mouth, eyes, and hands belong, if not the more " native " parts. This Protestant mission house is filled every Sunday with frenzied worshippers. Their zeal strikes the visiting Paul as a kind of delightful hypocrisy. Like the people of the adjacent

[31] *Ibid.*, p. 367.
[32] *Ibid.*, p. 210.

island of "Raiatair" (whom he has heard about), they pretend to be wrought up to madness by the preaching, but really
are not at all. Their "fits" are manifestations of a passionate
interest which is assumed for the sake of conformity.[33] Paul is
charmed, too, by the native warders of the church who go about
among the congregation to keep down the noise of conversation
at war with the sermon of the missionary. These disciplinarians
are making more noise than any others of the devout! It seems
to him, all of it, quite comical.[34] He hears the missionary's
flock *bleating* the hymns selected for the service; and he is
amused when he hears the missionary say more of steamboats,
lord mayors' coaches, and the way fires are put out in London
than of aught else! [35] Jack, the Hawaiian, translates for the
preacher, who concludes his sermon by excoriating the Catholic
priests in the neighborhood and by admonishing the congregation to bring plenty of food to his house.[36] How strange,
indeed, to think of London fires in church at Papeete; yet no
more strange, perhaps, than to think of Miss Ideea, with her
convenient double nature.

Melville romps here through some delightful incongruities.
But this mad disarray of opposing images is really not the end
of his reflection. He is moving toward the symbol of opposing
values. For he is immediately drawn to what we understand in
our century as an ethnological question: what he is looking at
and what he is trying to describe is the confusion set up in an
indigenous symbolic system when the symbols of an alien
culture are imposed upon the native religious expression of
the Tahitian. For this insight, to return to a novel earlier discussed, is exactly what Segalen has extended with brilliant success in *Les Immémoriaux*. With the same incongruity before
him, Segalen turns to a description of the confusion from the
Tahitian view. Again we see the flock of the missionary
assembled. When they are told that they must *eat God* in the

[33] *Ibid.*, p. 207.
[34] *Ibid.*, pp. 201–202.
[35] *Ibid.*, pp. 203–204.
[36] *Ibid.*, p. 205.

sacrament offered to them by the priest, they cannot understand: these strangers from unknown lands pretend to nourish
themselves upon their god; but the Maori men eat only of
happiness.[37] Baptism is even more incomprehensible: a man of
the community, Térii, is baptized and he is given the name of
Iakoba, but to his astonishment his body does not change in
form or color.[38] Further confusion attends upon the command
that the head and the heart, and not the entrails, as in old
Tahiti, must be revered as the noble parts of a man.[39] The
symbol of the Virgin is quite beyond reach: she is accepted as
Maria Paréténia (Mary of Britain), and no one knows why she
should be adored.[40] This confusion of symbols so clearly defined in Segalen's novel is the true object of Melville's study
of the incongruous.

It was perhaps inevitable that *Mardi* should have been exactly what it is: a large novel of multiple direction, very far
removed, indeed, from the fairly respectable narrative unity of
Typee and *Omoo*. We have here a record of revelation, an un-
covering, presumably, of the full store of images suggested by
the artist's usage in the two earlier works. It is also the record
of an emerging symbolism. This study will not undertake an
analysis of *Mardi* on these grounds. It should be said, however,
that this book is the most important of all American experimental literary works documenting the development of the
symbolistic imagination. One has in *Typee* and *Omoo* a clear
description of imagistic opposites. When, in *Mardi*, the artist
begins to develop the symbolism which is to follow, we lose the
clarity of description and are presented with various tangles
of potentially symbolic material. These materials are complicated enough in themselves; and since their confused masses
are rendered in an obtuse rhetoric to boot, we find them difficult. Polarity, however, may be defined in them, and at this
point one example will suffice.

In Chapter CVI of *Mardi*, the voyagers land on the island of
Maramma and encounter Pani, a blind priest, who offers to

---

[37] *Les Immémoriaux*, pp. 117, 126.
[38] *Ibid.*, p. 234.   [39] *Ibid.*, p. 245.   [40] *Ibid.*, p. 256.

guide them in the name of Alma to the temples of the realm. It is obvious that Melville has in mind here the blindness of the Christian episcopacy and that Alma, representing Christ, is distorted as a symbol of love and mercy by the perverseness of his ministers. Pani, for instance, demands an exorbitant fee for his service as a guide. The visitors refuse to pay; but, standing aside, they interest themselves in watching Pani extort money and strip clothing from various " pilgrims " who have come to seek his guidance through Maramma (here an allegorical representation of Rome or of some Holy Land on the journey to Heaven). Among the " pilgrims " is Fanna, a " hale matron " of considerable wealth (in the Polynesian sense of wealth). " Calling upon her attendants to advance with their burdens, she quickly unrolled them; and wound round and round Pani, fold after fold of the costliest tappas; and filled both his hands with teeth; and his mouth with some savory marmalade; and poured oil upon his head; and knelt and besought him a blessing." [41] The priest bestows the blessing and then proceeds to strip the clothing from an old beggar. A " sad-eyed maiden," standing near, mercifully covers the beggar with her cloak.

Melville tries here unsuccessfully to make a symbolic abstraction. Unlike the mature symbols which he later achieves, this extremely inept fusion results in a form which is awkward and really uninteresting. But the range of the elements which he tries to combine is startling. They may be designated in about this order: the emptiness of symbols of the Roman Catholic Church; the chicanery of priests and bishops; the Christian practice of making pilgrimages to distant shrines (for there was certainly no such practice in the islands of Polynesia) ; the wealth of the great Polynesian tribal families represented in rolls of *tapa* and in collections of human teeth; (the marmalade appears too obscure to trace) ; the Judaic rite of anointing with holy oil; the Catholic rite of Absolution; mercy and love as represented by the ministry of Jesus to the poor. Fanna and her train bearing precious gifts may possibly derive

[41] *Mardi*, vol. 2, p. 7.

from the story of the Queen of Sheba approaching Solomon (I *Kings*, 10). The interrelationship of these materials is crude, even in the closest scrutiny. As a symbol, the structure tends to spring apart and to lie in fragments. But the symbolistic direction of the artist is there, beyond question. The poles attracting opposite images are partially clear: the votive offering of a Polynesian worshipper (*tapa* and teeth) as opposed to the votive offerings of Judaic-Christian tradition (holy oil, the pomp and circumstance of Judaic-Christian pilgrims arriving with a show of worldly goods). The fragments of the symbol indicate that Melville, in drawing upon quite disparate imagistic areas, was trying to achieve an abstraction to stand for the whole human family. The awkwardness of the structure discourages analysis beyond this point, save the conjecture that Melville saw heaven as unattainable through the rites of any *traditional* religious symbolism, whether Christian or pagan.

I take it that all genuine symbols as abstractions make possible, as Wordsworth saw it, " the perception of similitude in dissimilitude " (*Preface* of 1800). But it is one thing to abstract from the really disparate natural forms contributing to a landscape (as in certain "spots of time " revealed in *The Prelude*) or from the contending dissimilarities of several sensations experienced at one and the same moment in a city; and it is another thing to abstract from opposite human values, where these values are already represented in countless disparate images swept up by sensuous experience. All great art renders a similarity which had not hitherto existed, in the real world. But the interplay of values which has been described is not a universal process in all symbolism. Interplay is a characteristic and special process in the art of primitivism.

What had happened to Melville's talent for abstraction through the " exercise " and the trial and error of *Mardi* is evident when one comes to his next work, *Redburn*, especially when one compares a passage here with the description of the derelict whaler at Papeete in *Omoo*. For now Melville's symbol of the ship carrying the human community is nearly completed. Control of the images has been established. This ship is to be transformed again and again. It is to become the *Neversink* of *White-Jacket*, the *Pequod* and the ships of the gams in *Moby-Dick*, the *San Dominick* of *Benito Cereno*, the *Fidèle* of *The Confidence Man*, the *Indomitable* of *Billy Budd*. As a symbol, it is not admissible to the group of avatars to be examined in the following chapters. But it is useful as a companion symbol in its distinctive mastery of clearly defined polarities. For each of these ships, symbols of the human community, contains, symbolically, the extremes of innocence and depravity, civilization and " savagery." In *Redburn* the young Wellingborough sees at Liverpool the *Irrawaddy*, newly arrived from Hindustan.

> The captain of the vessel was an Englishman, as were also the three mates, master, and boatswain. These officers lived astern in the cabin, where every Sunday they read the church of England's prayers, while the heathen [Lascars] at the other end of the ship were left to their false gods and idols.[42] And thus, with Christianity on the quarterdeck, and paganism on the forecastle, the *Irrawaddy* ploughed the sea.
>
> As if to symbolize this state of things, the ' *fancy piece* ' astern comprised, among numerous other carved decorations, a cross and a mitre; while forward, on the bows, was a sort of devil for a figure-head—a dragon shaped creature, with a fiery red mouth and a switchy-looking tail.[43]

This symbol, unlike those of *Mardi*, holds. Furthermore, Melville is more clearly aware of what he wants to convey. Now, it is highly probable that he did not see at Liverpool such a ship with a dual emblem of dragon, and cross and mitre. It may be doubted that any ship of any registration of the period would have been doubly marked with such pagan and Christian devices. But veracity, if it is of importance to maritime history, has no significance here. What we discover in the *Irrawaddy* is a characteristic obsession of Melville's feeling: the necessity of an art to encompass both the Oriental pole and the Occidental

---

[42] Melville's mature rejection of traditional Christian symbolism is not complete, I think, until he begins the composition of *Moby-Dick*. Note a passage in praise of churches in *Redburn*, Ch. XLI. The sensibility described is that of young Wellingborough, or, in fact, that of Melville himself at the age of 19.

[43] *Redburn*, pp. 219–20.

pole. The necessity is to be fully answered in the structure of the White Whale.

The duality of the *Irrawaddy* is clearly related to the method of *Moby-Dick*. Perhaps it is useful, finally, to call attention to the simple fact that this book, as one sovereign symbol of Ishmael's quest for new symbols of existential meaning, is attentive constantly to opposite values, from beginning to end. In New Bedford, Ishmael is confounded by opposites as he passes through the entry of the Spouter-Inn (Ch. III). On one wall hangs that strange dark picture of a Cape-Horner in a hurricane; its three masts are just visible above a yeasty, boiling sea, and a great whale is in "the enormous act" of impaling himself on the three mast-heads. On the other wall is a collection of "heathenish" clubs and spears, the emblems of Oceanic savages, and a harpoon that was found in the hump of a great whale attacked by whalemen once in Javan seas and slain, years afterward, off northwest Africa. Outside, in the street (near the very chapel where the word of the Christian God is preached), one can see actual cannibals, turned seamen, "many of whom yet carry on their bones unholy flesh" (Ch. VI). And long afterward, in space and time, Ishmael, the orphan of Ahab's world, clings to the coffin of Queequeg, the savage, in that desolate sea where the "devious cruising" *Rachel* comes searching for her missing children. Between Ishmael ashore at the Spouter-Inn and Ishmael adrift over the sunken *Pequod* lie the great symbols of opposites which the following chapters will discuss.

In conclusion, it is clear that Melville's tendency toward symbolistic polarity depends upon his persistent obsession with the primeval East; and it is generally true of Melville, as of Gauguin, Hearn, and Loti, to name other artists who follow him, that symbolistic polarity invariably means East (Oceania or the far Orient, or both) as opposed to West. The process toward the symbol now becomes demonstrable. The rich matrix of feeling in which the art symbol takes form is enlarged; it is given a new shape by the demands of feeling; it becomes heavy with both Western and Eastern "possibilities."

The " pulling " force is the awakening sense of deep time. The possibilities are the multifarious stores of experience in the image, all tending to cluster about the loci of opposing values. There, in the deep mind of art, a new reality is proposed. The sensibility presiding over this new growth is feeling informed by Ishmael's sense of loss among the expiring symbols of the fatherland. His native symbolism can no longer stand as a configuration of reality. Then the new reality must become the new configuration, if he is to represent the meaning of existence; and in the new art to which he dedicates his deepest acts of creation, the symbol compelling unity from a new disparity is formed. This disparity between East and West is new only in that it had hitherto been of no consequence in those earlier " Western ages " when Christian man could rest in the fatherland among symbolic structures the ultimate reality of which he was not moved by feeling to question.

It must seem, at this point of discussion, that I have used certain metaphors for the symbol which conflict. Initially, in my description of cultural failure, I spoke of the autotype (imagistic experience in Oceania and the Orient which produces facsimiles of feeling) as a die impressing material potentially sympathetic or susceptible to religious symbolism. Thereafter, I spoke of an art of primitivism which calls feeling to incarnation. In this chapter I have spoken alternately of an organic process in the symbolistic act, and of the polar structure produced by this process. Here, in my description of symbolic form, I have used terms appropriate to the image of the symbol as the " medal " employed in the introduction to these chapters. Lest it appear that these metaphors are haphazard and irreconcilable, I wish to make clear my distinction between the organic process of incarnation and the memorial character of the symbol as *fixed emblem*. Two levels of meaning are here involved. The first, the meaning of incarnation, is the concept that God is made manifest in embodiment. He appears in a visible form, which, being visible, was, is, or may be sensuously as well as spiritually known by man. Thus, in Christian dogma,

God has been seen on the earth, incarnate in the Son. Incarnation as concept underlies the symbols of sacrament. On the second level of meaning the symbol is the emblem of the concept. Thus, in the Christian Eucharist, the holy wafer is the emblem of God incarnate in the Son, the wine the emblem of the sacrifice of God for man. This is the minimum significance which the bread and wine, as tokens of the incarnation, may have in Protestant tradition. The maximum significance of these symbols as emblems appears, of course, in the Roman Catholic dogma of the Real Presence, in which concept and symbol become one in the faith that the consecrated bread *is* flesh and the consecrated wine, blood. The practice of intinction in the celebration of the Mass is a further extension toward unity, when the bread is dipped in the wine, and flesh and blood are unified. When one proceeds to the question of sacramentalism in art, it would be, of course, quite absurd to contend that any art symbol becomes the equivalent of these symbols of the Eucharist. It is nonetheless true that the concept of incarnation is again the substructure underlying sacramental symbols in art. Primitivism recognizes the human need for sacrament in its question: what are the symbolic forms which may represent the manifestations of God incarnate?

When these levels of symbolic meaning are understood, it is clear that the symbol in primitivistic art represents the concept of incarnation, organically conceived, and that in its *fixed form* it has its own special meaning which is the artist's reality as much as the elements of the Eucharist are reality to the wholly faithful Christian communicant. Each primitivist celebrates his own Mass alone, with his own symbols of meaning. And now, to dispense with any difficulty which may have risen from my seeming inconsistency in metaphor, I must recall the definition of sacrament earlier offered for use in this study. Sacrament is essentially a symbol of corporate subscription in any religious custom which expresses the concept that through corporateness the individual is made one with his fellows in communion with the deity.

Certainly corporate subscription to the symbol of art is nonexistent. Gauguin's *Ia Orana Maria* serves *fully* only Gauguin; Melville's Billy Budd serves *fully* only Melville. But this fact does not prohibit the symbol from the area of meaning described by sacrament. The symbol is the artist's compensation for lost sacrament. And the arresting character which it shows is its polarity, and hence its *impurity*, when it is compared with the purity, or better, oneness, of such a symbol as the Eucharist. In order to emphasize the difference strongly, a comparison of the Host with a hypothetical symbol from the religious art of primitivism will be useful. The imagistic origin of this Host cannot, I think, be denied. It is visually conceived from the broken bread of the Last Supper. But, in the theological traditions and dogmas of Christianity, the Host reaches the communicant as a pure symbol. It *means* God incarnate in the body of the Son, broken for man. It is the bread of the faithful through this breaking, and no other. It possesses, in its authority over a realm of feeling, a thorough symbolic oneness. But let it be supposed that the primitivist has substituted a sacrament of his own making in art. Both imagistic and symbolic purity would then disappear in the primitivistic symbol; complexity in the symbol would inherit in this loss of one value, and the symbol would propose, through its polarity, recognition of *more than one* manifestation of God incarnate. In this service of the symbol as an emblem of feeling conceptualized, the " impurity " of sacramental forms in primitivism is inevitable.

The epistemological character of this introduction will be justified, I think, as the method of the following analyses is revealed. The avatars to be examined will all show in some way polarity of values drawing imagistic facsimiles to opposing positions, and they will all appear as fashioned from archetypal material in the mind obsessed with the Orient. It would be foolish to claim that the sacramentalism of these avatars can be uniformly defined. I contend only that they are entirely susceptible to clear analysis which will lift them from ambiguity, and that they all show in some way the marks of the search for sacrament. The symbols tell us what the primitivist wants in sacrament: they tell us what he has lost and what he would newly put there, and in this revelation of feeling art becomes a form of knowledge. Melville compels to the incarnation of art his ideality of Polynesia as that realm of earth most able to offer proof for the divinity of man. Various readers of Melville will reach various judgments upon his success in giving form to this ideality. But since art is not answerable to any charge whatsoever of failing to present proof, I do not think it matters at all how successful, how consistent, how pure his sacramentalism referring to Polynesia and the Orient may be. What one wants in a study of art is mastery of the formal elements of symbols. In the examination of these elements, the conditions of cultural failure, the sense of deep Oriental time, the tendency toward symbolistic polarity determined by experience in the image are all subject to analysis. These conditions bring the symbols of primitivism into being. But the power of these symbols to interest us as works of art cannot, of course, have anything to do with their logicality, their mystery, or their ultimate effectiveness as substitutes for orthodox Christian sacrament. They are the artist's symbols for existential meaning; they are his reality.

Puer Aeternus:
Eternal Innocence

All that has been said of the Protestant mind in its man-God relationship of I-You is historical preface to neo-sacramentalism. The Protestant artist's sense of his impoverishment makes the new symbol of sacrament inevitable. Ishmael in the desert of I-You, in the "desymbolized" Protestant world defined by Jung, is the condition of the creative mind susceptible to obsession by the archetype. The first thing to acknowledge as fact in the nature of this archetype, whatever its content, is that the unconscious area it represents is neither Oriental nor Occidental. The true archetype is universal. Symbolic authority from any religious system may obscure it altogether. But the removal of this authority will uncover and at once permit it to assert itself. Theoretically, one may expect to find cults of snake-handlers in Borneo, in the Sudan, in Brazil at exactly the same moment he finds them, on some hot Sunday afternoon, in the pine flats of Georgia or South Carolina. The snake as archetype is everywhere known. There is nothing distinctly Oriental or South American or South Carolinian or what not about it. In the collective unconscious of universal man it is merely there. But in the sense of the avatar which has just been defined, it becomes Oriental (whether in the true Orient or not) when the artist, encountering it within his own feeling, shapes it in such a way as to give it a major Oriental reference. The images of Oriental origin which he employs establish this reference.

In the sense of Jung's theory, an *archetype of transformation* is a theme (the snake as one example) which marks the passing over of a commonly shared collective, without imagistic identity, from the areas of the unconscious to the areas of the conscious, wherein the collective is expressed in typical images. Jung's examples of such archetypes are extensive. In beginning a discussion of *puer aeternus*, the eternal youth, it will be useful to review some of these examples with specific reference to Melville. The archetypal richness of his work should be suggested, at least, even though it is certainly not my intention to offer a study of all the archetypal materials present in this art.

Melville may be thoroughly studied through Jung, of course, if one wishes to examine archetypes without attention to the nature of the unique symbol of the artist. I shall first quote some of Jung's examples, and then invite attention to some forms and incidents in Melville's work which may be studied in relation to Jung's distinctions. Jung writes:

The birds and mammals are various forms of the sanguine instincts, whereas the serpent, the saurians, and monsters personify primordial, cold-blooded animal nature, and, as adversaries of warm-blooded, emotional nature with its panic excitement, are anticipations of everything divinely pre-eminent. Cave and sea refer to the unconscious state with its darkness and secrecy . . . . Fire is emotional excitement or sudden bursts of impulse . . . . Weapons and instruments represent the will.

To the intermediate symbols belong . . . hanging, soaring, or swimming. Here, too, the tree has its place, or transformation into a tree, and represents rootedness, repose, growth, and a spreading forth in the upper regions of air and light, as also the union of sky and earth.

The hero and the *puer aeternus* may appear as themes throughout the whole process.[1]

My choice of themes from Jung's categories is deliberately limited, since I wish only to propose figures and episodes from Melville which appear promising for study. Melville's albatross of *Moby-Dick*, in the footnote to the chapter on whiteness (XLII), shows such a bird-archetype as an anticipation of the "divinely pre-eminent." (So, too, does the albatross of Coleridge's *Ancient Mariner* show the same "divinity.") Melville's obsession with the serpent appears at various points in his work in the form of the anaconda (to be discussed in a later chapter on imagery) ; and the sanguine instincts of mammals contending with the primordial, cold-blooded nature of the serpent may be seen in an obsessive image in *Redburn* (Ch. xx) of the whale swallowing Jonah "like an anaconda, when it swallows an elk and leaves the antlers sticking out of its mouth." Numerous descriptions of the sea, particularly those appearing in *Moby-Dick*, will provide examples of the "dark and secretive" unconscious. Ahab's address to the corposants (*Moby-Dick*, Ch. CXIX) and the fire of the try-works (Ch. XCVI) signify excitement and impulse. Ahab's will is represented by the harpoons. Billy Budd's hanging, Pip's descent through the primeval waters (*Moby-Dick*, Ch. XCIII) , White-Jacket's fall from the yard-arm into the sea (*White-Jacket*, Ch. XCII) all suggest Jung's intermediate symbols of hanging and swimming. The tree and its relation to the Christian cross will be interpreted in a chapter to follow. At this point Melville's notice of the tree tattooed upon the back of the mysterious Marnoo of *Typee* (Ch. XVIII)

---

[1] *The Integration of the Personality*, pp. 93–94.

may represent rootedness, repose, light (and the union of nature and man). These examples suggest the archetypal character of Melville's symbolistic expression. But it is the archetype of *puer aeternus* which presides over all of them. For it is the image of tattooed Polynesian and of innocent youth-outcast in the civilization of the Christian West, made one, which authorizes the symbols of sacrament displayed in Melville's primitivism.

Puer aeternus as Melville's full symbol is the emblem of corporateness, of communion with and in God. There can be no doubt of his obsession with sacrament, for he himself describes it in a confession to Hawthorne. As I shall presently show, the symbolic content of *puer aeternus* is the ideality of fraternal love between men, wherein the identity of one is discovered in the identity of the other. Melville's symbol is made of two disparate elements: the ideality of Polynesian friendship and the ideality of Christian communion in the Eucharist. It is perfectly clear in Melville's symbol that the inherited Christian ideality, no longer able of itself to command faith in a doctrinal reality, is brought to life in a new form by the addition of Polynesian reference. When this act occurs in Melville's art, it is perfectly clear, again, that the new sacramental symbol expresses a new reality: it means that the absolute self is relinquished to fraternal love and that the emphasis upon the self-act of Christ's suffering is exchanged for emphasis upon Christ as the innocent man among men. Despite Melville's professed resistance to Emerson's major theory, in this act he comes closer to Emersonian insistence upon Christ in the world, as a man, than any other American author.

Melville's concept of his relationship with Hawthorne is sacramental. Hawthorne has written to Melville his letter on *Moby-Dick* (November, 1851), that lost letter which every student of American letters would reclaim before any other American literary document, if he could. And Melville replies:

Whence come you, Hawthorne? By what right do you drink from my flagon of life? And when I put it to my lips—lo, they are yours and not mine. I feel that the Godhead is broken up like the bread at the Supper, and that we are the pieces. Hence this infinite fraternity of feeling.[2]

The confession speaks for itself, and I shall not labor it. Melville's reference to *feeling* here must be understood for what it means. The fraternity of feeling offered to Hawthorne is the fraternity of selfless innocence, not the fraternity of men wrested from evil by the suffering of God. Melville brings to Hawthorne the feeling of Polynesian friendship, *tayo*, the same feeling which shapes the full symbol of Billy Budd, both innocent Tahitian and Christ, made one. Billy is the apotheosis of *puer aeternus*.

1 Tayo

Melville's ideality of selfless acceptance is expressed in *tayo*. This Polynesian word means *friend* or *friendship*, but it names a relationship which Melville and other travelers in the Pacific have seen as uniquely Oriental. Its equal is not to be found in the West. The custom of *tayo* is one man's acceptance of another man as his equal sharer. In the bond between the two, what one possesses, the other possesses; what success one has, the other shares; what adversity one encounters, the other must bear. This relationship usually comes about in early youth, and it may continue through the lifetimes of the two so bound together. The marriage of each will normally follow, and the rearing of children; but these extensions of experience only widen the area of mutual responsibility in the bond which has been established. The ideality represented in *tayo* is distinctly Oriental. In it appears a union of two persons similar to that denoted by the sacrament of marriage in the Christian world. Ignorance of the meaning of *tayo* will, of course, permit vulgar errors in interpretation. Melville's confession to Hawthorne is no more than an expression of Melville's feeling about devotion between men as the release of self into selflessness. One may extend this fact by saying that he had the sense of men's

[2] Printed by Eleanor M. Metcalf in *Herman Melville: Cycle and Epicycle*, p. 129.

love represented by Christ and the apostles. Or the sense may be Chinese, as it is described by Saint-Denys: " Perfect solidarity, mutual support, the sharing of both good and bad fortune between friends joined by a sort of marriage; such is the germ of strong cohesion which from the earliest times has possessed the Chinese race. In modifying the form of the pact, the centuries have not altered its essence." [3] But this sense in Melville, whatever parallels may be found for it, was a sense developed through his Polynesian experience and through his quest for sacrament, the feeling of oneness in communion. Hawthorne could scarcely have known the origin of Melville's offering, which he could not accept with an equal fervor (for some have said, and perhaps rightly, that Hawthorne's decision to go to his consular appointment in Liverpool may have been to some degree influenced by a desire to escape Melville's intensity). The origin of Melville's ideality, as this took shape through his natural talent for friendship, was what he had seen and felt of Polynesian *tayo*. (When the prototypes of Polynesian culture are recalled, then this custom would seem to derive from the far Orient.)

Melville's definition of *tayo* appears in *Omoo* (Ch. xxxix). He relates that the arrival of his ship at Tahiti brought to the sailors troops of " tayos " " eager to form an alliance after the national custom, and to do our slightest bidding." He remarks that the annals of the islands preserve the histories of many " Damon and Pythias " friendships; and he speaks of Polynesian hospitality in the extension of *tayo* to the first white visitors reaching the islands. Then he turns to a description of the youth who was his faithful friend while he was ashore at Papeete.[4] But *tayo* is not new to him here. He had already acquired the sense of it in Typee Valley. His account of his friendship with Kory-Kory and other men of the tribe and his

---

[3] *Poésies de l'Époque des Thang*, preface: " Étude sur l'art poétique en Chine " (VIIe, VIIIe, IXe siècles A. D.), p. xxix.

[4] In the following chapter of *Omoo* (XL) Melville presents another *tayo*, one Kooloo, who is an opposite of Poky. Kooloo professes great friendship in order to cajole gifts from the sailors; he is quite faithless. Melville's play with the theme at this point means little when the significance of *tayo* elsewhere in his work is considered.

description of the mysterious youth Marnoo (*Typee*, Ch. xviii) show his earliest interest in the nature of Polynesian fraternity. It is abundantly clear, furthermore, that in his experience among the people of Nukuhiva he had already begun to think of that union in fraternal love which reaches its highest expression in the "marriage" of Queequeg and Ishmael in *Moby-Dick*.

The literature of primitivism shows frequent examples of thematic relationship between the *puer aeternus* and the friend. This archetype of fraternal love is a clear distinction of primitivism through the last century. Even in the work of authors in whom religious sensibility has no importance, the theme is present and potentially capable of what Melville does with it. The first of English "primitive" novels, Thomas Hope's *Anastasius* (acquired by Melville in 1849) [5] presents Spiridion, the childhood friend of the hero. Anastasius alternates between wishing to worship at the Christian altar with Spiridion and wishing to assert his freedom as a visitor in Islam. The love of Spiridion is ideal and selfless: "To see me wise, to see me happy, and that through his exertions; nay, to sacrifice, if necessary, his own repose and felicity on this globe to mine, became the only bliss Spiridion aspired to on this earth!" [6] Here *puer aeternus* as archetype follows the familiar theme: the youthful wanderer completes his identification of self in the friend, even though Hope's achievement amounts only to a representational token of sentiment. Another example may be found in the narrative of Jack London's adventurer David Grief. This crude and tedious hero-voyager in Polynesia is admired by Mauriri, a native youth of the island of Fuatino, who makes complete the Polynesian voyage of the narrative as David's faithful *tayo*.[7]

The friend as he is presented in these widely separated accounts does not reach the status of the true life-symbol. In the art of Melville a different resolution of the archetype

[5] See *Journal up the Straits*, ed. Weaver, p. 19.
[6] London edition of 1836, vol. 2, pp. 350–62.
[7] *A Son of the Sun*, p. 88.

takes place. The voyager and the friend tend constantly toward symbolic union; and the evidence of this tendency is apparent in the prefigurations of Melville's early work. The full symbol of the mature art is to be made of two elements: the ideality of Polynesian *tayo*, and the thematic figure, on the other hand, of the solitary voyager who may be described here as the " sailor savage," to use Melville's term from the image employed in the discussion of seamen carving the likeness of God (*Moby-Dick*, Ch. LVII) . The sailor savage is the " receiver " of *tayo* extended; and in Melville's final symbol, Billy Budd, the dichotomy is removed altogether as Billy himself becomes both wanderer and Polynesian friend.

It is obvious to every reader of Melville that the theme of the search for union in friendship is projected through nearly all his work. *Israel Potter, The Confidence Man*, and some of the stories should perhaps be excluded, since friendship in these pieces is not centrally encountered. But even here the theme of the voyager in solitary pursuit of reality through communion with his fellow beings continues. The other works are all in varying degrees concerned with the same theme. A review of the relationships of Ishmael which may be adjudged as expressions of reality through communion will be of interest here. They are found in these patterns: in *Typee*, Tom—Toby, Kory-Kory, Marnoo; in *Omoo*, Paul—Dr. Long Ghost, Poky, Shorty; in *Mardi*, Taji—Jarl; in *Redburn*, Wellingborough—Larry, Carlo; in *White-Jacket*, White-Jacket—Jack Chase; in *Moby-Dick*, Ishmael—Queequeg; in *Pierre*, Pierre—Charlie Millthorpe; in *Clarel*, Clarel—Rolfe, and the Lyonese. In each instance the pattern is of primary importance; in some of its uses it is essential in the structures of the works. When these patterns are studied for what they mean in the area of Melville's feeling as he described it to Hawthorne, they present the central fact of his primitivistic tendency: reality may be expressed through symbols of existential meaning which represent fraternal union.

Puer aeternus governs the pattern of the communal relationship. It becomes the avatar of reincarnation from the Orient when the themes of *tayo* and the innocent sailor savage meet in Billy Budd; and the prefigurations of both *tayo* and sailor point ineluctably to what is to come. The imagistic foundation of Melville's feeling for *tayo* is encountered very early in his work. The prototype of the Polynesian friend is Marnoo, the mysterious visitor to the valley of the Taipis.[8] Marnoo contributes to the symbol of fraternal love, as this fills the emptiness of Ishmael's I-You relationship with God. Marnoo as prototype and Marnoo transposed into Queequeg, for instance, mean feeling toward fraternal relationship. Furthermore, the sensuous character of images describing Marnoo tells us quite directly that impressive physical beauty, actually seen by the eye, orders the artistic form in which *tayo* is to be initially represented. The contention that the eye has seen the things which are abstracted by the imagination into symbols is equal, in my analysis of primitivism, to a law of the symbolistic process.

Marnoo (*Typee*, Ch. XVIII) arrives upon the scene quite suddenly. Young Tom fears that the stranger may persuade the inhabitants of the valley to do him harm, so great is Marnoo's obvious popularity in the community. But Tom is immediately seized with amazement at the beauty of the youth. His form has a matchless symmetry, his limbs are beautifully modeled; his beardless cheeks suggest the face of Apollo and are of a feminine softness; his hair, a rich curling brown, twines about his temples and his neck in close ringlets; and over his body spreads a richly profuse pattern of tattooing, the spine traced with the "diamond-checkered shaft" of the "artu" tree. The tattooing is of the brightest blue, contrasting with the light olive color of the skin; and over the loins Marnoo wears a slight girdle of white *tapa*. The visitor engages the inhabitants of the valley with his startling charm; and then he approaches Tom and asks questions of the youth. In his conversation with Marnoo, Tom learns that Marnoo is *tabu*. No one can harm him, since his person is held sacred by all the tribes of the Marquesas. Marnoo

---

[8] To Richard Chase belongs the distinction of having first recognized the symbolic importance of Marnoo. Chase sees in him Melville's first sketch of the hero-voyager, the man who accepts "the psychological and cultural substance of life" (*Herman Melville*, p. 4).

has been abroad, to Sydney, as cabin boy to the captain of a
trading vessel; hence his knowledge of English. We are not told
when he became *tabu* or why he enjoys this sacred distinction.
In his brief meeting with Marnoo Tom is fascinated. For here
is Melville's first encounter with Polynesian masculine beauty,
displayed in color, grace, and unstudied charm, which suggests
the store of images acquired through observation and a totally
receptive sensuous nature. Marnoo's tattooing seems, at this
point, to pass into the symbol of the Tree of Life; his *tabu* protects him from harm; the white girdle becomes a representational
mark of primitive innocence. Since he receives more attention
than any other character of *Typee*, that is, attention revealing
physical attributes, it may be proposed that his tattooing is
prototypic for the tattooing of Queequeg, and his *tabu* a prefiguration of the freedom and innocence of such a figure as
Jack Chase, who serves aboard an instrument of evil and suffering, the warship *Neversink* in *White-Jacket*. (Jack Chase is, in
turn, prototypic for Billy Budd.) The white girdle of Marnoo
passes into the symbolism of whiteness surrounding the figure
of Billy. Already one sees in Melville's ideality of *tayo*, as he
thinks of Marnoo's excellence, the vision of manly and youthful
friendship as a manifestation of God.[9]

Tayo has received in the *South-Sea Idyls* of Charles Warren
Stoddard the same notice which Melville gives it, save that
Stoddard's symbol of ideality does not pass from the area of
description into the area of the sacramental symbol, as Melville's is to do in *Billy Budd*. Stoddard's *tayo* is Kána-Anà in
the story "Chumming with a Savage." The same archetypal
theme of *puer aeternus* governs again. The meaning of *tayo*
is embodied in images expressing physical grace and beauty,
which in turn reflect innocence and purity. The voyager lands
at an unnamed island (Maui in the Hawaiian group?) and joins
a native community where people do not know " that it is one
of the Thirty-nine Articles of Civilization to bully one's way

---

[9] Thirty years after the composition of *Typee* Melville seems to recall the
beauty of Marnoo and the significance of *tayo* in a scene of *Clarel*. See his
description of the young Lyonese Jew (Part IV, Sec. xxvi, " The Prodigal ").

through the world." [10] His "fellow barbarians" hate civilization as much as the visitor and are "quite as idolatrous and indolent as I ever aspire to be." In this new vale of Typee, Kána-Anà is the faithful friend. Stoddard describes him with almost the same intensity which Melville feels for Marnoo. "His sleek figure, supple and graceful in repose, was the embodiment of free, untrammelled youth. You who are brought up under cover know nothing of its luxuriousness." [11] The effect of sensuous experience appears here in *luxuriousness*. But how really important is the distinguishing absence of tattooing! Melville's attention to this art of adornment has already been reviewed as one of the major consequences of his Polynesian voyage. Tattooing serves him so indispensably in his later symbolism that one may almost say it represents in his sensibility the total ideality of *tayo*, as well as the mystery of God in man.

2   *The Sailor Savage*

The prefiguration of *puer aeternus* as the sailor savage begins with Melville as Tom of *Typee*, the same savage who is to be

[10] *South-Sea Idyls*, p. 55.

[11] *Ibid.*, p. 26. For an account of *tayo* in the narratives of Louis Becke see "Te-bari, the Outlaw" in *The Call of the South* (London, 1908), pp. 191–202. The author is accompanied for two years by the faithful Suisuega-le-moni from Tanumamanono in Samoa.

I have omitted Robert Dean Frisbie from my discussion of the lineage of Ishmael (Chapter IV) because I do not find his studies of Oceanic life—excellent as they are—symbolistic in the expression defined. Furthermore, I consider him less authoritative than Louis Becke in his readings of the Polynesian personality. He is more clearly related to the art of Nordhoff and Hall than to that of Melville and his successors. Nonetheless, I must call attention to Frisbie's description of Polynesian friendship in *Mr. Moonlight's Island* (1939) as the most informative and accurate account in American literature. Frisbie uses the relationship of two native youths of Danger Island, George and Toa, as a theme of the narrative. He contends justly that the love conventions of Oceania are governed by *tabus*. George and Toa are united in *tayo*. Thus it is George's duty to separate Toa from his amatory relationship with one young woman of the community so that he may know the "salutary adventure of promiscuity" among many women (pp. 100–101). Later, in the chapter "Birth on a Coral Atoll," a child is born of Toa's adventure with the first woman of his experience; and it becomes the office of George, as the equal sharer in friendship, to support the mother in labor and to assist in the delivery of Toa's child.

named Ishmael in the first sentence of *Moby-Dick*. The ideality
of *tayo* provides the first element of the sacramental symbol
which Ishmael makes of his archetypal theme. The second element is provided by the sailor savage whom Ishmael meets.
He is the " savage " of Christendom, as Marnoo and his Polynesian brothers are the savages of the uncivilized (i. e., the non-
Christian) world. The sailor savage is called by Melville the
Handsome Sailor, as this epithet is given to Billy Budd. The
first of the handsome sailors encountered as the friends of
Ishmael is, of course, Toby of *Typee*. This character (Richard
T. Greene, Melville's shipmate on the *Acushnet*) is described
by Tom (as Ishmael) in an image which is the most usual of
all Melville's conditions of the hero. " He was one of that class
of rovers you sometimes meet at sea, who never reveal their
origin, never allude to home, and go on rambling over the
world as if pursued by some mysterious fate they cannot possibly elude." [12] Toby is " slightly made "; his dark complexion
is matched by the dark locks clustering about his temples and
the darker shade in his large black eyes (Ch. v). Melville's
description suggests the symbol to come as he interprets Toby's
voyage, the first voyage of the Handsome Sailor, as the journey
of the unknown wanderer. One is at once impressed with the
symbolistic tendency: to divorce the wanderer from the knowledge of his origin, to make his meaning as a human being
general rather than specific. It is this general reference which
Toby ever afterward possesses in Melville's recollection. Thus
Toby is transposed to the poetry of *John Marr and Other
Sailors* (1888) where he becomes Ned Bunn.[13] Ned's poem
appears in the " Minor Sea Pieces " published with " John
Marr ":

> Ned, for our Pantheistic ports:—
> Marquesas and glenned isles that be
> Authentic Edens in a Pagan sea.

Now Melville turns back to the sailor savage of *Typee*. In

---

[12] *Typee*, p. 40.
[13] See Howard P. Vincent's notes, *Collected Poems of Herman Melville* (Chicago, 1947), p. 472.

these " glenned isles " and " authentic Edens," this savage was free of bondage to the laws of the Christian pilgrimage. Like Marnoo, he was *tabu*; he was safe; no one could harm him. These lines of " John Marr " show Melville's own recognition of union between the Ishmael-voyager and his sailor savage companion:

> Twined we were, entwined, then riven,
> Ever to new embracements driven,
> Shifting gulf-weed of the main!
> And how if one here shift no more,
> Lodged by the flinging surge ashore?
> Nor less, as now, in eve's decline,
> Your shadowy fellowship is mine.
> Ye float around me, form and feature:—
> Tattooings, ear-rings, love-locks curled;
> Barbarians of man's simpler nature,
> Unworldly servers of the world.

(I have already disclaimed any concern with the disorders and encumbrances of Melville's verse.) The image of entwining here represents the symbolic fusion accomplished between Ishmael and shipmate.

The relation of the sailor savage to the sea influences Ishmael's devotion, beyond question. The archetypal significance of ocean as the element over which the voyager travels is that of timelessness—eternity. The sea is primitive and timeless; the ego is subsumed by the sea; and here man returns to his first objective in his atavistic longing for origins. All the major pilgrimages of Melville's books, save those of *Pierre, Israel Potter*, and *Clarel*, take place on water. The seaman becomes by association primitive and eternal like the sea beneath him. This feeling for the life of the mariner is, after all, the feeling of Conrad's artistic concept in his men of the sea, those, for instance, of *Typhoon*, and the feeling of O'Neill in his play *The Moon of the Caribbees*.

But to illustrate Melville's feeling here, Loti is particularly appropriate. *Pêcheur d'Islande* expresses the same feeling toward the sailor savage. Pierre Flottes offers a description of the *dénouement* of this novel which serves the study of Melville as

well as that of Loti. Yann, as Loti's symbol from the archetype
of *puer aeternus*, is the "savage" of the voyage (just as Melville's heroes all stem from the race of sea savages). Yann is
lost in the end to the sea, after sea and woman (Gaud, who
wishes to marry him) have contended for the possession of his
love. Flottes considers the conclusion of *Pêcheur* a superior
symbol. The drama of woman against sea is over, and Yann is
wedded to the ocean "with her virgin and generative joys of
force." [14] So it is, indeed, a symbol of arresting power.
Throughout the novel we have seen the "savagery" of Yann,
his sense of loss when he is ashore, his attainment of existential
meaning when he is sustained upon water. The sea seems to
give him his savage nature, for even in play his caress is often
very near brutal violence.[15] His heart is a virgin region, difficult
to govern, unknown.[16] Yann's brother, Sylvestre, tells Gaud
that Yann has promised himself in marriage to the sea,[17] and on
the appointed wedding night with Gaud (representing the ties
of home, identification with the land) the wind roars to remind
Yann of his betrothal to another.[18]

In my discussion of Loti in an earlier chapter, I suggested
that *Pêcheur* stands closer to *Moby-Dick* than any other novel
of its time. I had in mind particularly a similarity of artistic
vision: the sea "with her virgin and generative joys." It is this
mighty sea forming the nature of the man who sails upon her
waters that brings these two books together. They are united
in the archetype of *puer aeternus*, who is primitive like the sea
over which he wanders. For as unknown aeons of life sprang
from the mysteries of the sea's generation, in those darker
depths, so the sailor savage who sails over the surface, the man
who knows her upper and virgin joys, is man carrying in him
all the time of human history. Loti, like Melville, thought of
the tie, the "betrothal" of man to the sea as the oldest relationship of man to nature: civilized man is savage in his role as
mariner.

[14] *Le Drame Intérieur de Pierre Loti* (Paris, 1937), p. 111.
[15] *Pêcheur d'Islande*, édition Calmann Lévy (Paris, 1939), p. 13.
[16] *Ibid.*, p. 161.   [17] *Ibid.*, p. 72.   [18] *Ibid.*, p. 223.

Thus the theme of sailor savage is identified in Toby and in Ned Bunn; and nearly all the art that lies between the two shows this civilized savage again and again. When one proceeds to *Omoo*, he finds him in Dr. Long Ghost, Paul's companion ashore; he finds him, too, in Shorty, whom the two adventurers meet at Imeeo, near Papeete. Like Marnoo, Shorty is twenty-five. In his blond good looks and his radiant temperament, he is a prefiguration of Billy Budd, and he seems to reflect Jack Chase whom Melville, of course, had already known aboard the *United States* before he wrote *Omoo*. "His cheeks were dyed with the fine Saxon red, burned deeper from his roving life; his blue eye opened well, and a profusion of fair hair curled over a well-shaped head." [19] Like Billy Budd, he sings at work. Shorty passes symbolically into honest Jarl of *Mardi*. Now the sailor savage becomes a Scotsman who was yet "an old Norseman to behold" (*Mardi*, Ch. III). The love which binds him to Taji becomes the symbol of universal love. Jarl's language is a universal "Lingua-Franca of the forecastle." "Ah, Jarl! an honest, earnest wight; so true and simple, that the secret operations of thy soul were more inscrutable than the subtle workings of Spinoza's" (Ch. III). And Redburn, following *Mardi*, replaces the excellent Jarl with Larry, an ordinary seaman aboard the *Highlander*. (Harry Bolton, Wellingborough's English companion in Liverpool and London, who signs on for the return voyage, must be excluded here. He is a youth of the land and its vices, not the savage of sea-going life.)

Before leaving *Redburn*, this summary must digress for an interpretation of Carlo, the unlettered Italian boy who travels aboard the *Highlander* on the return voyage to New York. Carlo is not a sailor; but he belongs with the company of the hero-voyagers. There is much here that prefigures Billy Budd, and much that recalls Marnoo. Melville's portrait is the most sensuous of his art after the description of Marnoo, and it deserves careful study for what it reveals of the obsessive image.

[19] *Omoo*, p. 243.

The head was if anything small; and heaped with thick clusters of tendril curls, half overhanging the brows and delicate ears, it somehow reminded you of a classic vase, piled up with Falernian foliage . . . .

His whole figure was free, fine, and indolent; he was such a boy as might have ripened into life in a Neopolitan vineyard; such a boy as gypsies steal in infancy; such a boy as Murillo often painted, when he went among the poor and outcast, for subjects wherewith to captivate the eyes of rank and wealth; such a boy, as only Andalusian beggars are, full of poetry, gushing from every rent.

Carlo was his name; a poor and friendless son of earth . . . .[20]

Carlo is a musician. He had come ashore at Prince's Dock, Liverpool, some months before, from a vessel bound in from Messina, carrying with him a hand-organ; and with his music in the foggy streets of the port he had collected enough to pay his passage over the Atlantic. Aboard the *Highlander* he entertains the passengers and earns his board. The primitive excellence which he shows in every word and look and gesture is approximate to the perfection of Marnoo, Jack Chase, and Billy Budd.

But it is the obsessive image of Polynesian beauty which orders the ideality expressed in Carlo. Melville describes his eyes as shining " with a soft and spiritual radiance, like a moist star in a tropic sky," speaking of " humility, deep-seated thoughtfulness, yet a careless endurance of all the ills of life." [21] As the music of the organ is recalled, images of antiquity crowd upon Melville's mind, images of Saracens, Persians, of Greek and Judaic myth. The tribute to Carlo continues:

Play on, play on, Italian boy! . . . let me gaze fathoms down into thy fathomless eye;—'tis good as gazing down into the great South Sea, and seeing the dazzling rays of the dolphins there.[22]

These images of " moist star in a tropic sky " and of gazing through Polynesian waters at the dolphin illustrate Baudouin's

[20] *Redburn*, p. 319.
[21] *Ibid.*, p. 319.
[22] *Ibid.*, p. 323.

subjacent affective reality. Carlo is in part described for what he was; but he is in part rendered in an image which Melville had acquired in waters adjacent to the Polynesian youth, as he was seen in Nukuhiva and Tahiti. The image is the more striking when it is studied in its first form in *Typee*, in a scene immediately preceding the appearance of Marnoo. Young Tom, bathing with the "nymphs" of the valley, relates that they swam like a "shoal of dolphins," tumbling him about and ducking him (*Typee*, Ch. xviii). This blending of imagistic experience is vitally related to Melville's symbolistic process, in which the focal centers of opposing cultures are united in the concept. The sight of the innocent wanderer seems to invoke Polynesia immediately in the consciousness of Melville's art.

Thus, the same dolphin image appears in the description of Mortmain, the Swedish outcast of *Clarel*. Here the subject is a youth who was illicitly high-born and cast into the world with only wealth to sustain him. As the wanderer from society, he frequents the gray places of earth. Derwent, one of the pilgrims, offers consolation to Mortmain, "the dream of fair redemption": he tells of a wreck adrift which he once saw at sea, and of the rainbow cast over it from the spray of a gamboling dolphin (*Clarel*, Part ii, Sec. iv). The wreck represents Mortmain as the derelict of society, the dolphin the same "careless endurance" associated with Carlo. For it is Carlo who seems to be recalled in Melville's description of a Palm Sunday procession in *Clarel* (Part iv, Sec. xxxii), when the image is employed to describe a group of young singers, "a rainbow throng, like dolphins off Madeira." In the poem "Jack Roy" (*John Marr and Other Sailors*, 1888), the dolphin image returns with the same evocative power. Melville recalls another wanderer gifted with the careless endurance, the complete acceptance of Carlo; and once again the unreasoned perfection of Polynesian innocence becomes Melville's ideality of the sea-going hero. Jack "vaults over life" like that "iridescent arch," the rainbow cast by the dolphin. The associations revealed in these instances show that the dolphin is an emblem of Polynesian life and that the contexts in which it appears invariably mean the life of innocence and acceptance in contrast to the civilized life of law, convention, vice, egocentricity, Prometheanism.

After *Redburn*, the prefigurations of Billy Budd become still more clear in the sailor savages of *White-Jacket*. The inimitable Jack Chase as a prototype for Billy Budd is known to every reader of Melville. The significance of Melville's dedication of his last work to this comrade has long since been recognized. Jack is a scholar, a reader of Byron, Shakespeare, and Homer, and an ardent admirer of Camoëns; he is a linguist; he is a skilled mariner in his post at the fore-top; he is the perfect companion, " better than a hundred common mortals." [23] But most of all, he is the man of acceptance; like Jack Roy, he " vaults over " life. Ishmael on the *Neversink* finds him the master hero-wanderer. With him in the ship's company are two other youths, Peter and Frank, both known and admired by White-Jacket. Peter is a handsome lad of nineteen and a great favorite in his mess. He is flogged by the boatswain's mate for his " crime " of fighting on the gun-deck with John, a malignant rascal of the crew. The scene (Ch. XXXIII) prefigures Billy Budd's " crime " in striking down the malignant Claggart. Frank is another shipmate, a genial boy whom White-Jacket sometimes singled out for conversation, " a very handsome young fellow, with starry eyes, curly hair of a golden colour, and a bright, sunshiny complexion: he must have been the son of a goldsmith." [24] Billy Budd's physical attributes seem to take form from these images of Peter and Frank; his strength comes directly from Jack Chase just as his innocence, expressed in his singing, recalls the musical Carlo, and his Polynesian good humor, the ideality of *tayo*.

But for all Jack Chase's relationship to Billy Budd, who is really a younger and unlearned Jack, I do not think that Melville makes here as obvious a transfer as he does in creating Rolfe of *Clarel*. Rolfe is Clarel's companion, like the sailor savage, the man of perfect acceptance; and he is surrounded in

---

[23] *White-Jacket*, p. 14.
[24] *Ibid.*, p. 303.

Melville's description of him with the familiar images of Polynesia. He appears as the voyager into the waters of the tropics. He possesses a genial heart and an austere mind. He is a man given to study, but no " scholastic partisan." Clarel thinks of his union with Rolfe as the closing of two halves of an apple. These two natures are united under the sign of the tropics: " To him here first were brought together / Exceptional natures, of a weather / Strange as the tropics with strange trees, / Strange birds, strange fishes, skies and seas." [25] The " weather " is the area of feeling in which the communion of friendship is realized. This, again, is the friendship offered by Melville to Hawthorne.

The last of Melville's sailor savages for notice here, the friend who is no sailor at all, has the meaning of sanity as clearly distinguished from insanity. He is Charlie Millthorpe, the friend of Pierre Glendinning. Charlie is the sanity of primitive acceptance; Pierre, the real son of Ahab in Melville's art, is insanity, the overreaching absolutist who finds his end in an indifferent God.

> Thus does Pierre burn his *mementi*, the memorials of his past life: " Of old Greek times, before man's brain went into doting bondage, and bleached and beaten in Baconian fulling-mills, his four limbs lost their barbaric tan and beauty; when the round world was fresh, and rosy, and spicy, as a new-plucked apple;—all's wilted now!—in these bold times the great dead were not, turkey-like, dished in trenchers, and set down all garnished in the ground, to glut the damned Cyclop [sic] like a cannibal; but nobly envious Life cheated the glutton worm, and gloriously burned the corpse; so that the spirit up-pointed, and visibly forked to heaven! " [26]

These words are but Ahab's curses in another language: the oaths against life itself, the destruction of the quadrant, and that baleful wish for a bough of cherries before death comes to him under the furious lashings of the unconquerable God. How quietly Charlie Millthorpe, Pierre's friend of boyhood, he whose heart was " a far more excellent and angelical thing "

---

[25] *Clarel*, vol. 1, pp. 121–22.   [26] *Pierre*, p. 276.

than brain,[27] stands there opposite to this young Ahab. Not long before the end of his bitter quest Pierre reflects: ". . . the god that made [Charlie] Millthorpe was both a better and a greater than the god that made Napoleon or Byron.—Plus head, minus heart—. . . the heart's the preserving salt itself, and can keep sweet without the head." [28]

Heart, in this denunciation of head, means feeling distinguished from reason. *Tayo* and the sailor savage are Melville's prototypes of feeling. Each expresses an ideality made of the artist's experience, and each has its own store of images to describe the affective reality of that experience. It remains true, both in these prototypes and in the prefigurations of Billy Budd, that feeling (heart) governs with an undiminishing control; it is equally true that feeling controls in the master symbol, the avatar of Billy Budd. But some will say: this feeling is sentimental. So it may be to antagonists, if they are as well prepared to say that the sacraments of the Christian faith are the same. Whatever their judgments of sacrament may be, it happens that the elements of Billy Budd as a symbol are these provinces of feeling which have been described.

3 *Billy Budd*

It cannot matter whether *Billy Budd*, the story, is the capstone of Melville's art or not. Various critics have advanced it as Melville's testament of acceptance, his resolution of the problem of good and evil; and as many others have found it less important than *Moby-Dick* in this respect. It is studied here not as a moral allegory (allegory representing the life of reason, the life of the head), but as a full achievement of the symbolistic imagination governed by feeling. As the archetype of the primordial whale becomes the avatar of God the unknowable in *Moby-Dick*, so the archetype of *puer aeternus* becomes in *Billy Budd* the avatar of God the knowable through the communion of fraternal love, innocent, free of self-conscious-

[27] *Ibid.*, p. 389.
[28] *Ibid.*, p. 445.

ness, carelessly enduring. This avatar of Billy becomes sacrament in an art form when it is completed with the symbolic pole opposite to the state of innocence of *tayo* and the sailor savage. The new pole, represented in the execution of Billy by hanging from the main-yard-arm of the ship, is the crucifixion of Christ. Thus Billy becomes the symbol of sacrament in which the innocence of *tayo* and the innocence of the sailor savage (itself envisioned, as I have shown, through various Polynesian images associated with *tayo*) are unified with the innocence of Christ. The symbol takes the place of the Eucharist, even as it preserves the images of the cross in the yard-arm and the fleece of the Lamb of God, the vestigial emblems of an orthodox symbolism. At the moment of his execution Billy Budd represents the body of God. But I wish again to emphasize that the element of Christ in the symbol represents Christ the innocent among men, not the suffering Christ of the cross. The agony in Gethsemane, the ascent of Calvary, the cries from the cross have no place here. These hours of the Passion represent Christ in the act of reason and hence in Promethean suffering, Christ the tragic hero. Melville's rejection of the tragic hero, whom he studies in *Moby-Dick* and in *Pierre*, prefigures the rejection which he makes here. He presents, instead, Christ as the innocent among men, Christ freed of that dogma in which the emphasis falls most heavily upon Christ crucified. Thus this avatar of Billy as sacrament, with its reference to the pagan Orient of unreasoning acceptance, is heretical from the orthodox Christian view. It equates the ideality of Polynesian friend and the hero-voyager with the ideality of Christ. The equation is formed in the private domain of the artist's feeling.

Melville's dedication of *Billy Budd* to Jack Chase must now be regarded as an ascription of the sacramental symbol to Ishmael's fellow voyager bound to him in fraternal love. Early in the story Melville recalls a native African sailor whom he once saw in the street of Prince's Dock, Liverpool. He was magnificent in his impressive stature and in his abounding good humor. As he strode along, each of his shipmates crowding around him rendered a spontaneous tribute to this " black pagod of a fellow—the tribute of pause and stare, and less frequent an exclamation." These sailors " showed that they took that sort of pride in the evoker . . . which the Assyrian priests doubtless showed for their grand sculptured Bull when the faithful prostrated themselves." [29] We thus approach Melville's symbol through this adoration of the faithful, these who are the lawless, innocent wanderers, the priests of an image of God. When Billy is about to come aboard the *Indomitable* from the *Rights-of-Man*, we learn that he has been made the object of the same priestly adoration by the men of the ship from which he is transferred. On the *Indomitable* Billy wins the same devotion. Every reader knows his excellence. As foundling, exile, outcast, sailor, he is the apotheosis of the sailor savage: he is an Englishman of pure Saxon strain, touched by a Greek sculptor with the look of Hercules; " noble descent was as evident in him as in a blood horse "; [30] he might have passed for a statue of young Adam before the Fall; [31] he is free of self-consciousness; he is illiterate, but he can sing; he is an upright barbarian,[32] and to deal in double talk and insinuations of any sort is quite foreign to his nature.[33] " The sailor," remarks Melville later, " is frankness, the landsman is finesse." [34] The landsman's life is a chess game, which he plays out in tediousness and obliqueness by the light of a poor candle. Opposite to Billy's innocence and his barbaric perfection is the malevolence of Claggart with the finesse, the guile, and obliqueness of society. Once, it will be remembered, he looked upon Billy as though he could have loved him, " but for fate and ban." But Claggart (even as sailor) is the player of the chess game, hating with all the passions of the civilized world the spectacle of frankness. The structure of the story need not be retraced once more. All the values which it presents are familiar. I am concerned only with the nature of Billy as the

[29] *Billy Budd and Other Prose Pieces*, pp. 5–6.
[30] *Ibid.*, p. 16.
[31] *Ibid.*, p. 68.
[32] *Ibid.*, pp. 16–17.
[33] *Ibid.*, p. 12.
[34] *Ibid.*, p. 58.

sacramental symbol. The meaning of Melville's sailor savage emerges from its early prefigurations to its apotheosis in Billy's death.

Billy does not understand the chaplain who would prepare him for death because he does not understand, in turn, the meaning of Christian suffering and the fear of death. As the sailor savage of careless endurance, he is unable to contemplate absolutism or Prometheanism. To Billy, God has one meaning —love; but as Melville presents him, the love he knows is the love of his fellow sailors, as primitive men, not the love of landsmen in Christian civilization. The cry " God bless Captain Vere " as Billy mounts the ladder and submits to the noose is not the cry of a stupid youth; it is a cry of unreasoning accept-ance which reveals an ideality of complete selflessness. The Polynesian origin of Melville's concept is made known in the interview with the chaplain.

> If in vain the good chaplain sought to impress the young barbarian with ideas of death akin to those conveyed in the skull, dial, and cross-bones of old tombstones; equally futile to all appearance were his efforts to bring home to him the thought of salvation and a Saviour. Billy listened, but less out of awe or reverence, perhaps, than from a certain natural politeness. . . . And this sailor way of taking clerical discourse is not wholly unlike the way in which the pioneer of Christi-anity, full of transcendent miracles, was received long ago on tropic isles by any superior *savage* so called—a Tahitian, say, of Captain Cook's time or shortly after that time.[35]

As the account of this scene with the chaplain moves on, it is Billy's indifference to death which establishes him as the true spiritual descendent of the Polynesian savage. " This sailor way of taking the discourse " is the way of the sailor savage, and the way of the innocent Polynesian. Thus the object of life is the pagan act of loving, not the doctrinal Christian act of learning how to die in the sense of guilt and in suffering, and in answer to the preacher of redemption. By this one stroke Melville reveals his total feeling for the communion of man, and his

---

[35] *Billy Budd and Other Prose Pieces*, pp. 97–99.

scepticism toward doctrinal Christianity with its insistence upon absolute truth in the civilized world of Promethean anguish.

Thus Billy Budd, as the full symbol containing both Polynesian innocence and the original innocence of Christ in the world as man, hangs from the main-yard-arm in a new crucifixion. The civilized evil which raised him there and took his life is of God, too, as Melville had already presented the all-encompassing unknowable God in the White Whale. But it is evil, the reasons for which man may not know. Billy does not question them. In the limits of man's feeling there is only the capacity to know God in his manifestation as fraternal love. Billy is an avatar, one reincarnation of a God of limitless aspect. In other forms this God may destroy the man who seeks him through reason. Captain Vere's bondage to the absolute of man-made law is the proof of another form of God; so is Claggart's evil, made by "fate and ban." At four o'clock in the morning, as the dawn breaks from the east, Billy blesses Captain Vere and selflessly yields to death. But this death is met indifferently by an innocence that has never felt the sickness of ego. "The vapoury fleece hanging low in the East, was shot through with a soft glory as of the fleece of the Lamb of God seen in a mystical vision; and simultaneously therewith, watched by the wedged mass of upturned faces, Billy ascended; and ascending, took the full rose of the dawn." The sacramental crucifixion and ascension are marked by a strange murmur among the men. "Whoever has heard the freshet-wave of a torrent suddenly swelled by pouring showers in *tropical* mountains, showers not shared by the plain; whoever has heard the first muffled murmur of its sloping advance through precipitous woods, may form some conception of the sound now heard." [36]

It was inevitable that Melville should have returned here to the Polynesian image. What we hear is the sound of water falling from mountain escarpments in the Marquesas or Tahiti, after a sudden inland shower. Thus the obsessive vision of

[36] *Ibid.*, p. 105. Italics mine.

Polynesia marks the last pages which Melville wrote. His setting for the symbol of Billy in his crucifixion is attended by the sound of grief and reverence in the murmurs of his shipmates who, through the image, become Polynesian worshippers, emblems of *tayo*. Even the scene of the worshippers, touched with the light of the sun in a sacramental ceremony, had been prefigured long ago in *Mardi*. The voyagers with whom Taji travels land on the isle of Serenia (Ch. CLXXXVII). There one needs no temples, no shrines, no precepts; there only the love of Alma, the original Christ—Christ free of all dogma—is known. For Alma gave his laws to Mardi (Earth), not to Paradise; and in Serenia " reason no longer domineers." There the voyagers kneel before the old chieftain of Serenia, " and as the old man blessed them, the setting sun burst forth from mists, gilded the island round about, shed rays upon their heads, and went down in a glory—all the East radiant with red burnings, like an altar-fire." Melville had long ago visualized this last setting; only the sunset is exchanged for the dawn of Billy Budd's execution. For in this sacrament of an unsuffering youth, the symbol of Christ is made new again as Melville summons the ideality of Polynesian selflessness and the testament of innocence to the reality of man's communion in God.

VII

Polynesian Ethos

Ethos is the character of a community; it is the spirit which animates customs, especially moral attitudes and practices. Ethos as character is the expression of a governing morality. To this concept I add here the significance of ethos as wisdom which represents the particular genius of any community for expressing and acting out the values of its existence. In the historical sense, Gladstone, Disraeli, and Lincoln, as examples, are wise men through the expressions of communal values which their careers singularly provide. Each expresses in thought and action the moral attitudes commonly shared by the community which he represents. The contemporaries of these men who proposed in thought and action denials of these communal values are adjudged, in true historical perspective, as unwise in relation to their respective cultures. The expressions of a common morality in the acts of a dictator, let us say, no matter how odious these may be to a foreign observer, are wisdom in proportion to their faithfulness to the native moral attitudes motivating them. In the religious sense, the same concept of wisdom pertains. The priest, the man of holy orders, is wise in proportion to his expression of the custom and the morality which govern his dogma and his exemplary conduct, no matter, again, how antithetical this dogma may be to a priest or a communicant of an alien faith. Thus, the wise man, as the representative man possible for the expression of any communal (or tribal) wisdom, appears in the continuity of human consciousness as an archetype. He may be the " elder statesman " of any government or the ancient adviser to princes; he may be the witch-doctor of Madagascar, the Hindu ascetic sage, the Biblical Hebrew prophet, the Greek seer, the " elder " of any religious sect. Whoever he is, he is the wisdom of the community.

Polynesian ethos is the representative character of a people of primitive Oceania; the wise man expressing this ethos is the tribal sage. He is the apotheosis of primitive custom. In the art of Melville he is a character named Queequeg, who as the second of Melville's sacramental symbols, the second of the avatars discussed here, is made of the universal archetype of the wise man and the Polynesian ideality of wisdom which the artist imposes upon the archetype to give it form. It has been seen that *puer aeternus* impressed by the idealities of *tayo* and the sailor savage becomes a new symbol of sacrament which is exchanged for the symbol of the Christian Eucharist. The symbol made of the wise man impressed by Polynesian ethos, as understood by Melville, supplants the sacrament of holy orders of the Christian faith.

Billy Budd and Queequeg are Melville's true sacramental symbols as avatars of reincarnation from the Orient. The avatars which follow these in my discussion are related to sacrament, but their implications are primarily theological. By this statement I mean that if one examines Melville's sym-

bolism in relation to the seven sacraments of Catholic orthodoxy, he discovers that Melville's artistic consciousness and
religious sensibility are concerned only with the third and the
fourth. The experience of Melville as Protestant limits his
concern to the Communion and the office of the minister.
When he has arrived at satisfactory symbolic equivalents for
these, he turns to an expression of feeling toward the nature of
God, and the avatars which follow display, consequently, less
concern with symbolic expression of man's communion with
his fellows in God. As Polynesian *tayo* provides the great autotype for the making of sacrament from the archetype of the
youthful voyager, so Polynesian ethos provides the autotype for
a new sacrament made of the archetypal wise man and the
Christian symbol of the priesthood or the ministry.

At this point it must be clearly understood that Melville's
holy man is not a preacher. In my review of Melville's experience in Polynesia I proposed that the young voyager to the
Marquesas was attracted strongly toward the " ideal " disintegration of religious formalism in Typee Valley. He rejoiced to
find the idols in decay, for this freedom from an unyielding
tradition made possible the condition of the artist of the " Hawaiian " war-club or spear-paddle (*Moby-Dick*, Ch. LVII) , carving the likeness of his God as he pleased. Thus Queequeg does
not preach, and he worships his little idol in the Spouter-Inn
as he likes. He is a holy man free of holy orders. But this is
not to say that he expresses less wisdom in this condition of his
freedom. His every action is an expression of the ethos of his
people. Furthermore, Queequeg, in his one purely sacramental
act as the " obstetrician " delivering Tashtego from the great
sperm whale's head (*Moby-Dick*, Ch. LXXVIII) , officiates as wise
man, not as priest.

It seems to me that Melville committed an artistic error
when he chose Tashtego as the man to be immersed in the
oily skull of this whale. He ought rather to have let Ahab fall
into it! In this scene Tashtego is hauling up the precious oil
of the whale's head, bucketful after bucketful, from the great
" tun " of the skull. But suddenly he loses his hold on the

tackle and slips from his balance into this " Tun of Heidel-burgh " with " a horrible, oily gurgling." It is a perilous mo-ment. Then Queequeg comes to the rescue. With his " sword " he opens the head near its base and pulls out Tashtego, head foremost, from his oily tomb. The image of parturition is perfectly clear. But the head as a symbol is equally clear: it is the head of God, as though here, for the moment, Moby Dick himself had been captured and decapitated. Melville is think-ing, of course, of the sacrament of baptism, as the act of Chris-tian initiation into the knowledge of God. For he goes on to say that Tashtego might have perished in that head, just as the " many " who have fallen into " Plato's honey head, and sweetly perished there." But Queequeg does not bring Tash-tego from this baptism in God with prayers and benedictions. He rather assumes the symbolic function of freeing Tashtego from an oily death in the inscrutable mysteries of God, freeing him through pagan indifference to those enigmas which Mel-ville calls at the end of the chapter " the secret inner chamber and sanctum sanctorum." For Queequeg's wisdom is a Poly-nesian wisdom of acceptance which has already been seen in the ideality flowing into the symbol of Billy Budd. Logically regarded, Tashtego is not really the man who needs to be rescued. That man is Ahab. But such a " delivery " of Ahab would have obviated the whole artistic purpose of *Moby-Dick*, of course, even though some readers who hate the absolutism of Ahab might like to see him either brought to primitive acceptance or else drowned in the oil of God.

A second condition of Queequeg to bear in mind is that he inherits, in his form as Melville's wise man, the ideality of *tayo*. But in him it becomes a paternalistic *tayo*. Ishmael has wandered with his sailor savage's quest for fraternal love, and he has found it in the friends described in the last chapter. Now Ishmael is to receive *tayo* again, the devotion of Queequeg and half his worldly wealth as a pledge of that love. But he is to receive more as well. He is to be taught wisdom, particularly the wisdom of selflessness and the wisdom of how to accept God, and of how to die.

1   The Ideality of Queequeg

Queequeg as the holy man is patriarchal. At the outset, an impressive archetypal analogy for this patriarch may be comparatively studied in the art of Conrad; and it must be at once evident in the analogy that Conrad's symbol reveals the limitations of a lesser symbolistic imagination. The character about to be presented is rich only with the archetype of the wise man and Conrad's autotype of an old sailor who must represent scores of such men seen by the novelist during the years of his voyages. Here Conrad appears as the maker of a simple representational symbol rather than of the complex symbol of religious sensibility. The scene is the deck of the *Narcissus* in *The Nigger*. An old sailor is reading Bulwer-Lytton's *Pelham*.

> Old Singleton, the oldest able seaman in the ship, sat apart on the deck right under the lamps, stripped to the waist, tattooed like a cannibal chief all over his powerful chest and enormous biceps. Between the blue and red patterns his white skin gleamed like satin; his bare back was propped against the bell of the bowsprit, and he held a book at arm's length before his big, sunburnt face. With his spectacles and a venerable white beard, he resembled a learned and savage patriarch, the incarnation of barbarian wisdom serene in the blasphemous turmoil of the world.[1]

Conrad's Singleton resembles a savage patriarch; Melville's Queequeg, in the realm of the symbolist's feeling, *is* this man of wisdom, the incarnation of barbarian serenity. Melville certainly thinks of Queequeg as a priestly man in the opening chapters of *Moby-Dick*, as will be seen. But he is actually faithful to the archetype which appears in this character of Conrad: barbarian wisdom rather than religious formalism is his symbolistic objective.

In confronting the archetype to be resolved in the fixed symbol, Melville depends upon a counter-reference, an opposing symbolic pole, in many of his descriptions of Polynesian char-

---

[1] *The Nigger of the "Narcissus,"* in *Collected Works* (London, 1950), vol. 18, p. 6.

acters. He is fond of referring to what he imagines to be the
oldest and most " ideal " prototype of Occidental wisdom, this
prototype conveniently counterbalancing the Oriental prototype in Polynesian ethos: he refers to Greek beauty and wisdom.
Let us suppose that Queequeg is one of the " tattooed Greeks "
in the following passage from *Clarel*. At the monastery of Mar
Saba, Clarel's companion Rolfe (Jack Chase transformed) reflects upon the Easter rite of the Syrian-Greek church and the
religious " festivals " of the Polynesians (Part III, Sec. xvi) :

> Never I've seen it; but they claim
> That the Greek prelate's artifice
> Comes as a tragic after-piece
> To farce, or rather prank and game;
> Racers and tumblers round the Tomb:
> Sports such as might the mound confront,
> The funeral mound, by Hellespont,
> Of slain Patroclus. Linger still
> Such games beneath some groves of bloom
> In mid Pacific, where life's thrill
> Is primal—pagan; and fauns deck
> Green theatres for that tattooed Greek
> The Polynesian.—Who will say
> These Syrians are more wise than they,
> Or more humane?

The Greek prelate's " artifice " is the Syrian-Greek rite commemorating the visit to the Holy Sepulchre. Melville, through
Rolfe, speculates upon the origin of the rite in the religious
pre-Christian festival games of ancient Greece. The racers and
tumblers receive their symbolic equivalents in the " games "
(probably Melville is thinking only of tribal dances) of the
" tattooed Greek," the Polynesian. Apart from the interesting
question proposed at the close of this passage, as this relates to
Melville's rejection of fixed truth and religious absolutism, the
meaning of " primal thrill " depends upon ancient Greek and
Polynesian juxtaposed. If we then suppose, for the moment,
that Queequeg is one of these strange Greeks in a " green
theatre " of some island in Oceania, we see that Melville thinks
again in this character of the primitive man of acceptance who

has no concern for a ritualistic commemoration of suffering. The formalism of his religion is only " game " and no more. Undoubtedly, much of this Greek-Polynesian reference in *Clarel* was determined by Melville's recollection of Polynesia as he passed through the Aegean on his voyage of 1856-57. The Cyclades, northeast of Crete, reminded him of Polynesia " reft of palms," the island of Syra, of " leisure, merriment, peace," of love as " righteousness." [2]

Melville had used this Greek reference as early as his description of Marnoo in *Typee*, when he speaks of the youth as a Polynesian Apollo. This tendency toward Greece as the prototype may seem entirely unimportant to us (the simile of Apollo being exceedingly commonplace in popular speech) until it is noticed elsewhere in the literature of primitivism. Fenollosa shows it in his description of Japanese culture: " [W]e have here . . . a flash of human genius at highest tension, which in our records only the sensitively organized Greek, and that for only a few centuries, ever reached. The land itself . . . is as broken into islands, peaks, and promontories as the Greek Archipelago, but swathed with a far richer garment of semi-tropical foliage. The charm of the South Sea Islands is all here without their excessive enervation." [3]

In Martinique, Lafcadio Hearn, seeing in a tanning yard a young mulatto wearing only a clout about his loins, thought of the satisfaction of a sculptor shaping a fine Mercury with a cast of such a body.[4] Henry Adams, admiring the Siva dance of Samoa, found the dancers " all absolutely Greek in modelling and action, with such freedom of muscle and motion as the Greeks themselves hardly knew." [5] Safroni-Middleton, describing the grace and manly beauty of Hawahee, the Oceanic hero of his novel *Sestrina*, returned to the art of the Greek sculptor in the same comparison.[6] These examples show that as the

[2] See *Timoleon*, the collection of poems published in 1891 (vol. 16 in Constable edition), pp. 288–90: " The Archipelago " and " Syra, A Transmitted Reminiscence."

[3] *Epochs of Chinese and Japanese Art*, vol. 1, p. 52.

[4] *Two Years in the French West Indies*, p. 48.

[5] *Letters*, ed. Ford, vol. 1, p. 419. To Elizabeth Cameron, Apia, October 9, 1890.

[6] *Sestrina: A Romance of the South Seas*, p. 219.

observer in the Orient, the West Indies, or Polynesia is confronted with the antiquity of primitive grace which he is to
describe, he turns to a pagan Greek ideality (the Golden Age)
as a prototypic analogy from his own culture in its oldest
heritage.

The sign of Melville's symbolistic treatment of primitive
ethos is the appearance of what I shall call here the *element* of
Queequeg. By this element I mean, of course, ideality. As
ethos, it becomes a symbol when it attains multiple meaning.
The element of Queequeg as wisdom is the force which creates
the avatar of sacrament, the master symbol of the Polynesian
sage, the holy man. An understanding of the facts of this
symbol must depend upon complete mastery of the attributes
of Queequeg, as Melville presents these through the first twenty
chapters of *Moby-Dick* (particularly Chapters III–XXI). In beginning an examination of the character, I take as my directive
Melville's own pronouncement which recalls, of course, his very
earliest preoccupations with opposing values already discussed
in the preceding comments on obsession with the East. In the
" Nightgown " chapter of *Moby-Dick* (XI) he writes: " [T]here
is no quality in this world that is not what it is merely by contrast. Nothing exists in itself." It follows that the symbol is
the instrument which shows the reality of existence in contrast.
Queequeg himself is made of contrast: he is at one and the same
moment the princely son of a cannibal king and a whaleman's
" harpooneer." Thus, if one takes the little black Yojo idol of
Queequeg and one of Ahab's harpoons as two devices used by
Queequeg the man, the one represents pagan acceptance of
God, the other stands for Ahab's absolute will in reasoned non-
acceptance. Polynesian ethos appears in the little idol, and
" Christian folly " in the harpoon. The reality of Queequeg as
a symbol is discovered in the ethical " native " conduct of
Queequeg so strangely placed before the stern, unyielding coun-
tenance of Christian absolutism.

Melville reaches here and elsewhere his real meaning in his
view of the opposites that exist in God: light is light because
darkness defines it; pagan acceptance, by the same token, is

pagan excellence because "darkness" in absolutism exists to define it. Queequeg is Melville's idealized wise man for this world, the human being who accepts in quiet serenity the enigma of God's contradictions. As one approaches the greatest of all Melville's symbols in the White Whale, he sees the greatest of all Melville's answers (and the answers of all true primitivists) written in the stars: God is in himself multifarious and contradictory. Every quality of God is what it is by contrast. Thus, God is the symbol of all being.

As soon as we discover Queequeg with Ishmael at the Spouter-Inn, we see that his skin is not wholly strange. We have seen something like it before, on the body of Marnoo of *Typee*. Marnoo's skin fits better and is more beautifully adorned, it may be noted, since it covers the archetypal body of the idealized youth. Queequeg's skin may seem rather ill-fitting and rough, and his "pattern" ugly, by contrast; but then its service is to cover the wise man. The purplish-yellow hue of Queequeg is his prevailing color. When we study him through Ishmael's description, we see that his arms, his chest, and his back are covered with a checkered design which gives him the appearance of wearing patches or sticking-plaster (Ch. III). His arm matches the patchwork quilt on the bed. His legs are covered with a design of the palm tree, and Ishmael thinks he sees frogs running up the trunks. The checkered trunk of the "artu" tree which covers the back of Marnoo is the nearest of all the designs of tattooing (described before *Moby-Dick*) to these devices displayed by Queequeg. I do not mean to press Marnoo as a prefiguration unduly: but a close examination of his relation to wisdom as well as to *tayo* suggests that the design of the tattooing here is an imagistic expression of an ideality passing into Queequeg. After *Moby-Dick*, especially in *Israel Potter*, tattooing appears as a device related to wisdom in the sage of Melville's own society. Queequeg stands between Marnoo and John Paul Jones of *Israel Potter* in the configurations of archetypal wisdom. As we contemplate the strange bedfellow of Ishmael, we see again Melville's love of the incongruous. What can be more arresting than the incongruity of Queequeg's putting on his *squeaking* new leather boots as he dresses his elaborate and colorful figure on his first morning with Ishmael? Bad examples of the bootmaker's art, encasing those legs adorned with the trunks of palm trees and green frogs! But, for that matter, consider incongruity again when Captain Bildad, feeling some serious responsibility for the soul of this cannibal about to sail in his ship (Ch. xviii), thrusts a religious tract into the hands of Queequeg.

The avatar, as a reincarnation from the Orient, does not derive its power from veracity; we cannot hold it to fact. This is plain truth. But it happens here that Queequeg's tattooing is fact. My authority is the reliable Louis Becke who describes in his story " The Vision of Milli the Slave," a youth of the island of Tetuaroa, near Tahiti. This youth, Narü by name, must be very like a more youthful Queequeg at home, even to his " top knot " (which Melville preserves in the odd coiffure of Ishmael's companion).

> Round his waist was a girdle of bright yellow strips of plantain leaves, mixed with the scarlet leaves of the *ti* plant; a band of pearl-shell ornaments encircled his forehead, and his long, black hair, perfumed with scented oil, was twisted up in a high spiral knob, and ornamented with scarlet hibiscus flowers. Across one broad shoulder there hung a small, snowy-white poncho or cape, made of fine tappa cloth. . . . On each leg there was tattooed, in bright blue, a coco-nut tree, its roots spreading out at the heel and running in wavy lines along the instep to the toes, its elastic stalk shooting upwards till its waving plumes spread gracefully out on the broad, muscular calf.[7]

An ethnologist will have to separate the prototypes of Queequeg into Marquesan and Tahitian; but it is my suggestion that he is made of both. Marnoo of Nukuhiva figures in Queequeg's wisdom and in his ideality of *tayo*, and undoubtedly some tattooed Tahitian chieftain (as described here by Becke), in his design of palm trees and his manner of dressing his hair. (Ishmael tells us that Queequeg has nearly no hair on his head

---

[7] *Ridan the Devil and Other Stories* (London, 1899), pp. 93-94.

except the top-knot; and presumably we are to understand this as a sign of Queequeg's age, or of his station in a tribe where shaving the head was reserved for "royalty.")

But there is more veracity here than appears in the design of tattooing; and again Becke furnishes an account which is serviceable in establishing the facts of Queequeg. Becke's character is a "gentleman" of the island of Kusaie, in the East Carolines, who appears in at least three stories as a chieftain named Kusis. He is the headman of the village called Leassé. In the story "The Supercargo," he appears, in Becke's description, as "one of Nature's nobleman . . . courteous, dignified, brave and truthful."[8] Another sketch, called "Kusis," presents him as "the finest specimen of Micronesian native, physically and socially."[9] In a third sketch, "Leassé," Kusis is again presented as a model of wisdom, bearing, and decorum.[10] Kusis, in all three instances, appears as the representative man of wisdom from his community. In the skills of hunting and fishing, he is the apotheosis of native grace. As head man of the village, he epitomizes the justice and the humanity represented in the communal life of his people. In his position as head of his family, he is wise, gentle, hospitable. Like Melville's Queequeg, whom he follows by almost half a century, he is the representative of a primitive ethos. And for an analysis of Queequeg he performs the inestimable service of establishing as fact much of the humanity that is contained in Melville's symbol.

These attributes of Queequeg are born of fact. We can no longer be sure of fact, in truth we may be most suspicious, when we come to Queequeg's behavior as a holy man. The one certainty of Queequeg as this man of Polynesia is apparent in Ishmael's introductory description of his friend. Queequeg, we are informed (Ch. x), is discovered by Ishmael sitting before the fire at the inn and whittling away with his jack-knife at the nose of his little black Yojo (that black "Congo" idol that

[8] *Under Tropic Skies* (London, 1905), p. 211.
[9] *Ibid.*, pp. 167–68.
[10] *Rodman the Boatsteerer* (London, 1898), pp. 298–304.

had so astonished Ishmael on his first night with the savage).
Here Queequeg is another carver of God in a likeness which
suits his fancy. He is first cousin, if not brother, to the spear-
fisherman or the sailor savage carving out the likeness of his
God to please himself, as this symbol is to be later presented in
Moby-Dick. This savage independence is reflected in Queequeg's off-hand treatment of the idol when he has finished
" sacrificing " a piece of ship's biscuit to it on that first night.
He merely " bags " it again in the pocket of his " grego " (wonder of wonders, really a hooded jacket worn in the Levant)
without so much as a backward glance, and hops into bed!

For the rest, we are not looking at Polynesian " holy duties "
at all. In the first place, no one could have found an idol in
the shape of Queequeg's Yojo anywhere in Polynesia, even in
those days when artifacts were still to be had in trade for some
trinket from a seaman's chest. This idol is not a *tiki* of Polynesia. It is really, as Ishmael says, African. In the second place,
when Ishmael finally turns aside from his Presbyterianism to
worship with Queequeg, as holy man, he kindles the shavings
for the strange " altar fire," offers burnt biscuit, " salaams "
twice, and kisses the nose of Yojo (Ch. x). This scene is almost
as crowded with incongruities as the scene of Fanna in *Mardi*
earlier described. The burnt biscuit is a substitution for the
consecrated Host of Christian ritual; beyond that, it is very
clear that the major reference of Queequeg's idol as a symbol
is to the Moslem world. So Ishmael *salaams* instead of *kneels*.
The image, of course, is perfectly appropriate, for before the
Pequod sails, Queequeg conducts a " Ramadan," a day of
fasting and humiliation, before this idol (Ch. xvii). *Ramadan*
is the ninth month of the Mohammedan year, a month set aside
for atonement on each of its days. The intensity of Queequeg's
concentration as he goes about his " humiliation " (so wrapt
that he does not move when Ishmael enters the room) recalls
the rite of such exacting disciplines of the Orient as Yoga, and
Zen Buddhism. The complexity of Queequeg as a symbol seems
nearly inexhaustible. One begins with his true Polynesian (his

factual) attributes, his tattooing, his decorum. Then one proceeds to his incongruous foreign dress, and his mysterious cloak
from the Levant. When finally he reaches Queequeg's idol, he
finds not a Polynesian phallic *tiki*, but a pigmy figure from the
Congo.

We go on to the burnt biscuit of the ceremony, a ship's biscuit offered as the bread of life to an African idol belonging to
a Polynesian tattooed man! We follow the ceremony of Queequeg as a holy man into his Mohammedan Ramadan. But these
are by no means all the elements of Queequeg as a symbol. This
wise savage has also known holy water in Polynesia. Here, on
Queequeg's home soil, we encounter a rite which is as far from
fact as Queequeg's tattooed palm trees are near to it. Queequeg, says Ishmael, was a native of Kokovoko, " an island far
away in the West and South," and he was the son of a king;
in fact he came of a line of thirty pagan kings, and he felt somewhat defiled by his life in the Christian world and thought he
could not go back to succeed his father until he " felt himself
baptized again " (Ch. XII) . With this introduction to guide us,
we hear a story told to Ishmael by Queequeg. At home on
Kokovoko people " express the fragrant water of young cocoa-
nuts into a large stained calabash like a punch-bowl." Once,
when Queequeg's sister was being married, a sea captain was
invited ashore for the festivities. The captain seated himself
between the High Priest and Queequeg's father, the king.
After the " grace " was said, the High Priest opened the ban-
quet by dipping his " consecrated and consecrating " fingers
into the bowl before the beverage was circulated among the
guests. The captain, however, being unaccustomed to local tradition and wishing to oblige with some sort of conformity,
proceeded to follow the High Priest by washing his hands in
the bowl. And, says Queequeg, " Didn't our people laugh? "
Melville has in mind here the *kava* ceremony customarily insti-
tuted in tribal practice throughout Oceania. His substitution
of coconut water is purely notional. At this point he is recalling the tree which he presents as the Tree of Life in his
discussion of the Coco-palm in *Omoo* (Ch. LXIX) and in his

description of Queequeg's tattooing. Thus the water of young coconuts here represents the vitality of the Tree of Life. There is no Polynesian custom whatsoever which even suggests the Christian rite of consecrating holy water by the fingers of a priest. Melville here adds to the elements of the symbol which have already been reviewed. He makes the holy water of the Christian church the " holy water " of the Polynesian Tree of Life, and he offers this to us in a ritual which is expressly intended to recall Christian practice. Now the real meaning of the scene emerges: it is sacred water in the sense that it has no absolute meaning at all. Hence the laughter that breaks forth as a man of Christendom makes the mistake of washing his hands in it. Through the feeling apparent here Melville intends a new sacrament of primitive wisdom to supplant the old.

Finally, the most wonderful thing about Queequeg is Melville's completion of his attributes in giving him the ideality of *tayo*. Ishmael joins himself to this savage who has been described (Ch. x) as always " entirely at his ease; preserving the utmost serenity; content with his own companionship; always equal to himself." And, wonderful to relate, the pledge of Queequeg's *tayo* is one half his worldly goods, in particular, one half his *thirty dollars in silver*. For thirty pieces of silver Judas Iscariot sold Jesus Christ into the suffering of the cross. But Queequeg has no more reference to suffering on the cross than Billy Budd. Melville's willful selection of thirty pieces of silver presents here Queequeg's non-apostolic, non-Christian friendship in an undying bond of selfless love. Immediately before his freely extended act of the gift, he and Ishmael have pressed their foreheads together and embraced in pledge of this love. Immediately after the silver is poured into Ishmael's pockets, the youth turns to salaam before Queequeg's idol.

I was a good Christian; born and bred in the bosom of the infallible Presbyterian Church. How then could I unite with this wild idolator in worshipping his piece of wood? But what is worship? thought I. Do you suppose now, Ishmael, that the magnanimous God of heaven and earth— pagans and all included—can possibly be jealous of an insig-

nificant bit of black wood? Impossible! But what is worship?
—to do the will of God?—*that* is worship.

It is the will of God, continues Ishmael, that we should accept
our fellowmen. It is the will of God, in the larger meaning of
this passage when the symbols of Melville's sacrament are sum-
moned to it, that we should accept, like Queequeg, the unknowable universe, "entirely at ease," serene, always equal to
ourselves.

For this is Melville's ideality of Polynesian ethos. "No
more," says Ishmael, "my splintered heart and maddened hand
were turned against the wolfish world. This soothing savage
had redeemed me" (Ch. x). Howard P. Vincent is certainly
correct when he remarks that "Queequeg's poise is implicitly
a criticism of the neurotic divagations of 'civilized man.'" I
doubt his accuracy when he continues in saying that Melville
portrays Queequeg unsentimentally, that he "had known such
men well in the Typee Valley." [11] Certainly Queequeg is sentimentally portrayed; he is built of feeling. But in the vast complexity of this symbol is all the evidence we need that such a
man never really existed in Typee Valley, or anywhere else.

Aboard the *Pequod* Queequeg is, of course, "balanced" by
his two harpooneer shipmates, Tashtego and Daggoo. But what
need be said of them? They are only very pale reflections of
the symbol of Queequeg. They serve as characters necessary to
the structure of the book, standing as they do in trinity with
their three cup-bearers, the mates, Starbuck, Stubb, and Flask.
Tashtego, even though he is the one selected to nail the flag of
Ahab to the masthead as the *Pequod* sinks, is never really developed as either symbol or character; nor is Daggoo, that coal-
black Negro savage, "an Ahasuerus to behold." When one
passes from Queequeg to the other pagan harpooneers in the
trinity, it is apparent that he has passed as well from the realm
of Melville's feeling which inspires the ideality of the true symbol. Tashtego and Daggoo are not archetypal wise men at all;
they are characters introduced for the sake of structure. We

---

[11] *The Trying-Out of Moby-Dick* (Boston, 1949), p. 76.

should be glad we have them. Their presence shows us quite clearly that Melville is governed in his symbolistic act by the power of the autotype, the directly sensed personal experience.

2 *Indifference to Death*

Aboard the *Pequod* Queequeg performs his sailor-whaleman's duties; he sustains with his companionship and devotion and wisdom the young whaleman-novice Ishmael; he rescues his fellow Tashtego from his oily captivity in the head of a great whale. But his significance as ethos, after we leave him awaking at the Spouter-Inn from his Ramadan, appears only once more, and then with the sovereign power of Melville's greatest art. He falls ill and he approaches death. " Now, at this time it was that my poor pagan companion, and fast bosom-friend, Queequeg, was seized with a fever, which brought him nigh to his endless end " (Ch. cx). The *Pequod* (Ch. cix) is moving into the waters between Formosa and the Philippines (the " Bashee Isles "). Ahab has been studying charts of the islands of Japan. Starbuck has reported to Ahab that the oil is leaking from the casks in the hold; the casks need to be re-hooped, he tells the captain. If this work is done, Ahab must leave off searching for whales, in particular his great white enemy, for a week or so. The oil is leaking at a great rate, and Starbuck warns Ahab that in one day a year's taking may escape. Ahab has driven Starbuck away at the point of a loaded musket, with roaring contempt for the warning and as well for his obligation to the owners of the ship awaiting her return to Nantucket. " There is one God that is Lord over the earth," he screams, " and one Captain that is lord over the *Pequod*."

How like the recapitulation of a serene *andante* midway in the strident dissonances of a symphonic poem comes the tranquil vision of Queequeg in his illness immediately after these agonies of Ahab. Queequeg the wise, in perfect peace upon these vast Oriental seas. Poor Queequeg to Ishmael, who has seen him " bitterly sweating all day in that subterraneous confinement " of the ship's hold. For Ahab did, indeed, follow the advice of the mate; and when it was found that the leaking casks were the most deeply buried of all the great " ground-tier butts," then all the hold had to be cleared. Into that midnight of the *Pequod*'s vitals Queequeg was ordered to go; and there he labored, half-clothed, and caught a chill.

How he wasted and wasted away in those few long-lingering days, till there seemed but little left of him but his frame and tattooing. But as all else in him thinned, and his cheek-bones grew sharper, his eyes, nevertheless, seemed growing fuller and fuller; they became of a strange softness of lustre; and mildly but deeply looked out at you there from his sickness, a wondrous testimony to that immortal health in him which could not die, or be weakened. And like circles on the water, which, as they grow fainter, expand; so his eyes seemed rounding and rounding, like the rings of Eternity. An awe that cannot be named would steal over you as you sat by the side of this waning savage, and saw as strange things in his face, as any beheld who were bystanders when Zoroaster died. For whatever is truly wondrous and fearful in man, never yet was put into words or books. And the drawing near of Death, which alike levels all, alike impresses all with a last revelation, which only an author from the dead could adequately tell. So that—let us say it again—no dying Chaldee or Greek had higher and holier thoughts than those, whose mysterious shades you saw creeping over the face of poor Queequeg, as he quietly lay in his swaying hammock, and the rolling sea seemed gently rocking him to his final rest, and the ocean's invisible flood-tide lifted him higher and higher toward his destined heaven.

No praise need be recorded for this commanding apotheosis of Queequeg as the man of holy wisdom. Melville wrote here one of the greatest symbolic scenes in the history of religious art. I submit that it is a pure example of the highest *poesis*. But the fact of the symbol must govern attention in criticism, not that appreciation which is the responsibility of the individual reader. I wish to point out, at once, that this description of the pagan approach to the mystery of death lacks, most conspicuously and tellingly, a single reference to Christian fortitude, this description so rich in its invocations of the wisdom of antiquity—the wisdom of the Persian Zoroaster, the wisdom of the Neo-Babylonian Chaldee, the wisdom of the Greek, the wisdom of the Polynesian. The dying eyes of Queequeg round like circles on water, round and grow full with the immortal health which lives in him. In this wonderful moment he becomes the health of the human soul. Health is exchanged for mere wisdom, the health of a wise and fearless acceptance of God, the fixed truth of whom may never be known by man. Supremely sweet and quiet man of healthy soul, rocking in his sea-hammock aboard the ship of Ahab, the God-defying and God-bullying captain of Christendom! Man was meant to die in innocence and acceptance. For the near-death of Queequeg is really the death of Billy Budd, in the symbolic sense, as well.

Queequeg then orders his coffin from the ship's carpenter. He confides in his shipmates: he wants, he says, one of those "little canoes of dark wood" which he had chanced to see in Nantucket, for he shudders at the thought of being buried in his hammock. There is some "heathenish, coffin-colored old lumber" aboard the ship, which on a previous voyage had been cut "from the aboriginal groves of the Lackaday islands." This wood the carpenter fashions into the little canoe desired. Melville intends, of course, to represent here a Polynesian mortuary canoe (while Queequeg thinks of a coffin which he has seen in New England). But it cannot be of wood cut in a New England forest; it must be made of a tree of an aboriginal Oriental grove. One thinks at once of some forest of the Marquesas, even though the Lackaday Islands are possibly the Laccadives, off the coast of India.[12] A French ethnologist, C. de Varigny, has written of mortuary custom in Oceania that the dead, after being swathed in bands of cloth, are put to sea in canoes with prows pointed toward the west. The equatorial currents bear these craft over great distances, and often such canoes have been seen on open seas far from their points of origin.[13] Melville's discussion of Marquesan mortuary practices in *Typee*

[12] See Willard Thorp's edition of *Moby-Dick* (New York, 1947), p. 448, fn. 3.
[13] "L'Océanie Moderne," *Revue des Deux Mondes*, 3ᵉ période, vol. 85, p. 422. Varigny refers here particularly to Marshallese custom.

does not mention mortuary canoes, although there is some notice of wrapping the body of the dead " in new white tappa " (Ch. xxvi). But the absence of the custom in the pages of *Typee* is of no consequence. It is clear that he knows of these canoes when he has Queequeg call for his " Nantucket " coffin. For when the coffin is finished by the carpenter and brought to Queequeg, the sailors place in it at Queequeg's direction his harpoon iron, a boat paddle, biscuits, a flask of water, a bag of woody earth (for his altar fires to Yojo?), and a piece of sail-cloth for a pillow. Then Queequeg is lifted into the coffin and directs that his little black idol be brought from his sea-bag. Lying serenely with arms crossed on his breast and clasping Yojo, he calls for the lid to be placed over him. Satisfied then, he murmurs " Rarmai " (" It will do; it is easy.")

One cannot venture more than the suggestion that this " last " utterance is the pagan equivalent of the Christian " It is finished." The simplicity of each sentence spoken at the moment of surrender to death (or almost the moment for Queequeg) seems to invite comparison. If Melville intended " Rarmai " to supplant " It is finished," then the meaning here is no more than an extension of what has already been observed through the facts of the symbol: the " ease " of Queequeg's life and " death " as distinguished from the suffering of the Christian hero. It is evident that Melville deals here very purpose-fully with the moment; and it is evident, too, that Queequeg does not die at this point because his departure would destroy the double trinity of harpooneers and mates which must be pre-served until the *Pequod* sinks. But it is Queequeg's last scene; and it is very much as though Ishmael had learned here his final lesson from this man of wisdom.

What Queequeg has taught Ishmael is freedom from con-sciousness of self. This is the " freedom " which we see as Queequeg lies complacently in his coffin, yet alive and entirely perceptive, and still to recover from his fever. His indifference to death is, as Melville intends us to read it, Polynesian. Sir James Frazer bears Melville out, at least in this concept of Marquesan serenity before death. Melville gives us something which he felt; Frazer gives us fact. " The Marquesans have, or used to have, a sovereign contempt for death, and do not fear its approach. When a native felt that he must die, he took it calmly and ordered his coffin, which he caused to be brought to the house while he was still in life. The coffin is hollowed out of a single log and resembles a canoe. If the sick man after all recovered, the coffin was kept in a corner of the house till it was wanted." [14] The " immortal health " of Queequeg is the health of a soul free of self-insistence and full of its own sense of participation in the soul animating all men and nature; and his " dying " words mean unreasoned acceptance of death by a self which demands no knowledge of its own identity.[15] This is the opposite of the Christian self triumphant over life and suffering.

The literature of primitivism is very often reflective upon this pagan acceptance of death. Its concern with the Marquesan attitude, apart from this symbolic representation in the art of Melville, is of especial interest here. Loti and Stevenson were both impressed with the complacency marking the last days of Queen Vaekehu of Nukuhiva. (See Chapter III of this study.) In his *Rarahu* Loti says of the old queen in her last illness: " One sees rarely in our civilized world any scenes as impressive; in that bare hut, unknowing of all the lugubrious furnishings which add in Europe to the horrors of death, the pain of that woman revealed a poetry unknown, full of a bitter sadness [i. e., bitter to Loti in his retrospection] . . . the approach of death caused her no terror." [16] The bitterness of Loti's account of the death of Vaekehu is the unrest of civilized man before the spectacle of primitive wisdom in acceptance. With less reflection but more attention to fact, Stevenson wrote in his account of the Marquesans: " For ten years Queen Vaekehu had dunned the fathers [i. e., implored the French priests of the island]; at last, but the other day, they let her have her will, gave her her coffin, and the woman's soul is at rest." Stevenson

---

[14] " *The Belief among the Polynesians,*" *The Belief in Immortality and The Worship of the Dead*, vol. 2, pp. 352–53.

[15] On the lack of self-consciousness in primitive man see Lucien Lévy-Bruhl. *The " Soul " of the Primitive*, trans., Lilian A. Clare (New York, 1928), p. 201.

[16] Ed. Calmann Lévy (1923) , p. 110.

continues in the same passage to speak of the Marquesan's indifference to his coffin, very close here to Frazer's observation, and of his sometime recovery in full sight of this emblem of death.[17] Here Stevenson is the reporter, not the poet. One might better offer Hearn's admiration of the Japanese as a fit parallel for Loti's feeling (and Melville's). For Hearn means exactly what Loti means of Vaekehu and what Melville means, symbolically, of Queequeg. "None love life more than the Japanese; none fear death less. [sic] Of a future world they have no dread; they regret to leave this one because it seems to them a world of beauty and of happiness; but the mystery of the future, so long oppressive to Western minds, causes them little concern." [18]

Thus, Melville's Queequeg symbolizes in his acceptance of death a kind of wisdom and innocence which may be related to ethnological fact. This is the wisdom of Polynesian ethos which protects and sustains Ishmael; this is again the wisdom which saves Ishmael as the waters of the sea close over the sinking *Pequod*. In the epilogue to *Moby-Dick* Ishmael tells us that he was drawn toward the " closing vortex " by the half-spent suction of the descending ship. The image he uses to describe his whirling motion as he is drawn toward the center of the vortex is the torture of Ixion on the wheel. At the vital center, the black bubble bursts upward; " and now, liberated by reason of its cunning spring, and, owing to its great buoyancy, rising with great force, the coffin life-buoy shot length-wise from the sea, fell over, and floated by my side." This is Queequeg's coffin-canoe, and on it Ishmael floats for a day and a night. " The unharming sharks, they glided by as if with padlocks on their mouths; the savage sea-hawks sailed with sheathed beaks." Then the *Rachel* draws near and picks him up at last, and only he lives to tell the story. The consistency of Melville's symbolic theme of Queequeg is thus confirmed in Ishmael's final act. Here in the broad water-courses, the illimitable solitudes traversed by Ahab, where God's predatory

[17] *In the South Seas*, pp. 32–33.
[18] *Glimpses of Unfamiliar Japan*, " Shinjū," vol. 1, p. 286.

sharks and menacing hawks could have ripped this lone survivor in pieces, it is the sustaining influence of Queequeg that
protects Ishmael. So is the Ishmael-voyager sustained in a world
of egomaniacs, of countless Ahabs destroying themselves and all
humanity compelled into their services in a futile quest for the
absolute truth of God. It is the wisdom of Queequeg, the immortal health of him, that saves the innocence of Ishmael. Long
ago, at the Spouter-Inn, Ishmael had felt " a melting " in him toward his new friend. The " soothing savage " had redeemed him
from the wolfish world (*Moby-Dick*, Ch. x). Now in his lone-
liest hour Ishmael is redeemed again with the peace of that
same Queequeg, always serene in a furious world, through this
symbol of a drifting canoe.

3 *Queequeg and the Archetypal Sage*

The archetype of the wise man apparent in Queequeg is a
derivative from the collective unconsciousness underlying the
expression of primitivism. When Ishmael makes the unusual
observation at the Spouter-Inn that " Queequeg was George
Washington cannibalistically developed," we are startled. Why
should Washington occur to him? The answer to this question
is found in the description which the wise man receives at other
points in the literature of primitivism and in other instances of
Melville's own artistic experience with this archetype. The
image of Washington for Queequeg is, in artistic meaning,
exactly equal to similar images employed by other authors describing the dignity and the wisdom of Polynesians. Notice,
for instance, Henry Adams writing of Samoans. " We entered
the nearest hut [at Tutuila], and put on our best manners,
which were none too good, for the natives had manners that
made me feel withered prematurely in association with the
occupants of pig-sties. Grave, courteous, with quiet voices and
a sort of benevolence beyond the utmost expressiveness of Benjamin Franklin, they received us and made us at home. The
cabin was charming when one looked about it." [19] Safroni-

[19] *Letters*, ed. Ford, vol. 1, p. 416. To Elizabeth Cameron, Apia, October 9,
1890.

Middleton in the Marquesas records his impression of a chieftain named Hafiao: " I remember him well, because he was such an intellectual-looking old fellow and looked very much like Gladstone, but he was more powerfully built and of course brown skinned." [20] When these descriptions are compared with the picture of Queequeg as Washington, it is apparent that the objective of the imagination is to provide an illustration of the wise man from the artist's parent culture which will explain the wisdom recognized in the Polynesian sage. Thus the symbol from Oceania, and the Orient, as well, may be strengthened with reference to an American or a British wise man; and the sage selected from the history of the artist's country may be strengthened, in the same manner, by reference to Oriental wisdom. Adams's and Middleton's Samoans and Marquesans are only symbols in the making; Melville's Queequeg, with all his other symbolic meanings, is Washington cannibalistically developed only for good measure!

The general observation may be offered here that when the primitivist intends a symbolic description of his own ethos, he depends upon images or concepts from his particular obsession with the Orient. This dependence has already been suggested in the notice of Melville's " Hinduish haze " over the rich lands of Pierre Glendinning's ancestral Saddle Meadows in the Berkshires. One encounters here an " Orientally " inspired concept rather than a personally acquired image. But the interesting distinction is that where we have in the " Hinduish haze " only the suggestion of an Oriental antiquity, in Melville's wise men we discover an Oriental reference which defines ethos with ethos. Thus the description of Benjamin Franklin in *Israel Potter* invokes the Orient, as well as the tribes of Israel, the pastoral setting of Greek wisdom, and the Italian prince of the Renaissance. Franklin here abdicates his real place in history; he is no longer the simple representative of colonial America.

The first, both in point of time and merit, of American envoys was famous not less for the pastoral simplicity of his

[20] *Sailor and Beachcomber*, p. 159.

manners than for the poetic grace of his mind. Viewed from a certain point, there was a touch of primeval orientalness in Benjamin Franklin. Neither is there wanting something like his scriptural parallel. The history of the patriarch Jacob is interesting not less from the unselfish devotion which we are bound to ascribe to him, than from the deep worldly wisdom and polished Italian tact, gleaming under an air of Arcadian unaffectedness. The diplomatist and the shepherd are blended; a union not without warrant; the apostolic serpent and dove. A tamed Machiavelli in tents.[21]

Franklin as an embodiment of the sage comes from the same archetype of the wise man which is really the essential stuff of Queequeg. What better argument may exist to refute authoritatively the claims of criticism which reduces all archetypal expression to undistinguished *trauma* than the symbolic variety which an artist such as Melville imposes upon the basic archetype? The symbol of Franklin is individuated in exact relation to what Melville, the artist, uniquely feels. Melville here represents patriarchalness in the sense of political acumen and statesman-like wisdom. The symbol with its multiple reference gives us exactly that representation. In Queequeg patriarchalness is represented in the sense of personal nobility, spiritual health, gentleness, faith, selflessness. The difference between the symbolic significance of Franklin and that of Queequeg is at once obvious. The symbolic Franklin appears in an area of Melville's art which is essentially nonreligious; Queequeg emerges at the center of Melville's meaning as artist, his religious act of creating new symbols of sacrament. The one is a symbol marked with an Orient which is conceptual; the other is an embodiment of Polynesian wisdom, its form achieved through the autotypic power of Melville's full store of images directly acquired in his experience with Polynesian ethos.

All these archetypal symbols are uniquely fixed in artistic form. But if one wishes to see the archetype of the wise man in less distinctive guise, he has in Melville's work at least one example for study. He is the old Dansker of *Billy Budd*, known

[21] *Israel Potter*, p. 59.

to his shipmates as " Board-her-in-the-smoke." Among the crew
of the *Indomitable*, he is the " salt seer," as Melville calls him.
In the narrative he has the function of a Teiresias of the British
Navy. He is the dispassionate observer of Billy's innocence and
Claggart's evil. He it is who warns Billy that " Jimmy Legs "
(Claggart) is "down upon him." He is oracular, as Melville
intends him; he is the " old sea-Chiron " who thinks that for
the nonce " he had sufficiently warned his young Achilles." In
his role as the seer, the old Dansker is the voice of fate. But
this old veteran of weathered face, of a complexion like parch-
ment, of many scars is, more particularly, a pure distillation of
the ethos of the mariner's custom, of the culture of all men who
go down to the sea in ships.

> Now the first time that his small weasel eyes happened to
> light on Billy Budd, a certain grim internal merriment set
> all his ancient wrinkles into antic play. Was it that his eccen-
> tric unsentimental old sapience, primitive in its kind, saw, or
> thought it saw, something which in contrast with the war-
> ship's environment looked oddly incongruous in the Hand-
> some Sailor? [22]

The primitive wisdom of the ancient Dansker is the least
symbolized wisdom appearing in Melville's art. It matches the
primitive flowing sea beneath the *Indomitable*; it has no form
save the shadowy outline of an old sailor who is dusk to the
sharp light in which Billy, Claggart, and Captain Vere are
shown. The Dansker is wise with the weary wisdom of the
Furies and the Norns, heavy with the knowledge of human
error and distorted purpose. I can think of no character in
literature nearer this hoary old seer of *Billy Budd* than Shakespeare's Old Man who enters with Ross after the murder of
Duncan in *Macbeth* (Act II, Sc. iv) or Marlowe's Old Man who
comes to warn Faustus (Scene XIV). With either or both of
these he is the seer of primordial wisdom. In the art of Melville
he is the character who stands nearest to the pure archetype;
he is the least symbolic sage, and the only one who may be

[22] *Billy Budd and Other Prose Pieces*, p. 38.

assigned to that area of dream content in which archetype and nothing else is seen.

Among all these men of wisdom, whatever their symbolic forms, Ahab of *Moby-Dick* has no place. He is insanity as distinguished from sapience. He is knowledgeable in nothing save his own demoniacal purpose. Opposite to Queequeg, he is a gigantic symbol of the sickness of the self, the disease of the egoist-absolutist of Christendom. If immortal health shines in the dying Queequeg, then mortal illness festers in Ahab. He is the hater of that " heartless, proud, ice-gilded world " hated, in turn, by Pierre Glendinning.[23] True, Melville intends us to see Ahab as an ancient. In perfect consistency with the whole range of imagery in *Moby-Dick* which evokes antiquity, we are given an Ahab who had such vital strength in him when the White Whale sheared off his leg that his shipmates were forced to lace him, raving, into his hammock; and that strength lurked in his *Egyptian* chest (*Moby-Dick*, Ch. xli). But Ahab's strength is not the strength of endurance or wisdom. It is the misspent power of a whole human history of absolute defiance of God. Long ago he had transferred to the White Whale all the maledictions of humanity. Upon the white hump of Moby Dick " he piled . . . the sum of all the general rage and hate felt by his whole race from Adam down; and then, as if his chest had been a mortar, he burst his hot heart's shell upon it " (Ch. xli). Not one of Ahab's purposive and fully reasoned acts shows wisdom. We see him as the expression of civilized man's colossal error. Clearly *Moby-Dick*, the work, itself a vast symbol, shows here the counter-being of Queequeg. To go back to Melville's reflection as he presents Ishmael at the Spouter-Inn, " there is no quality in this world that is not what it is merely by contrast." The wisdom of Queequeg is the wisdom which is just for man. But, as Melville saw it, the master paradox of life is that we cannot know the nature of justice and nobility until folly and the overreaching pride of the ego explain this nature by contrast.

[23] *Pierre*, p. 126.

4   *Fayaway and Related Figures*

Melville's representation of Polynesian ethos appears in his symbolic figures of men. Fayaway and the girls of *Typee* are the only women of Melville's work who contribute to the projection of ethos as the life-symbol; and it may be reasonably proposed that Fayaway might be removed from the novel without serious loss. Fayaway is related to Polynesian ethos through her gift of unstudied grace and physical and temperamental charm. We meet her first in the eleventh chapter of *Typee*. Her complexion is a " rich and mantling " olive; her teeth are dazzling white, like the milk-white seeds of the " arta," a fruit of the valley (the fruit probably of the " artu " tree which appears in the tattooing of Marnoo) ; she has strange blue eyes with unfathomable depths; she is delicately tattooed, with three dots on each lip, and two slight bands on the shoulders; she shows in every movement the " unstudied grace of a child of nature "; she is unclad " for the most part," but occasionally she wears a tunic of white *tapa*; she is adorned with flowers. The facts of Fayaway are probably that she was as beautiful as she is in the description, and that she was " given " by the tribe to young Tom for his pleasure. This " giving " of a girl companion to a visitor was as much traditional Polynesian custom as the offering of *tayo*. But except for the contribution which Fayaway makes to the elusive Yillah of *Mardi*, she survives scarcely at all after *Typee*. The only instances of her return I shall note in a concluding comment on Marianna of the story *The Piazza* and Ruth of *Clarel*.

In the history of primitivism Fayaway is almost certainly the prototype and the consciously selected model for Loti's Rarahu of Tahiti. In Rarahu, Fayaway's narrow bands of tattooing reappear on the ankles; but on the lip are three dots, almost imperceptible (exactly as described by Melville) , like those worn by the women of the Marquesas.[24] With Rarahu, Loti bathes in a fresh pool fed by a stream falling in a cascade.[25] The scene

[24] *Le Mariage de Loti* (ed. Calmann Lévy), p. 9.
[25] *Ibid.*, pp. 14–15.

recalls that of " Fayaway's Lake " as described by Melville in
Typee (Ch. xviii) . Rarahu, living later than Fayaway in a
century of missions, can read the Tahitian Bible and the words
of the Maori language. "A great many maidens in our countries of Europe are less cultivated assuredly than that savage
child." [26] The reflection matches Tom's observation of the
superb bearing of Fayaway in *Typee*. Thus does Loti " hesi-
tate " to " marry " Rarahu at the express invitation of none
other than Queen Pomare; [27] and thus does he succumb.[28]

Both Melville and Loti (whether the latter borrowed the
technique or not) are here engaged in a symbolic representation of ethos. Fayaway and Rarahu both come in the end to a
celebration of the freedom of Oceanic marital custom; and this
amounts to the free and easy grace of Maori women represented
in Gauguin's *Noa Noa*, and in the symbol of his Marquesan
picture *The Call*, as one example. Loti abandons the symbolic
potentialities of Rarahu when he leaves his finished novel. It
is Melville's distinction that Fayaway survives the years as an
ideality related to the meaning of *tayo* and to the wisdom of
Queequeg. Although she is not at all essential to Melville's art
in the symbolism of Billy Budd and Queequeg, she is very well
remembered. She, too, is innocence and acceptance, and, one
may say, the honesty of sensuous and even sensual experience
received without the plagues of a conscience hounded by the
spectre of original sin.

For it is a striking fact that the woman represented by Fayaway is the only woman in whose company the Ishmael-voyager
rests easily. This fact is borne out in the story *The Piazza*
(1856) , Melville's recollection of a summer walk in the hills
near Pittsfield. He leaves his house, he says, to seek Edmund
Spenser's fairyland; for he imagines that Una (Truth) and her
lamb dwell in the ferns of an adjacent hillside. " A sultry hour,
and I wore a light hat, of yellow sinnet, with white duck
trowsers—both relics of my tropic sea-going. Clogged in the

[26] *Ibid.*, p. 14.
[27] *Ibid.*, p. 25.
[28] *Ibid.*, pp. 116-18.

muffling ferns, I softly stumbled, staining the knees a sea-green." [29] These ferns recall the lush grasses and foliage surrounding the village of the Taipis. Then he continues:

> Pausing at the threshold, or rather where threshold once had been, I saw, through the open doorway [i. e., of the hut in which Marianna lives], a lonely girl, sewing at a lonely window. A pale-cheeked girl, and fly-specked window, with wasps about the mended upper panes. I spoke. She shyly started, like some Tahiti girl, secreted for a sacrifice, first catching sight, through palms, of Captain Cook . . . .

A brief and simple conversation ensues. Marianna, looking down from the hillside at the house of her visitor, has often supposed that some rich and happy man lived there. The question comes in reply to her: Why do you suppose some happy one? The legend closes with this reflection: " But, every night, when the curtain falls, truth comes in with darkness. No light shows from the mountain. To and fro I walk the piazza deck, haunted by Marianna's face, and many as real a story." [30] Truth comes in with darkness, and recollection. This is Fayaway transposed, by way of Tahiti, to the upland meadows of Pittsfield, Massachusetts; and in this transposition she has passed through Yillah of *Mardi* who was also a Polynesian girl " secreted for a sacrifice " (Ch. XLI). Her visitor is Tom of *Typee*, Paul of *Omoo*, Taji of *Mardi*, all these voyagers mindful now, long afterward, of the truth of primitive ease, of Polynesian ethos, all these made one in this man of Pittsfield, haunted by " many as real a story."

Fayaway is seen again, and for the last time, in Ruth of *Clarel*. As Ishmael in the person of Clarel looks at the young Jewess by the wailing wall, he reflects:

> Hebrew the profile, every line;
> But as in haven fringed with palm,
> Which Indian reefs embay from harm, . . .
> Red-budded corals in remove,

[29] *The Piazza Tales*, p. 12.
[30] *Ibid.*, p. 18.

> Peep coy through quietudes above;
> So through clear olive of the skin,
> And features finely Hagarene;
> Its way a tell-tale flush did win— [31]

Ruth, the only woman in the wasteland of *Clarel*, recalls the haven of Fayaway, even though the image is disguised with the reference to *Indian* reefs. The clear olive skin is the " rich and mantling " olive complexion of Fayaway, combined here with the image of coral seen under the water of a tropical reef. Ruth, like Marianna, is another emblem of the survival of primitive grace in Melville's return to Polynesian ethos. Slight, indeed, are these women related to Queequeg and to the sailor savage. But if one wishes to name the opposite of Fayaway, as Ahab is the opposite of Queequeg, let him choose with unquestionable justice that gentlewoman hypocrite of Christian society, Mrs. Glendinning of *Pierre*. As the women go, she too is man's insanity to heaven's sense.

---

[31] *Clarel*, vol. 1, p. 68.

VIII

Whiteness

It is perhaps no more than coincidental that Théophile Gautier's " Symphonie en Blanc Majeur " (1849) [1] and Melville's famous chapter on the whiteness of the White Whale (1851) are separated by only two years. Gautier's poem is the first important experiment of the Parnassian school in rendering the essence of color or hue by means of a " symphonic " union of poetry, painting, and music. It introduces an exotic tradition which extends into the color symphonies of John Gould Fletcher (noted in the first chapter of this study). In Gautier's white scene we are given the transmutations of an

[1] Published in *Émaux et Camées* in 1852. I am indebted to Miss Marian Monaco of Connecticut College for her suggestion that this " white " poem of Gautier might be profitably compared with Melville's chapter.

exotic woman from Germanic swan maiden and undine to the Madonna of the Snows, through the shifting white subtleties of down, pith of reed, alabaster, sea foam, ivory. Gautier's effect seeks to render the essence of whiteness. Yet the Romantic insistence of the Parnassians upon seeing color or hue as in reality a compound to be described in terms of mutation, or of the multiple values contained in it, is worth relating to Melville's obsession with whiteness. When Gautier renders white in the " symphony " as an aggregate of values rather than as an absolutely pure quality, he stands at the threshold of a symbolic use of whiteness encountered in primitivism. Given a poet of primitive feeling in this instance, we should then find the exoticist's purpose of creating artistic effect or mood abandoned for the moral requirements of the symbolistic imagination. At this threshold Gautier is interested, however, in no more than imagistic projections of the mutations of whiteness; and so the poem becomes a shifting pattern of images presenting varying objects commonly regarded as white. It is thus another design in the *émaux* of its companion pieces in Gautier's volume *Émaux et Camées*, of 1852. Melville, at the same time, arrives, certainly without any knowledge of Gautier, at the same symbolistic threshold. But the mutations of white pass beyond the method of exotic effect, and become symbolistically representative of Melville's primitivistic theology.

Whiteness, as the third of Melville's avatars from the Orient, is the sign of the all-encompassing God. It stands for what Melville calls at the conclusion of the thirty-fifth chapter of *Moby-Dick* " the inscrutable tides of God "; and it is of these tides as well that the great White Whale himself is the quintessential emblem, the iconographic representation. This avatar of whiteness demonstrates the same polarity which has been seen in the symbols of sacrament. It possesses a like degree of autotypic reference to the Orient. It accompanies sacrament, just as the white of the Paschal Feast establishes an emblematic setting in Catholic ritual. The fullness of its moral import is Oriental in its symbolic reference to a God containing in himself the chaos of contradictions, the whole state of being-in-

contrast which was defined in the preceding analysis of Queequeg. It is the perfect " hue " for a sacrament of pagan acceptance, and it is the perfect symbol of the relativist's theory as
the antithesis of the absolutist's dogma. This is the symbolic
meaning of Melville's contemplation of whiteness, as the opposite of Gautier's exotic meaninglessness. Yet, in passing from
this notice of Parnassian poetry, it is interesting to observe that
Melville begins his analysis of whiteness in *Moby-Dick* (Ch.
XLII) with the same imagistic technique which Gautier employs.
He begins by considering the color properties of white objects,
whiteness " as in marbles, japonicas, and pearls "; from this
point he proceeds to a consideration of the ritual value of white
objects in the cultural history of man. This symphony in white,
composed as it is in the area of primitivistic feeling, thus is
inevitably written into a multiplistic symbol of moral reference,
not into an affective tonal picture.

The renowned ambiguities of the chapter on the whiteness
of the Whale are old problems in the canon of Melville's
critics. Whiteness, writes Melville, has been sacred to Persians,
Romans, American Indians, Christian priests; but mingled with
its history of noble and sublime associations is its history of
violence and dread.. Melville himself confesses to his own
awareness of whiteness as an archetypal obsession: " Therefore, in his other moods, symbolize whatever grand or gracious
thing he will by whiteness, no man can deny that in its pro-
foundest idealized significance it calls up a peculiar apparition
of the soul." Again in the same chapter he returns to the
theme of the archetype: " But not yet have we solved the
incantation of this whiteness, and learned why it appeals with
such power to the soul; and more strange and far more portentous—why, as we have seen, it is at once the most meaning
symbol of spiritual things, nay the very veil of the Christian's
Deity; and yet should be as it is, the intensifying agent in
things the most appalling to mankind." " Of all these things,"
says Ishmael in conclusion, " the Albino whale was the symbol."

The meaning of these observations is considerably extended
by the notice that all the hues of the visible world which are

contained in "the concrete of all colors" are but the outer deceits of that deified Nature who "absolutely paints like the harlot," covering "the charnal house within." The import of this controversial and disturbing image is fully revealed by Melville some years later in the opening of Marianna's story, *The Piazza*. Before he ascends the mountain to visit this "Tahitian" girl of the Berkshires, he walks on the porch of his house. "I could not bear to look upon a Chinese creeper of my adoption, and which, to my delight, climbing a post of the piazza, had burst out in starry bloom, but now, if you removed the leaves a little, showed millions of strange, cankerous worms, which feeding upon those blossoms, so shared their blessed hue, as to make them unblessed evermore." [2] This Chinese creeper, imagistically rendered as it is, stands for this same deified, painted Nature visibly beautiful, invisibly repulsive. It is the sign of that archetypal whiteness calling up "a peculiar apparition of the soul." As the veil of the deity, it is more than the pure radiance of the Christian "hue." It is the white sign of the God of all being who has borne such Oriental names as Bhagavat, Brahma—the God of endless contradiction. There is, of course, a disparity between the Melville of the directly revealed private emotion, as in the reflection upon painted Nature and the description of the flowering vine, and the Melville who creates the symbol of pagan acceptance in Billy Budd and Queequeg. The one reveals the disillusionment of the man born within the traditions of absolutism; the other reveals the ideality of the artist, Ishmael.

But the real problem in interpreting whiteness does not lie in the dichotomy between Melville's private emotion as a man of Western civilization and his ideality as symbolist. We seek to know the meaning of whiteness as the sign of theology. This is the theology of feeling, quite apart from the traditional theologies of intellection and dogmatism; and Ishmael, in making this theology, selects from feeling what, in the light of his experience, seems to him a just description of the nature of God. Thus, Melville's dependence upon observation and feel-

[2] *The Piazza Tales*, p. 8.

ing brings him to his essential apostasy: he rejects the dogma of Christian faith in his proposal that the truth of God's nature was not, and could not have been made fully manifest on earth. For the full nature of God was unknowable even to the Son; hence, Christianity cannot present through dogma any *fixed* truth. Before further comment, the nature of this apostasy, as Melville presents it in *Clarel*, must be examined.

At the outset, it is clear that Melville, like the " new " philosopher of the twentieth century, is entirely aware of the unending act of symbolization in human history: old symbolic systems disappear and new ones inevitably follow. Thus Derwent in *Clarel* speaks:

> Suppose an instituted creed
> (Or truth or fable) should indeed
> To ashes fall; the spirit exhales,
> But reinfunds in active forms.[3]

This recognition, with its attention to " inactive " forms (symbols) , explains the heretical thought presented in Part I of the poem in an impressive section called " The Arch." Here Melville speaks through the youth Celio, an apostate of Rome, who seeks in the Holy Land a new affirmation of the Catholic creed, which he cannot accept. As evening falls over Jerusalem, Celio walks across the city to the Via Crucis, to the arch named Ecce Homo, at the spot where Christ was relinquished by Pilate to his enemies. Then follows Celio's solitary reflection:

> No raptures which with saints prevail,
> Nor trouble of compunction born
> He felt, as there he seemed to scan
> Aloft in spectral guise, the pale
> Still face, the purple robe, and thorn;
> And inly cried—*Behold the Man!*
> Yon Man it is this burden lays:
> Even He who in the pastoral hours,
> Abroad in fields, and cheered by flowers,
> Announced a heaven's unclouded days;
> And, ah, with such persuasive lips—

[3] *Clarel*, vol. 2, p. 105 (Part III, Sec. xxi) .

Those lips now sealed while doom delays—
Won men to look for solace there;
But, crying out in death's eclipse,
When rainbow none His eyes might see,
Enlarged the margin for despair—
My God, My God, forsakest Me?

Upbraider! we upbraid again;
Thee we upbraid; our pangs constrain
Pathos itself to cruelty.
Ere yet Thy day no pledge was given
Of homes and mansions in the heaven—
Paternal homes reserved for us;
Heart hoped it not, but lived content—
Content with life's own discontent,
Nor deemed that fate ere swerved for us:
The natural law men let prevail;
Then reason disallowed the state
Of instinct's variance with fate.
But Thou—ah, see, in rack how pale
Who did the world with throes convulse;
Behold Him—yea—behold the Man
Who warranted if not began
The dream that drags out its repulse.

. . . .

'Tis eighteen cycles now—
Enigma and evasion grow;
And shall we never find Thee out?
What isolation lones Thy state
That all we else know cannot mate
With what Thou teachest? Nearing Thee
All footing fails us; history
Shows there a gulf where bridge is none!
In lapse of unrecorded time,
Just after the apostles' prime,
What chance or craft might break it down?
Served this a purpose? By what art
Of conjuration might the heart
Of heavenly love, so sweet, so good,
Corrupt into the creeds malign,
Begetting strife's pernicious brood,
Which claimed for patron Thee divine?

Anew, anew,
For this Thou bleedest, Anguished Face;

Yea, Thou through ages to accrue,
Shalt the Medusa shield replace:
In beauty and in terror too
Shalt paralyse the nobler race—
Smite or suspend, perplex, deter—
Tortured, shalt prove a torturer,
Whatever ribald Future be,
Thee shall these heed, amaze their hearts with Thee—
Thy white, Thy red, Thy fairness and Thy tragedy.[4]

This passage, with its description of the abyss between God
and Christ, the professed manifestation of God, is the most important theological statement Melville ever made. Proceeding
from Melville's image of creeds falling into ashes, one reaches
in the soliloquy of Celio a direct description of the great Redemption symbol in decay. It is not the historicity of Christ
which is rejected, but the terror of absolutism. The promise
of the Gospel and the promise of the Cross are irreconcilable,
as absolutes, with the nature of a supreme God endlessly eluding the " man-dreamed " revelation of the promises. To follow
the text: man before Christ was content with life's discontent;
" natural " law prevailed; and after Christ the hope of an absolute knowledge of God as mercy and justice convulsed the
world; Christ's earthly love was corrupted into creeds malig-
nantly breeding strife in the name of Christian patronage; the
anguished face now becomes the face of Medusa capable of
paralyzing with terror the race of man living in the aspiration
of the promises; Christ, upbraided by the tortured Celio, becomes the torturer of man in the contradiction of *whiteness*
in His fairness, *red* in His tragedy.

None of this reasoning will deny what has been earlier said
in the analysis of Christ in the symbol of Billy Budd. It is again
obvious that the fairness of Christ is the fairness of a man
among men, living in the bond of human love. But beyond this
fairness is the tragedy of Christ *as represented by the dogma of
creeds* (it is impossible to overemphasize this distinction), the
tragedy of man who seeks to define the totality of God and who

---

[4] *Clarel,* vol. 1, pp. 52–54.

dares to give to man the absolutes of God which become promises of God's benevolence. In simple terms, the passage is Melville's contention that Christ in his ministry to men did not
know the inscrutable nature of God, and Melville's denial that
Christ among men was the manifestation of the *totality* of God.
Thus the ideality of the Christ of the Redemption and the
perpetuation and interpretation of this ideality in the dogma
of sects are rejected as the over-aspiration of Christian absolutism. White at the conclusion of the passage is purity, the
purity of love among humanity, and this is of the incomprehensible God; red is the tragedy of over-aspiration and absolutism, and this, too, is of the same incomprehensible God. Since
God is all things and conditions, he is simultaneously love and
hate, beauty and terror, white and red, and all the paradoxes,
the contrasts, the disparities, the poles of the universe.

The whiteness of Christ is comprehensible to man. It represents man's proper sacrament of love in an existence which
cannot be fully understood through the courses of human
reason. For this existence, originating in God, contradicts, in
its own interior forces, the power of love, and is itself a reflection of the contradictions which God encompasses in himself.
The red of Christ is the "unnatural" tragedy of over-reason,
the futile and unproductive tragedy of attempting to master
God. This red is the tragic Christ established by Christian
theology and apostolic dogma. Melville tells us through Celio
that the whiteness of Christ's *feeling* of communion among men
is the only attribute of God's whiteness which man may *know*.
Beyond is the supreme whiteness of God, containing in itself
without distinction the red of Christ, as well, and all the hues
of universal being.

For Melville begins to fashion his theology in *Mardi*, as he
begins to make symbols for his God; and thus no one need be
astonished at the theology of *Clarel*. Here, through the wisdom
of his old Polynesian "philosopher," Babbalanja, discoursing
over the calm waters of an unknown Pacific lagoon, Melville
reflects upon the Oriental being of Oro, god of Polynesia. This
Oro (as we know through ethnology, the illustrious descendent

of the Hindu Brahma) is the God of Mardi (the world). So comes the wisdom of the sage (*Mardi*, Ch. CXXXV):

> Nay; for the Searcher of the cores of all hearts well knoweth that atheists there are none. For in things abstract, men but differ in the sounds that come from their mouths, and not in the wordless thoughts lying at the bottom of their beings. The universe is all of one mind. Though my twin-brother sware to me, by the blazing sun in heaven at noonday, that Oro is not; yet would he belie the thing he intended to express. . . . Let us be content with the theology in the grass and the flower, in seed-time and harvest. Be it for us to know that Oro indubitably is. . . . Sick with the spectacle of the madness of men, and broken with spontaneous doubts. I sometimes see but two things in all Mardi to believe:—that I myself exist, and that I can most happily, or least miserably exist, by the practice of righteousness. All else is in the clouds; and naught else may I learn, till the firmament be split from horizon to horizon.

Melville's assignment of these words to an old and wise Polynesian requires no interpretation. The " righteousness " by which one lives most happily or least miserably is, in this theological beginning, primitive acceptance of that Being (Oro or God) who will never be known to man; and it is the righteousness of human love.

1 *Animism*

W. H. Hudson is the only primitivist who derives from Melville's reflections upon whiteness. In an essay of *Idle Days in Patagonia*, which he calls " Snow, and the Quality of Whiteness," he refers to Melville's famous chapter of *Moby-Dick* as " perhaps the finest thing in the book." [5] I have already commented on the nature of *Green Mansions* as a primitivistic document. The South American locus of the work excludes

---

[5] *The Collected Works of W. H. Hudson* (London, 1923), vol. 16, p. 104. It is strange that students of Melville have overlooked this instance of Melville's influence. H. Cahoon appears to be the only student of Hudson's chapter, in a brief essay " Melville and W. H. Hudson," *American Notes and Queries*, vol. 8, pp. 131-32.

it from the concerns of this study. Furthermore, animism, rather than Christian and Oriental thought, governs its symbolic form. Thus animism directs Hudson's examination of man's reaction to the whiteness of snow: ". . . that mysterious something that moves us at the sight of snow springs from the animism that exists in us, and our animistic way of regarding all exceptional phenomena." [6] Animism Hudson defines as "not a doctrine of souls that survive the bodies and objects they inherit, but the mind's projection of itself into nature, its attribution of its own sentient life and intelligence to all things —that primitive universal faculty on which the animistic philosophy of the savage is founded." He continues: "Poets [using the figure, e. g., ' rejoicing sun '] speak not in metaphor, as we are taught to say. . . . In moments of excitement, when we revert to primitive conditions of mind, the earth and all nature is alive and intelligent, and feels as we feel." [7] In his discussion of whiteness Melville proposes that the mariner, looking out at midnight upon the phantom of whitened waters, is struck with fear, not from the danger of hidden rocks but from this spectacle of hideous whiteness. He will not rest until the blue water is under him again. This fear of the seasoned mariner Hudson interprets as animism: ". . . to his animistic mind that whiteness was nothing but the sign of ocean's wrath —the sight of its tremendous passion and deadly purpose proved too appalling." [8] Ocean receives and puts on the sentient being of the mariner who is appalled at the incomprehensibility apparent in this reflection of his own dread.

Hudson and Melville agree in this genetic area of animism. Melville means exactly what Hudson means when he remarks in his chapter: "Bethink thee of the albatross, whence come those clouds of spiritual wonderment and pale dread, in which that white phantom sails in all imaginations? Not Coleridge first threw that spell; but God's great, unflattering laureate, Nature." For this animism is nothing more than the commonly shared archetype of whiteness. The essential difference between Hudson and Melville—and here the one illuminates the other—

---

[6] *Ibid.*, p. 110. [7] *Ibid.*, p. 111. [8] *Ibid.*, p. 113.

is that Hudson's approach is nonmoralistic in feeling, Melville's, both moralistic and theological. Hudson attempts in his study of the snows of South American mountains to grasp the conditions of an animistic approach to nature. Melville, sharply denoting here the difference between his own reading and such an approach as that of Hudson, emerges from his examination of the archetype into an immediate symbolic representation of the nature of God described by whiteness. This ultimate destiny of Melville, the theologian, comes into view here with dramatic power. Whiteness becomes " the most meaning symbol of spiritual things." Proceeding beyond his view of that deified Nature that paints like the harlot with all the " broken " hues of the universe, Melville concludes with his consideration of " the mystical cosmetic which produces every one of her hues, the great principle of light, forever . . . white or colourless in itself." " Pondering all this, the palsied universe lies before us a leper; and like wilful travellers in Lapland, who refuse to wear coloured and colouring glasses upon their eyes, so the wretched infidel gazes himself blind at the monumental white shroud that wraps all the prospect around him."

This conclusion is rich with meaning. The universe is all-white; the wretched infidel-traveler is the man of folly, such as Ahab, who may gaze himself blind at the white enigma about him. The coloured glasses suggest that the wise traveler may save his vision by directing it to its proper *human* limitations. Melville's encounter with archetypal whiteness brings him to the theological meaning of his Whale, the symbol of the incomprehensible God.

2   *The Vortex*

" So, floating on the margin of the ensuing scene, and in full sight of it, when the half-spent suction of the sunk ship reached me, I was then, but slowly, drawn towards the closing vortex. When I reached it, it had subsided to a creamy pool." These words of Ishmael, from the epilogue to *Moby-Dick*, describe the maelstrom in which the *Pequod* sinks. The sky-hawk has been impaled upon the spar with the flag nailed there by Tashtego; the "yawning gulf" has been closed by the shroud of the sea. In a moment Ishmael is to be saved by Queequeg's coffin thrust up from that "vital centre." This vortex is the most familiar of Ishmael's critical experiences. But there are four others, at least, in the same pattern. A close study of these, with the master scene at the close of *Moby-Dick* at hand, reveals the meaning of the vortex as symbol. The presence of whiteness in this symbol relates the meaning of the crisis to the meaning of God-in-whiteness. In its symbolic function, the vortex displays some of the most intricate complexities to be found in Melville's feeling as artist, and it is constantly related to the theological significance of whiteness as both archetype and avatar. A chronological arrangement of its recurrences in Melville's work shows, furthermore, another master pattern of prefiguration, one such as has been studied already in the pro- totypes and inheritors of the sailor savage. The symbolic form of the vortex is obsessive.

A general principle for the reading of this symbol may be initially stated: the vortex represents descent into the water, the emblematic essence of God. Ishmael in relation to the vortex, the descent, is Ishmael in view of God the unknowable. The parts of each variation upon the vortex as pattern specify aspects of the total theological meaning.

Ishmael's first encounter with whiteness as the emblem of God is discovered in Taji's Yillah of *Mardi*. At the close of *Mardi* it becomes apparent that Yillah, through the experimen- tation of this first symbolistic work, has assumed the meaning of Truth. It will be recalled that Taji has thrown off the blandishments of the enchantress, Hautia, who, in her flowers and her sensual delights and her serpentine magic that threatens to "drink up" Taji's soul, may remind us of some hybrid crossing of Richard Wagner's Venus and Keats's Lamia. In this final chapter of *Mardi*, Taji, fleeing Hautia, gains a "twilight arch" in a cliff along the sea. Passing through, he comes upon a transparent lake, where conflicting currents meet and wrestle in the turbulent confluence of lake and sea. There in the deepest eddies, a gleaming form circles: it is " white and vaguely Yillah." Taji plunges in, but the currents are "as fierce headwinds off capes, that beat back ships." In this vortex Yillah eludes him. But now at the close of the book and of this voyage to Mardi (the world) he becomes his own soul's emperor; he " abdicates," he says, and puts to sea. The currents have swept Yillah oceanward, and Yillah he will pursue.

I have earlier cited this conclusion of *Mardi* as Melville's scene of departure upon the sea of symbol-making. At the same moment, it is Ishmael's departure upon the quest for the meaning of primitive innocence in the totality of God. Yillah has been described earlier in this study as of semi-divine origin (from the Polynesian legend of Hina). At the close of *Mardi* she becomes a symbol of the essence of waters and takes her place, in a family union strange indeed, with the White Whale, the sharks, and the sailor savage who sail upon the surface of the deep, that mysterious face of God himself. She is a symbolic experiment in describing the essence of God; but unlike the whiteness of Moby Dick, hers is the whiteness of Truth, itself contained in the all-color of God. Taji's pursuit of Yillah, at this point in Melville's career, becomes the prototype of Ahab's pursuit of Moby Dick. Thus Ishmael begins his symbol-making as absolutist, as the man dedicated to the pursuit of absolute truth, even though he begins in love, not in the vengeance of Ahab. Ishmael as Taji at the close of *Mardi* confesses that the whiteness he sees in the vortex is endlessly elusive to man. Its absoluteness may never be grasped, but he will pursue. Ahab, the fool of truth, denies the elusiveness of absolute knowledge to the final moment when he drowns with the *Pequod*, sucked down in the God-made vortex of her death. By the time Ishmael has arrived at the narration of Ahab's quest, he has cast off the absolutism of Taji's aspiration.

In the chapter (XCII) immediately preceding the close of *White-Jacket*, Melville reaches the second vortex of the symbolic pattern associated with this experience. White-Jacket is on the weather-top-gallant-yard-arm, reeving the line through the block. Suddenly the ship plunges, and he is pitched from the yard to fall a hundred feet into the sea. The heavy skirts of his white jacket, muffling him, have broken his hold upon the sail. As he falls, " through the eddying whirl and swirl of the Maelstrom air," time seems to stand still. His " braided, blended emotions " are " icy cold and calm." As he " gushes " into the sea, his soul seems to be flying from his mouth. Then he sinks below the surface, and bounds back, after some terrifying moments of wondering whether he lives or is dead. The seamen on the ship toss out a line. But the white jacket, soaked with the water, pinions him like a feather-bed. He takes out his knife, slashes off the obstacle of the jacket, and swims away towards a life-buoy astern of the frigate. " Sink! sink! oh shroud! thought I; sink forever! accursed jacket that thou art! " The seamen, thinking that the sinking jacket is a white shark, cast harpoons at it, and so the accursed garment disappears from sight as the youth is picked up by a cutter and returned safely aboard.

In the presence of whiteness as symbol we return to a pattern of meaning introduced in Taji's pursuit of Yillah. The voyager is again in or near the maelstrom. At the close of *Mardi* he has dedicated himself to the pursuit of elusive whiteness. At the close of *White-Jacket* he casts off whiteness to survive. In the fall from the yard-arm he sinks through " a soft, seething, foamy lull." A current seems to hurry him away. He hangs " vibrating in the mid-deep." Like Pip of *Moby-Dick*, he has descended into the primal waters. And into these he would sink forever, should he allow the white jacket to pull him down again. The whiteness which the youth wears to this point of liberation is Taji's sign of whiteness from *Mardi*, the " white " hero who in turn seeks the whiteness of Yillah. But the Ishmael-voyager emerges from the sea-change of *White-Jacket* liberated from dedication to the search for absolute truth; he is freed into the ideality of primitive innocence.

Were it not for the analogies which exist between the " falling scene " of *White-Jacket* and the epilogue of *Moby-Dick*, these conclusions could not be so firmly asserted. But beyond this vortex common to both in the ceremony of innocence—in the one, the hero liberated from absolutism, in the other, the sole survivor sustained on the " buoy " of Queequeg's coffin— is the device of the shark. The sinking white jacket seems a shark to the seamen aboard the *Neversink*, and they pierce it with harpoons. This seeming shark attends Ishmael's peril. But like the whiteness of God, it is other than what it seems. So, too, are those *unharming* sharks that swim about Ishmael, as the presence of Queequeg's coffin " padlocks " their mouths, other than what they seem. They come from God, they are manifestations of God. Earlier in the story, they have fed voraciously upon the blubber of a slaughtered whale, moored to the side of the *Pequod*, have fed with that voraciousness by which all Nature lives (Ch. LXIV). Their meaning as truth cannot be grasped. They are only unharming through the power of a man of primitive innocence (Queequeg) who is dragged to the sea-floor by the obdurateness of Ahab. Ishmael, unquestioning, through the example of his pagan friend, is safe as he floats over the waters where that creamy white pool has closed the vortex. In this third experience with the maelstrom, Ishmael, the symbolist-voyager, is again preserved. But this time there is no whiteness to be cast off. To plunge into the depths is to descend into the insoluble mysteries of God. Here Pip's descent into the great deep (*Moby-Dick*, Ch. XCIII) illustrates the concept governing the symbol. Pip, from that hour of his " drowning " in " the unwarped primal world " where he saw " God's foot upon the treadle of the loom," had appeared mad to his shipmates of the *Pequod*. But the fortunate Ishmael survives upon the surface, sustained by the coffin of Queequeg, that noble pagan indifferent to divine mysteries, indifferent to death.

The symbolic experiences of both White-Jacket and Ishmael are combined intricately in the fourth instance of the vortex to be reviewed here. The scene occurs in *Clarel*, Part III, in the section called " Man and Bird " (xxvii). The pilgrims to the monastery of Mar Saba have fallen into the company of another traveler, an old mariner from Lesbos; and this " good gossip," as he is called, tells an anecdote. It is the story of a young sailor alone at the mast-head, strapping a block for the halyards.

As he works, the sailor suddenly feels the fanning of wings over his head. He looks up, into the eye of a large bird, red-billed and black.[9] To his amazement, this demon creature begins to peck and tear at his woolen cap. He loses his stay on the mast, and falls, pursued by the bird. Like White-Jacket, he is hurled into the sea, and as he sinks below the surface, he hears the piercing " gird " (the sneering cry) of the bird bearing away the cap in his beak. When the sailor bounds to the surface, he swims toward the ship. Now his shipmates, thinking that they see a shark astern, fire a harpoon. Their catch is the sailor, whom they drag aboard. The man is water-logged with the spongy lumps of quilted patches on his shirt and trousers. He lies inert. And then he confides that the taunt of the thieving bird was more bitter to him than the brine of the sea. The bird, he deemed, was the devil, who carried off his soul in the old cap.

This interlude of *Clarel* is obviously made of elements from the final scenes of *White-Jacket* and of *Moby-Dick*. The fall from the mast, the descent through the air and into the sea, the rising to the surface, the harpooning of the " shark," even the water-soaked clothing all come from the incident of White-Jacket's fall from the yard-arm. The bird at the mast-head and its shrieks recall the scene of the *Pequod's* sinking, as Tashtego nails the standard to the spar. The manipulation of whiteness, in the *seeming* body of the shark, against the blackness of the bird is of interest here. The sky-hawk of *Moby-Dick* is called a part of heaven. The *Pequod*, like Satan, will not sink until she has dragged this token with her and helmeted herself with it. In this incident from *Clarel* the bird is black, of the devil, and the cap snatched away, says this man of Lesbos, was the soul. The " gird " of the creature is a transposed sound: it comes from the " archangelic shriek " of the sky-hawk in *Moby-Dick*. To humanity, which is shark and which is man? Which is archangelic bird, a part of heaven, and which the demon black thing, the agent of Satan, that snatches away the prize of the soul? Melville's use of clothing here in the sense of spiritual

---

[9] Very probably the " man-of-war's hawk " described in *Typee*, Ch. II.

being is exactly the same use which he has earlier made in *White-Jacket*. The clue to meaning in this rather difficult passage in *Clarel* is found in the assertion by the narrator that the black creature of the air, attacking the sailor, pecked at his brain (presumably through the holes of the old woolen cap). And at this moment the sailor lost his stay on the mast, and went plunging through that vortex of air and sea. The image of the brain here introduces the folly of human reason. As soon as the sailor wonders what power has attacked him, he falls, and makes the same descent into the waters which White-Jacket experienced. In comparison with the descent of Tashtego aboard the sinking *Pequod*, the descent of the sailor in this scene from *Clarel* means again human powerlessness in the vortex of reason. For though Tashtego has nothing to do with reason, it is Ahab's folly which drowns him. And it is from this vortex that Ishmael is saved by his own *unreasoning* acceptance, learned from the example of Queequeg. The sea-hawk of *Moby-Dick* and this black demoniac bird of *Clarel* are one in the multiplicity of the same God. The clothes of White-Jacket, the woolen cap of the sailor from this anecdote of the man of Lesbos, the sharks swimming about Ishmael and the sharks " seen " in these water-soaked victims of the vortex are all symbolistically interrelated.

The fifth instance of the vortex appears in *Billy Budd* (Ch. XXIII). Billy has been hanged, and his body is laced into his shotted canvas hammock for burial. As white as the white of his clothing, the hammock becomes his shroud. The whiteness of innocence is in this sign of Billy Budd, for all his other signs are white as well. His is the last vortex. As the man of innocence, condemned to death by human processes reflecting in themselves the inscrutability of God, the coexistence of good and evil, beauty and hideousness, the body of Billy is now given to the mysteries of " primal waters," the ultimate God. A " peculiar commotion " in the water as the hammock disappears beneath the surface attracts " certain larger sea-fowl." They wing so near the hull of the *Indomitable* that the bony creak of " their double-jointed pinions " is audible; and as the ship passes on, they circle the burial spot " with the moving shadow of their outstretched wings and the cracked requiem of their cries." The bird of God marking the vortex has been seen before. White or black, it is the token of the mystery of descent into the waters. But now the whiteness of Yillah has been exchanged, through all the intervening mutations of the vortex, for the whiteness of Billy Budd. Ishmael, the maker of this last of Melville's symbols, stands now far from the moment of Taji's vision of glimmering whiteness in the depths. He is the Ishmael of acceptance. Billy in life was the innocent man among men. This was and is the only truth that can be known. It is in this innocence that he " ascends " from his execution. But in the mystery of that God who permits the triumph of evil over innocence, he is buried, with only the memorial cries of sea-birds to mark the point of his descent. A quiet sea rolls on, and it is full day: ". . . the circumambient air in the clearness of its serenity was like smooth white marble in the polished block not yet removed from the marble-dealer's yard." How distant is this aerial whiteness and serenity from the whiteness of Milton's " pure marble Air "! " Down right into the World's first Region " comes the fallen Lucifer in his flight precipitant, making his oblique way " amongst innumerable Stars " (*Paradise Lost*, III, 562-64). The opalescence through which Lucifer travels is only the palest extension of that divine, refulgent light coming from the Christian God of all light and goodness, the everlasting conqueror of darkness and evil. Such is the difference between Melville's relativism, his " great principle of light " encompassing all the hues of the universe, and the absolutism of Milton, in this metaphor of God's marble-white air.

3 Autotypes of Whiteness

The origin of the vortex, with its images of hanging and falling and swimming, is archetypal. The theology which these scenes as symbols represent is directed toward the Oriental concept of all-encompassing deity. Whiteness becomes the third of Melville's great avatars when it is rendered through the autotypes of his experience. His use of whiteness in the following examples of autotypes is generally connotative of innocence and goodness, although I shall note exceptions. It is understood by this time that the whiteness of innocence belongs to the all-whiteness of God, even as all the hues of the universe must belong there.

The first view of whiteness which we have in Melville's work is a vision of Marquesan beauty. Young Tom, looking from a mountain height into the valley of the Taipis, believes that he has had a glimpse of the gardens of Paradise (*Typee*, Ch. VII). " From the spot where I lay transfixed with surprise and delight, I looked straight down into the bosom of a valley, which swept away in long wavy undulations to the blue waters in the distance. Midway towards the sea, and peering here and there amidst the foliage, might be seen the palmetto-thatched houses of its inhabitants glistening in the sun that had bleached them to a dazzling whiteness." [10] This is the beginning. Presently young Tom observes that white is the sacred " colour " among the Marquesans. When he visits the mausoleum of a deceased warrior chief (Ch. XXIV), he finds the sign of the inscrutable *tabu* " in the shape of a mystic roll of white tappa, suspended by a twisted cord of the same material from the top of a slight pole planted in the enclosure." His later account of his interview with Marnoo (Ch. XVIII) reveals whiteness in the observance of the *tabu* protecting this handsome stranger: Marnoo wears " a slight girdle of white tappa, scarcely two inches in width, but hanging before and behind in spreading tassels." Both Stewart and Porter bear Melville out in their accounts of the ceremonial use of white. Stewart describes a dancing youth adorned with a sash of this native white cloth; [11] Porter speaks of men of high station wearing cloaks of " a white cloth, in appearance somewhat like paper " and carrying handsome white fans.[12] These persons were undoubtedly *tabu* in the manner of Marnoo. Sir James Frazer has recorded that Marquesan

[10] This dazzling whiteness of thatch is presented in the same manner by C. S. Stewart, *A Visit to the South Seas*, vol. 1, p. 211. Stewart is describing life on Nukuhiva.

[11] *Ibid.*, vol. 1, p. 235.

[12] *Journal of a Cruise Made to the Pacific Ocean*, vol. 2, p. 10.

banqueting halls for men (which should be here compared with
Melville's "Ti") were marked by long pennants of white
cloth attached to posts of the house, these signifying the *tabu*
cast upon these retreats.[13] The observations of Melville's young
Tom are here very clearly validated, from his first view of
glistening white roofs among the trees. Whiteness is sacred in
the Marquesas, and it is the emblem of innocence to the
Ishmael-symbolist. It is the sign of divinity.

Yet this whiteness is interchangeable in its symbolic meaning. Note, for instance, what Melville is willing to do with the
primitive connotations of white in his chapter of *Moby-Dick*
called "The Candles" (Ch. CXIX). In the pallid light of the
corposants glowing on the yard-arms Queequeg's tattooing
"burned like Satanic blue flames on his body," and the parted
mouth of his primitive companion Tashtego "revealed . . .
shark-white teeth." Thus it is not at all strange to find Fedallah,
the evil alter-ego of Ahab, wearing yet another whiteness: he
has "one white tooth protruding from its steel-like lips"; over
the "ebonness" of his costume rises "a glistening white plaited
turban, the living hair braided and coiled round and round
upon his head" (*Moby-Dick*, Ch. XLVIII). Fedallah is seen by
Ishmael in a later description as a creature of "those insulated,
immemorial, unalterable countries, which even in these modern
days still preserve much of the ghostly aboriginalness of earth's
primal generations" (Ch. L). His whiteness is Oriental, as is
the ancient Polynesian whiteness which Tom has seen displayed
in Typee Valley. But Fedallah's whiteness is of evil. Both
manifestations represent the mysteries of God. If white denotes
"sacredness" from all these Oriental autotypes (for I venture
that Melville had seen Parsees as well as the noblemen of Polynesia), then it reveals innocence in one direction, evil in
another. Fedallah is the mysterious agent who confirms Ahab
in his absolutist's evil, his insane resolve to pursue and to
conquer the mysteries of the White Whale.

The union of opposites in Melville's symbol of whiteness has
been correctly interpreted by M. O. Percival, who notes that in

[13] *The Belief in Immortality and The Worship of the Dead*, vol. 2, p. 342.

whiteness good and evil are held together "in a mysterious unity beyond the power of the finite mind to comprehend." [14] But every use of white does not, of course, represent the union. Pure good appears in the radiance of Marquesan whiteness. Again, good is clearly discernible in Melville's description of the white albatross, in his footnote to the chapter on whiteness. Through the purity of this creature, dashed upon the main hatches, Ishmael, bowing as Abraham before the angels, has lost " the miserable warping memories of traditions and towns." Melville complements this tribute to white purity with his reflection upon the legend of the White Steed of the Prairies in the same chapter, that creature " a most imperial and arch-angelical apparition of that unfallen, western world, which to the eyes of old trappers and hunters revived the glories of those primeval times when Adam walked majestic as a god." Or there is the picture of white sails glistening about Liverpool harbor in *Redburn* (Ch. XLVII) , " like a great Eastern encampment of Sultans " in the clear morning air. Only Conrad's description of the *Narcissus* under full sail in the moonlight can match the purity of this morning whiteness of ships at Liverpool: " The moonlight clung to her like a frosted mist, and the white sails stood out in dazzling cones as of stainless snow." [15] These are not symbols of the union of opposites. They are emblems of purity, of oneness. Not until we come to Moby Dick himself do we discover the full meaning of " Oriental " whiteness as avatar. In the White Whale, as I shall show, the values are combined.

Finally, there is Melville's use of whiteness in Billy Budd's costume on the night before his execution. Soon the chaplain will come to him, and Billy will reply like some innocent Tahitian of Captain Cook's time. Billy lies on the gun deck, under the threatening blackness of guns and carriages. " In contrast with the funereal tone of those surroundings the prone sailor's exterior apparel, white jumper and white duck trowsers, each more or less soiled, dimly glimmered in the obscure light

[14] *A Reading of Moby-Dick* (Chicago, 1950), p. 57.
[15] *The Nigger of the " Narcissus,"* in *Collected Works* (Dent), vol. 18, p. 145.

of the bay like a patch of discoloured snow in early April lingering at some upland cave's black mouth. In effect he is already in his shroud or the garments that shall serve him in lieu of one " (Ch. xx). Through the Polynesian reference of Billy's innocence, the whiteness of his uniform takes up again, in the autotype, the meaning of Marquesan whiteness. It is the symbol of Billy's primal innocence, as much as the burial of Billy in whiteness is a symbol of the all-whiteness, the all-color of God, as much as that circumambient air in its smoothness of white marble holds the white light of the incomprehensible deity.

Melville's theology represented in whiteness contends against the folly of over-reason. It presents the non-Christian concept that the God of endless contradiction may be known only through as much of radiance as man may discover in the beauty of his fellows and as much of darkness, as much of " primal " shadow and aboriginalness, as much of evil as may be described. For in his supreme and endless whiteness God contains all. Out of this theology come the symbols which are to be defined in the following chapters of this study. They are symbols of the multiplicity of God; and they all show in some way, as avatars, as reincarnations from the Orient, the timelessness of God in whom the signs of both the primitive and the civilized endlessly cross each other and are contained. God is represented in the fairness of Christ, but he is represented at the same moment in the shadow of some Eastern mystery, or in what man understands as the evidence of evil. The appearance of the two together, to recall once more the unknowable Oro of Mardi, is the appearance of what God " indubitably is." " All else is in the clouds; and naught else may I learn, till the firmament be split from horizon to horizon." Ishmael, now theologian, must pray only as Pip prays in *Moby-Dick* (Ch. xl) : " Oh, thou big white God aloft there somewhere in yon darkness, have mercy on this small black boy down here; preserve him from all men that have no bowels to feel fear." [16]

---

[16] The theological implications of Ishmael's voyage, with its final haven in the symbolism of *Billy Budd*, have been perceptively recognized by W. H. Auden in his poem " Herman Melville."

IX

Shadows and
Erotic Symbols

God manifest in primitive innocence is, at the same moment, God manifest in primal mind and in primitive eros. The avatar to be discussed in this chapter is that of primal mind, of dark blood-consciousness. In the symbolic structure of Melville's art it has its own validity. It is the symbol of the dark, instinctive mind living and generating in another area of that great whiteness which has just been described. There it is contained in God with the " lighter," more radiant symbols, the avatars of sacrament represented in the ideality of *puer aeternus* and of Polynesian ethos. Again, both archetype and autotype appear in the forms of the primitivist's symbolistic rendering.

Again, the avatar describes religious feeling. If Billy Budd and Queequeg are light to the darkness of Ahab and Pierre, then, as primitivistic symbols, they are light to the dark of other areas of primitive mind and feeling. In this second sense, they do not oppose the absolutism of the tragic Christian hero. They rather stand in contrast to other primitive emblems. The sign of Billy Budd is primitive white; but there are primitive " hues " as well which belong to the primal mind idealized in him. It has been said that the symbols of sacrament project the artist's ideality. It follows now that ideality is exchanged for pure symbolic description, and that the description becomes the application of Melville's Oriental theology to his making of a record of the multifarious God evident to man. The symbols which come into being in this province of Melville's art, especially those of remarkable erotic content, acknowledge the multiplicity of primal mind. They support anew what has been said of Melville as relativist. The first fact for attention is that they take form through autotypes revealing Melville's sensitivity to " dark " and to erotic circumstance in his experiences as the voyager. They are, of course, all particularly attractive to Freudian critics. It is my intention to analyze them through the method which has already been established. Freudianism can in no sense account for the relationship between these autotypes and the theology which Melville's symbols describe.

The closing scene of *Mardi* presents Taji pursued by three " pale sons " of Aleema, the priest slain long ago by Taji in his act of freeing Yillah. As shadowy beings and specters, they are appropriate examples of the shadow which distinguishes Melville's dark symbols to follow. They enter the art of Melville through those autotypes of the journey which are highly informed with emotion but which never reach the sharp delineation to be found in the symbols of the sailor savage and the Polynesian wise man. The avatar of primal mind is inevitably spectral. It has been seen that certain memorials of Melville's Christian heritage are brought to the service of the symbols of sacrament. The sharpness of Melville's meaning in these forms derives from the condition of a mind of Christian civilization predisposed to that ideality expressed in *tayo*, for instance. The condition urges the symbolist to look for what the feeling *toward* communion seeks to find. When it comes to the symbolist confronting the emblems of primitive mind which have no counterparts in his remembered heritage, the sharpness of symbolic form disappears. He merely assimilates what he can of the unknown as he finds it in the Orient.

Thus we get symbolic descriptions of sensuous impressions which relate generally to the primitivist's concept of primal mind. This statement would seem to admit to some ambiguity as characteristic of these spectral symbols. I do not think it does, however, since the symbols all represent the intention of the artist to suggest the mystery of the Oriental, the primal being of God.

1 *Fedallah*

The attributes of Fedallah, generally regarded as the alter-ego and the tempter of Ahab, are familiar to all readers of *Moby-Dick*. This Parsee, this Zoroastrian fire-worshipper, is the only one of Melville's characters fully representing the shadow of primal mind. As attendant to the fire-worshipping Ahab, the worshipper of the corposants and the blazing try-works, he is the force of destruction through which Ahab is confirmed in his insane hatred. Fedallah's fire is of hell itself, the fire of destruction existing in the universe of God. His signs are all of the inscrutable. He is such a creature, says Melville (Ch. L), as "civilized, domestic people in the temperate zone" see only in their dreams, a creature "from the ghostly aboriginalness of earth's primal generations." He appears sinister to every man of the crew. The mate, Flask, expressing his dislike of this incarnation of "the devil," calls Stubb's attention to Fedallah's one protruding white tooth, "that tusk of his . . . carved into a snake's head" (Ch. LXXIII). He is "funereally invested" with Chinese clothing, all of black cotton; and over this darkness glistens his plaited white turban (Ch. XLVIII). He it is who sights the spirit-spout from the look-out, on that calm moonlit night " when all the waves rolled by like scrolls of silver . . . and a silvery jet was seen far in advance of the white bubbles at the bow " (Ch. LI). The spout seems " some plumed and glittering god uprising from the sea." Fedallah is wont to watch by night instead of day. Ahab orders a lowering, but the spout disappears. Thereafter it is seen again, this spout " jetted into the clear moonlight, or starlight," standing out to sea, off the *Pequod's* bow. It is the snowy jet of Moby Dick, eluding Ahab as the snowy whiteness of Yillah eludes Taji. It is the apparition of the great whale, luring the ship toward her destruction in " the remotest and most savage seas." It is the apparition understood by the spectral Fedallah, and pursued by the crazed Ahab.

Fedallah is the Parsee of India. But there seems little doubt that he is made, as well, of the prototypic Bembo, the New Zealand harpooneer aboard the *Julia*, bound for Papeete as the narrative of *Omoo* begins. This dark, moody savage, wholly unrelated to the family of Queequeg, is described as a dark and sinister figure (*Omoo*, Ch. III). He is a Maori cannibal obsessed with dark hatred for the white crew of the ship; and acting as mate in command (Ch. XXIII), he attempts in his savage hunger for vengeance to wreck the *Julia* on the reef of Tahiti. His hostility, his darkness and mystery, and his isolation from the crew of the ship all prefigure the dark primitive attributes of Fedallah. This much, at least, of Melville's autotype passes into the mystery of the Parsee; for Bembo is fashioned of that area of Melville's actual experience which is the source of Dr. Long Ghost and the other " real " characters of *Omoo*.

The quality of Fedallah which fascinates is his indefiniteness; and it is the same quality which informs all Melville's shadowy symbols of primal mind. The aboriginalness of Fedallah is archetypal; it eludes the power of reason. The element of the miraculous in the spirit-spout of Moby Dick, as this phantom watches from his look-out, complements the element of the immeasurable in Fedallah. He is the link between Ahab and the murky depths of both the conscious and the unconscious.

That white, vaporous column that jets up in the moonlight from the sea is a sign of his meaning. Thus it is that he is the master of Ahab's whale-boat and the master of the phantom boat-crew. His are the eyes through which Ahab sweeps the seas for Moby Dick. Through him Ahab passes into the dark realms, the great deeps of God in which all human existence is involved through its dim awareness of its origins. Fedallah is consciousness of those deep primal waters where Pip descended and saw the matrix of creation. Ahab's alter-ego Fedallah may be; but his phantom quality is, more significantly, the shadowy sentience and the knowledge of the mysteries which Ahab aspires to know but can never master. Fedallah is Ahab's guide into the depths of Oriental time, into the aboriginalness of God. He is the mentor of Ahab, just as, in a different meaning of the Orient, Queequeg is the mentor of Ishmael. W. H. Auden is of the opinion that " Queequeg and Fedallah are opposites in their relation to Christianity. . . . Queequeg is the unconscious Christian, Fedallah is the unconscious anti-Christian, the tempter of Ahab." [1] Auden is right in seeing Fedallah and Queequeg as symbolically interrelated, although I doubt that Melville had unconscious Christian or anti-Christian in mind. A close examination of Fedallah in relation to Ahab shows that this phantom Parsee, with his heritage of Zoroastrian mysteries, is intended to establish polarity in the symbol of Ahab himself. Ahab becomes, through Fedallah's influence, at one and the same time the absolutist of Christendom and the explorer wandering among incomprehensible mysteries of God which the Orient *feels* in its vast age. Such is Fedallah's meaning as shadow, specter, phantom; and such is his service to Ahab. Through him we enter the shadows of the Oriental deity.

2 Altars and Stones

> Altars such as Cain's
> Still find we on far island-chains
> Deep mid the woods and hollows dark,
> And set off like the shittim Ark.

---

[1] *The Enchafèd Flood* (New York, 1950), p. 124.

These words of Rolfe in *Clarel* (Part II, Sec. x) recall Melville's Polynesian experience. The stone altars remembered here, in the reference to far island-chains, must certainly be inspired by those monumental ruins discovered on Nukuhiva by Tom of *Typee* (Ch. xxi). Melville says that he came upon a scene in the Marquesan forest which reminded him of Stonehenge and " the architectural labors of the Druids." Then he proceeds to describe the great stone terraces overgrown by trees and vines and remarks that these " dumb stones " were probably placed there three thousand years ago. He is awed, as though he stood at the base of the great Pyramid of Cheops. One of the striking characteristics of the landscape of *Typee* appears here as well: the massiveness of stone outcroppings overgrown with the profusion of jungle plants. Melville appears in these descriptions as particularly sensitive to the antiquity of stone everywhere about him; and it is not surprising to find his feeling for archaic emblems establishing a relationship between ancient nature and ancient religious experience. Through these autotypes of Polynesian landscape and Polynesian ruins he descends into the shadowy aboriginalness of God.

Animism, of course, projects this feeling for the archaic religious significance of stone.[2] In *Mardi* at least two stone images and altars appear. The first of these is the shrine of the god Keevi, placed in a natural niche of a cliff walling in the valley of Monlova (Ch. xcii). This " god of Thieves " has five eyes, ten hands, and three pairs of legs. He is probably more nearly akin to the Hindu representations of Siva than to any image which Melville might have seen in Polynesia. The second is a large image of dark-hued stone in the holy Morai (burial ground) of Maramma (Ch. cix). This image of Doleema, so called, represents a " burly man " with " over-

---

[2] The poetry of Robinson Jeffers, with its frequent symbolism of archaic stone, will illuminate the animism of Melville. See, for instance, " Oh, Lovely Rock," in *Such Counsels You Gave to Me* (New York, Random House, 1937): ". . . this age will die,/ And wolves have howled in snow around a new / Bethlehem: this rock will be here, grave, earnest, not passive: the energies / That are its atoms will still be bearing the whole mountain above: and I, many packed centuries ago, / Felt its intense reality with love and wonder. . . ."

grown head." The abdomen is hollowed out, and in the cavity are placed elements of human sacrifices. These deities in stone are perhaps unmatched in the literature of primitivistic art. Oddly enough, there seem to be no others comparable to them anywhere, save in the musical statues of Samuel Butler's *Erewhon*. Readers of Butler will recall those barbarous images, " neither Egyptian, nor Assyrian, nor Japanese " and yet akin to all. The heads of these massive stone figures are open like organ pipes through which they catch the wind and sound horribly with its blowing.[3] Both these and the massive images described by Melville are animistic as emblems of the artist's feeling.

But the haunting mystery of stone, related to primitive cairns and altars, is encountered in Melville's symbols more directly as the shadow cast into glens and valleys, the places of antique rite. An example of the shadowy place of stone from *Mardi* illustrates this judgment and suggests the archetypal feeling which underlies the description of all rock and stone masses related to the forest and the jungle. I return here to the chapter setting forth the image of Keevi (XCII). It is my suggestion that an autotype is present in the description and that it is the facsimile of an ascent to the great Pali (cliff) falling away from the pass in the mountains rising behind Honolulu, on Oahu. The travelers begin the ascent to the shrine of this Keevi. The fine valley of Monlova (Manoa?) ascends with a gentle gradation. (Melville here thinks of Nuuanu Valley as the approach to the Pali; but, perhaps from inexact memory, he confuses the name with another term from the topography of Oahu.) Then the valley contracts; the cliffs advance. The travelers come to a narrow space shouldered by buttresses of rock. Through the cleft opening in the shadows they look into blue sky. If the trade-winds blow through this defile, says Melville, you would think the god pushing you with his hands, so powerful is the current of air. And then, at the summit, the travelers look down the sheer descent of a thousand feet to the wide plain below. Here fifty rebel warriors, driven back by a superior force, once sprang to their deaths; " but their

[3] *Erewhon or, Over the Range* (London, 1923), pp. 32–33.

souls ascended ere their bodies touched." The geography of the scene and its history are those of the Pali of Oahu. Both geography and history Melville probably learned during his visit to Honolulu in the summer of 1843. The presence of the god in the wind, the image of the rebel warriors ascending to immortality from the fatal leap over the cliff, the defile of massive crags make together the experience of a religious pilgrimage. The image of stone, with its primitive mystery of the animist's God, predominates. Out of the shadow of stone the travelers advance into the presence of a god, himself enshrined in the stony walls of Monlova.

After Yillah has been rescued from the priest Aleema, and at some time before she vanishes into the lagoon, Taji recounts something of her early life in the glen of Ardair (*Mardi*, Ch. L). This valley, shut in by "hoar old cliffs," cannot be very far from the glen of the Taipis or from those Tahitian valleys explored by Paul and Dr. Long Ghost. Here Melville describes a great stone of the shadows which is later to be transposed in its animistic meaning, if not its exact shape, to the shadowy forest of *Pierre*. At the end of the valley, he says a great rock hurled from an adjacent height had fallen in a narrow space between the overhanging cliffs. There it remained fixed. "Aerial trees shot up from its surface; birds nested in its clefts; and strange vines roved abroad, overrunning the tops of trees, lying thereon in coils and undulations, like anacondas basking in the light." Beneath this rock was a wall of stones, and through its crevices appeared the sea in the far distance. Near the foot of the wall was a deep pool fed by the waters of a brook. The rocks about the pool had been worn into a "grotesque resemblance to a group of giants." Here in this pool Yillah would bathe. The shadow of this place, the home of Yillah, the essence of waters, repeats the mystery of the ancient deity of nature already seen in that tangled mass of vines, trees, and sacred stones on the island of Nukuhiva. The feeling of the primitivist was never more clearly marked with animism, with the awesomeness of the " sacred glen " than here.

This mythical Ardair, with its probable combination of many

Polynesian autotypes, is far from the Berkshire hills of Massachusetts. Yet the similarity of the great stone of Ardair to the
" Hanging Memnon Stone " visited by Pierre Glendinning in
his search for the god of nature seems undeniable. Pierre, dis-
tracted by what he has learned of his father's duplicity, seeks
the divinity of the forests; and he seeks death. He plunges deep
into the woods and does not pause until he has come to a great
mass of rock " huge as a barn . . . overarched by beechtrees and
chestnuts." This rock is irregularly wedge-shaped, and somewhere near the middle of its under side it rests on a second
sharpened rock protruding from the ground. On this one frail
point of contact the whole enormous mass is balanced; it hovers
at one end near the soil, without touching it, and at the other
it projects over a space high enough to admit a man.[4] This
Memnon Stone would seem to be a primitive altar for Pierre.
For here he crawls beneath the stone and awaits a " primitive "
death. Then a " down-darting " forest bird startles him from
his vigil, and as though warned by a sign from the nature god,
he eludes his " fate." (A comparison of this forest bird with
another, from the literature of exotic primitivism, is here irre-
sistible: the forest bird of Wagner's *Siegfried*, its voice of premonition from the forest gods, its attendance upon the primitive religious act of the " natural " hero.) At the very least,
it is clear that Melville intended to invest this scene with a
primitive religious significance. It cannot matter whether the
autotype used in the description of the Memnon Stone was
shaped from some of those Polynesian scenes of deep, rocky
glens or whether it came into Melville's mind from an actual
setting in the Berkshires. The point here is simply that Melville's attribution of primitive, animistic meaning and religious
significance to rocks and to glens shut in by stone escarpments
reveals his symbolic approach to the deity of shadows. Through
it he attains a representation of primal religious consciousness.
In these examples from *Mardi* and *Pierre* it is clear that the
rocky scene means the same in each case. The one is the home
of Yillah of the waters, Yillah contained in the primal being of

[4] *Pierre*, p. 185.

God; the other is the objective of the pilgrim Pierre who would leave, if he could, all consciousness of his Christian self in the same all-containing God-being.

The Polynesian glen, with its rocks and shadows, is one of the most frequently recurring of Melville's symbolistic patterns. As will be shown presently, it reappears with unmistakable authority in the most important symbolic chapter of Melville's art, " A Bower in the Arsacides " of *Moby-Dick*. If psychologists intend to resolve Melville's symbols in terms of dream content, it would seem that these obsessive images of glens, rocks, and shadows cannot be surpassed in the promise of the material which they offer. In the last paragraphs that Melville wrote, rock and shadow appear again. Billy Budd, lying on the gun deck in his white jumper, resembles a patch of snow at the mouth of some black, upland cave.

3   Eros

It was in the cool shadows of a rocky glen that Melville first received in pure sensuousness the primitive abandonment of Polynesian life. The chapter evaluating Melville's experience in Typee Valley has suggested the setting and established the meaning of the experience. The feeling of the artist was literally made there, in those brief days and the ones which followed on Tahiti. Shadow and stone and their meanings of primitive deity became autotypes which are combined with the meaning of primitive eros. For the step from the stone altar to the god of fertility and erotic love, the god of the dark consciousness, is a short one. Arvin has recognized Melville's discretion in his account of eros. He observes that Melville had looked upon " a frank and astonishingly free celebration of the power of Polynesian Eros, an unashamed and sometimes orgiastic sensuality." Undoubtedly he had. Arvin continues: " It was the happy and harmless sensualism of a culture that had not yet undergone the penalties or enjoyed the rewards of social complexity and psychological maturity, and Melville was debarred, as a writer for the general public, from reproducing all that he had certainly observed; he had to content himself with discreet intimations." [5] Some of these intimations I shall review here as symbols derived from the sexual iconography of Polynesia.

It would be dishonest to deny Melville's symbolic account of Polynesian eros. In the beginning it ought to be said that one aspect of his view of God, however unpalatable this may be to some readers, is similar to that aspect spoken of by D. H. Lawrence in a letter of 1922 addressed to Willard Johnson.

> The old, dark religions understood. "God enters from below," said the Egyptians, and that's right. Why can't you darken your minds, and know that the great gods pulse in the dark, and enter you as darkness through the lower gates. Not through the head. [6]

Such gods of the lower gates had ruled in the Polynesian that Melville knew in the vale of the Taipis, at least. The facts of Marquesan culture at the time he visited Nukuhiva will allow no other conclusion. E. S. Craighill Handy's study of Marquesan legends establishes the facts of ethnology. Handy found that the sex motif is (or today, more properly, *was*) more dominant than any other. He concluded: "The sex interest shown in their folk lore demonstrates the Marquesans to have been healthy in mind—there is none of the morbid dwelling on erotic detail characteristic of the folk lore of certain other races more effetely civilized." [7] The legends presented by Handy celebrate the gods of the lower gates dreamed of by Lawrence. Nukuhiva was created by the God Tiki, [8] the great original of all *tikis*, it may be assumed. It is interesting to observe, with Arvin's recognition of Melville's discreet intimations in view, that scented oil in these legends is used to anoint the wife before sexual union. [9] Melville's account of his anointment with the

[5] *Herman Melville*, pp. 56–57.

[6] *The Letters of D. H. Lawrence*, ed. Huxley, p. 564. Written at Taos, New Mexico.

[7] *Marquesan Legends*, Bernice P. Bishop Museum Bulletin 69 (Honolulu, 1930), p. 5.

[8] *Ibid.*, p. 122.

[9] *Ibid.*, p. 101.

fragrant oil of the " aka " at the hands of Fayaway and her companions (*Typee*, Ch. xiv) invites some speculation here upon the nature of his " intimations." He says merely that he forgot all his troubles and buried for the time every feeling of sorrow, in this " luxury " provided by his female companions.

4 *The Lizard*

The sensual power of eros is symbolized first by Melville through the image of the Polynesian lizard. In his discussion of the origins of Polynesian culture, Handy distinguishes between an original Tahitian culture (influencing original patterns of the Marquesans) and the " Arii " culture introduced by a race of conquerors at an undetermined time in history. Handy's conclusions concerning the elements of the original culture and the Arii are established upon his study of artifacts and legends. Tane, god of light (and probably Melville's " god " represented in Taji of *Mardi*), is of the basic culture; Taaroa, the god of waters, is of the Arii. Handy's studies of animal motifs show, among other interesting conditions, that the lizard, venerated by both Tahitians and Marquesans contemporary with Melville, became " sacred " under the Arii culture. Formerly it had been considered demonic.[10] Melville understood (and almost miraculously, it would seem, when one remembers the brevity of his days ashore in Polynesia) that the lizard among these islanders had a special religious significance. He probably knew, at any rate, as much as William Mariner, the visitor to the Tonga Islands, who observed that among the Tongans the lizard (with the porpoise and a species of water-snake) was believed to be the incarnation of a primitive god.[11] But Melville's artistic employment of the lizard illustrates again the subjacent affective reality (cf. Baudouin) which governs in the acquisition and the later use of an image from experience. (Here comparison should be made with the

[10] *The Problem of Polynesian Origins*, p. 7.
[11] John Martin, ed. and comp., *An Account of the Natives of the Tonga Islands* [arranged from Mariner's accounts] (Edinburgh, 1827), vol. 2, pp. 100–101.

dolphin image earlier reviewed in the discussion of Carlo of
Redburn.) Experience in the image determines the meaning
which it will later project through its form in art. Thus Melville's lizard is associated with eroticism.

One must go back to Typee Valley once more to see the
source of this autotype. Here Melville discovered the Marquesan lizard, " a beautiful golden-hued species " of about five
inches in length (*Typee*, Ch. xxix). He recalls how these
creatures showed their glittering sides among the spears of grass
and along the shafts of the trees. Furthermore, they were perfectly tame and fearless and often overran the youth, who rested
" in some shady place," until he was covered with them. The
memory of tropical ease in the shadows of the glen turns with
sensuous delight to the beauty of these golden lizards. The
same association with the image appears in Loti's description
of the Tahitian lizard in *Le Mariage de Loti*. Loti's place of
rest is the glen where he passes the hours with Rarahu (his
Tahitian Fayaway). The Tahitian lizard is blue as turquoise,
and it moves over the tranquil lovers, in company with large,
resplendent butterflies.[12] The lizard in the settings of both
artists becomes the image of delight to the senses. It is associated with pleasure and abandon and later, in Melville's art at
least, with sensuality.

In his description of Queequeg at the Spouter-Inn, Ishmael
says nothing of lizards in the pattern of the tattooing covering
his friend. But in his later account of Queequeg's descent into
the hold, at that point when the *Pequod's* " ground-tier butts "
of oil must be lifted to reveal the leaks in the store, Ishmael
notes that as the savage was crawling about in the dampness
and slime he looked " like a green spotted lizard at the bottom
of a well " (*Moby-Dick*, Ch. cx). This image seems doubly
appropriate for Queequeg. It recalls his Polynesian home.
Furthermore, it suggests the Marquesan practice of tattooing
the lizard upon the faces of men, as recorded by Handy.[13] (At
the same moment Handy notes that women had " birds and

---

[12] *Le Mariage de Loti* (ed. Calmann Lévy), p. 53.
[13] *Tattooing in the Marquesas*, p. 15.

fish behind their ears and on their legs.") Thus Queequeg, as Melville's symbol of Polynesian ethos, is identified with a distinguished image of sensuous delight recalled from the glens of Typee Valley. The green spots of Queequeg as the lizard do not disturb the original image of the golden creature of *Typee*. They suggest only Queequeg's tattooed pattern of dark green frogs running up the trunks of young palms covering the legs; of this wise savage the image of the lizard becomes another token.

We cannot know exactly what sort of experience Melville intended by inference to describe through those curious chapters of *Redburn* in which young Wellingborough is " kidnapped " by his friend, Harry Bolton, and carried off to a mansion in the West-End of London (Chs. XLV, XLVI). The sumptuous establishment (" Aladdin's Palace ") which they visit is a gambling house; the description suggests also the atmosphere of an elaborate bordello. Wellingborough, trusting his new friend to guide him through London, is dazed by the splendor of the reception rooms. Then Harry suddenly departs for a mysterious engagement, leaving Wellingborough to await him in a luxurious apartment of the house. As the youth sits alone in reflection through the midnight hours, he wonders at his surroundings:

> But spite of these thoughts, and spite of the metropolitan magnificence around me, I was mysteriously alive to a dreadful feeling, which I had never before felt, except when penetrating into the lowest and most squalid haunts of sailor iniquity in Liverpool. All the mirrors and marbles around me seemed crawling over with lizards; and I thought to myself, that though gilded and golden, the serpent of vice is a serpent still.[14]

We are not told what is meant by " sailor iniquity." This must rest as one of Melville's intimations. But his use of the lizard in an image of *Pierre* suggests that in *Redburn*, as well, the figure as a symbol has erotic connotations. Thus Pierre speaks:

---

[14] *Redburn*, p. 303. The visit to the gambling house is discussed by W. H. Gilman in his *Melville's Early Life and Redburn* (New York, 1951), pp. 192–98. Gilman concludes that this journey to London with Harry Bolton may be imaginary.

" Love's museum is vain and foolish as the Catacombs, where
grinning apes and abject lizards are embalmed." [15] In both
Pierre and *Redburn* the morality associated with the lizard is
that of the character's attitude. Pierre is the young moralist-
absolutist; Wellingborough Redburn is an unknowing young
sailor on his first voyage from home. Melville, as the narrator,
stands behind each. The only matter of importance here is the
association in the mind of the narrator. The lizard represents
erotic adventure.

Now if it be thought that the image of a lizard might reasonably mean the same in the work of any artist, let one example
from Hawthorne be examined. In *The Marble Faun* (Ch.
XXVII) the " curse " of Donatello's " death " in life causes all
nature to shrink from him. In the presence of his friend, Kenyon, Donatello withdraws into a thicket and attempts in vain
to recall the life of the earth. But no living thing makes itself
known to him, save a brown lizard rustling away through the
sunshine. " To all present appearance, this venomous reptile
was the only creature that had responded to the young Count's
efforts to renew his intercourse with the lower orders of nature."
Donatello trembles in grief; and Kenyon, though doubting the
" strange, natural spell " which Donatello is said to have over
nature, attempts to comfort him. The elaborate supernatural-
ism of this scene reflects no affective power of the image upon
Hawthorne, save its connotation of subtle evil, its suggestion of
reptilian life. This brown lizard is a simple representational
image. It has no double meaning of both reptilian life and
sensuous or erotic adventure. Melville's image, with its multiple reference to Polynesian eros (in the sense here of abandonment) and to some subtly profligate life which he witnessed in
London (and to the " sailor iniquity" of Liverpool) is distinguished by the character of the genuine symbol. The autotype of Polynesia, with its association of experience in the
image, governs the ulterior meaning of the adventure with
Harry Bolton.

It is a thing most strange, indeed, that Émile Verhaeren

[15] *Pierre*, p. 275.

should more closely match Melville's meaning in the lizard than any other contemporary artist. Verhaeren's symbol would seem to stand as evidence of a manifest archetype. In that dark period of Verhaeren's career, the period of his foundering in nihilism recorded in the poetry of *Les Soirs*,[16] we see the collapse of his faith in the traditions of society and religion. But the preface to this darkness is the sensualism of *Les Flamandes*, his first volume of 1883. In this poetry he introduces his sensual mistress Kato, and she becomes the symbol of his quest for the dark gods of blood-consciousness. With the same meaning she passes into the later collection of *Au Bord de la Route* (1891). Here, in the "Cantiques" from "Les bords de la nuit," she becomes the apotheosis of sensual abandon. He addresses her:

> With nailed feet of bronze and staring eyes
> As of great lizards
> My desires, long and green, crawl toward your body,
> Drinking the gold of light.
>
> And you stretch out, lascivious and gigantic, rebelling,
> Drinking the golden light of great lizards,
> As my desires return
> To their first ardor.[17]

The passion of the lover is received by the loved one; the body of the mistress receives the ardor of golden light, here combined symbolically with the emblem of the lizard of desire. The situation of the poem suggests incompleteness: desire will return to its first ardor and the meeting will be repeated. The power symbolized in the lizard is to be recalled again. It would be foolish to contend that Melville, even by intimation, suggests the intensity of these lines. Yet the striking similarity between his symbol of the Marquesan lizard and this golden reptilian symbol of Verhaeren's abandon proposes a strong affinity between the two in the quest for the religious meaning of sexual ardor.

[16] See Stefan Zweig, *Émile Verhaeren* (Boston, 1914), p. 57.
[17] "Cantiques," no. 2, of "Les bords de la nuit" in *Poèmes* (Mercure de France, 1895), p. 28.

5 *Tiki*

The symbol of the lizard leads finally to a consideration of Marquesan symbolism, and the phallicism of *tiki*. Michel Leiris, in a masterly study of Marquesan art, has written of phallic symbolism in the iconography of this province of Polynesia:

> Whatever question there may be of a statue, of a piece of jewelry, of a design in tattooing, of a decorative motif of whatever category, the Polynesian word *tiki* applies in general to human figurations. In common use throughout all Polynesia, the term signifies the phallus; it designates all the images of the gods (in stone, in wood, in jade, either carried on the person or fixed in the ground) and it is moreover the name of a mythological deity [cf. Handy's account of Tiki, the creator of the Marquesas]. . . . He [Tiki] is the creator, he who gives form and feature to the child in the womb. He is equally an agrarian god. One finds his image everywhere, in fact to such an extent that he is combined with every human image: upon clubs in the form of canoe paddles (of which the upper part represents on its two sides a human head with eyes often appearing as smaller heads), weapons which are now no more than weapons of show; upon the footed points of stilts with which the youths engage themselves in tilting matches; upon pestles of stone which are used for grinding food (pestles decorated with a single or a double head, often also simply phallic) ; upon ear ornaments in ivory such as those brought home by the great navigator Cook.[18]

This report establishes the phallic symbolism, for instance, of the " idol " described by Melville in the twenty-fourth chapter of *Typee*, that decayed old god, green with moss and age, which tumbles upon Kory-Kory and receives a beating for its decrepitude. Melville says of it: " The image itself was nothing more than a grotesquely shaped log, carved in the likeness of a portly, naked man with the arms clasped over the head, the jaws thrown wide apart, and its thick, shapeless legs bowed

---

[18] " L'Art des Îles Marquises," *Cahiers d'Art*, vol. 9 (1934), pp. 185–88.

into an arch." Midway in the same chapter Melville describes the spear paddle and the war club of Kolory, that "Knight Templar" of the valley, the paddle carved at the lower end into a "heathenish looking little image," the club with an upper part "intended to represent a human head" and swathed round with bits of white *tapa*. These symbols of *tiki* agree with the devices examined by Leiris; and it would appear certain that Melville observed among the Taipis dozens of objects designed and carved in this phallic iconography.

But the critical problem here is not one of establishing the veracity of Melville as an ethnologist, interesting as this is; it is one of demonstrating the relationship of the Marquesan *tiki*, as an autotype, to his erotic symbolism. The first fact to be noted is that *tiki*, as the assimilated image, merges with the impression of Polynesian sensualism apparent in Melville's feeling informing his symbols. The second fact is that this image thus contained in sensualism passes into the theology represented by whiteness and by Moby Dick. *Tiki* means pagan vitality; it means as well the acceptance of life represented in Polynesian ethos. In it rests the emblem of man's nature, as a living being in the flesh. Against it Melville poses the image of Ahab's injury in the groin (*Moby-Dick*, CVI), sustained before the *Pequod* sailed from Nantucket, when his ivory limb (not Moby Dick's ivory, of course), displaced by some casualty, had "stake-wise" smitten him. He poses the image of Ahab as he was first "dismasted off Japan," his leg sheared off by Moby Dick (Ch. XXVIII). He poses those "dark" sacramental images from a distorted Christian rite, when Ahab addresses his "sweet cardinals" (his harpooneers), and bids them drink from those "murderous chalices" in solemn covenant of vengeance upon the white monster (Ch. XXXVI). In this black mass on his quarter-deck, Ahab, dismasted and pierced by the god who may never be known till the firmament splits asunder, stands as symbolic Western man shorn of his native power and fertility of primitive being. (This, even though the old man, according to Peleg (Ch. XVI), has had a child by that sweet girl he married after his first encounter with the White Whale.) Ahab is civilized man shorn of the vital being represented in the ethos of *tiki*. The quest for ultimate knowledge and absolute truth ends in distortion and utter ruin. For the quest is the denial of the nature of man.

Melville establishes his master symbol of Polynesian *tiki* midway in the chartless course of Ahab's search, in the chapter called " The Cassock " (xcv) . The mincer comes forward and removes the dark pelt from the " symmetrical unaccountable cone " of a dead whale. Longer it is, this " grandissimus," than " a Kentuckian is tall," and jet-black it is " as Yojo, the ebony idol of Queequeg." Such an idol as this, says Melville, was found in the secret groves of Queen Maachah in Judaea, and was burnt for an abomination by her son, Asa, as recounted in the fifteenth chapter of the first book of *Kings*. The pelt removed, the mincer turns it inside out, like a pantaloon leg, and hangs it in the rigging to dry. After a time, it is taken down, and the mincer, removing some three feet of it at the pointed extremity, cuts then two slits for arm-holes and slips himself bodily into it. " The mincer now stands before you invested in the full canonicals of his calling. Immemorial to all his order, this investiture alone will adequately protect him, while employed in the peculiar functions of his office." Thus appareled, he cuts the blubber of the whale into thin slices for the try-pots.

As avatar, the cassock of the mincer is supreme, and is rivaled only by the Oriental meaning of Moby Dick himself, For this cassock is patterned after the garment of the Christian priest who extends the sacrament of the deity in flesh, as the mincer cuts the flesh of the whale, the essence of the sea's mysteries; and in the same moment it is the apparel of God in the *tiki* of Polynesia and the greater Orient. It presents a superior example of symbolic polarity in primitivistic art. Freud's observation upon the primitive practice of dressing the human body in the skin of the totem (i. e., of the animal venerated as the incarnation of the primitive god) should be noted here, even though there is no reason to suppose that Melville knew of this practice or of any totemism. Since Freud here reports ethnological fact, the observation is pertinent: " A member of a clan seeks to emphasize his relationship to the totem in varied significant ways; he imitates an exterior similarity by dressing himself in the skin of the totem animal, by having the picture of it tattooed upon himself, and in other ways." [19] But Melville is not reporting ethnological fact. He is creating another symbol of his art from the autotypes of his Polynesian experience and his remembered Christian heritage.

To recall the protruding tooth of Fedallah, carved into a snake's head, it is interesting to note here, in conclusion, that this phantom through which we entered the realm of shadows and exotic symbols, this ghost of Oriental aboriginalness, bears in this tooth the sign of a most aboriginal symbolic device. H. M. Westropp has reported that before the Hebrew legend of the fall, the serpent was a symbol of wisdom.[20] I doubt that Melville intended wisdom through Fedallah, since Fedallah leads Ahab to his death; but Melville appears to have understood that in the symbol of the snake, apart from its Hebraic and Christian meaning, he had touched the primal God of the ages, supreme in the universe long before Jehovah was thought of. In the symbol of the cassock for the mincer he plunges as deeply into Oriental time as the imagination can go. For here he gets back to a primitive religion symbolizing the energy and the fecundity of all nature. Primitive religions, as Westropp observes, consist fundamentally " in the reverence and worship paid to nature and its operations." [21] Here primitivism as art reaches the base of religious history; it plumbs to the bottom of religious feeling. And if it be that the ancient symbol of the cross was once involved in the still more ancient symbol of the phallus, darkly representing in umbrageous glens and altars of stone the procreative powers of nature, of eternally renovating life,[22] then the avatar to follow in the succeeding chapter re-

[19] *Totem and Taboo*, trans. A. A. Brill (New York, 1931), p. 182.
[20] *Ancient Symbol Worship* (with C. S. Wake, New York, 1875), p. 39.
[21] *Ibid.*, p. 27.
[22] *Phallism* (London, 1889), p. 67. This study, published anonymously, makes considerable use of Baring Gould's *Origin of Religious Beliefs*.

veals the same depths. For cross came from tree and the most
primitive forms of animism, before that totemism noted by
Freud existed. In his symbols of the cross Melville gets down
to the base anew. It is finally suggested here that the aboriginalness of Fedallah, the primal shadows of stone, the sensualism of
Marquesan iconography all point to the same state of man:
the human being existing without the burden of civilized man's
over-reason.

X

Tree and Cross

Yggdrasill, tree of life, is the great mountain ash of the primitive Norseman, his symbol of the universe. In the feeling of at least two primitivists, Melville and Hearn, Yggdrasill is the coconut palm. Melville's description of the palm in *Omoo* (Ch. LXIX) presents it as the Polynesian Tree of Life. It supplies food, shelter, ointment; it provides the material of the islander's house; it yields oil to embalm the dead. But it is its " sacredness " that passes into the avatar of tree and cross in Melville's art. The religious significance of the tree dominates the description of this chapter:

In pagan Tahiti a coco-nut branch was the symbol of regal authority. Laid upon the sacrifice in the temple, it made the offering sacred; and with it, the priests chastised and put to

299

flight the evil spirits which assailed them. The supreme
majesty of Oro, the great god of their mythology, was declared in the coco-nut log from which his image was rudely
carved. Upon one of the Tonga Islands, there stands a living
tree, revered itself as a deity.

Melville's appreciation ends with a scene in a palm grove,
planted by the first Pomare of Tahiti at Papeete. It is a "witch-
ing place," filled with a strange silence. Overhead are "ranges
of rustling green arches." The place is "a hall of pillars," with
"stately aisles intersecting each other." These images of a
church or a ceremonial hall relate the description, through
striking similarity in feeling, to Hearn's view of the same tree.
Hearn begins by reflecting upon the terror which he once felt
in the presence of Gothic architecture. He was aware that the
secret of the terror "somehow belonged to the points of the
archings." But the secret was not revealed until the early hours
of a tropical morning some years later (in Martinique?).[1] What
he calls the "monstrous fetish"[2] of Gothic architecture was
then supplanted by the majesty of a palm grove:

> Each stone-grey trunk is a perfect pillar,—but a pillar of
> which the stupendous grace has no counterpart in the works
> of man. You must strain your head well back to follow the
> soaring of the prodigious column ... through abysses of green
> twilight, till at last—far beyond a break in that infinite inter-
> weaving of limbs and lianes which is the roof of the forest—
> you catch one dizzy glimpse of the capital: a parasol of emer-
> ald feathers outspread in a sky so blinding as to suggest the
> notion of azure electricity.[3]

It is the opening of this spacious "roof," contrasted with the
closing arches of the Gothic cathedral, that conveys the religious
significance of the palm. Both Melville and Hearn bring to
their descriptions of the tree—Melville with his "factual" account and Hearn with his impressionistic imagery—the animism
of that primitive mind which made a god in Yggdrasill. But the

[1] *Shadowings* (London, 1900), p. 216.
[2] *Ibid.*, p. 222.
[3] *Ibid.*, pp. 217–18.

palm, of course, refers to a primitive sensibility far removed from Scandinavia. In the symbolistic imagination of Melville it stands for the sensuous experience of the Polynesian voyage. The scene in the palm grove of Papeete becomes a master autotype.

Susanne Langer has spoken of symbols of multiple meaning in this judgment:

> Many symbols . . . may be said to be " charged " with meanings. They have many symbolic and signific functions, and these functions have been integrated into a complex so that they are all apt to be sympathetically invoked with any chosen one. The cross is such a " charged " symbol: the actual instrument of Christ's death, hence a symbol of suffering; first laid on his shoulders, an actual burden, as well as an actual product of human handiwork, and on both grounds a symbol of his accepted moral burden; also an ancient symbol of the four zodiac points, with a cosmic connotation; a " natural " symbol of cross-roads . . . and therefore of decision, crisis, choice; also of *being crossed*, i. e. of frustration, adversity, fate; and finally, to the artistic eye a cross is a figure of a man. All these and many other meanings lie dormant in the simple, familiar, significant shape.[4]

In the sense of this reading of multiple association evoked by a traditional symbol, all the experimental symbols of Melville represented in avatars are " charged " symbols. This Melville admits to when he says in the chapter on whiteness: " Of all these things the Albino whale was the symbol." But Mrs. Langer's example of the cross is especially useful here since it provides an approach to Melville's avatar of tree and cross as a heavily burdened (preferred here to " charged ") emblem. For tree and cross are locked together in this avatar; and the symbolistic associations which each possesses play constantly into the other. Note, for instance, the immediate association which is established between tree and cross in a brilliant image from the sixth paragraph of the first chapter of *Moby-Dick*. The narrator is speaking of the power of water upon the imagination of the artist. " Meditation and water are wedded forever." To

[4] *Philosophy in a New Key*, pp. 284–85.

illustrate, let us take an example of an artist, says Melville. The elements of a landscape are before him; but he cannot paint unless his eye is fixed upon some "magic stream." Of these elements are the trees. There they stand in the landscape, "each with a hollow trunk, as if a hermit and a crucifix were within." What appears at first baffling in this image of the crucifix within the tree (if one pauses at all to consider) becomes entirely clear when it is understood that *tree* instantly evokes *cross*, even in so seemingly casual a usage. I shall return later to this fusion of tree and cross. For the moment, this initial image from *Moby-Dick* provides a beginning.

It should not be supposed that the vitality of the tree as a pagan symbol reëstablishes the symbol of the Christian cross of suffering. Frustration and crisis are represented in the avatar of Melville's art, when primitive sensibility, represented by the tree, *crosses* some emblem representing the Christian sensibility of Western civilization. But the Christian cross as the symbol of the Redemption "thought out" in the ways of traditional theology disappears. Thus Melville comes to describe in *Clarel*, with remarkable dramatic power, the waning of the Christian symbol. In the section which he names "The Inscription" (Part II, Sec. xxxi) he presents a scene by the Dead Sea. The travelers pass a large rock rising from the shore; on its face they see a strange message written in chalk, and midway in the script, a drawing of the constellation the Southern Cross. A priest among them is induced to translate the inscription. It was written, he says, by one who bewailed the loss of this " altar " (and here one notes Melville's return to primitive stone) ; the "Slanting Cross" (i. e., the *slanting* position of this constellation on a diagonal to the eye of the observer) becomes the only remaining symbol, and this too fails. For the inscription continues:

> Emblazoned bleak in austral skies—
> A heaven remote, whose starry swarm
> Like Science lights but cannot warm—
> Translated Cross, hast thou withdrawn,
> Dim paling too at every dawn,

> With symbols vain once counted wise,
> And gods declined to heraldries?
> Estranged, estranged: can friend prove so?
> Aloft, aloof, a frigid sign:
> How far removed, Thou Tree divine . . . .

The "translated cross" is the symbol of the Redemption, now as remote as the great constellation that guides the southern mariner on his voyage. The memorial of the Christian cross of suffering recedes "dim paling at every dawn" like the starry crucifix hung in the inscrutable heavens. This cross, which lights but cannot warm, is the symbol of a feeling which has expired. (It is unnecessary to be disturbed here by an apparent inconsistency between this reflection of the cross of suffering and the ideality of Melville's symbol of *puer aeternus*. The element of Christ in Billy Budd supplants the traditional symbolic element of the redemption in the cross which, in Melville's feeling, has lost its authority over religious sensibility.)

Melville's meaning here is supported by Verhaeren, who describes the same exhaustion of feeling in his "Quelques-uns" from the collection *Au Bord de la Route* (1891). His people are of those Europeans who stand upon the brink of nihilism defined by Nietzsche:

> In them, now, nothing ever stirs;
> No desires, no regrets, no alarms;
> They have even lost, alas, the fine dream of the Crosses,
> Lost, too, the last hope reaching out towards red death.[5]

It is worth noting here that Verhaeren's obsessive use of the image of *carrefour* (cross roads) in relation to the cross at other points in the poetry is an excellent illustration of Mrs. Langer's theory that the "charged" cross evokes images of zodiac points and becomes itself a symbol of decision and crisis. Melville's distinction in his view of the Southern Cross in *Clarel* derives from his relation of symbolic authority and vitality to the life of feeling (*warmth*). His symbol of the starry cross is his own, and it clearly bears the mark of the autotype, the memory of

[5] Rendered by Eden and Cedar Paul, trans. Baudouin's *Psychoanalysis and Aesthetics*, p. 153.

the voyager in southern seas who has looked upon that slanting constellation through the long watches of the night.

The association of tree and cross is archetypal. Daniel G. Brinton, writing of primitive man's "arboreal home," discusses the origin of tree worship. First came the simple symbol of the tree which was the protector. Later the tree was represented by a sacred pole as an object for worship. Then came the cross. " In early art the cross as a sacred design is often derived from the conventional figure of a tree, and symbolizes the force of life, the four winds, rain, and the waters." [6] This is the cross which unites with the tree in Melville's avatar, not the cross of Christian theology. Yet this avatar of tree and cross, because it springs from a mind informed with the traditions of Christian symbolism, takes into itself the conflict between acceptance and over-reason and so attains the polarity of form which we have come to expect. Should there be some persons who may say that Melville is merely translating in this avatar what he has read of primitive religions, let it be remembered that the sciences of ethnology and anthropology were scarcely learned enough in his day to have provided very much fact about the primitive cross. The archetype here rising from primal mind fills the breach opened through cultural failure, that waning of the cross described in *Clarel*.

1 *Animism*

Just as Melville's approach to whiteness is frequently animistic, so his approach to the living tree of primal nature appears as the same. In a preceding chapter I commented upon Melville's curious behavior at Pittsfield on that summer day of 1855, when he mystified his visitors by telling them that he spent much time " patting " the trees. This probably seems to us pure spoofing. Yet this madness, or tomfoolery, has a curious relationship to Melville's symbolized feeling for the life of the tree. The assertion that his approach to the tree as the object

---

[6] *Religions of Primitive Peoples* (New York, 1897), p. 152.

for study is essentially animistic can be amply documented. Since I am quite sure that Melville's description of trees in his symbolic key chapter to the meaning of Moby Dick as God (" A Bower in the Arsacides ") is not intended as satire upon some mad group of transcendental Pantheists, I am unwilling to read other portions of other texts as satire. In this chapter of *Moby-Dick* he writes: " The wood was green as mosses of the Icy Glen; the trees stood high and haughty, feeling their living sap " (Ch. cii). This is attribution again of the sentient life to the life of nature. To recall the image appearing before the eye of the painter in the first chapter of *Moby-Dick*, the tree with its hermit and crucifix within is a tree endowed with sentient life. This sentience is, of course, the same as that discovered in the Old English poem *The Dream of the Rood.* The tree feels its burden of sorrow and mystery when it is cut from the forest; and as time passes and it becomes the wood of the Cross, it gains a soul.[7]

Much depends upon what one intends to do with a passage from *Mardi* in which we hear the wisdom of Babbalanja again. Is this Babbalanja speaking, or Melville, and if Melville, is he the animist or the satirist? I choose Melville and the animist, as I have earlier chosen Babbalanja's discourse upon Oro as Melville's early theological pronouncement. This I accept, then, and in so doing accept even Melville's " seriousness " on that summer day at Pittsfield. Babbalanja addresses Media (Ch. cxliii) :

> Think you, my lord, there is no sensation in being a tree? feeling the sap in one's boughs, the breeze in one's foliage? think you it is nothing to be a world? . . . Mardi is alive to its axis. When you pour water, does it not gurgle? When you strike a pearl shell, does it not ring? Think you there is no sensation in being a rock?—To exist is to be; to be, is to be something.

This is that same Babbalanja who has spoken earlier of Oro. " But since evil abounds, and Oro is in all things, then he

---

[7] See the preface of Albert S. Cook, ed., *The Dream of the Rood: An Old English Poem Attributed to Cynewulf* (Oxford, 1905), p. lii.

cannot be perfectly good " (Ch. cxxxv) . These are the words,
spoken through Babbalanja, of Ishmael, the symbol-maker of
Moby Dick. So, too, are the sensations of being a tree meant
by Ishmael to represent the sentient unity of life in Oro. To
feel the life of the tree and the rock, to acknowledge the multiplicity of God through both good and evil is to be Oriental.
I take Melville literally, for what he says.

Thus do forests feel the cold of New England as the palm
tree feels the light and warmth of the south. In the story *The
Tartarus of Maids* Melville's Ishmael-narrator travels through
this winter scene: " The forests here and there skirting the
route, feeling the same all-stiffening influence, their inmost
fibres penetrated with the cold, strangely groaned—not in the
swaying branches merely, but likewise in the vertical trunk—as
the fitful gusts remorselessly swept through them." [8] Thus does
Pierre Glendinning find the forest trees his comforters as the
remorseless world of civilized duplicity bears in upon him.
" This day I will forsake the censuses of men, and seek the
suffrages of the god-like population of the trees, which now
seem to me a nobler race than man. Their high foliage shall
drop heavenliness upon me; my feet in contact with their
mighty roots, immortal vigour shall so steal into me." [9] These,
too, are examples of animism; and undoubtedly others could
be discovered in Melville's descriptions of forest journeys. They
reveal primitive feeling toward the tree as living object. They
point to the archetypal relationship of tree and cross which, in
the symbolistic process, passes under the authority of autotypes
from Melville's experience. The avatar of tree and cross presents a further symbolic description of the Oriental deity manifest to man.

2   The Cross in Primitive Setting

The tree in the designs of tattooing displayed by Marnoo and
Queequeg illustrates the association in the image which the

[8] *Billy Budd and Other Prose Pieces*, p. 241.
[9] *Pierre*, p. 150.

cross as a burdened (or "charged") symbol is to reveal. Beginning with the primitive symbol of the tree as endowed with sacred attributes or with deific properties, the imagination of the symbolist transfers this simple significance into the area of tattooing. As this process takes place, tattooing becomes multiple in meaning. It presents the iconography of the tree in the primitive religious sense, and it also signifies the wisdom of the Polynesian whose body it adorns. In the examples of Marnoo and Queequeg (and one may supplant these by attention to other designs of tattooing examined by Melville in the Polynesian romances), tattooing as symbol is completed at this point. Tree, innocence, and ethos are combined in the symbol of the design. When this symbol, here yet singular in its relatively pure Polynesian reference, assimilates additional meanings from the realm of Christian iconography, it attains the full burden of opposed values determining its character as avatar. It becomes another art form of inner polarity such as has been discovered in the symbol of Billy Budd, or in the *tiki* fashioned in the symbolistic method of *Moby-Dick*. An extending pattern of prefiguration and artistic fulfillment in the representation of the cross in tattooing may be traced through the courses of Melville's symbolism. I shall take up examples from this pattern in the chronological order in which they appear.

When Taji sails into the waters of Mardi, his companion is honest Jarl, an old seaman from the isle of Skye. After Yillah has been rescued and brought aboard the *Chamois*, Taji records that she often gazed in fascination at the "characteristic device" on the arm of Jarl. The design presents "our Saviour on the cross, in blue; with the crown of thorns, and three drops of blood in vermillion, falling one by one from each hand and foot" (Ch. XLVII). Another design in tattooing has been earlier presented by Taji in the description of the old islander Samoa, aboard the *Parki* (Ch. XXX). Taji says simply that Samoa was covered on one side of his person, and blank on the other. According to Braswell in his study of Melville's religious thought, we are to see a particular meaning in the difference between Jarl's origin and the Oceanic derivation of Samoa.

"These two characters may be taken to reflect the northern Christian heritage and the South Sea pagan influence that were at work on Melville's will when his real development began." [10] There can be no objection to the view that Melville intended a contrast between these two ill-matched shipmates. But the image of Jarl's tattooing is the only object of real interest in these early scenes of *Mardi*, excepting, of course, the symbol of whiteness which appears in Yillah. For in Jarl's tattooing Melville reaches his first expression of feeling invoked by the image of the Christian cross, or the crucifixion, represented through a primitive art which he had long ago (on Nukuhiva) come to accept as the emblem of Polynesian ethos. It is unnecessary here to summon fact in the history of tattooing among sea-going men of Western civilization during the last century and a half, save to call attention to what I suppose to be common knowledge: tattooing as an ancient art of Oceania, particularly of Melanesia and Polynesia, and of Japan supplied the original technique which, in the Western world, was put to its hundreds of uses, from the indelible outlines of pornographic inscriptions and drawings to the most pious emblems of orthodox religious faith. In short, there would have been, probably, no tattooing in the Western world without the Oriental craft which inspired it. There can be not the slightest doubt, I think, that Melville's unusual fondness for tattooing as a device for the symbol stems from his feeling about its primitive origin. When this feeling is related to a vast area of recollection in which the bodies of not only Polynesians but also unknown scores of Melville's shipmates bear the elaborately wrought sign of primitive man, it cannot seem strange that the symbolist is obsessed by the possibilities of tattooing for multiplistic representation. Jarl and Samoa may represent opposing values. But it is the image of Jarl's tattooed drawing of the crucifixion, executed in the tradition of an art from the non-Christian world, seen here in the primitive setting of Polynesian waters and in the presence of Samoa, and, more important, wondered at by a primitive girl-goddess who herself represents Polynesian legend—it is this

---

[10] *Melville's Religious Thought*, p. 88.

image that relates the cross to the primitive setting where it first took form in the imagination of man.

In his short narrative sketch *Daniel Orme* Melville again uses the cross in tattooing. In the symbol of this old man we reach the full maturity of the artist in completing a form to contain the tokens of primitive ideality and the forces of existence which oppose it. Compared with the theology expressed in *Clarel* through the meditation of Celio at the Arch, this " crossed " image of the crucifixion on the body of Daniel Orme represents pagan acceptance through the connotations of tattooing, the Christian promise of the Redemption, and this promise slashed by the co-existing forces of violence and evil. On Daniel's " secret bosom " is discovered

> a crucifix in indigo and vermillion tattooed on the chest and on the side of the heart. Slanting across the crucifix and paling the pigment there ran a whitish scar, long and thin, such as might ensue from the slash of a cutlass imperfectly parried or dodged. The cross of the Passion is often tattooed upon the sailor, upon the forearm generally, sometimes, though but rarely, on the trunk. As for the scar, the old mastman had in legitimate naval service known what it was to repel boarders and not without receiving a sabre mark from them.[11]

Braswell has said of this symbol: " Into these few sentences Melville compressed the most moving part of his own religious history." [12] No more moving, perhaps, than the meditation of Celio at the Arch or the " crucifixion " of Billy Budd. But Braswell is substantially right in this conclusion. Melville's " religious history " is the evolution of the theology demonstrated in the multiplicity of whiteness. God is here, in every element of this symbol: in its reference to primitive man, in its figure of the Man of the Cross, crucified by the emblem of war and violence, as though to negate, with an imperious divinity, the total meaning of human innocence. This scar is the brand of God, the same brand which Ahab has felt in the loss of a leg

[11] *Billy Budd and Other Prose Pieces*, p. 120.
[12] *Melville's Religious Thought*, p. 125.

and a wound in the groin and in that pale, thin scar that runs the length of his face. For the symbol of Daniel Orme is made even larger when it is compared with these signs of Ahab. In his earliest years at sea Ahab, even he, must have been the innocent sailor savage. But having been cursed by the disease of over-reason, he lost the wisdom of primitive acceptance. God brands all. So Melville seems to say in the symbol of a cross (this time without tattooing) on the body of Israel Potter. On Copps' Hill, overlooking the Charles at Boston, Israel fought in the Revolution and sustained a "slit" upon his chest. In that same war he fought again on the *Bonhomme Richard*, and in the engagement with the *Serapis* received a traversing cutlass wound. Thus he became "the bescarred bearer of a cross." [13] Israel, another Ishmael who asks of the world security and rest, wanders with this token of divine incomprehensibility carved into his flesh.

Again, the old sailor among the travelers of *Clarel*, provides a third symbol of the cross in tattooing. Melville's feeling here is so closely related to, so clearly prophetic of the feeling of Yeats in "The Second Coming" that I must call attention to similarities. Yeats's familiar lines describe the close of one symbolic cycle and the beginning of another, the symbols of a new era which no one can know.

> The Second Coming! Hardly are those words out
> When a vast image out of *Spiritus Mundi*
> Troubles my sight: somewhere in sands of the desert
> A shape with lion body and the head of a man,
> A gaze blank and pitiless as the sun,
> Is moving its slow thighs, while all about it
> Reel shadows of the indignant desert birds.
> The darkness drops again; but now I know
> That twenty centuries of stony sleep
> Were vexed to nightmare by a rocking cradle,
> And what rough beast, its hour come round at last,
> Slouches towards Bethlehem to be born?

Not in that unknown "rough beast" is the shape of Melville's prophecy descried, but in the "nightmare" named by Yeats in

[13] *Israel Potter*, p. 222.

these lines and in his earlier statement in the same poem, that
" The ceremony of innocence is drowned." For Agath points
toward the gray hills beyond the travelers' rest to " that upland
dim: . . . the wreck—Jerusalem " (*Clarel,* Part IV, Sec. i) . As
this " wrinkled son of ocean " points the bearings south and
north, he reveals his tattooed arm stretched forth from a loose
sleeve:

Upon the forearm did appear
A thing of art, vermil and blue,
A crucifixion in tattoo,
With trickling blood-drops strange to see.
Above that emblem of the loss,
Twin curving palm-boughs draping met
In manner of a canopy
Over an equi-limbed small cross
And three tri-spiked and sister crowns:
And under these a star was set:
And all was tanned and toned in browns.

(*Clarel,* Part IV, Sec. ii)

Agath tells his companions, as they ask for an explanation of
this design on his arm, that it was all " sketched out " one
Christmas Day off Java Head. After some discourse from Rolfe
upon the meaning of these devices in the age of the Knights
Templar, it is explained that the palm-leaves signify Judaea,
the crowns the magi, and the star the star of the Nativity. The
travelers appoint old Agath as the guide to Bethlehem and resolve " to follow the star on the tattooed man " (*Clarel,* Part IV,
Sec. ii) .

Here, again, is the primitive Polynesian art of tattooing
wedded in the flesh of man to the symbol of the cross. But the
image of Jerusalem, the " wreck," and the strange admonition
from Derwent to the travelers, to follow the star of the tattooed
man to the place of the Nativity, bespeak the theological meaning of Agath's symbol. The sense of Melville meets that of Yeats:
the ceremony of innocence is drowned. For Agath confesses
that the design sketched upon his arm was acquired in his
youth, when he had no thought of its meaning. The signs of the

Passion which it contains were merely inherited from older sailors. They were branded upon innocence, in this sense, just as the innocence of Jarl and of Daniel Orme and of Israel Potter was branded. Melville does not envision a Second Coming. But he proposes in this scene that the star appearing in the design of a primitive art, with all the richness of meaning which that art has now come to possess, must lead the travelers to Bethlehem. The anticipation of Yeats is, of course, expressed elsewhere, in Celio's meditation at the Arch and in the symbol of the translated cross waning in the southern constellation. Even Yeats's image of the "rough beast" seems to be prefigured as Derwent of *Clarel* thinks of the "shapeless birth" of the future (Part III, Sec. v). The cross belonged to primitive man before it belonged to Christianity. But the difference between Melville and Yeats is clear. Melville constantly reveals, under his sacramental signs, the persistent meaning of the *original* cross; Yeats sees no return to an earlier symbolic cycle, for whatever "rough beast" is to be born is to be the symbol that was never seen before. The beast is the future, heavy with symbolistic possibilities. The only Second Coming which Melville conceives of is the second coming of Christ in his fairness, his innocence among men, Christ freed of the symbolic accretions of nineteen centuries of reasoning theologies. That is what he means by saying that Tahiti was the only fit place for Christ in advent.

The cross is related to these signs of a Polynesian iconographic craft. It is also related, apart from its bond with the tree, to the majesty and the humility of nature. In majesty it appears once, at least, in the spirit-spout of a great whale of the Japanese sea. Morquan, an ancient whale called the King of Japan, reigns there. His lofty jet, they say, "at times assumed the semblance of a snow-white cross against the sky" (*Moby-Dick*, Ch. XLV). Is he Moby Dick, under another name? That spirit-spout casting the mystery of God aloft, that moonlit column of mist comes from the depths of time and has been seen to form itself into an ancient cross. And in humility this wondrous sign is borne, as well, upon the shoulders of that lowliest of beasts, the ass.

Melville uses the figure of the cross on the shoulders of the ass in two symbolic descriptions. It appears first in the account of the Chola widow in the last sketch of *The Encantadas*. The story of Hunilla, with its tale of tragedy as she helplessly watches her husband drown at sea, ends in the return of this Mayan woman to her native village. She passes " into Payta town riding upon a small gray ass; and before her on the ass's shoulders, she eyed the jointed workings of the beast's armorial cross." [14] It was this symbolic token of Hunilla's tragedy and humility that Melville's editor, Charles Briggs of *Putnam's*, admired and that James Russell Lowell called " the finest touch of genius he had seen in prose." [15] Melville returns to the same symbol in *Clarel* (Part II, Sec. i) when he describes the mount of the traveler, Nehemiah:

> The ass, pearl-gray,
> Matched well the rider's garb in hue,
> And sorted with the ashy way;
> Upon her shoulders' jointed play
> The white cross gleamed, which the untrue
> Yet innocent fair legends say,
> Memorializes Christ our Lord
> When Him with palms the throngs adored
> Upon the foal.

The Christ of this passage is the Christ of " fairness," of innocence and love. It is of the greatest consequence that Melville chooses here the primitive pre-Christian cross. It is subjacent to the primitive humanity of the original Christ. It embodies the ideality of acceptance and humility, the same ideality which appears in the legend of the Chola widow and in the great symbols of sacrament which precede it in Melville's art. This primitive cross of Oriental time, transplanted here to the shoulders of the ass, means Oriental ethos. In it the unaccountable God of all-being is accepted; and through it the iron nails of Christian suffering, theologically emphasized, are denied. The Christian " burden " of life and the complexities of reason

[14] *The Encantadas* in *The Piazza Tales*, p. 235.
[15] See von Hagen's edition of *The Encantadas* (1940), p. 108.

and dogma are refuted. The Christ of the Palms is the Lord of love, as though Christ were bound to man in *tayo*, the ideality of Polynesian friendship.

It is immediately obvious that Melville's emblem of the cross on the shoulders of the ass recalls Wordsworth's description appearing in " Peter Bell."

'Tis said, meek Beast! that, through Heaven's grace,
He not unmoved did notice now
The cross upon thy shoulder scored,
For lasting impress, by the Lord
To whom all human-kind shall bow.

(Part III, ll. 236 ff.)

Wordsworth's poem, with its similarity to Buddhistic ethic and its reflection upon the place of man in nature, is of all English " Romantic " art the symbolic work closest to the basic tenets of Oriental theology. It is so closely related to Melville's symbol of humanity in the ass that we may propose a direct indebtedness of Melville in artistic method.

Both Wordsworth and Melville may be compared, finally, with the recent French poet Francis Jammes, friend of Loti, Péguy, and Claudel. The " primitivism " of Jammes is, of course, totally unlike the primitivism analyzed in this study. This poet's mind and feeling are wholly Catholic, and there is no question here of primitivistic symbols which replace the symbols of orthodox doctrine and ritual. But the feeling of Jammes for the essential and the vital in nature, so like the feeling of St. Francis, is animistic in the manner of both Wordsworth and Melville. The garden prays; the fields and pastures *feel* their life-giving sap.[16] As Léon Moulin observes in his preface to the poetry of Jammes, this verse is full of " atavistic reminiscences." [17] And it is this atavism, certainly, that is expressed in the feeling of the " Prière pour aller au Paradis avec les Ânes ":

---

[16] See Joseph W. Beach and G. Van Roosbroeck, " Francis Jammes, Primitive," *The Sewanee Review*, vol. 28 (1920), p. 177.

[17] Preface to Jammes, *Choix de Poèmes* (Paris, 1946), p. 15.

. . . grant that, leaning toward that abode of the soul on
your divine waters, I may be like the asses, who will carry
their humble and sweet poverty to the radiance of eternal
love.[18]

Atavism here leads to the original Christ of humility and love,
and Jammes is the inheritor of a primitive symbol essential to
both Wordsworth and Melville.

Tree and cross become one in Melville's avatar contained,
like the avatar of dark, primal mind, in the theology of whiteness. The vitality of the tree which became the cross is the
vitality of man's life in nature. The primitive cross represents
the gift of life. The Christian cross, with its theologically fixed
denial of innocence in the world and its symbols of suffering
in the barren wastes which must be traversed before the life
eternal, represents death in the tragedy of over-reason. The
final chapter of this study will trace Melville's quest for the
original Christ in the Holy Land. Perhaps *Clarel*, as the poetic
record of the pilgrimage, is important as a theological document
chiefly because of its concluding implications: the mystery of
God, who permits those acts that slash the symbol of the tattooed cross with the scar of war, that brand the sailor Israel
Potter with the crossed scar of suffering, will never be unfolded.
In the end man must accept the mystery, and when he accepts
it, he must deny that Christ interpreted by the theology of
Christendom, and the symbols of that Christ who suffers in
this theology for the sake of eternal life for man are together
the quintessential meaning of human existence. For nineteen
centuries of Christian history, as Melville saw them, prove
nothing, and God is still unknown. Truth is relative. For
Melville, the primitivist, the meaning of Christian sacrament
must become the meaning of a new sacrament in art. His is
the way of the Protestant artist. His relation to Yeats need not
here be further emphasized. His agreement with Verhaeren,
less widely read than Yeats, is worth equal attention. Stefan
Zweig has defined the meaning of Verhaeren's apostasy: " All

[18] *Choix de Poèmes*, p. 137.

religions, all dogmas, are . . . transitory . . . ." He quotes these lines from Verhaeren's *Les Moines*:

> For there is nothing other than art on this earth
> To tempt a strong and solitary brain
> And gray it from its red and tonic spirit.[19]

The red spirit is the vitality of the maker of art, and the making of art is the graying of the creative mind. Out of this gray comes Melville's White Whale, an icon of the God endlessly elusive of man's reason.

[19] *Émile Verhaeren*, p. 51.

XI

The Dragon Whale

Moby Dick is Melville's icon of the God described in the theology of whiteness, of primal mind, of tree and cross. In his multiplicity of meaning the White Whale is the most complex single symbol in the history of American art. He is the base of a primitivistic symbolism of existential courage, and he is the master American token of art as religion. It is at once evident, after the preceding discussions of sacrament and avatar, that the Whale is the supreme reincarnation from the Orient. He is the feeling of Ishmael, the westward mariner, brought to form. Certainly the archetypes of primeval waters have entered his enormity. But he is Melville's own, in the sovereign power of an individuated art through the great autotype of the monster whale. Thus is Moby Dick heavy with man's universal poetry of unknown generative seas, heavy with Melville's own inclination toward Oriental wisdom; but he is enormous also with an American whaleman's memories of the monster's breachings through the solitary vastness of the Pacific. Melville's dependence upon Owen Chase's narrative of the sinking of the *Essex*, in 1820, by a vindictive " white whale " and his reflection upon the legends of the monster Mocha Dick are well known.[1] The artist takes his place here with the myth-makers of the American frontier. But Moby Dick as a symbol is unique. He must remain an object for endless study, because all meanings are contained in him. There can be no question of Melville's intent: he purposed that Moby Dick should be ambiguous. Yet this Whale is a nonambiguous ambiguity. The form which he assumes in the hands of Melville is clear. This must be described as an avatar entirely susceptible to analysis. For Melville in himself felt Moby Dick to mean to him what his own artist's theology had evolved.

But who would prevent or deny the various meanings of Moby Dick to other spectators? Moby Dick is the ambiguity of God. If he means endlessly to critics and other students, then he means exactly as Melville intended him to go on meaning. In the introduction to this study it was stated that the facts of the symbolic process may be isolated and named through comparative readings within symbolic systems, the organic wholes of artistic expression. I think it certain that the facts of Melville's feeling about his whale may be demonstrated with complete clarity. The facts of the other symbols of his theology and the facts of the whale's form make this simple assertion irrefutable. It does not follow, nor should it, that other meanings of Moby Dick would be unacceptable to Melville. Richard Chase, I think, does no violence to Melville the artist when he says that " the White Whale is the transmutation of the implicit spiritual meaning of free enterprise." [2] But Chase's read-

---

[1] See A. B. C. Whipple, *Yankee Whalers in the South Seas* (New York, 1954), pp. 17–40 for an account of the *Essex*. See also Whipple's discussion of Melville, pp. 40–56.

[2] *Herman Melville*, p. 101.

ing here, and readings from various critics who see the monster as either implacable evil or elusive good are all descriptions of affective power in the form itself. The effects upon the critic's sensibilities are interesting; but they have little to do with the fact of Melville's feeling. Great art, as was earlier contended, endures because it lends itself to the hues of any passing sensibility. It goes on meaning all things to all men. The responsibility of criticism remains fixed: to establish the facts of what it meant to its maker.

It may be proposed that Melville's whale is the most striking nonanthropomorphous God-symbol from serious religious art in the recent history of the Christian world. Moby Dick as icon has no predecessors in that Western tradition which permitted, in its own cultural failure, the genesis of Ishmael. For it is upon this question of anthropomorphism, more than any other, that Melville's drive toward the God-symbol, and that of a generation of primitivists, depends. To some students a possibility of refuting this statement must inevitably appear in the account of Father Mapple's " Jonah " sermon (*Moby-Dick*, Ch. IX) . God is there, a person in his ancient Hebraic-Christian form. He sends the whale to swallow Jonah, to test the sinful man's capacity to repent. God is certainly not the whale. His Truth is the Truth of " righteous " men; and Scripture (written by men) is his word. But who can escape noticing here Jonah's descent into the boiling sea in Melville's account, as though Jonah were another of those mastmen who plunge into the vortex of the incomprehensible God of the waters? And who can deny Melville's own dramatic talent for representing a Calvinistic sermon which, as a device of dramatic narrative, has its own relationship to the " righteousness " of Peleg and Bildad and to the implacable purpose of Ahab? The anthropomorphism of the sermon is not the conception of Melville's religious symbols. Here, as elsewhere in primitivism, the waning of the anthropomorphous God is reflected. The Judaic lore of man in the image of God, as an anciently installed symbolism, certainly exerted no power upon the creative acts of Gauguin or Loti or Hearn or Henry Adams. In the case of Melville this lore was exchanged for the primitive symbol of the whale, in the personal art of creating a new image of God. Can Melville's confession of feeling in his journal of 1856–57 mean other than his own awareness of the waning of the ancient symbol? Journals, it should be remembered, are not usually written as dramatic and narrative art. Melville stands here in the stony darkness of the Pyramids of Giza.

> I shudder at idea of ancient Egyptians. It was in these pyramids that was conceived the idea of Jehovah. Terrible mixture of the cunning and awful. Moses learned in all the lore of the Egyptians. The idea of Jehovah born here.[3]

The "idea of Jehovah" is the symbol of the Hebraic anthropomorphous God inherited by Christianity. Melville acknowledges this as a master symbol in decline. But it happens that Melville, among other primitivists who acknowledge the same waning power of the symbol, is singular in his achievement of a personally wrought form to supplant the old. Again, and now finally in this discussion of avatars, the symbol proceeds from feeling. Melville is unable to accept Hebraic-Christian anthropomorphism; and the White Whale comes into being.

1   Moby Dick's Elements of Antiquity

The ballast of Moby Dick, his weight of primitive meaning which the primitive waters must *feel* in his divings and breachings even as the "dusky air" of Chaos-Hell *felt* the unusual weight of Milton's Lucifer rising from the flood, his whale's enormity is, of course, Melville's feeling for Oriental time. We should expect Moby Dick to be the most heavily burdened of all the symbols. Ishmael tells us what this feeling is (and here Melville probably recalls a journey of his boyhood to Illinois and the ancient waters of the Mississippi). At this point in the voyage of the *Pequod*, the sperm whale is described. This monster is all over "obliquely crossed and re-crossed with numberless straight marks in thick array." His pattern of these scorings

---

[3] *Journal up the Straits*, ed. Weaver, p. 58.

seems to be engraved upon the body itself. It is hieroglyphical.
" By my retentive memory of the hieroglyphics upon one Sperm
Whale in particular," says Ishmael, " I was struck with a plate
representing the old Indian characters chiselled on the famous
hieroglyphic palisades on the banks of the Upper Mississippi.
Like those mystic rocks, too, the mystic-marked whale remains
undecipherable " (Ch. LXVIII). The allusion to these American
Indian rocks reminds him of another thing, too. He thinks of
the resemblance of the " engraved " sperm whale to the scored
rocks of the New England sea-coast, those rocks which Agassiz
supposed to have been scraped and gouged in contact with vast
floating icebergs. The American reference of the description is
entirely relevant to all that is elsewhere, for the sake of the
whale's ancient mysteries, to be invoked from the Orient. It
is part of the ballast assembled by Melville from as many quarters of antiquity as he could plunder.

Both F. O. Matthiessen and D. H. Lawrence have defined the
primordial nature of the White Whale. Matthiessen thought of
the energy antedating man: " Melville keeps coming back to
the primitive, pre-human energies that are represented by the
whale." [4] Lawrence, in the hit-or-miss commentary of the
essays on American literature, hits the area of the true mark
when he says that Moby Dick is the " deepest blood-being of the
white race . . . our deepest blood-nature." [5] Moby Dick is all
these energies: prehuman chaos-force, blood-consciousness of
earliest man, blood-consciousness inherited by the race called
white. He is the timelessness of God, containing in himself all
the measurements of man's time. Thus the head of the sperm
whale hanging at the waist of the *Pequod* drips blood as the
head of Holofernes bled from the girdle of Judith; at the same
moment, it seems the head of the Sphinx in the desert (Ch.
LXX). It rose from that primitive sea described in an image of
the same chapter earlier noted in this study: that ancient Oriental ocean " where an intense copper calm, like a universal
yellow lotus " more and more unfolded " its noiseless measure-

[4] *American Renaissance*, p. 437.
[5] *Studies in Classic American Literature*, pp. 238–39.

less leaves." We should be prepared for these ranges of time displayed in Melville's vaulting images. As the symbol begins to take form before the *Pequod* sails from Nantucket, Melville fashions his net to drag the very bottom of the seas of time. The intrepid men of Nantucket, he says, have declared everlasting war upon " the mightiest animated mass that has survived the flood." " That Himmalehan [sic] salt-sea Mastodon, clothed with such portentousness of unconscious power, that his very panics are more to be dreaded than his most fearless and malicious assaults " (Ch. xiv). The " unconsciousness " of the monster is the primitive energy of God, God read daringly by an apostate Christian who rejects the traditional God-prototype of the image of man and accepts God as the power represented endlessly by the signs of all religions since time began. He is the God of Judith, the cryptic Sphinx, the mastodon portentous as the Himalayas, and the essence of those waters coppered with an intense Buddhistic calm. He is the God of the minaret, as Tashtego mounts the great " tun " of the whale's head, and stands there like " some Turkish Muezzin calling the good people to prayers from the top of a tower " (Ch. LXXVIII). He is all these.

Each reader must dredge with Melville. The names of God in the whale are the intersections of archaic meanings in the symbol as avatar. Out of primitive prehuman energy came the mind of man to measure time; and out of man's blood-consciousness came the necessity for naming his God. Arvin suggests that Melville would have profited by some anthropological knowledge unfamiliar to him: ". . . he probably did not know, literally, that for many primitive peoples—for peoples as remote from one another as the Annamese, the Tongans, and the Unalit Eskimos—the whale is, or once was, the object of a solemn cult . . . ." [6] There can be no doubt, certainly, that this fact would have appealed to Melville. But the totemism of this simple primitive symbol would have taken its place as only a beginning in fact. For Moby Dick in his fullness becomes the whole of man's religious history.

---

[6] *Herman Melville*, p. 185.

All this meaning, of course, eludes Ahab, the absolutist of Christendom. To Ahab, the White Whale is only absolute malignity, this and no more. " That intangible malignity which has been from the beginning; to whose dominion the modern Christians ascribe one-half of the worlds; which the ancient Ophites of the East reverenced in their statue devil; Ahab did not fall down and worship it like them; but deliriously transferring its idea to the abhorred White Whale, he pitted himself, all mutilated, against it " (Ch. XLI). For Ahab, not Ishmael instructed in the wisdom of Queequeg, is the true God-hater. He lives in an equation with a God whom he sees as pure evil. As the hater rather than the worshipper of evil, he is the Gnostic turned heretic. In his folly of over-reason, born of that distorted Christian absolutism which engendered his hatred of the thing he cannot understand, Ahab denies the relative truth of God. Of Moby Dick all things are true, according as the mind of the Almighty sees itself, not as the mind of man aspires to order it to conformity. Ishmael as Taji of *Mardi* has said of the great Oro only that he indubitably *is*. It must then follow that the timelessness of God, named in the chronology of human culture with a thousand different names and through a thousand different formal theologies, is but the *being* of Oro, or the being of his parent Taaroa, or the being of the father of all Oriental gods, the Hindu Brahma.

2 *Moby Dick as Hindu Deity*

Melville uses two frames of reference to establish the Oriental meaning of Moby Dick: he makes the body of the whale—any great whale—one with the body of the Hindu Vishnu incarnate in the form of leviathan, and he constructs a primitive " shrine " of the skeleton in a " reconstituted " Polynesian valley. The second of these symbolic methods will be considered in the section immediately to follow, an analysis of Melville's meaning in his Bower of the Arsacides. Reference to Hindu mythology appears in two key descriptions of the whale as the deity of waters. Hinduism, and Polynesian landscape combined with

the bony memorials of the sea monster together determine the
character of Moby Dick as avatar; for it is clear that every
account of the whale, of whatever sort, presented by Melville
leads to Moby Dick and is contained in his multiplicity of
meaning. Thus Moby Dick becomes Vishnu reincarnated and, at
the same time, the whale deity of a mythical Polynesian valley.
By the same token, of course, he contains the emblems of the
spirit-spout, and the white vapory cross of old Morquan, King
of Japan. The polarity of the symbol is endlessly apparent.

The first of the descriptions of the Hindu whale appears in
the chapter treating certain " Monstrous Pictures of Whales"
(Ch. LV). Melville begins with the Hindu " base " in an account of the oldest of all representations.

> Now, by all odds, the most ancient extant portrait anyways
> purporting to be the whale's, is to be found in the famous
> cavern-pagoda of Elephanta, in India. The Brahmins main-
> tain that in the almost endless sculptures of that immemorial
> pagoda, all the trades and pursuits, every conceivable avo-
> cation of man, were prefigured ages before any of them
> actually came into being. No wonder then, that in some sort
> our noble profession of whaling should have been there
> shadowed forth. The Hindoo whale referred to, occurs in a
> separate department of the wall, depicting the incarnation
> of Vishnu in the form of leviathan, learnedly known as the
> Matse Avatar. But though this sculpture is half man and
> half whale, so as only to give the tail of the latter, yet that
> small section of him is all wrong. It looks more like the
> tapering tail of an anaconda, than the broad palms of the
> true whale's majestic flukes.

From this point Melville proceeds to review the iconography
of the whale in a score of representations ranging from the
leviathan of Hebraic lore to the semiscientific "cetology" of
Scoresby, Beale, Cuvier, and others. This chapter of pictures
is actually an extended essay retracing the emergence of the
whale as archetype from its genesis in the depths of the Hindu
unconscious. The tapering tail which bothered Melville as he
looked at a representation of the " Matse Avatar " could have
led him to the archetype antedating the great basic whale (ac-

knowledged in Chapter LXXXII of *Moby-Dick*). For here he saw the vestigial emblem of the Oriental chaos-dragon, not the tapering tail of the anaconda. The picture which Melville was looking at is a plate to be found in William Maurice's *Indian Antiquities*.[7]

Vincent has established Melville's debt to Maurice; and further searching for pictorial material which may have gone into Melville's account is not very likely, I think, to yield anything new. It appears that Melville had read Mickle's essay " Inquiry into the Religious Tenets and Philosophy of the Brahmins," appearing with the translation of Camoëns in Chalmers's *English Poets*.[8] From this he may have derived his initial idea of mural painting and sculpture in the caves of India. But in passing to Maurice's account of Vishnu in the form of a fish, Melville makes the error of placing a whale among the symbolic devices displayed at Elephanta. The Vedic art of these cave chambers actually does not contain a whale. Vincent has concluded, and I think accurately, since my own search for a whale in the accounts of Elephanta provides nothing, that Melville made too rapid a transition from Maurice's own description of Elephanta to the account of the Matse Avatar in the same source. Furthermore, as Vincent notes, Melville's spelling *Matse* is used by no other authority available when *Moby-Dick* was written.[9] There seems no doubt that Melville's description of Vishnu as the great fish derives from the plate appearing in Maurice's account and that the error in placing the fish (whale) in the " primal " caves of Elephanta comes about not only through haste in studying the source but also through his obsession with the whale as the first incarnation of deity.

[7] *Indian Antiquities: or Dissertations . . . of Hindostan* (London, 1800), vol. 2, the plate opposite p. 261. The legend reads: " The first Indian Avatar, denominated that of Matse; representing the incarnation of Veeshnu in the form of a Fish: [and] in the opinion of S[ir] William Jones, pointedly allusive to the General Deluge."

[8] Camoëns as used in the description of Jack Chase of *White-Jacket*. The essay of William Julius Mickle on the Brahmins appears as a supplement to the translation of the *Lusiad* in Alexander Chalmers's *The Works of the English Poets* (London, 1810), vol. 21, pp. 713–33.

[9] See Vincent's discussion in *The Trying-Out of Moby Dick*, p. 278.

For it was the idea of Vishnu (the Preserver contained in the all-being of Brahma) as first incarnate in the whale that seized Melville's symbolistic imagination. Maurice describes Vishnu's " Matse Avatar " as the first; so does Chambers's famous and widely read encyclopaedia speak of the first avatar, Vishnu " in the form of a fish, blazing like gold, extending a million leagues." [10] Chambers cites Sir William Jones's translation of the *Bhagavad Gita*, in which Vishnu appears as a fish in the deluge, as the source of the description. It would be interesting to know how much of Oriental scripture from Jones's translations (if any) Melville may have read. Jones's essay " On the Chronology of the Hindus " tells of the demon Hayagríva (Siva?) who, having plundered the sacred Vedas from the custody of Brahma, caused the race of man to become corrupt. Vishnu in the form of a fish then appeared to a good and righteous prince and instructed him to go aboard a ship, with all his wives and with holy men and pairs of animals. A flood to engulf the corruption of men brought about by Hayagríva was to cover the earth. After seven days the ocean began to overflow the coasts, and the prince with his retinue entered the ark. Then Vishnu, in the form of a vast fish, caused the ark to be tied " with a great sea serpent, as with a cable, to his measureless horn." After the rains had ceased, Vishnu killed the demon Hayagríva and recovered the Vedas from the deep, instructed the prince in divine knowledge, and appointed him the seventh Menu. [11]

Although Melville thinks of the ancient *Pequod* with her trophies of antiquity (*Moby-Dick*, Ch. XVI) as the emblem of a universal human community, and of the White Whale as pursued by this community through the will of Ahab, the story of the primitive Hindu ark towed by Vishnu in his avatar of great fish proposes a striking question for speculation. The wisdom at the bottom of the sea in the lost Vedas is certainly

---

[10] Very probably read by Melville: article no. 66, " Hindoo Superstitions," vol. 4, pp. 9–11 in *Chambers's Miscellany of Useful and Entertaining Knowledge* (Boston [1847-48?]).

[11] *The Works of Sir William Jones* (London, 1807, 13 vv.), vol. 4, pp. 10–12.

the wisdom which Moby Dick and all his enormous brothers possess as well. If the translations of Sir William Jones figure in the making of the whale-god, it must certainly follow that Melville's symbolic reference to Vishnu's first avatar is brought to the symbol of Moby Dick through his contemplation of Vedic wisdom lying on the sea floor and belonging only to the vast fish sounding to its primitive mysteries. To think of Vishnu in his first avatar as fish means to think of the first wisdom of creation, everlastingly unknown to man in its ultimate truth.

Melville returns to the primordial Vishnu-as-fish in his eighty-second chapter. He is talking of the honor and glory of whaling. Among other wonders, he recalls the story of St. George and the Dragon; and he is convinced, he says, that this dragon was really a whale. For " in many chronicles whales and dragons are strangely jumbled together, and often stand for each other." He continues:

> Nor do heroes, saints, demigods, and prophets alone comprise the whole roll of our order. Our grand master is still to be named; for like royal kings of old times, we find the head-waters of our fraternity in nothing short of the great gods themselves. That wondrous oriental story is now to be rehearsed from the Shaster, which gives us the dread Vishnoo, one of the three persons [Brahma, Vishnu, Siva] in the godhead of the Hindoos; *gives us this divine Vishnoo himself for our Lord*; [12]—Vishnoo, who by the first of his ten earthly incarnations, has for ever set apart and sanctified the whale. When Brahma, or the God of Gods, saith the Shaster, resolved to recreate the world after one of its periodical dissolutions, he gave birth to Vishnoo, to preside over the work; but the Vedas, or mystical books, whose perusal would seem to have been indispensable to Vishnoo before beginning the creation, and which therefore must have contained something in the shape of practical hints to young architects, these Vedas were lying at the bottom of the waters; so Vishnoo became incarnate in a whale, and sounding down in him to the uttermost depths, rescued the sacred volumes. Was not this Vishnoo a whale-man then? even as a man who rides a horse is called a horseman?

[12] Italics mine.

The account, of course, is exceedingly close to that of Jones. But Melville goes beyond his original in his later completion of the symbol. He thinks of his own White Whale as more than the incarnation of Vishnu, restorer of primal wisdom. Moby Dick becomes Brahma incarnate, encompassing in his vast being both Vishnu (the Preserver, goodness) and Siva (the Destroyer, evil). Moby Dick is the keeper of infinite and time-less wisdom; he is also the unreasoning force of chaos, the de-stroyer of the Ahab-absolutist who seeks to know him, and the incomprehensible executioner of innocence. In his divings and breachings, in his terrifying whiteness, he merely *is*, in all his mysterious reality of being. The great fish of the Hindus be-comes the primal God. This is the whale of the primitivist. How far he is from the whale of Jonah, Melville himself tells us in the satire of his next digression (Ch. LXXXIII). Jonah *probably* took refuge in the floating body of a dead whale or climbed aboard a passing ship with a whale for its figure-head! This rejection of an old symbol of man punished for his sins in the belly of the whale follows Melville's fusion of Hindu elements in his master symbol. In this fusion he has rejected even the Hindu Trinity. He has reached an equivalent of the primal Polynesian Taaroa, father of all Oceanic gods.

3 In a Bower of the Arsacides

Moby Dick as Vishnu incarnate is followed by Moby Dick enshrined. It does not matter that the bones of this shrine cannot be explicitly named as the skeleton of Ahab's great adversary. They are the bones of a mammoth sperm whale, and they are the symbols of the master symbol. They are Moby Dick ashore. Ishmael, in his reflection upon his voyages as a whaleman, comes now to the " recollection " of a Bower in the Arsacides (Ch. CII). I have earlier called this chapter the most important symbolic description in Melville's primitivism. It is such because it summarizes all the theology embodied in the avatars of this man's art.

Ishmael tells us that he was once entertained by his friend

Tranquo, King of Tranque, one of the Arsacides (in the Mediterranean). In his recollection he spends part of the "Arsacidean holidays" in the royal palm villa at Pupella, not far from Bamboo-Town, the capital. Among the wonders which he sees is a collection of "matters of barbaric vertú" assembled by the King: "carved woods of wonderful devices, chiselled shells, inlaid spears, costly paddles, aromatic canoes; and all these distributed among whatever natural wonders, the wonder-freighted, tribute-rendering waves had cast upon his shores." Chief among these is a great sperm whale, found dead and stranded upon the shore "with his head against a cocoa-nut tree, whose plumage-like, tufted droopings seemed his verdant jet." The body has been stripped of "its fathom-deep enfoldings" and the skeleton, after being dried in the sun, has been transported to the glen of Pupella, "where a grand temple of lordly palms now sheltered it." The ribs of the vast shrine were then hung with trophies and the vertebrae carved "with Arsacidean annals, in strange hieroglyphics." In the skull the priests maintain an aromatic flame "so that the mystic head again sent forth its vapoury spout." All around are the mosses of the Icy Glen, and there "the trees stood high and haughty, feeling their living sap." Beneath them "the industrious earth was as a weaver's loom." There "the great, white, worshipped skeleton lay lounging." Vines grow over him; "Life folded Death, and Death trellised Life." In the skull is an altar, and here Ishmael enters, seeking the source of the smoky jet. Then he brushes aside the vines on the ribs and walks the "shaded colonnades" with a ball of twine. Soon the line plays out; and having seen no living thing within, Ishmael retraces his steps and emerges. He enters again, this time with a green measuring-rod, to make some "admeasurements." The priests in the skull berate him for his audacity in presuming to measure their god. Measurement is for them alone. His measurements obtained, Ishmael withdraws; and these, he says, he had tattooed upon his right arm. He did not trouble himself with odd inches, since he wished the other parts of his body to remain a blank page for a poem he was then composing. So ends his account of his visit to Tranque, and he proceeds thereafter to give us the dimensions. He cannot account for the terminal vertebrae, since these were missing. Some little cannibal urchins, the priest's children, had stolen them to play marbles with. " Thus we see how that the spine of even the hugest of living things tapers off at last into simple child's play " (Ch. CIII) .

In this wonderfully intricate completion of Moby Dick as symbol, Melville brings together the elements of whiteness, primal mind, primitive tree. The Arsacides are not Mediterranean at all in this description. They are Oceanic islands. As Vincent has so correctly observed, " the valley of Tranque is like no valley along the Mediterranean coast but is obviously a Marquesan or Tahitian valley from Melville's own memorable past." [13] We return here to the thick shade of the familiar ravine. The whole drama of completing the symbol in this scene is played against the background of the tropical valley as a master autotype. I have intended what must seem overelaboration in the preceding summary because nearly every element of the description is of primary significance in relation to symbolic elements already familiar in this analysis.

First we discover Polynesian artifacts in the collection of Tranquo, reminding us of those spear-paddles made by the Polynesian artisan carving the likeness of his god. Next comes the image of the dead whale with his head against the Polynesian Tree of Life. The annals carved on the vertebrae evoke the mysteries of " first wisdom." In the wood where the skeleton reposes in its whiteness the trees *feel* their living sap. The vines that cover the white bones become one with death, and death is folded in life. Then Ishmael, wandering within like Theseus in the labyrinth of the Minotaur, finds no living thing. Returning again to measure with a green stick, he is accosted by the priests who suppose that they alone know how to measure God. But Ishmael escapes with some measurements, which he proceeds to record on his flesh in tattooing!

Nearly every Oriental emblem save *tayo* is contained here. Even Queequeg is recalled, as King Tranquo laughs when

[13] *The Trying-Out of Moby Dick*, p. 356.

Ishmael professes amazement that a chapel should be regarded by the sovereign as an object of " vertú " for a collection of curios. Within the walls of this transposed Polynesian valley gleams a symbol of man's first theism. Once, at the beginning of time, death and life were one in the temple of whiteness; the living tree and the green loom of the earth were more sacred than the altar; the " priest " who professed to make the total measurement of God his trade was a mere eccentric; the only dimensions which were to be recorded by anyone were the inexact measurements of a sailor savage with a green stick of the living earth; and these dimensions were to be preserved only in the primitive art of tattooing. The implication here is that the priests have measured nothing save their own altar constructed in the skull. It follows that when professional theology seeks to measure God, it measures futilely. Whatever meaning of God man may aspire to make his own comes through primitive man's " measurement "; and whatever record of measurement man may preserve is to be recorded on the tattooed skin of Ishmael, the mariner.

So appears the significance of Moby Dick's skeleton if one could capture him dead and bleach his bones upon the land and enshrine him beneath the tufted droopings of the palm. With his emblems of antiquity, with his head full of the primal, unspeakable Vedic lore of Vishnu as the fish of the deluge, with all his mysteries of Arsacidean annals, his connotations of primitive and dark mind, his everlasting whiteness—with all these he is the Oriental Moby Dick, the God forever unknowable.

4 *The Dragon as God*

Through the facts of these materials brought to the avatar described in Moby Dick one reaches the *transitus* into ultimate meaning. Here pure archetype reigns. The autotype of the great sperm whale disappears, and both artist and spectator are drawn into the darkest depths where poor Pip lost his reason in the awful presence of primal creation. We see through the murkiness of deep Oriental time the parent of great fish and whale, the symbolic progenitor, the ancient chaos-dragon. Melville seems to have been only darkly aware of what he had touched in Moby Dick when he spoke of " whales and dragons strangely jumbled together." At that moment when Melville sounds to the sea floor with Vishnu incarnate in Moby Dick, he reaches the domain of the old sea-dragon; and there he feels the antiquity of his God. E. M. Clerke, in a summary paragraph of his study of Eastern dragon myths, has written the following account of the ancient sea-lord of creation in Buddhist cosmogony. I propose his description of the god of the primal waters as a statement of exactly what Melville reached in Moby Dick.

> Hence in Buddhist cosmogony, water is the active agent in the destruction and restoration of the universe through vast alternate cycles; since on its brooding surface forms the protoplasmic scum, whence by the potential energies of matter, the germs of all life are evolved once more. Its mysterious symbol—the Dragon of the Great Deep, typifying both the waters below, which are the cradle, and those above, which are the nurse of the earth—was, therefore, originally worshipped as the most beneficent of the nature powers, as he still is throughout China, where he is regarded as the dispenser of all happiness and prosperity.[14]

Melville's feeling for the division of waters here represented is familiar to every student. It is his habit to think of the surface waters of the dolphin (and of the shark as well), the illuminated waters which are familiar to man, and the deep waters which are the cradle, the loom, the area of indescribable propulsive force. Every one of his descriptions of falling into the vortex shows this division in some way, and *Moby-Dick* is constantly informed with the feeling which the division suggests. We should approach the White Whale as the keeper of both upper and lower reaches. He is the fashioner of cycles, he is the master of his own potential energies, he is the lord of protoplasmic scum, the eternal builder and the eternal destroyer. But essentially he is the benefactor as the *giver of life*. That

---

[14] "Dragon Myths of the East," *Asiatic Quarterly Review*, vol. 4 (1887), p. 100.

Melville should have grasped this Oriental concept, and, in so doing, have supplanted the old Western mythology of the dragon as evil is an outstanding fact of his symbolistic process.

Acknowledgment must, of course, be made of Melville's indebtedness to the legend of Jonah. But I have earlier proposed his use of this mythology as purposive satiric phantasy on Hebraic lore. This I maintain again when I suggest that the whale of the Bible which *means* to Melville is the leviathan of the Book of *Job*. It is this whale that, as Clerke notes, embodies the Vedic dragon metaphor.[15] Leviathan, as Job is commanded to contemplate him, is the dragon of creation, not that convenient agent of a God who intends to terrify Jonah into repentance. Two authorities who have studied Job's leviathan in his basic meaning agree initially that the monster is the Nilotic crocodile under another name. Edgar C. S. Gibson investigates the master force contained in the symbol of the verse *Who are ready to rouse up Leviathan* (3: 8). He relates this to the mythology of the eclipse. " The verse . . . can only be explained as an allusion to an ancient mythological notion (found also among the Indians), according to which eclipses were produced by a mythical dragon or monster of the sky which swallowed up sun or moon, and so created darkness." The same belief, he notes, is found among the Chinese.[16] This account of the dragon as the adversary, the maker of darkness, extends Clerke's description of the benefactor to a duality agreeing with Melville's multiple meaning in the White Whale. James Strahan provides an interpretation of leviathan, however, which is clearly descriptive of Melville's experience with the archetype. Strahan's comment is directed to the descriptions of leviathan appearing in the concluding chapters of the Book of *Job* (40: 15–41: 34).

> . . . [I]t has been the generally accepted opinion that Behemoth is to be identified with the hippopotamus, and Leviathan with the crocodile, two Nilotic animals which ancient writers often name together. Some modern critics—notably

[15] *Ibid.*, p. 103.
[16] *The Book of Job* (New York, 1899), p. 15.

Gunkel and Zimmern, Cheyne and Toy—have propounded
the theory that the beasts described are not real animals but
mythological monsters. Gunkel regards Leviathan as the
chaos-dragon, Tiâmat, and Behemoth as Kingu her consort
[n. 1, *Schöpfung und Chaos*]. Cheyne finds in both descriptions a fusion of Babylonian and Egyptian semi-mythical
elements.[17]

A digression upon the origins of leviathan in the East would be
extraneous here, since I cannot presume to scholarly interpretation; furthermore, my objective is to define feeling in the
genesis of the symbol of primitivism, not the mythological
derivations of Job's whale-dragon. Tiâmat, even though female,
is undoubtedly the chaos-dragon of Vedic and Chinese lore
described by Clerke. Melville, in his contemplation of the
whale-archetype, experiences in his feeling a clear transmutation of myth. The anthropomorphous God of Job passes into
the multiplicity of leviathan and becomes, at least for Melville
as the maker of the White Whale, the old dragon-benefactor of
Indian and Chinese mythology worshipped as the giver of life.

Melville's " encyclopaedic " knowledge, as I have earlier said,
cannot be fully checked. I do not know what he had read. At
the same time I am sure that what he reaches in the ultimate
meaning of the symbolic whale is in full agreement with what
Clerke says of the dragon. This meaning is again defined when
the symbol of Moby Dick is related to Fenollosa's dragon-of-
the-waters as he reconstructs this symbol from the iconography
of Chinese art. Fenollosa analyzes here certain symbolic forms
from the art of the Hai Dynasty (B. C. 2205–1707) and the
Shang (B. C. 1706–1122). He concludes:

> Another Pacific feature in the decoration of these bronzes
> is the fish, or marine monster, the ancestor of the Chinese
> dragon, which is identical with forms found from the South
> Pacific Islands to North-Eastern America. This sea-creature
> has a head unlike a fish, with curved snout, opened nostrils,
> sometimes with tusks, and a curving tail also unlike a fish.
> Yet it is often found in connection with forms that are clearly

[17] *The Book of Job Interpreted* (Edinburgh, 1913), pp. 337–38.

fish-like. It occurs in New Zealand and Micronesian art, carved on the handles of utensils, gourd bottles, and woven into stuffs; and it reappears in almost identical forms in Alaskan patterns. Its shape, identical on the early Chinese bronzes, is probably their dragon; only we see here that a " dragon " means no lizard monster of Western tradition, but a semi-fish-like or possibly seal form—evidently a spirit symbol connected with water.[18]

In the same comment Fenollosa observes that " this dragon-world underneath the sea is part of Primitive Chinese myth." And we are reminded later by the same token that " Chinese art is first Pacific, second Mesopotamian, third Indian Buddhist." [19] I take it that in naming the monster of Hai and Shang memorials as the ancestor of the Chinese dragon, Fenollosa had the " refined " dragon of later epochs in mind. For the original fish of the bronzes is the original chaos-dragon, represented in this primitive Chinese iconography and in the earliest art of nearly all peoples dwelling on the Pacific rim or on the islands of Oceania. He is the essence of generative waters. Fenollosa's great original symbol interprets the deepest meaning which Moby Dick embodies. The White Whale inherits from the first of all symbols of God conceived in the vast mind of the Orient and in the time-buried origins of Oriental feeling. As the master avatar of Melville's art, he is a reincarnation of the old chaos-dragon.

In this analysis of the dragon whale I have intended to reach the facts of Melville's primitivistic feeling. I must contend again that whatever any student wishes to find in Moby Dick would probably not be unacceptable to Melville. The old dragon of the waters, like the great Oro, originally contains all states of being. He prefigures all, and he holds all of incalculable time in him, the great cycles of creation and destruction, birth and rebirth. Coleridge's profound and beautiful speculation in " Frost at Midnight," it will be recalled, is a supreme example of the Romantic mind grappling with the idea of the dynamic God, the God who has still to complete creating him-

---

[18] *Epochs of Chinese and Japanese Art*, p. 10.
[19] *Ibid.*, p. 27.

self.[20] But this intellection, heroic as it is, cannot be proposed as an equivalent of Melville's symbolistic act in the realm of feeling. Even the dynamism of Coleridge's idea yields finally to the old notion of anthropomorphism, I think. At some future time God will be complete and absolute and *known*. There are no such promises in Melville's future. The ultimate God lies yesterday, this day, and forever beyond the reach of man's mind. I take that God to be " the God beyond theism " named by Tillich in *The Courage to Be*. When this fact of Melville's master symbol has been understood, the distance between the symbol of Christ as the man of innocence among men and the symbol of the unknowable God beyond him is illuminated with flashing brilliance. Melville becomes, through the artistic heroism of making Moby Dick, the man of Oriental acceptance in the realm of his ideality. And in that becoming he confirms the symbols of his theology and his sacrament. As artist, he passes into the future of the twentieth century, into the next era of the desymbolized Protestant world; and there Verhaeren and Yeats, to name only two symbolists of that future, have fortified his meaning.[21]

The foregoing discussions have analyzed the major Oceanic and Oriental symbols of Melville, and cognates of these symbols wherever these appear in the art of recent primitivism. The symbols have been presented as avatars since, as the facts of origin and meaning demonstrate, they are reincarnations in art of Oriental prototypes. I have intended to distinguish clearly between archetypes and autotypes as these shape the symbol in the religious act of achieving equivalents for the " lost " symbols represented in cultural failure. These avatars contribute to the definition of recent primitivism. Furthermore, they define

---

[20] Ll. 58–62: " . . . so shalt thou see and hear / The lovely shapes and sounds intelligible/ Of that eternal language, which thy God/ Utters, *who from eternity doth teach / Himself in all, and all things in himself.*"   (Italics mine.)

[21] Other critics have, of course, recognized Moby Dick as Melville's image of God. The first of these was Olson (*Call Me Ishmael*, p. 82). Both Chase (*Herman Melville*, p. 49) and Thompson (*Melville's Quarrel with God*, p. 204) have followed with the same conclusion. It is good to have these critical opinions in agreement. But the ways by which each was reached, all at variance with the method of this study, will not be reviewed here.

genuine art with its power to create individuated form; they set it apart from a commonly shared universality of "dream content," and from exoticism and its instances and techniques invoking the bizarre and the strange. The genetic facts of existential primitivism establish its character as that of a new religion.

The community of all genuine primitivists in the recent history of Western art may be visualized through a metaphoric use of one of Melville's scenes in *Moby-Dick*. In the sixty-first chapter Stubb kills a sperm whale. Ishmael's account proposes once again that sacramental acts engage the imagination of the artist. For Stubb is later to eat of the body of that whale, and Ishmael is to exclaim: " That mortal man should feed upon the creature that feeds his lamp, and, like Stubb, eat him by his own light " (Ch. LXV). When the whale is finally given his death wound, a red tide pours from his sides like brooks down a hill. His tormented body rolls in his blood, seething far behind in the wake of the *Pequod*. And all his captors are bathed in the reflected color of that gore. " The slanting sun playing upon this crimson pond in the sea, sent back its reflection into every face, so that they all glowed to each other like red men." Certainly there need be no insistence here upon symbolistic intent. The scene can as well be of the " functional " level of the book which reports with consistent directness upon the science of whaling. Yet these men of the *Pequod* are made red, all one, in the aura of that primal blood of life. Each, save Ahab and his attendant Fedallah with his spirit crew, is a sailor savage free to carve the likeness of the whale and the likeness, therefore, of his god. In the God-stained light of that evening sea each becomes one with his fellows in his redness and in his acceptance of the blood-mysteries of the lord of the primitive waters. He stands before an ancient sign of sacrificial blood, and on his countenance he wears the color of primitive man's blood nature, even that redness which courses vastly within the inscrutable whiteness of Moby Dick.

PART FOUR

IMAGES
FROM THE URWELT:
THE WORLD BEFORE
CIVILIZATION

XII

The Sea and Aqueous Images

The world of the dragon, the realm of primal and generative waters, describes the deepest reach of the symbolistic imagination in primitivism. It is the symbol of the *Urwelt* (to use the more convenient German term), the *original world* shaped from the original universe. Just as this *Urwelt* lies below even the Oriental antiquity of the great Vishnu as whale, so is the " Urishness " of the primitivist the deep below his Orientalism. It is the feeling which he has toward the base of all time in the nature of God. As the maker of symbols he relates his feeling to the Orient because the culture of that region is the

oldest which he can touch. It gives him the possibility of referring to the greatest depth of recorded history and tradition.
But he can dream beyond that depth, and in that dream his
Urishness directs him to images which, having no particular
symbolistic direction, are merely the tokens of his particular
vision. Thus Ishmael on the sea dreams of its deepest and least
known generative waters out of which rose the continents and
islands, and on the land, of the primal world of the jungle and
the rain-forest and of the original life of ancient earth.

This dream of a world before civilization is the characteristic
sign of Ishmael as imagist. His constancy in the dream is revealed in the metaphor of his art. Even though he had never
created a single life-symbol to define his feeling, the Urishness
of his imagination would still be there. But in the area of
imagery where experience is made known, the archetype disappears. Thus it may be said, in beginning a study of primitivistic imagery, that *any description of sensuous experience
rendered through a metaphoric reference which is not governed
by archetypal patterns emerging through cultural failure is, in
the idiom of primitivism, imagistic.* This chapter and the next
are intended as examinations of genetic fact in an area of the
imagination which is adjacent to the area of the symbolistic
process. But it is understood initially that this adjacency refers
to the Urwelt behind the symbols, the great heterogeneously
figurative background against which these symbols are displayed. It must be understood, too, that no measurement can
be made of conscious as opposed to unconscious imagistic usage.
It may very well be that in imagism the primitivist, however
knowing he may have been of his symbolistic intent, is like the
turtle who never once sees the strange and beautiful markings
on the hump of his shell. They are a part of him, even though
he cannot admire them as we do.

In the preceding analyses of avatars, the objective was one
of reaching conclusive readings. The examination of imagery
to follow is intended as suggestive, since the appearance of autotypes in metaphor is too extensive to attract exhaustive comment, *ad nauseam*. The important problem would seem to be

one of determining why certain images become obsessive and why these appear selectively in the acts of artistic creation. This problem belongs to psychologists rather than to critics and aestheticians. One may say simply that images are retained because of accidental association, and let it go at that. But I think we may speak initially of two possible conditions in primitivistic imagery: first, images bear the characteristics of symbols in their artistic potentialities, and second, they are mysteriously retained and employed because of certain factors in emotive experience which make them particularly attractive and memorable at the time they are received. What these factors are I shall not attempt to say, save that they are the qualities of any Oriental setting signifying " liberation " from the traditional cultural background of the primitivist-voyager. This sense of liberation is revealed in Melville's preference for Polynesian metaphor, in Hearn's preference for the image inspired by Japanese landscape and Japanese custom. And if we take Gauguin's range of color as an equivalent of imagery in language, we see that the brilliant contrast of Tahitian and Marquesan light and shadow is in the same way obsessive; so are the details of native dress and the familiar contours of Polynesian landscape.

Of a third condition of primitivistic imagery there can be little question. This is the condition of a native, inherent taste for the incongruous. My metaphor of the undiscerning turtle will serve again. The artist with his Urishness is inevitably concerned with expressing his sense of the incongruous. The incongruity lies in the juxtaposition of images from primitiveness with images from the world of civilization. But there is a question whether the turtle knows the extent of what he carries in his treasure of figures of either kind.

Melville's fascination with mixed cultural values has already been fully discussed. It appears in his symbolistic experiments from their first forms, and equally in the nonsymbolistic act of establishing incongruity between the image and its companion figures. This act, of course, is innately poetic, since it seeks to render unity from a sharply differentiated sensory manifold.

Note, for instance the incongruity suggesting poetic method in the following description from *The Confidence Man*. Sensation is first revealed in an autotypic image from a Polynesian reef and is immediately extended by an image of *coolness* distinguishing the complex affectation of " civilized " behavior. The character described here is a " stranger " aboard the *Fidèle*. " At last, setting down the goblet, and gently wiping from his lips the beads of water freshly clinging there as the valve of a coral-shell upon a reef, he turned upon the cosmopolitan, and, in a manner the most cool, self-possessed, and matter-of-fact possible, said . . . ." [1] The quality of water clinging to the mouth as the valve of the coral shell to the reef fixes the idea of coolness and then passes, through incongruous association, into the cool decorum of the man. At this point in *The Confidence Man*, with its bitter denunciation of a civilization negating everything represented in the ideality of Melville's symbolism, we are as far from Polynesia as the Mississippi itself is from Papeete.

Yet the autotype still governs; and it is hardly possible to guess how much of this incongruous state of things is unconscious in artistic method and how much is studied. In Melville's work it is a sign of poetic endowment, this almost instinctive act of making what Mrs. Langer calls " crazy " associations. (See Chapter II of this study.) The " craziness " of the following image in *Mardi* shows that the taste for imagistic incongruity was developing as the power to render symbols began to take form. Babbalanja and Mohi are discussing crocodiles, which are said (like the whale) to yield ambergris. Babbalanja observes: " No wonder, then, their flesh is so fragrant; their upper jaws as the visors of vinaigrettes." [2] The vinaigrette image comes obviously from some observation Melville had made of a bottle of aromatic vinegar with a cap reminding him of the visor of a helmet. What can be more incongruous than this combination of the crocodile's upper jaw and the sharply pointed, " threatening " visor of the bottle? Certainly the asso-

---

[1] *The Confidence Man*, p. 257.
[2] *Mardi*, vol. 2, p. 63.

ciation is "crazy." But it is just this craziness which sets up images from Melville's Urishness where one would least expect to find them.

The origin of primitivistic imagery, like that of symbols, is emotive. In Melville's artistic method, the seemingly incongruous position of images recalling the sea and Polynesia usually denotes a double point of view, as though the artist were looking away from the thing or the situation described toward its opposite in the Oriental setting recalled. One must go back in examining this phenomenon to Melville's contention in beginning his description of Queequeg, that nothing exists "but by contrast."

1 Primitive Waters

The great September waves breaking at the base of the Neversink Highlands, far in advance of the swiftest pilot-boat, carry tidings. And full often, they know the last secret of many a stout ship, never heard of from the day she left port. Every wave in my eyes seems a soul.[3]

This early passage from *Mardi* is the first revelation we have of Melville's feeling for the primitiveness of ocean. It has what may be called the inevitable stamp of the Urwelt in the image of cosmic movement. Its distinction is metaphoric. September sea, with its suggestion of volume and weight rolling upon the highlands from some mid-ocean vortex of equinoctial storms, is heavy with secrets, heavy with the meaning of life and death. Apostrophe and personification, as Byron might have used these, do not appear at all. Melville's image is not related to any literary convention. It is a spontaneous expression of Urishness. The elemental character which it displays may be defined in a comparison of these waves with the "scrolls of silver snowy sentences" used by Hart Crane in his familiar "Voyages II."

> And yet this great wink of eternity,
> Of rimless floods, unfettered leewardings,
> Samite sheeted and processioned where

[3] *Mardi*, vol. 1, p. 56.

Her undinal vast belly moonward bends,
Laughing the wrapt inflections of our love;

Take this Sea, whose diapason knells
On scrolls of silver snowy sentences,
The sceptred terror of whose session rends
As her demeanors motion well or ill,
All but the pieties of lovers' hands . . . .

Mark how her turning shoulders wind the hours,
And hasten while her penniless rich palms
Pass superscription of bent foam and wave,—
Hasten, while they are true,—sleep, death, desire,
Close round one instant in one floating flower.[4]

The metaphor of Crane's poem is central in aesthetic method; it is developed and extended idiomatically in such fashion that the poem as a form achieves a wrought, a deliberately " artistic " appearance. The spume of the sea-troughs becomes the written secret of the manuscript, the " superscription." The development of the metaphor becomes highly purposed, and we discover our chief pleasure in contemplating the poem through the marvelous intricacy of its imagistic structure. Certainly a kind of primitivism is revealed here; and there would seem to be little question that Crane is about the work of creating artistic form through the autotype of his own experience with spume and cascading foam and scroll-like waves. But his poem has little of Urishness. Melville's September sea is an image of primitivistic feeling. It receives no poetic development; it is merely an " original " image, an image from which the artist with Crane's intent will proceed to fashion a poem. In its clear, " original " state it is simple and direct rather than intricate.

---

[4] *Collected Poems*, ed. Waldo Frank (New York, Liveright Publishing Corp., 1933). The feeling of salt sea as the beginning is found in a passage from Robert Dean Frisbie's *Island of Desire*, marked with an intensity recalling that of Melville. " Then, for a little time, I stood still, allowed my mind to go blank, and sensed the strange and sequestered beauty of this uninhabited place. I sensed the presence of the familiar spirit of peace in the fragrant odor from the land, in the sustained drone of palm fronds, the clamor of birds, the deep undertone of reef combers rising and falling and mingling with the other sounds in a kind of fugue that expressed the loneliness and beauty of primitive things." (See p. 149.)

Through it we look into the distances of the background against which the intricacies of Melville's symbols are achieved.

The sudden and then brief appearance of such images as this of the primitive sea is characteristic of primitivism as art. The imagery to be examined here should be regarded as emblematic of the world beyond the theology of symbols, and much of this is thrust into view without the artist's attention to questions of relevance in form, as deep strata emerge in outcroppings on the earth's surface, these to the eye of the practiced geologist all memorials of the prehistoric world which they reveal. Olson believes that we may name one " important single fact about Melville ": it is that " the beginning of man was salt sea, and the perpetual reverberation of that great ancient fact [is] constantly renewed in the unfolding of life in every human individual." [5] If it is not *the* fact, then it is one of the important ones.

The same Urishness which governs Melville's feeling here is the imaginative domain of other artists in primitivism. Loti's feeling for the generative waters of ocean has already been noted. In *Pêcheur d'Islande* he reaches the definition of this feeling through the images employed in his closing chapter. Yann is claimed in death by the sea and is " married " to the waters. It is the same sea of Melville's *Mardi,* the sea of secret-freighted waves. One night in August, far from the sombre coasts of Iceland, in the midst of a raging storm, Yann " celebrated his marriage with the sea."

> With the sea who once had been also his nurse; she it was who had cradled him, who had made him the strong adolescent,—and then she who had claimed him, in his superb strength, for herself. A profound mystery enveloped the rites of the monstrous marriage. . . . At the moment when he abandoned himself, his arms open to receive her, [he uttered] a deep cry like that of a dying bull, his mouth already full of water, his arms open and rigid forever.[6]

The scene discloses the same emotion which informs the last

[5] *Call Me Ishmael*, p. 13.
[6] *Pêcheur d'Islande* (Calmann Lévy), pp. 272-73.

page of *Moby-Dick* through one striking similarity: these waters are generative in their all-containment of life and death. Melville's closing description reads: " Now small fowls flew screaming over the yet yawning gulf; a sullen white surf beat against its steep sides; then all collapsed, and the great shroud of the sea rolled on as it rolled five thousand years ago." To say simply that the sea images of *Mardi* and *Moby-Dick* and of *Pêcheur d'Islande* are images of death is to ignore their complete meanings. They are openings upon the vistas of timelessness, in which death and life are made one, exactly as death and life are one in the emblems of Melville's whale-temple of the Arsacides. They are tokens of the *foundations*, in Melville's words from *Moby-Dick*, " the unspeakable foundations, ribs, and very pelvis of the world." [7]

To Leconte de Lisle this sea is timelessness in the same sense. In " Les Clairs de Lune " he pictures the waters which inherit all time. The poem opens with this setting of waste and desolation in moonlight:

> This is a world misshapen, rugged, dull, livid,
> The monstrous spectre of a universe destroyed
> Thrown as a wreck to the Ocean of emptiness,
> Hell petrified, without flame and without tumult,
> Flowing and eddying in the undisturbed night.[8]

This is the primal water which created all life, and must claim all life in the end. Death by water, commonly regarded as one of the major obsessions of the poet in the twentieth century, is foretold in these images of the sea from primitivism. The sea as shroud over Melville's *Pequod*, the sea as fatal mistress and bride in the life and death of Loti's Yann, the sea as the flowing and eddying night of chaos in the imagery of Leconte de Lisle— all these, and a whole range of imagery tending toward the same feeling (as in Whitman's " Out of the Cradle " or Arnold's " Dover Beach ") , demonstrate the continuity of the poetic descent into the deep. For death by water in our recent poetry means essentially the return of life to the matrix of creation. It

---

[7] Vol. 1, p. 166.
[8] *Poèmes Barbares* (Lemerre), vol. 1, p. 178.

carries with it none of the connotations of Christian baptism. It is the ultimate destiny of life, born of the timelessness of sea, bearing upon its face in birth the prefiguration of its watery death.

The primitivism of Isadore Ducasse (Lautréamont) would show perhaps little relationship to that of Melville were it not for the imagery of the sea which distinguishes the opening scenes of the *Chants de Maldoror*. For this imagery equals that of Loti in interpreting the sea realm revealed by Melville's figures. The similarity of the following passages (written in 1869) to descriptions of the primitive sea from Melville and Loti is at once clear; and they might have come from any other primitivist. "Ancient ocean . . . you call again to the memory of your lovers . . . the rude beginnings of man when he became acquainted with grief, which leaves him no more. . . . Ancient ocean, nothing is impossible in what you hide in your being of future avail to man. You have already given him the whale. You do not easily relinquish to the eyes of science the thousand secrets of your inmost organization: you are modest." Man, even with his science, cannot measure the dizzying depth of these abysses.[9] Acquaintance with grief appears here in its non-Christian sense. It is the grief of man's knowledge of his own momentary time contained in the secret, the unknown timelessness of ocean. This doom of humanity and the promise of man's future flow together in the same watery being.

Ducasse and Melville are united in the character of the image again through the reference which each makes to the sea as the bearer of human error and violence. It is the primitiveness of the sea which underlies the tragedy of Billy Budd; and in at least one instance Melville presents this fact of feeling in the image. Captain Vere, standing aside from the drum-head court convened to judge Billy, paces the cabin athwart and climbs the "slant deck in the ship's lee roll; without knowing it symbolizing thus in his action a mind resolute to surmount difficulties even if against primitive instincts strong as the wind and

---

[9] *Oeuvres complètes* (ed. Soupault), pp. 60–62.

the sea." [10] This primitive ocean beneath him is the energy of indifferent good and evil, and against this he is powerless. It sustains the human forces of naval power, with its acts of violence represented in the execution of Billy. In the same manner Ducasse describes the " patriarch observer " of the waters. He is " the contemporary of the first epochs of our suspended globe." He smiles in pity even as he permits naval wars upon his waters. He hears the commands of the officers, the cries of the wounded, the volleys of the cannon. The tumult of annihilation endures only a few seconds. Then the ocean takes all this into his vast belly, through his formidable mouth. The poet addresses his patriarch deity: " [Thus] . . . you unroll, from the heart of a sombre mystery upon the sublime face [of ocean], your incomparable wastes." [11] In these images Ducasse stands with Melville at the threshold of making the god-symbol of the great waters. Who can tell what this hand, so abruptly withdrawn by the early death of the poet, might have fashioned beyond the imagery of Maldoror? The unrolling of the wastes is the same unfurling of the essential mystery which we discover in Melville's great September waves leaping against the highlands.

Melville's imagery of the primitive sea, in this elemental context, need not be discussed further. It exemplifies the first of the two possible conditions in primitivistic imagery: images bear the characteristics of symbols in their potentialities. But Melville's art in primitivism transcends the imagistic rendering of sea distinctive in the art of Ducasse, Leconte de Lisle, and Loti. It transcends the same kind of symbolic potentiality which is impressive in Hearn's description of the Caribbean as he first saw it in the summer of 1887, en route to the Lesser Antilles: " All this sensuous blending of warmth and force in winds and waters more and more suggests an idea of the spiritualism of elements,—a sense of world-life." [12] This again is the cosmic imagery of Urishness. It was Melville's distinction,

[10] *Billy Budd and Other Prose Pieces*, p. 85.
[11] Oeuvres complètes (Soupault), p. 65.
[12] *Two Years in the French West Indies*, p. 19.

among these artists, to have made the symbol of his White Whale as *all* primitivistic feeling toward the Urwelt brought to form. Melville's own images as tokens of that feeling, and the images of all primitivists related to him, together represent the original mysteries of timelessness; and it is the symbols standing before these token figures that tell us the meaning of the imagery. Thus Moby Dick interprets all else: Loti's sea reclaiming the life which it cradled, the dark wastes of Leconte de Lisle's sea of death, the enormous maw of the sea opening to receive Ducasse's naval battle. And all these, in turn, demonstrate the meaning of Moby Dick. Beyond these equations, Hearn's tropic sea of world-life is matched by Melville's " eternal August " sea of the tropics, when the *Pequod* sails through days like heaped-up goblets of Persian sherbet, and when " the witcheries of that unwaning weather " turn in upon the soul (Ch. xxix). For this warm sea of world-life, of " the bright Quito spring," is but another domain of Moby Dick.

It is obvious that the use of the autotype of primitive sea must be limited. Man, since he belongs to the land, makes analogies among his fellow human beings through images of the land. Thus the islands of the sea-realm, themselves the progeny of the sea and yet the lands of men, appear in primitivistic art as sources of imagery displaying autotypes of a more various character. In turning from the sea itself to the reef and the lagoon which the sea forms, we understand that the oceanic Urwelt still dominates the imagination. For these islands rise from the vastness of water. Thus Loti reflects upon the union of land and sea in Tahiti: " Consider the cliffs of basalt, the forests hanging to the sombre mountains, and all this, lost in the midst of that majestic and limitless solitude: the Pacific." [13] Hearn at La Soufrière in Santa Lucia of the West Indies feels the same primeval oneness: " You behold before you a geological dream, a vision of the primeval sea: the apparition of the land as first brought forth, all peak-tossed and fissured and naked and grim, in the tremendous birth of an archipelago." [14]

[13] *Le Mariage de Loti*, p. 35.
[14] *Two Years in the French West Indies*, p. 95.

Stevenson, who remarked that the first sight of a Polynesian island is an experience like no other which civilized man may encounter, wrote of his first view of Nukuhiva: " Except for the *Casco* lying outside, and a crane or two, and the ever-busy wind and sea, the face of the world was of a prehistoric emptiness; life appeared to stand stockstill, and the sense of isolation was profound and refreshing." [15] This *prehistoric emptiness* is the feeling of Urishness expressed by Loti and Hearn. It is revealed in the same dominant imagery by Melville in his recollection of Tahiti seen from sea.

> It is one mass of shaded tints of green, from beach to mountain top; endlessly diversified with valleys, ridges, glens and cascades. Over the ridges, here and there, the loftier peaks fling their shadows, and far down the valleys. At the head of these, the waterfalls flash out into the sunlight, as if pouring through vertical bowers of verdure. Such enchantment, too, breathes over the whole, that it seems a fairy world, all fresh and blooming from the hand of the Creator. [16]

Out of the unknown vulcanism of submarine mountains rose these islands of Tahiti, Nukuhiva, Santa Lucia. In the domain of the primitivist's feeling they are essences of sea-mystery, and their coral beaches and still, reef-locked pools were made of those endlessly generative waters.

2   *Reef and Lagoon*

The most impressive single figure employed by Melville from his store of aqueous images—that store which I shall not attempt to catalogue here—is the form of the coral reef. The appearance of this reef as an autotype, superimposed upon a various array of impression and circumstance from the civilized world, is one of the brilliant signs of Melville's art. In my evaluation of Melville's sensuous experience in Polynesia, I spoke of his impressions from Oceanic landscape as derivations of an importance equal to that of his knowledge of native custom and

[15] *In the South Seas*, p. 22.
[16] *Omoo*, pp. 76–77.

religion. The autotype of the Polynesian valley has been described in the preceding analysis of symbols. The facsimile of the reef is employed as an image strengthening some concept or description which seems to the artist to require a visual representation of *enclosure* or *fortification*. The reef recalled is thus the barrier of encircling coral rock. It encloses the calm waters inside; it fortifies the land against the lashings of the sea.

I shall not differentiate extensively between the two major sources of the autotype. Every traveler in the Pacific will recognize at once the barrier reef of the volcanic island as one of these, the encircling reef of the atoll as the other. Since the atoll invariably possesses a lagoon locked in by the reef, I propose this formation as the preferred of the two sources, even though Melville was thoroughly acquainted with Nukuhiva and Tahiti, both volcanic. Yet it is worth noting that he thinks of the atolls of the Gilbert Islands in *Mardi*. In the early chapters of this work we are told that the *Parki* is bound for the vicinity of the Kingsmill Chain (Gilberts) and that Taji's encounter with Samoa has confirmed his intention to touch there (Ch. xxx). Presumably Mardi is located somewhere in these waters, and they may very well be seas actually crossed by Melville after his departure from Tahiti in November, 1842, aboard the *Charles and Henry*. He was, at any rate, entirely familiar with the structure of the atoll, notably represented by the Marshalls, the Gilberts, and Kapingamarangi.

The reef as the barrier encircling either atoll or volcanic peak is the physical form which passes into the obsessive image. Melville's use of the reef becomes almost instinctive when he wishes to represent encirclement of an object situation or a character. Thus, on the first page of *Moby-Dick* he describes the island of Manhattan, " belted round by wharves as Indian isles by coral reefs—commerce surrounds it with her surf." Experience in the double image appears immediately; and it is important to note the appearance of a related double reference in the image of the tree following this reef image, the tree with its hollow trunk containing a crucifix. (See Chapter x of this study.) Manhattan becomes the island of New York seen through the frame of the Pacific reef. In the same manner, the tree of the landscape painter is represented as the familiar tree by the brook, regarded through imagery as the Tree of Life. These images are signs of the whole imagistic structure of *Moby-Dick*, to say nothing of their reference to the symbolistic method of the work. An understanding of their implications is indispensable in proceeding toward an evaluation of Melville's later primitivistic character.

For this reef image recurs with a constantly accreting meaning. It appears in its ultimate significance at the beginning of *Clarel*. The mind of the student-voyager is studied in this fashion:

> These under-formings in the mind.
> Banked corals which ascend from far,
> But little heed men that they wind
> Unseen, unheard—till lo, the reef—
> The reef and breaker, wreck and grief.
> But here unlearning, how to me
> Opes the expanse of time's vast sea!
> Yes, I am young, but Asia old.
> The books, the books not all have told.[17]

The reef, mounting through the waters of the mind, is to be both the barrier against the sea and the rock of death to the islander who ventures into the ocean beyond it. Interpreted through its Oceanic images, this passage means that Clarel (the Ishmael voyager) creates in the scepticism of his quest the reef of his own destruction. The reef is the boundary between the " inner " life of primitive acceptance and the " outer " life of over-reason, of man's aspiring search for absolute truth. But even if this meaning were not so clearly set forth, the venture of Clarel described in this metaphor would still demonstrate clearly the immeasurable power of Melville's retained experi-

---

[17] *Clarel*, vol. 1, p. 5. This atoll metaphor for intellect may be seen again in a poem of Alex Comfort, " The Atoll in the Mind," reprinted by Oscar Williams in *A Little Treasury of Modern Poetry* (New York, 1952, pp. 627–28). Here the mind's stone tree grows up from deep waters; it becomes an island above, open to the sun; it bears " slender trunks " by the lagoon; then mind appears as two trees, one reaching upward into light and air, the other " rooted among the bones."

ence. This image, like that of the coral shell clinging to the reef in the figure from *The Confidence Man*, suggests the nature of Melville's obsession. It was perfectly natural that he should think of Clarel's mind as the emblem of all human reason, building itself endlessly toward the surface, and in itself creating the rock of its own destruction. The initial reef image explains the artistic purpose of *Clarel*, the work; for it must be remembered that the poem ends with Clarel's rejection of reason and his acceptance of only the " primitive " heart.

The reef appears in its fullest significance in *Pierre*. The youth has renounced his heritage and has taken refuge in New York, where he sets to work upon a book which is to expose the nature of truth.

> [Pierre] . . . perceiving, by presentiment, that most grand productions of the best human intellects ever are built round a circle, as atolls (*i. e.*, the primitive coral islets which, raising themselves in the depths of profoundest seas, rise funnel-like to the surface, and present there a hoop of white rock, which though on the outside everywhere lashed by the ocean, yet excludes all tempests from the quiet lagoon within), digestively including the whole range of all that can be known or dreamed; Pierre was resolved to give the world a book, which the world should hail with surprise and delight.[18]

The lagoon image specifically expresses Melville's entire artistic ideality. The meaning of the reef encircling the inner calm is too clearly established by its meanings elsewhere to be accepted in any other sense. For the speaker here is the Ishmael-symbolist, not Pierre Glendinning. No primitivist, in recognition again of a simple fact, is to be reborn a primitive man. He remains the man of intellect, the man finding his ways out of cultural failure through his art. The ideal of this art is the stillness of the lagoon, fortified with its hoop of white rock against the incomprehensibilities of the wild sea beyond. The lagoon is the calm of the man who has found his reality. Pierre's giving the world a book means Ishmael's giving himself

[18] *Pierre*, p. 394.

the symbols of his reality, formed by his art from the chaos of
the primitive sea dashing upon the reef. Pierre's failure is
seen in his failure to reach the lagoon. Having taken leave of
that green island, that " insular Tahiti " in the soul of man
(the innocence named by Melville in *Moby-Dick*, Ch. LVIII) ,
Pierre does not reach a new haven in this lagoon of the artist,
and so perishes at last, like Ahab, in the deep.

The autotype impressed here upon the moral significance of
Melville's Pierre is equaled by the facsimile of Stevenson's
experience in the same image. The reef of the atoll appears
in *The Ebb-Tide*, at that moment when the tormented Herrick,
indentured aboard the pirated *Farallone*, sails into the still
lagoon of Attwater's island kingdom.

> He tortured himself to find analogies. The isle was like
> the rim of a great vessel sunken in the waters; it was like the
> embankment of an annular railway grown upon with wood:
> so slender it seemed amidst the outrageous breakers, so frail
> . . . he would scarce have wondered to see it sink and dis-
> appear without a sound and the waves close smoothly over
> its descent.[19]

The lagoon is sequestration and refuge from the meaningless
chaos of his outcast's life, from the unreality of his world.
Herrick stands transported. " In the gratified lust of his eye
he forgot the past and the present; forgot that he was menaced
by a prison on the one hand and starvation on the other; forgot
that he was come to that island, desperately foraging, clutching
at expedients." [20] That same hoop of white coral, laid like a
magic talisman upon the chaos of Pierre's tragic folly, is impressed by the hand of Stevenson upon the meaninglessness of
a quite comparable folly embodied in Herrick. In each instance
of art represented here, the primitivistic image of encircling
reef outlines the meaning of civilization with its codes, its
measurements of success and failure, its moral chicanery, its
masochistic torments, as these are embodied in the character
described. Remove the autotype of the Oceanic reef, and in

[19] *Works* (Scribner, 1922), vol. 18, p. 108.
[20] *Ibid.*, p. 110.

the disappearance of the double image the precise meaning of the folly and the tragedy vanishes. Melville's use of the reef in *Pierre* confirms his intention in his other uses of the same image; Stevenson's dependence upon the image in completing his artistic realization of Herrick extends the significance of Melville's facsimile from the Pacific.

The concluding image for discussion may be proposed as a perfect example of Melville's transposed facsimiles of the Oceanic reef and lagoon. The transposition is so direct, its method so clearly allied to Melville's reception of the Polynesian experience in pure sensuousness, its demonstration of sensitivity to color so remarkable that any analysis would seem superfluous. The sense of liberation attendant upon the acquisition of the image at Tahiti and the taste for the incongruous certainly direct its appearance in the imaginative realm. But the poetic clarity which it attains is so supreme as to lift it from its associations with every image standing about it. The double vision of its metaphor is that of a pure poetry freed of all morality, all artistic purpose. It is a figure of the beauty of existence, and nothing more. Melville establishes and records the autotype clearly in the pages of *Omoo*. He is describing an hour of looking down into the " marine gardens " of Motoo-Otoo, the " private " island of Queen Pomare. It is a " white, moonlight night."

> Right in the middle of Papeete harbour is a bright, green island, one circular grove of waving palms, and scarcely a hundred yards across. It is of coral formation; and all round, for many rods out, the bay is so shallow that you might wade anywhere. Down in these waters, as transparent as air, you see coral plants of every hue and shape imaginable—antlers, tufts of azure, waving reeds like stalks of grain, and pale green buds and mosses. In some places, you look through prickly branches down to a snow-white floor of sand, sprouting with flinty bulbs; and crawling among these are strange shapes—some bristling with spikes, others clad in shining coats of mail, and here and there, round forms all spangled with eyes.[21]

[21] *Omoo*, p. 192.

On a November night in 1849, seven years after that November of his departure from Tahiti, Melville attended the Royal Lyceum Theatre in London with two fellow travelers of his recent voyage from New York.[22] There he entered the shilling gallery and experienced an impression of the brilliant audience below him which must immediately have joined the scene of the marine gardens of Motoo-Otoo in the deep recesses of memory and imagination. The full image in its double reference appeared some four years later in the sketch called *The Two Temples*.

> The height of the gallery was in truth appalling. The rail was low. I thought of deep-sea-leads, and the mariner in the vessel's chains, drawing up the line, with his long-drawn musical accompaniment. And like beds of glittering coral, through the deep sea of azure smoke, there, far down, I saw the jewelled necks and white sparkling arms of crowds of ladies in the semicirque. . . . [The orchestra plays] As the volumed sound came undulating up, and broke in showery spray and foam of melody against our gallery rail, my head involuntarily was bowed . . . .[23]

The character of poetry in this achievement of the double image, with its autotypes of Tahitian reef and the *grand monde* of opulent London, need not be explained. The waters of the Pacific lagoon flow over the brilliant semicirque, and the hemispheric distance between these two worlds is removed in the Urwelt of the sea. Among Melville's aqueous images, the lagoon scene of the theater is rivalled only by the brilliance of that hoop of white coral rock impressed upon the chaotic, " ocean-lost " Pierre Glendinning.

Other primitivists have experienced something akin to Melville's sensuous hours over the sea-garden waters of Motoo-Otoo.

[22] See Leon Howard, *Herman Melville*, p. 142. Howard, following the account of this incident in Jay Leyda's *Melville Log*, states that the three friends saw Madame Vestris and her husband, Charles Mathews, in a play and an extravaganza by J. R. Planché. Melville, in his narrative account, states that the performance was one by Macready as Richelieu.

[23] I use here the manuscript of the sketch (dedicated to Sheridan Knowles), deposited in the Melville Papers, Metcalf Collection, Houghton Library, Harvard. The excerpt appears on leaf 15.

Stoddard, in his sketch called " A Canoe-Cruise in the Coral Sea," has described the same buds of coral, blossoming in the ripples of warm lagoons.²⁴ O'Brien, traveling in the Paumotus, confessed that as he looked down into the crystal depths of the lagoons and into the sky above he saw for an instant the shape of a great city, " its lofty trade battlements, its crowded streets, the pale, set faces of its people, the splendour of the rich houses, and the squalor of the tenements." In Polynesia one found the opposite of these: there man had hardly touched the primitive work of nature.²⁵ The phantasy passed as quickly as it came, and the fragments of coral on that ever-changing reef seemed to him " pieces of the primitive foundation." ²⁶

These are images of the sea as the mirror. All life is there, and all death, and thus all time. As *Moby-Dick* opens, Ishmael thinks of the legend of Narcissus (in that same initial paragraph in which the oneness of tree and cross is recalled) —Narcissus " who because he could not grasp the tormenting, wild image he saw in the fountain, plunged into it and was drowned." That same image we see, he says, in all rivers and oceans. " It is the image of the ungraspable phantom of life; and this is the key to it all." Water bears forever in its depths the illusoriness of all life; and every image of reef and lagoon, every image of existence lifted from the great original depths must descend finally into that illimitable, ancient world of ocean.

²⁴ *South-Sea Idyls*, p. 175.

²⁵ *Atolls in the Sun*, p. 34.

²⁶ *Ibid.*, p. 45. Robert Dean Frisbie describes the reef scene in *The Island of Desire*. The lagoon is brilliant in moonlight: " In the shallow places the white sand bottom was of the light blue of a clear summer sky, with here and there growths of coral, shadowy fish moving among the coral forests." (See p. 31.)

He never felt twice the same about the flecked river,
Which kept flowing and never the same way twice, flowing

Through many places, as if it stood still in one,
Fixed like a lake on which the wild ducks fluttered,

Ruffling its common reflections, thought-like Monadnocks.
There seemed to be an apostrophe that was not spoken.

There was so much that was real that was not real at all.
He wanted to feel the same way over and over.

He wanted the river to go on flowing the same way,
To keep on flowing. He wanted to walk beside it,

Under the buttonwoods, beneath a moon nailed fast.
He wanted his heart to stop beating and his mind to rest

In a permanent realization, without any wild ducks
Or mountains that were not mountains, just to know how it
would be,

Just to know how it would feel, released from destruction,
To be a bronze man breathing under archaic lapis,

Without the oscillations of planetary pass-pass,
Breathing his bronzen breath at the azury centre of time.

Wallace Stevens
"This Solitude of Cataracts"
The Auroras of Autumn

XIII

Original Nature

The man of bronze from the art of Wallace Stevens is a poet's symbol of human life at the timeless center where all outward-moving time originated. His man-of-now walking by the river is the symbol of man caught in time, searching vainly for the fixity of a reality that is never fixed, for the end of momentary things. The power of this contemporary poetic statement requires no definition. I relate it here to the imagery of the Urwelt because the way of this saunterer by the river, this man of solitude, is the way of the imagist in primitivism. The

360

" azury center " he will never see; but the way toward it is the way to that timelessness which he imagines in the distant, submerged silence of the past. His dream is of original nature, the nature of the land that was born of sea. It is not for him to say bluntly and finally with Thoreau: " I have seen how the foundations of the world are laid, and I have not the least doubt that it will stand a good while." [1]

Moving landward from the sea, Ishmael searches for the life of ancient earth, the large animals of blood-consciousness, the land monsters akin to the enormous whale, or prehistoric with him in his origins. The air of the land where Ishmael finds them smells of creation. And along his course he leaves the tokens of his dream, his dark emblazonry of images. They are the signs of the dream, covered here and there with the heavy shadow of primordial gloom. As emblems, they are art forms like the tokens of Sidney's dream in the *Arcadia*—those dream fragments which delighted Virginia Woolf, as though she wandered in a garden of " marble steps green with moss " and " lovely broken faces " of classic statues.[2] But Sidney's images are memorials of the Renaissance humanist with his vision of the Golden Age. The signs of Ishmael's dream are images from his feeling toward an uncivilized world. For Ishmael, with his characteristic solitude, makes his way from civilization toward an age when no man was, save that original bronze man at the center of time.

Melville's images of the primitive sea are usually formed, as I have shown, by autotypes from the Pacific voyages. In one province of his images of the original land, the autotype again appears: he transfers his impressions of the giant tortoise of the Galapagos Islands to an imagery of ancient stoniness and desolation, and ponderous age. Other areas of the Urwelt are represented by forms which come into being through what I have earlier called popular report. The primitivistic imagination discovers its material in the recorded facts of paleontology and

---

[1] *A Week on the Concord and Merrimack Rivers* (New York, 1921), pp. 125–26.
[2] See Mrs. Woolf's essay " The Countess of Pembroke's Arcadia " in *The Second Common Reader* (New York, 1932), p. 48.

zoology. Melville and Leconte de Lisle, who seem to work with
the same hand in their brilliant displays of primitive animal
life, reveal, for instance, a common feeling for the wildness of
panthers and tigers, for the hot life felt by these beasts. But
the feeling, of course, does not derive from observation of animals in the jungle or in cages. It is generated in the drift of
mind toward the past and in that curious ability to take scientific fact and to feel through it the ancient hot-bloodedness, the
sinewy movement, and the elemental instincts of these creatures.

Much of this feeling must be related to animism in the
primitivistic imagination, as represented in Melville's feeling
for the primitive cross in the tree. Outside the range of symbolistic intent, this animism means simply the desire of the
artist to feel the life of the object, to relinquish self in the
sentient being of primitive existence. The contemporary German primitivist, Hermann Hesse, has described the nature of
Buddhistic animism in his recent *Siddhartha*, an imaginative
account of the Gautama who began his religious experience
as an Indian prince. With his friend Govinda, the youth
practices the self-denial and meditation of Samana, the discipline of directing the imagination toward non-human life.

> A heron flew over the bamboo wood and Siddhartha took the
> heron into his soul, flew over forest and mountains, became
> a heron, ate fishes, suffered heron hunger, used heron lan-
> guage, died a heron's death. . . . And Siddhartha's soul
> returned, died, decayed, turned into dust, experienced the
> troubled course of the life cycle. He waited with new thirst
> like a hunter at a chasm where the life cycle ends, where
> there is an end to causes, where painless eternity begins. He
> killed his senses, he killed his memory, he slipped out of Self
> in a thousand different forms. He was animal, carcass, stone,
> wood, water, and each time he reawakened.[3]

---

[3] *Siddhartha*, trans. Hilda Rosner (New York, 1951), p. 16. Hesse's Orientalism stems, in part, from the German academic tradition, distinguished by
such eminent Sanskritists as Max Müller, in part from his own experience in
India. His work is the only aspect of German primitivism which is relevant to
this study. The long regimen of Germany in Oceania (c. 1870–1918) and the era
of German entrepreneurs in Asia produced no German art, except Hesse's

This passage describes an Oriental discipline of escaping self. The process of the imagination required is one of concentration outside the self upon the life of the object. For the man of civilization this is a deliberate return to primitive animism. I do not propose that either Melville or Leconte de Lisle intended such a discipline. But the animistic nature of the process is the nature of the total artistic process in each mind.

Robert Hamilton, a recent critic of W. H. Hudson, finds the most impressive accomplishment of Hudson's art in a passage from *Hampshire Days*. It is a description of emotion and thought aroused by an ancient burial place of the prehistoric dead on the Hampshire downs. Here Hudson achieves in a linguistic form of remarkable intensity an atavistic identification of himself with the men who built these ancient monoliths and barrows.[4] Hamilton concludes: "All Hudson is here: his feeling of unity with the earth—the bliss of lying for ever in that rude, wild place, with the stonechat and rabbit for company, and the adder curled up in his empty skull; his contempt for materialism; his religious doubt—the old problem of immortality that had vexed him since childhood; and the atavistic primitivism that inspired the whole tremendous passage."[5] If Hesse reaches the meaning of Buddhistic animism in *Siddhartha*, it is clear that Hudson exemplifies that poetic atavism which has marked Western literature so variously in the last one hundred years. The Urwelt of the primitivist may be discovered in both, for in the feeling of animism and of atavism the imagination turns from the selfhood of its possessor and seeks the feeling of unity, whether of Hesse's Prince Siddhartha in suffering heron hunger or of Hudson himself in his trans-

---

which may readily be identified as primitivistic. There is, however, a large body of German travel literature, fashioned very much in the literary manner of the earlier traveler to America and Oceania, Friedrich Gerstäcker. This material is reviewed in part by Winfried Volk in a German dissertation *Die Entdeckung Tahitis und Das Wunschbild der Seligen Insel in der Deutschen Literatur* (Heidelberg, 1934). Volk's bibliographical account of Gerstäcker is interesting. So is the discussion of "Tahitian influence," by way of travel literature, upon Mörike. But the literature discussed here does not relate to existential primitivism. It belongs properly to the literature of exoticism.

[4] *W. H. Hudson: The Vision of Earth* (London, 1946), p. 81.
[5] *Ibid.*, p. 84.

mutation into the dry bones lying in an ancient barrow. This feeling is the climate of imagination in which the images of an original, timeless world are formed.

1 *Forests*

Howard has suggested in his biography of Melville that the Ahab-like Jackson aboard the *Highlander* in *Redburn* " perhaps inspired Joseph Conrad later to write *The Nigger of the 'Narcissus.'* " [6] The suggestion recalls Leyda's proposal at the conclusion of *The Melville Log* that Conrad was " touched off " by Melville. I have attempted to clarify the essential differences between Melville and Conrad in earlier comment. The question of " influence " does not figure in my discussion. At this point, it is rather Conrad's meeting with Melville in the province of Urishness which requires attention.

If Conrad is not the maker of primitivistic symbols, he is in this instance, if no other, the sharer of Ishmael's journey toward the Urwelt. As his character Marlow departs for his adventure upon the fateful river, he feels " as though, instead of going to the centre of a continent . . . [he] were about to set off for the centre of the earth." And it is the ancient rain-forest of Africa more than the satiety of Kurtz, gorged to his black fill upon primitive lusts, that is the real heart of the darkness. Marlow watches the primitive African coast slipping by the French steamer as he approaches his port. " The sun was fierce, the land seemed to glisten and drip with steam." [7] Ashore, and now in command of the wrecked river steamer, he waits for a shipment of rivets to repair that useless " carcass " of his craft. The great wall of vegetation encircling him seems " a rioting invasion of soundless life, a rolling wave of plants . . . ready to sweep every little man " of them from his existence. Then, " a deadened burst of mighty splashes and snorts reached us from afar, as though an ichthyosaurus had been taking a bath of glitter in the great river." [8] Traveling that stream is " like

---

[6] *Herman Melville*, p. 135.
[7] *Heart of Darkness* in *Works* (London, 1923), vol. 6, p. 60.
[8] *Ibid.*, p. 86.

travelling back to the earliest beginnings of the world, when vegetation rioted on the earth." [9] At last approaching the domain of Kurtz, Marlow and his men become " wanderers on prehistoric earth, on an earth that wore the aspect of an unknown planet."

But a protest must come at once: Conrad's feeling in the supreme art of these passages is exactly that feeling of horror which presides over the death of Kurtz in the sickening abundance of these jungles. It is, indeed. I do not intend to suggest that Conrad's imagery is employed through the same drift of feeling which governs the art of Melville and Leconte de Lisle. At the same time I am also mindful of the fact that Melville meets Conrad in this element of horror as he conceives his African blacks of *Benito Cereno*. One must wonder how much Conrad knew of this story of Melville as Marlow sees that threatening black head upon a pole near Kurtz's dwelling, that head staring with open eyes toward the river and the approaching steamer. For it is the head of the black Babo fixed on a pole and staring across the valley toward Mount Agonia [10] that one last sees in Melville's tale. The black head, full of its blacker secrets, is assuredly in each imagistic use the sign of primitive man's disdain of his civilized inheritors.

Forest and sea are the root emblems of the primal world. This two-fold antiquity is defined by Melville in the following passage from *Pierre*:

> Still wandering through the forest, his eye pursuing its ever-shifting shadowy vistas; remote from all visible haunts and traces of that strangely wilful race, who, in the sordid traffickings of clay and mud, are ever seeking to denationalise the natural heavenliness of their souls; there came into the mind of Pierre, thoughts and fancies never imbibed within the gates of towns; but only given forth by the atmosphere of primeval forests, which, with the eternal ocean, are the only unchanged general objects remaining to this day, from those that originally met the gaze of Adam. For so it is, that the apparently most inflammable or evaporable of all earthly

---

[9] *Ibid.*, p. 92.
[10] *The Piazza Tales*, p. 170.

things, wood and water, are, in this view, immensely the most
endurable.[11]

In this forest interlude we see the emblem of man who turns
from the " traffickings " of society to the timelessness of the
elemental earth. The passage is dominated by the contemplation of time. Forest and ocean burn and evaporate in *time
passing*, and still in their very physical states are imperishable
in *timelessness*. This is the " view " named by Melville. At this
point, if at no other, Pierre is the equivalent of the man walking by the river in the poetic setting of Wallace Stevens, and the
gaze of Adam is the gaze of the bronze man at the center of time.

Leconte de Lisle's dream of the Urwelt reveals the same
animism which has been seen in Melville's journey to those
original trees of the Arsacides, " feeling their living sap." It is
again animistic in the sense of Hesse's account of Siddhartha
meditating on the life of the heron. The animism expressed
in " Les Jungles " is entirely clear. Here the poet seeks the
feeling of the beast, with that " peaceful " animal breast " hot
as a furnace."

> The panther creeps on guard with arching back;
> The muscular python, with scales of agate,
> Slips his flat head quietly under the sharp cochineal figs;
> And in the air, where his circular flight has blazed,
> The cantharis vibrates about the striped [serpent] king.[12]

In this *Schwüle* of the jungle the poet recreates imagistically
the feeling of original life. It is not in the least strange that
he comes in " La Forêt Vierge " to dream of the primitive rain-
forests through a poetic feeling totally disagreeing with that of
Conrad, even as he reveals the same panorama which Conrad
unveils through the journey of Marlow. He reaches, like Melville, the Urwelt described by Conrad, but with an opposite
intention in the journey. For here the forest, " the mother of
lions," is invaded and destroyed by a ravening civilization, by
men who are more savage than the beasts of its jungles.

---

[11] *Pierre*, p. 196.
[12] *Poèmes Barbares* (Lemerre), vol. 1, p. 203.

Upon that hot shore where your rugged groves
Bend the sultry dome of their primeval verdure,
Fonts of great fragments of shade encompassed with light,
Where your pensive elephants meditate;

[There] as an inroad of advancing ants
That are crushed and burned and yet forever approach,
The waves will bring to you, the king of ancient days,
The destroyer of your woods, man with pale countenance.

This ravaging man, having gnawed at and destroyed the life of the world where his race swarms, finally clings at " the full breast " of the forest and leaves there the disease of his own death.[13] In this conclusion the difference between Conrad and Leconte de Lisle appears with striking clarity. The jungle of the poet is endangered by the bestiality of civilization; the jungle of Conrad stands as the image of a huge and menacing primordial nature, heavy with ancient lusts, where the redeemed man of civilization lives in imminent peril of returning to the first darkness of his origins.

2   *Animal Forms*

Leconte de Lisle is indispensable in a reading of Melville's imagery, indispensable, at least, in any critical process which is directed to an arrangement of forms which may permit the comment of art upon art. I propose that Melville's figures of large creatures from the original forest are equaled only by those of Leconte de Lisle among his contemporaries. Nor is there any later artist—American at any rate—who shares Melville's feeling for the Urwelt save Marianne Moore. This poet's miraculous " recreations " of ancient life in " The Jerboa " and " Elephants," to name only these, must surely gain in meaning when they are compared with the imagery of Melville and Leconte de Lisle. I understand Miss Moore's poetic objective as the valid art of imagining the sentience of the object—and how far she stands here from the externalities presented by the exoticist!

[13] *Ibid.*, p. 188.

What one finds in Leconte de Lisle's poetry is *an animistic entrance into the life of the object*. This entrance may be studied in such pieces as " Les Larmes de l'Ours " from the *Poèmes Barbares*. But his figures of marching elephants are still more attractive.

> With fan-shaped ears and trunk between tusks,
> With eyes closed, they make their way. Their bellies throb
>   and steam,
> And their sweat, fired in the [hot] air, rises in mist;
> And a thousand ardent insects hum about them . . . .
>
> Heavy with fortitude and slowness, they pass
> As a black line on illimitable sand;
> And the desert takes up again its immobility
> As the heavy voyagers withdraw beyond the horizon.[14]

These images of " throbbing bellies," of sweat kindled into steam, and of ponderous bodies " heavy with fortitude and slowness " describe the adventure of the artist's imagination: his objective is the sentience of the beast. They make the feeling of jungle and desert, and of the primordial past which the elephant carries in his steaming body.

Melville's entrance into the same world is recorded in two images taken here at random from *Moby-Dick* and *The Confidence Man*. Ahab, remonstrating with Starbuck, who questions the chase of the White Whale, cries to the sunset clouds, those " Turkish cheeks of spotted tawn ": " The pagan leopards —the unrecking and unworshipping things, that live; and seek, and give no reasons for the torrid life they feel." [15] This image of torrid leopard life comes from the Ishmael-narrator, not Ahab. The sentience which it reveals is extended in a description of the serpent in *The Confidence Man*. The stranger imagines the feeling of the rattlesnake.

> When charmed by the beauty of that viper, did it never occur to you to change personalities with him? to feel what it was to [be] a snake? to glide unsuspected in grass? to sting,

14 *Poèmes Barbares* (Lemerre), vol. 1, pp. 184–85.
15 *Moby-Dick*, vol. 1, pp. 204–205.

to kill at a touch; your whole beautiful body one irridescent scabbard of death? In short, did the wish never occur to you *to feel yourself exempt from knowledge, and revel for a while in the care-free, joyous life of a perfectly instinctive, unscrupulous, and irresponsible creature?* [16]

These images of sinuous movement, of the body as the scabbard, of exemption from knowledge, of " joyous " existence, recreate the jungle of Leconte de Lisle. They are the marks of entrance into the world of pulsing life.

An image from *Moby-Dick* introduces Melville's feeling for the jungle setting: "Warmest climes but nurse the cruellest fangs; the tiger of Bengal crouches in spiced groves of ceaseless verdure." [17] It is entirely characteristic of Melville to use the tiger again (and this time with an image of the reef) to suggest the relation of civilization to the life of the Urwelt. Here he is contemplating the bivouac of a regiment of the Civil War.

> No sleep. A sultriness pervades the air
> And binds the brain—a dense oppression, such
> As tawny tigers feel in matted shades,
> Vexing their blood and making apt for ravage.
> Beneath the stars the roofy desert spreads
> Vacant as Lybia. All is hushed near by.
> Yet fitfully from far breaks a mixed surf
> Of muffled sound, the Atheist roar of riot. [18]

The appearance of both jungle and surf in this passage again represents the constancy of Ishmael's dream. The Urwelt stands behind nearly every vision of civilized man. These tigers *feeling* dense oppression in *matted* shades come of that same Urishness which fashions the imagery of Leconte de Lisle's " La Panthère Noire." In this similarity one reaches at once the difference between the poet's nonsymbolistic imagination and Melville's

[16] *The Confidence Man*, pp. 251–52. (Italics mine.)
[17] *Moby-Dick*, vol. 2, p. 276.
[18] "The House-Top, A Night Piece" (July, 1863), in *Battle Pieces and Aspects of the War*, p. 64. The image of tigers "vexing their blood" is matched by a similar image in Henry Timrod's poem "Charleston" (composed 1861 [?], published 1873). "And down the dunes a thousand guns lie couched, / Unseen, beside the flood—/Like tigers in some Orient jungle crouched,/ That wait and watch for blood."

recurrent tendency to symbolize from every setting and situation. The one is the imagist of primitivism, the other the symbolist who sees an endless descent from primitiveness to civilization. Leconte de Lisle's panther represents pure blood-consciousness which Melville thinks of, symbolistically, as vestigial
in man.

> The queen of Java, the black huntress,
> Returns with the dawn to the lair in which her young,
> Glistening among bones, mew in hunger,
> Some crouching upon others.
>
> She drags after her the remnants of her chase,
> A portion of a fine stag which she has eaten in the night;
> And on the flowering moss a dreadful track,
> Red, and still warm, follows her.[19]

Stanley T. Williams, in a recent study of *Benito Cereno*,
speaks of the axiomatic quality of Babo's evil as carrying within
it all Melville's interest in primitivism, from *Typee* to *Billy
Budd*. " Everything on the *San Dominick* proclaims the ascendency in the universe of natural, primitive, evil man and his
easy victory over the obsolete armor of the past." [20] I do not
think that we are to regard the primitive African of this tale
as a personification of *all* evil as understood by Melville; he is
no more evil than the civilized makers of wars and the lusts of
wars burning in the hot nights of bivouacs. But every other
aspect of this clear judgment is unquestionable fact. The primitive ascends everlastingly, in Melville's universe. It was perfectly consistent that Melville should pose the overrich fecundity of the *San Dominick's* slumbering negress, " sprawled like
a doe in the shade of a woodland rock " and nursing her vigorous infant in her sleep,[21] against the pale, vitiated form of
Benito as the emblem of a dying civilization. Here again Melville's study of reality through contrast appears. The universe
is primitive at its core, and every appearance of civilized man

[19] *Poèmes Barbares* (Lemerre), vol. 1, p. 199.
[20] "'Follow your Leader': Melville's 'Benito Cereno,'" *The Virginia Quarterly Review*, vol. 23 (1947), p. 76.
[21] *The Piazza Tales*, p. 105.

is in some way demonstrable as what it is through its relation to the core. It is Melville's awareness of the "ascendency" of the primitive that directs his imagination toward a seemingly incongruous use of animal forms. Every student may discover the total range of these for himself. I suggest here only their nature and their range; again, a catalogue of images would be superfluous.

There are certain forms which appear to be obsessive. To begin with, there is the bear. In *Redburn* a congregation of harbor pilots at Liverpool, shaggy fellows in shaggy coats, seem to be a "fireside of bears wintering in Aroostook." [22] As Ishmael arrives at the Spouter-Inn in *Moby-Dick*, the crew of the *Grampus*, recently returned to New Bedford, tramp through the entry. Their beards are stiff with icicles, and they seem "an eruption of bears from Labrador." [23] Ahab, captain of that ship appareled with her trophies of antiquity, lives in the world, says Ishmael, as the last of the grizzly bears lived in settled Missouri; [24] and Daniel Orme, the old mariner bearing his scarred cross, silently couches on the gun deck between black cannon, like "the Great Grizzly of the California Sierras, his coat the worse for wear, grim in his last den, awaiting the last hour." [25]

The figure of the elk provides another opening upon the same primitive world. The image of this animal is used by Melville to describe ships in collision, or in deadly struggle with the forces of the sea, and to suggest the hugeness of battle between two bull whales. The ship as the elk first appears in *Redburn*: ". . . sometimes two vessels coming together, jib-boom and jib-boom, with a sudden shock in the middle watch of the night, mutually destroy each other; and like fighting elks, sink down into the ocean, with their antlers locked in death." [26] This elk appears again in the poetic description of the doomed ship in "The Haglets." It is only one form of original nature

[22] *Redburn*, p. 160.
[23] *Moby-Dick*, vol. 1, p. 17.
[24] *Ibid.*, vol. 1, p. 190.
[25] *Billy Budd and Other Prose Pieces*, p. 119.
[26] *Redburn*, p. 119.

used to represent the elemental fury of the sea, the image of the condor of the Andes being another (and the return of the cross here in primitive setting should also be noted) :

> The spars, athwart at spiry height,
> Like quaking Lima's crosses rock;
> Like bees the clustering sailors cling
> Against the shrouds, or take the shock
> Flat on the swept yard-arms aslant,
> Dipped like the wheeling condor's pinions gaunt.
> A lull! and tongues of languid flame
> Lick every boom, and lambent show
> Electric 'gainst each face aloft;
> The herds of clouds with bellowings go:
> The black ship rears—beset—harassed,
> Then plunges far with luminous antlers vast.[27]

A third imagistic use of the elk unites the emblems of sea and land as Melville describes the contests of whales in the mating season: "They fence with their long lower jaws, sometimes locking them together, and so striving for the supremacy like elks that warringly interweave their antlers." [28]

Except for that "down-darting bird" of the forest which breaks Pierre's suicidal meditation at the Memnon Stone, the birds of Melville's imagery all relate to the massiveness of the Urwelt. The favored use of the hawk is especially impressive in *Moby-Dick*: the riddle of Fedallah's death in the pursuit of the White Whale is said to "peck" at Ahab's brain "like a hawk's beak." [29] This figure foreshadows the man-of-war bird pecking at the brain of the old sailor Agath of *Clarel*. And it is the sky-hawk that is nailed to the mast by Tashtego as the *Pequod* sinks to her death. The great albatross is the most impressive bird of *Moby-Dick*, however. This example of Melville's imagery used in creating his symbol of whiteness derives, of course, from the Pacific voyages. His feeling for the albatross in its solitariness and its mystery may be interpreted through Leconte de Lisle's poetic approach to the same subject:

---

[27] In *John Marr and Other Sailors* (1891).
[28] *Moby-Dick*, vol. 2, p. 140.
[29] *Ibid.*, vol. 2, p. 353.

Alone, the king of space and of shoreless seas
Flies against the assault of savage gales.
Like an arrow strong and sure, without hesitation,
Its point flung from the livid mist,
On his rigid wings of iron
He splits the whirlwind of the hoarse expanses,
And, tranquil in the midst of terror,
Appears, passes, and disappears in majesty.[30]

The equivalent of this great sea bird is found in Melville's imagery of the original land. At one point in *Moby-Dick* he thinks of the " Catskill eagle " of some souls, the eagle " that can alike dive down into the blackest gorges, and soar out of them again and become invisible in the sunny spaces. . . ." [31] The image suggests the solitariness of the albatross. In his later use of the condor, he displays the same feeling; and it may be proposed here that Melville uses a facsimile of this giant of the Andes from impressions received when the *United States* put in along the western coast of South America in 1844. The great bird appears as Melville describes in *The Piazza* a mountain shadow advancing over the land, " stealing on, as cast by some gigantic condor, floating at brooding poise on outstretched wings." [32] The feeling expressed in the image, particularly in its element of " brooding poise," is so close to the spirit of Leconte de Lisle's condor of the *Poèmes Barbares* that, once again, I call attention to the work of this poet as a preface to Melville's imagery. These lines from the " Sommeil du Condor " are finally useful, in an examination of Melville's forms of animal life, as imagistic patterns suggesting the indispensability of Leconte de Lisle. For he might have used Melville's image of " brooding poise "; it is certainly this feeling of the Urwelt which he brings to poetic form in the Andean condor:

He rears his muscular and naked neck,
He rises, beating the bleak snow of the Andes,
With a hoarse cry he mounts where no wind reaches,

---

[30] " L'Albatros " in *Poèmes Tragiques* (Lemerre), p. 75.
[31] *Moby-Dick*, vol. 2, p. 182.
[32] *The Piazza Tales*, p. 14.

And, far from the black globe, far from the living stars
He sleeps on full wing in the icy air.[33]

3   The Anaconda

The most curious single circumstance of Melville's imagery
of the Urwelt is his obsession with the anaconda, the great
constrictor of the equatorial jungle. He may have seen one of
these creatures in captivity. But it is fact, at any rate, that he
had read accounts of this monster. For once it is possible to
show exactly how Melville's reading was used in the processes
of his imagery. In *White-Jacket* (Ch. XLI) he tells us that while
the *United States* was at anchor in the harbor of Rio de Janeiro,
he passed his time reading in the ship's library. Among the
books which attracted him was Robert Knox's *Captivity in
Ceylon, 1681*.[34] He says that he liked its "stories about the
devil." In Knox's account he would have read the following
description:

> Of Serpents, there are these sorts. The Pimberah, the body
> whereof is as big as a man's middle, and of a length pro-
> portionable. It is not swift, but by subtilty will catch his
> prey; which are Deer or other Cattel; he lyes in the path
> where the Deer use to pass, and as they go, he claps hold
> of them by a kind of peg that grows on his tayl, with which
> he strikes them. He will swallow a Roe Buck whole, horns
> and all; so that it happens sometimes the horns run thro his
> belly, and kill him. A Stag was caught by one of these
> Pimberahs . . . his tayl . . . encompassing a Tree to hold
> the Stag the better.[35]

The term *anaconda* seems not to have been used in such seventeenth century accounts as that of Knox. It appears, however,
in Dobson's *Encyclopaedia* (1798) ; and it is probable that
Melville saw this account as well, since the "pimberah" of
Ceylon is certainly the reptile described. Dobson's commen-

[33] *Poèmes Barbares*, vol. 1, p. 194.
[34] *White-Jacket*, p. 208.
[35] *An Historical Relation of Ceylon* (Glasgow, 1911), p. 47. This edition re-
prints *verbatim* the London edition of 1681 read by Melville.

tator writes: "ANACONDO, in natural history, is a name given in the isle of Ceylon to a very large and terrible rattlesnake, which often devours the unfortunate traveller alive, and is itself accounted excellent and delicious fare." [36] Melville's anaconda probably owes his name to Dobson; and he may also have in him some parts of a large serpent of the Amazon described by La Condamine in Pinkerton's *Voyages and Travels* (1813): ". . . but the most rare and singular of all is a large amphibious serpent, from twenty-five to thirty feet long and more than a foot thick . . . ; it is called Tacu Mama, or the Mother of the Water by the Americans of Maynas." [37] Pinkerton also includes an account of Brazil by Nieuhoff containing some notice of a serpent called Kobre Dehado by the natives, which was known to swallow a whole roebuck.[38] This vast collection of Pinkerton is an excellent example of the literature of travel available to Melville, whether or not he was anywhere indebted to its descriptions of this South American relative of the Singhalese anaconda. If Melville read any of Pinkerton, it is clear that the scene which seized his imagination was that described by Knox, of an enormous snake swallowing a deer. The monster itself, as he imagined it, became one of his chief images representing original nature and antiquity.

Thus in *Redburn*, where we have already the image of those two colliding ships as fighting elks, Melville makes a direct transference of the account of the " pimberah " which he found in Knox's *Captivity in Ceylon*. He is thinking of Jonah: ". . . perhaps, thought I, the whale, which, according to Rabbinical traditions was a female one, might have expanded to receive him like an anaconda, when it swallows an elk and leaves the antlers sticking out of its mouth." [39] Can there be any question of Melville's imagistic habit? The seeming incongruity of this image of triple reference—whale, serpent, elk—becomes, on

[36] *Dobson's Encyclopaedia* (Philadelphia, T. Dobson, 1798), vol. 1, p. 648.

[37] John Pinkerton, ed., *Voyages and Travels in All Parts of the World* (London, 1813), vol. 14, p. 247. Note the archetypal relationship between this Amazonian keeper of waters and other monsters of the deep, e. g., Moby Dick as dragon.

[38] *Ibid.*, p. 714.   [39] *Redburn*, p. 123.

examination, a most clear example of coalescence in the imagistic process. Whale, serpent, and elk, as figures of the original world, are united.

At other points the anaconda itself governs the image. A squid floating on the surface of the sea in *Moby-Dick* seems to Ishmael " curling and twisting like a nest of anacondas." [40] As Melville recalls the great-fish avatar of Vishnu represented in the plate from Maurice's account, he remembers that the tail is more like that of the anaconda than the true whale's flukes.[41] In *The Encantadas* he suggests the primitive setting of old Oberlus of Galapagos by calling him a Lord Anaconda ruling his " plebeian garter snakes," those sailor-deserters coerced into his service.[42] In the story called *The Happy Failure* the tubing and piping of a great machine for draining marshes contrived by a visionary inventor looks like " a huge nest of anacondas and adders." [43] In *The Tartarus of Maids*, as Melville makes his way through those winter woods where he sees the icy trees *feeling* the cold, he comes upon a fallen hemlock, " darkly undulatory as an anaconda." [44] Among these images, even that of a great machine to drain swamps, Ishmael's vision of the Urwelt persists. Finally, in his use of the anaconda to represent Ahab, Melville reaches his fullest expression of the obsessive power which this ancient serpent figure exerted upon his imagination. The sailors aboard the *Pequod* have been talking of Ahab's purpose against Moby Dick. The little black Pip shrinks in fear under the windlass. He cries out:

> White squalls? white whale, shirr! shirr! Here have I heard all their chat just now, and the White Whale . . . but spoken of once! and only this evening—it makes me jingle all over like my tambourine—that anaconda of an old man swore 'em in to hunt him! [45]

Ahab as the anaconda is Ahab swallowing all life; and gorged

[40] *Moby-Dick*, vol. 1, p. 351.
[41] *Ibid.*, vol. 1, p. 332.
[42] *The Piazza Tales*, p. 242.
[43] *Billy Budd and Other Prose Pieces*, p. 215.
[44] *Ibid.*, p. 241.
[45] *Moby-Dick*, vol. 1, p. 221.

with that life he alone possesses the temerity to hunt the God of the universe, Pip's God of whiteness. On that same voyage Ishmael, the symbol-maker, described this same God in his appalling white form, as the achievement of the primitivist's theology and his art.

4 The Giant Tortoise

At some time between November, 1841, and February, 1842, according to Anderson, Melville visited the Galapagos Islands.[46] If the image of the anaconda shows the power of retained impression from the realm of popular report, the image of the giant tortoise of the Galapagos is the clearest example we have of the autotype from the "original" land appearing in metaphoric reference. Russell Thomas has shown the use which Melville made of published accounts of these islands as he went about drafting the stony sketches of *The Encantadas*.[47] But it is Melville's own impression of Galapagos and its monsters that is made into images. It becomes the strongest of all his autotypes of the primeval world, save that of the sea and the master autotype of the great whale. His reading merely supports the impression.

The best of recent accounts of the Galapagos group is Victor von Hagen's, as this appears in the preface to his edition of *The Encantadas*. He notes that no water is readily available, and that the passing Humboldt current gives the whole area a permanent autumn temperature. As one walks over the shore, those very stones which reminded Darwin of the iron furnaces of Wolverhampton give off a metallic clatter. Apart from the lumbering tortoise, one finds some large iguanas with spiked heads and sullen visages, tokens of a time when the principal animals of the world were reptiles. He suggests, better than any other traveler (and eminent scientist in this case), the primordial twilight atmosphere which Melville achieves in his art.

[46] *Melville in the South Seas*, p. 52.
[47] "Melville's Use of Some Sources in *The Encantadas*," *American Literature*, vol. 3 (1931), pp. 432–56.

The sketches are poetically conceived and endowed with an unusual imagistic richness. Consider the following, for instance: " Like split Syrian gourds left withering in the sun, they are cracked by an everlasting drought beneath a torrid sky. ' Have mercy upon me,' the wailing spirit of the Encantadas seems to cry, ' and send Lazarus that he may dip the tip of his finger in water and cool my tongue, for I am tormented in this flame.' " [48]

Melville, like every traveler before him, describes the enormous size of the tortoise, lying inert and seemingly dead among the rocks of Albemarle Island. He is fascinated by the idea of his great age, as though all the stony sleep of calcareous and igneous rock were deeply fixed in him. He watches his lumbering, ponderous gait as he drags his enormous bulk over the blasted wastes which are his home. Here Melville projects the life of feeling into a creature of the natural world whose ancestors existed before the whale came to dominate the seas. He touches the world of ancient reptilian life. Almost immediately the image of the creature, carrying in his shell and hide the ancient dust of forgotten continents, brings Melville to the threshold of symbolism through its symbolistic potentialities. Thus he thinks: " Their crowning curse is their drudging impulse to straightforwardness in a belittered world." [49] For he has stood there and watched them moving in their dark primordial gloom seen through their weak little eyes, watched them butting against the rocks, and lying inert beside these barriers as though dead.

What " obstacle," indeed, did he think of in the years afterward? The autotype blazes here, as though he stood again under the burning sky of Albemarle and looked at those ungainly monsters. So does he recreate experience in *The Encantadas*, experience which is one with that primordial sea-feeling he has known in prospect of his acres from the verandah at Pittsfield. Only now he thinks of the everlasting primitiveness of every vision of land.

[48] *The Piazza Tales*, p. 182.
[49] *Ibid.*, p. 191.

Nor even at the risk of meriting the charge of absurdly believing in enchantments, can I restrain the admission that sometimes, even now, when leaving the crowded city to wander out July and August among the Adirondack Mountains, far from the influences of towns and proportionally nigh to the mysterious ones of nature; when at such times I sit me down in the mossy head of some deep-wooded gorge, surrounded by prostrate trunks of blasted pines, and recall, as in a dream, my other and far-distant rovings in the baked heart of the charmed isles; and remember the sudden glimpses of dusky shells, and long languid necks protruded from the leafless thickets; and again have beheld the vitreous inland rocks worn down and grooved into deep ruts by ages and ages of slow draggings of tortoises in quest of pools of scanty water; I can hardly resist the feeling that in my time I have indeed slept upon evilly enchanted ground.

Nay, such is the vividness of my memory, or the magic of my fancy, that I know not whether I am not the occasional victim of optical delusion concerning the Gallipagos [sic]. For often in scenes of social merriment, and especially at revels held by candle-light in old-fashioned mansions, so that shadows are thrown into the further recesses of an angular and spacious room, making them put on a look of haunted undergrowth of lonely woods, I have drawn the attention of my comrades by my fixed gaze and sudden change of air, as I have seemed to see, . . . heavily crawling along the floor, the ghost of a gigantic tortoise, with ' Memento * * * ' burning in live letters upon his back.[50]

The " evilly enchanted ground " is enchanted in the sense of Conrad's African jungle; and *memento* here must mean the atavistic remembrance of civilized man who carries within him the dark sense of his ancient origins. Time that was is made one endlessly with time that is, in Ishmael's dream. Whatever evil enchantment there was in the beginning remains evil enchantment forevermore. It was God-made, with whatever there was of primitive good, as in the birth of that first verdure of Polynesia. Desolation and fruitfulness are one, as death and life are one in the symbol of the whale-shrine of the Arsacides. It is with this feeling of aboriginalness that Melville contem-

[50] *Ibid.*, pp. 186–87.

plates the poverty of London slums in *Israel Potter*. Here humanity stumbles over the rocks of the tortoise. " The black vistas of streets were as the galleries in coal mines; the flagging, as flat tombstones, minus the consecration of moss, and worn heavily down, by sorrowful tramping, as the vitreous rocks in the cursed Gallipagos, over which the convict tortoises crawl." [51] The evil enchantment returns, reminding us of the primitive world that stands behind every scene of civilization. It is the master analogy, the link with the Urwelt approached through an imagination turned upon the distances of time receding forever toward the timeless center.

As a governing autotype, the tortoise returns once more after Israel Potter's story. Melville describes the Encantadas again in *Clarel*. The island monster emerges this time in an even richer imagery. Here, in the interlude of the journey to Bethlehem called " The Island," Melville presents him under " cobwebbed cactus trees." The shells of his own dead kindred lie about him, here where he reigns in his white armor for another hundred years of stumbling sluggishly upon the rocks. The old timoneer finishes his story of the blasted isles, and then comes Clarel's (and Ishmael's) analogy:

> What may man know?
> (Here pondered Clarel;) let him rule—
> Pull down, build up, creed, system, school,
> And reason's endless battle wage,
> Make and remake his verbiage—
> But solve the world! Scarce that he'll do:
> Too wild it is, too wonderful. [52]

I have contended in this study that images interpret symbols. In this image of the Galapagos tortoise rendering metaphorically the course of man's over-reason, Melville arrives at the meaning inherent in all the great symbols of his sacrament and his theology. Clarel's meditation upon the tortoise is Melville's own: reason may not solve the world. Nor will it solve the nature of God, whatever creeds and systems are de-

[51] *Israel Potter*, p. 212.
[52] *Clarel*, vol. 2, p. 172 (Part IV, Sec. iii).

vised to measure it. The Urwelt of images stands for the mystery of all genesis. Man as man in his true nature and his true destiny can aspire only to recognize the wildness and the wonder of existence here named by Clarel. That is all, and that is the supreme all which Melville's symbols of sacrament and theology mean as forms from the feeling at the base of primitivistic art.

For Ishmael, the voyager, sets the whole universe upon the ancient tortoise. From *The Encantadas* come these images inspired by the primitive Orient.

> Yea, they seemed the identical tortoises whereon the Hindu plants this total sphere . . . .[53]

> With them I lost myself in volcanic mazes; brushed away endless boughs of rotting thickets; till finally I found myself sitting cross-legged upon the foremost, a Brahmin similarly mounted upon either side, forming a tripod of foreheads which upheld the universal cope.[54]

There he reaches the end of his journey into time; he can go no farther toward the timeless " bronzen " center. The tortoise, revealed as the concealing foliage is brushed aside and the centuries are plundered, is the last emblazoned figure commemorating the quest. At the foundation of the universe, the tortoise is older even than the whale in which Vishnu came to earth to search the depths of the waters for the sacred Vedas. He is older than every other emblem of Ishmael's art; and on his back rests all—the wildness and the wonder, the sorrow and the desolation of man's God-made existence.

[53] *The Piazza Tales*, p. 190.
[54] *Ibid.*, pp. 191–92.

PART FIVE

ENTOMBMENT:
CHRISTIANITY
REVISITED

In a gown, the color of gall and poison,
The corpse of my reason
Floats on the Thames . . .

Reason dead of too much knowing,
Of too much wishing to hew out the cause,
On a pedestal of black granite,
Of every being and of every thing,
Reason dead, atrociously,
Of an empoisoned knowing,
Dead of a delirious frenzy
Toward an absurd and red empire . . .

These are wharves and barracks,
Wharves without end, and their street-lamps,
Impassive and slow spinners
Of a shadowy light:
These are sadnesses of stone,
The house of brick, the castle-keep in darkness
Whose windows, dull eyelids,
Open into the fog of evening;
These are the great dock-yards of madness,
Full of dismantled barks
And broken spars
Beneath a sky of crucifixion . . .

In a gown of lifeless jewels solemnizing
The hour of purpling [dusk] on the horizon,
The corpse of my reason floats on the Thames.

It floats away, toward the chance
Of darkness and of mists,
To the dead clamor of dull alarms,
Leaving behind the guardianship of towers,
Unsatiated leaving the vast city of life;
It disappears into the unknown dark
To lie in the tombs of evening,
Down there, where the empty spaces, slow and strong,
Open their boundless orifices,
Engulfing for all eternity:
The dead.

Émile Verhaeren
" La Morte "
Les Flambeaux Noirs

XIV

The Infernal City

> These are the great dock-yards of madness
> Full of dismantled barks
> And broken spars
> Beneath a sky of crucifixion.

These poetic tokens of ruin are the symbols of Verhaeren's despair in London—London with its black wharves where street lamps in mist are the slow spinners of fatal shadow. The spars are the broken, the " lost," symbols of redemption, and crucifixion is the sign of the city where every bark is dismantled, immobile, aspirationless, save in that broken spar against a sky of anguish. This image of the crucifixion recalls at once Melville's starry cross of *Clarel*, the waning light of the " lost " sign, the Southern Cross of the mariner. Five years after the appear-

ance of " La Morte," with its image of cadaverous reason floating on the Thames, Verhaeren published *Les Villes Tentaculaires* (1895). We may call the poetry of this volume the most
relentlessly condemning description of the city in modern
literature. The city is the annihilator of humanity, a tentacular
monster draining life of meaning, and poisoning what it does
not assimilate.

In this realm of poetic feeling (Verhaeren's or any other)
London and Paris, as only as two examples, have been transformed from their earlier characters as cities apotheosizing the
culture of a race. In the glut of materialism and in the decline
of the culture-symbols which formerly gave them the authority
of a supreme racial (and national) meaning, they have become
amorphous organisms spreading their tentacles over the land,
stinging and crushing their human prey, and digesting their
spoil in a foul nest of stone. To the maker of primitivistic art,
the city is the emblem of cultural failure, and the symbols
which he creates to describe this failure are in their elements of
feeling the direct opposites of symbols expressing the ideality
of the Ishmael-voyager. For, as recent primitivism is defined in
its true character through its symbols inspired by the Orient
and through its imagery of the Urwelt, so is it defined again
through its unremitting denunciation of the city as the supreme
modern evil. Verhaeren's London, where the poet wandered
in that time of his religious despair and of his search for oblivion in prodigious lust, became, as Baudouin observes, the
prototype of the " tentacular towns." [1] The images born of that
experience in London became the master images of the denunciation. Verhaeren is the spokesman not only of his own despair
but also of the hatred felt by Melville and Rimbaud and a new
generation of moralists most recently represented by Schweitzer.
The corpse of the reason floating on the Thames is more than
the symbol of urban disease and indigence. It stands for
modern man stripped of his symbols of existential meaning.
This is the import of Melville's denunciation in *Israel Potter*:

---

[1] *Psychoanalysis and Aesthetics* (Paul), p. 133.

" London, adversity, and the sea, three Armageddons, which, at one and the same time, slay and secrete their victims." [2]

The achievement of authentic primitivism is seen in its symbols of ideality. Just as these proceed from religious feeling, so do the primitivist's symbolic and metaphoric descriptions of cultural failure derive from the same area of the imaginative life. For though denunciation alone cannot represent to any just criticism the real content of primitivistic art, the inexorable rejections of an exhausted culture displayed by the artist are the concomitants of his symbolistic acts reaching toward ideality. The symbols of denunciation are formed equally of feeling. Their distinction lies in the poetic intent which shapes them; they arise from a descriptive and reportorial purpose. The Orient disappears, and with it the characteristic polarity which has been seen in Melville's symbols of sacrament. Ideality is exchanged for poetic synthesis. The symbol remains multiple in its containment; but now it is confined to one culture, the artist's own inheritance, and to the poetic act of rendering symbolic shape from a manifold of impression all related to the facts of urban existence in Western civilization. Art in these opposite symbols from the world of the damned ceases to be religion (unless one intends to call the despair which they express a religious feeling) ; art is now simply an abstract representation of cultural failure, the failure of culture as religion. (Tillich's thesis must be recalled again: religion is the substance of culture, and culture is the expression of religion.)

1 The Tombs of Evening

The poet's reason, in Verhaeren's poem, turns toward the tombs of evening. The shadow and the darkness represent the entombment of modern man destitute in a civilization existing blindly, living a death-in-life. Even Conrad who could write of the Thames in *Heart of Darkness* as the river of messengers, " bearers of a spark of the sacred fire . . . the seeds of common-

[2] *Israel Potter*, p. 213.

wealth, the germs of empires " [3]—even this Conrad felt the air of the tomb. Thus Marlow reflects as he returns to London from the jungle of Africa:

> I found myself back in the sepulchral city resenting the sight of people hurrying through the streets to filch a little money from each other, to devour their infamous cookery, to gulp their unwholesome beer, to dream their insignificant and silly dreams. They trespassed upon my thoughts. They were intruders whose knowledge of life was to me an irritating pretense, because I felt so sure they could not possibly know the things I knew.[4]

In *The Nigger of the " Narcissus "* the same feeling reappears as the ship makes her berth at London dock. Through that " precious and disgusting " air, full of the smell of things costly and things filthy, the *Narcissus* comes to rest, and there she ceases to live: ". . . the shadows of soul-less walls fell upon her, the dust of all the continents leaped upon her deck, and a swarm of strange men, clambering up her sides, took possession of her in the name of the sordid earth." [5] These are Conrad's notices of spiritual death; the tombs of evening become, in relation to Verhaeren's image, the stony places of sequestration where human beings escape the great life-issues, issues such as those expressed in the meaning of the *Narcissus* alive upon the sea, or those appearing to the individual (in the sense of this study, the artist) confronted with the necessity for some solitary and heroic action.

A recent statement of W. H. Auden is directly applicable in a study of modern primitivism. Auden extends the meaning of Schweitzer as he accounts for Ishmael's flight to sea. There is nothing in the city which can satisfy Ishmael because the symbols of the city as an emblem of a racial culture have disappeared.

> Urban society is, like the desert, a place without limits. The city walls of tradition, mythos and cultus have crumbled.

[3] *Works* (London, 1923), vol. 6, p. 47.
[4] *Ibid.*, vol. 6, p. 152.
[5] *Ibid.*, vol. 18, p. 165.

There is no direction in which Ishmael is forbidden or forcibly prevented from moving. The only outside "necessities" are the random winds of fashion or the lifeless chains of a meaningless job, which, so long as he remains an individual, he can and will reject. At the same time, however, he fails to find a necessity within himself to take their place. So he must take drastic means and go down to the waters . . . .[6]

The waters in this connotation are the realms outside the city and its impoverishment, the realms where Ishmael discovers, or seeks to discover, substitutes for the lost tradition represented in crumbling walls. Presumably, to have lived in the Vienna of Haydn and Mozart would have been to live in a city apotheosizing a national culture (religion) through its secure symbols. The possibility of an Ishmael turning in sanity from this city would seem to us to have been nonexistent. The power and the authority of this Viennese culture will account, at any rate, for the absence of existential primitivism during the period of their sovereignty over certain imaginative domains of art. To continue this analogy from the provinces of music, one may see what happens to the cultural possibilities of Ishmael by studying the creative act of Igor Stravinsky in 1910, when he turns to the feeling inherent in *Le Sacre du Printemps*. This work, like the *La Mer* of Debussy, cannot in any sense be claimed by exoticism. It is primitivistic in that it presents the same world of the Urwelt discovered through the images of Melville and Leconte de Lisle. Ishmael, here at work in the art of music, deserts the mythos and the cultus of cities: he takes drastic means and goes down to the waters.

Most of us can agree with Auden: we expect Ishmael every day to turn from our contemporary urban culture. For, if the life of feeling in any large metropolitan area of this moment may be particularized, it is probably true that the primitivist discovers three groups of city dwellers: a small number who, through religious orthodoxy or unusual discipline in some creative undertaking, are in possession of at least minimal symbols of existential meaning; a preponderant group who either

[6] *The Enchafèd Flood*, p. 37.

live with some sort of Nietzschean courage to be, or merely exist irrationally; and then some citizens who, having the means of buying oblivion, succeed in avoiding the demands of religious (and cultural) sensibility through a deliberate and studied hedonism (not very different from the hedonism which Verhaeren attempted). The disparity among these hypothetical groups will, of course, extend as the city increases and, within its traditionless and tentacular form, continues to dissolve the symbolic unity which urban culture once possessed.

Melville saw as much, certainly, as Schweitzer and Auden have recognized. It is the distinction of these later figures only that they are very recent observers who have defined our cities for us. Schweitzer, in his examination of the decay of civilization, observes that " the capacity of the modern man for progress in civilization is diminished because the circumstances in which he finds himself placed injure him psychically and stunt his personality." [7] In *Clarel* (Part IV, Sec. xxi) Melville understands the same psychic injury:

> Debased into equality:
> In glut of all material arts
> A civic barbarism may be:
> Man disennobled—brutalised
> By popular science—atheised
> Into a smatterer— [8]

Civic barbarism as the " disennobling " of man is the reduction of human dignity to minute and inconsequential issues. To be brutalized by popular science is to be made a worshipper of mechanisms, to be made into a smatterer of the city, grubbing among objects and devices which are in themselves meaningless. It is, in Conrad's sense, " to dream insignificant and silly dreams." It is to sleep in Verhaeren's tombs of evening

> Down there, where the empty spaces, slow and strong,
> Open their boundless orifices,
> Engulfing for all eternity:
> The dead.

[7] *The Decay and the Restoration of Civilization*, p. 15.
[8] *Clarel*, vol. 2, p. 250.

2   *City of Dis*

Melville's autotypes of the city (from the indigenous group discussed in Chapter III) relate primarily to his experiences in Liverpool (1839), in London (1849), in Jerusalem (1857), and in New York. Jerusalem will be discussed in the following account of the journey to the Holy Sepulchre; the images from the other three sources belong to the description of the infernal city. The appearance of these autotypes in images rather than in symbols should be acknowledged before the discussion proceeds. Melville does not anywhere match, for instance, Verhaeren's symbol of the cadaverous reason floating on the Thames. Melville is the preëminent symbolist only as idealist, although I shall conclude here with an analysis of the bell-tower as one example of his symbolism informed by the culture of cities in Western civilization. Autotypes of the city are usually employed in the method of imagistic description appearing in *Redburn, Pierre*, and *Israel Potter*, Melville's major studies of urban society. The city of the Roman god of the underworld, Dis, establishes a relationship of all the autotypes to mythology, as proposed by Melville's reading in Dante.[9] Thus it is Dante's description, which Melville had read as he completed *Mardi* (1848), that governs his view of London as the city of the damned.

Walking across the bridges of the Thames on a gray November day of 1849, he thought of an analogy which he recorded in his journal: " —a city of Dis (Dante's) clouds of smoke— the damned—coal barges—coaly waters . . . ." [10] The scene is thereafter transferred to *Israel Potter*. Israel watches " that hereditary crowd—[a] gulf-stream of humanity—which, for continuous centuries, has never ceased pouring like an endless shoal of herring, over London Bridge." [11] The bridge itself becomes an emblem of mourning. " Hung in long, sepulchral

---

[9] *Inferno*, Canto VIII. Melville began to read Dante in 1848.
[10] Manuscript Journal 1849, Melville Papers, Metcalf Collection, Houghton Library, Harvard, Entry of Friday, November 9, 1849.
[11] *Israel Potter*, p. 210.

arches of stone, the black, besmoked bridge seemed a huge scarf of crape festooning the river across." [12]

Something of this same November scene appears later in *The Two Temples*, the sketch in which Melville gives us the meaning of Ishmael, as he exchanges the artist's representation of the Nativity for the " true Hagar and her Ishmael " in the " gorgeous dungeon " of Grace Church. (See Chapter III.) Here he describes a solitary youth in London on a Saturday night. He looks down from the window of his room on the " muddy Phlegethon of the Thames." Then he reflects, in the manner of the outcast Israel Potter. " Better perish mid myriad sharks in mid Atlantic, than die a penniless stranger in Babylonian London. Forlorn, outcast, without a friend, I staggered on through three millions of my own human kind. The fiendish gas-lights shooting their Tartarean rays across the muddy sticky streets, lit up the pitiless and pitiable scene." [13] This vision depends upon the image of Dis from Dante. But there is the more impressive fact that in feeling it equals Verhaeren's recollection of the Thames, even in the street lamps as the spinners of fatal shadow.

These images of London come from impressions received by Melville at a point midway between the composition of *Redburn* and the achievement of the symbols of *Moby-Dick*. In the recent history of English and European poetry they are not at all remarkable. John Gould Fletcher provides a comparable description of the same city in the " Elegy on London ": the " iron roar " of traffic over London Bridge is heard again; the poet sees the " pale grey street façades "; he studies the life that flows " stiff and secret, / Cringing, pathetic," life that beats " like lava upon the stone." [14] Across the Channel, Verlaine had already said as much for the city of Paris in the " Parisien Nocturne."

If Melville's descriptions in comparison with other literature of the last century are not unusual, they are at least formed in

   [12] *Ibid.*, p. 211.
   [13] Manuscript of " The Two Temples," Melville Papers, Metcalf Collection, Houghton Library, Harvard, Leaf 13, Leaf 11.
   [14] Section I, in *Selected Poems* (New York, 1938), pp. 171–75.

the same sentience which dominates in the masterly poetic comment of Verhaeren. Furthermore, in their tacit admissions that the life of the city eludes any rational measurement toward existential meaning, they anticipate the characteristic attitude of Franz Kafka: there is no meaning which may be ascribed to the life of modern man victimized by his own culture. Such, I take it, is the significance of meaninglessness described by Kafka in *The Castle* and *The Trial*.

New York belongs to the same dominions of Dis. Melville's condemnation of the American monster is familiar to all readers of *Pierre*. As Pierre Glendinning and Isabel enter the city, the rough cobblestones under the carriage wheels are the hearts of the dead.[15] The side-streets running into the thoroughfare are " thin tributaries " to the great Orinoco, coming from " far-hidden places," from " dark beetling secrecies of mortar and stone." [16] Later Pierre stands in the watch-house, and Melville's artistic vision, now heightened by his maturing descriptive power, reveals a province of his art which is entirely separate from the symbolism of *Moby-Dick*. It is a vision of multi-farious, compressed humanity, as though the cornucopia of the city had dumped all its sordid burden into the dark confines of a police-station. " In indescribable disorder, frantic, diseased-looking men and women of all colours, and in all imaginable . . . grotesque, and shattered dresses, were leaping, yelling, and cursing around him. The torn Madras handkerchiefs of negresses, and the red gowns of yellow girls, hanging in tatters from their naked bosoms, mixed with the rent dresses of deep-rouged white women . . . ." [17] " On all sides, were heard drunken male and female voices, in English, French, Spanish,

---

[15] *Pierre*, p. 321. Melville seems in this image to be clearly indebted to Shelley. See " Adonais," Section 24. Urania, flying to the side of Adonais in death, travels through the city:

> Out of her secret Paradise she sped,
> Through camps and cities rough with stone, and steel,
> And human hearts, which to her aery tread
> Yielding not, wounded the invisible
> Palms of her tender feet where'er they fell. . . .

[16] *Pierre*, p. 322.
[17] *Ibid.*, p. 335.

and Portuguese, interlarded now and then, with the foulest of
all human lingoes, that dialect of sin and death, known as the
Cant language, or the Flash." [18]

Here Pierre, as Melville conceives his narrative, enters civilization. At this moment, as he seeks the aid of the police in
finding his kinsman of the city, he begins his own city life of
sequestration. Pierre, at last immured in that mass of stone
which Melville sardonically calls "The Church of the Apostles," becomes Pierre scratching at the book which is to astonish
the world. He is not a Bohemian hero as dreamed up in some
romance of Mürger, nor is he Melville's sardonic portrait of
the young artist in a city garret. He is more nearly a Kafkan
man of the city whose pursuit of truth is meaningless since
truth itself, in this idiotic center of Western civilization, has
no meaning. Hence the irrational, the "idiotic" circumstance
of Pierre's death in a city prison. As Ahab, the fool of truth, is
the God-hating theologian doomed to an at least distinguished
death in the sea-realm of Moby Dick, so Pierre, the fool of truth,
is the man of the city doomed to an existence and a death without meaning. For the truth which Pierre seeks is no more than
the irrationality of a chaotic urban culture.

The city of Dis proclaims the passing of the great Christian
symbols of existential meaning. For, in the sense of both
Verhaeren and Melville, the tentacular town is the governor
of the total culture. All men serve it, and to sustain it the most
inhuman of human acts are performed. It is the meaning of
meaninglessness, and the sign of an exhausted civilization.

3   The Bell-Tower

The archetype of the tower requires a thorough critical examination. But no attempt can be made here to suggest the
wide incidence of this figure in the recent literature of the
Western world. Readers of Hart Crane, of Yeats, and of Dylan
Thomas know it; but so does every careful reader of Romantic
and Victorian poetry. It is not at all surprising that Melville

[18] *Ibid.*, p. 336.

should have discovered the tower, or that Verhaeren should have used it. As an archetype, it has a very rich manifestation. My purpose here is to examine Melville's tower as the important symbolic form which he derives from his experience with the city. Once again the limited claim of the archetype upon critical attention is evident. The tower, of course, is put to as many artistic uses as there are individual poetic temperaments to bring it into view. Again the argument for art as universal dream and myth is thoroughly refuted. Richard Chase, whose recent interpretation of Melville's story *The Bell-Tower* is the only published critical analysis of any consequence, elects the Freudian position of reading art as a description of traumatic states from infantile sexuality. The conclusion of the story is a dream of castration.[19] This interpretation overlooks the real element of Melville's tower symbol, and its relation to his feeling for the modern city. Furthermore, it proposes the interesting possibility of reading every archetypal appearance of the tower in recent literature as sexually derived dream content surviving from infancy.

If Chase's reading is accepted, then we may proceed to regard "The Broken Tower" of Hart Crane as an elaborately extended image of phallic worship. These lines from the poem contain the essential matter of the piece and reveal the metaphoric idiom which distinguishes it.

> The bell-rope that gathers God at dawn
> Dispatches me as though I dropped down the knell
> Of a spent day—to wander the cathedral lawn
> From pit to crucifix, feet chill on steps from hell.
>
> Have you not heard, have you not seen that corps
> Of shadows in the tower, whose shoulders sway
> Antiphonal carillons launched before
> The stars are caught and hived in the sun's ray?
>
> The bells, I say, the bells break down their tower;
> And swing I know not where. Their tongues engrave

---

[19] See fn. 3, ch. II. Another of Chase's Freudian views in this study is that Melville, in recounting his fear of cannibalism among the Taipis, betrayed in *Typee* an early fear of castration (*Herman Melville*, p. 12).

Membrane through marrow, my long-scattered score
Of broken intervals . . . And I, their sexton slave!

Oval encyclicals in canyons heaping
The impasse high with choir. Banked voices slain!
Pagodas, campaniles with reveilles outleaping—
O terraced echoes prostrate on the plain! . . .

And so it was I entered the broken world
To trace the visionary company of love, its voice
An instant in the wind . . . .[20]

No argument will here be offered for the superiority of Crane's
bell-tower. I am not here concerned with a judgment of the
poem as art. But it is perfectly clear that this work is a valid
lyric expression of the elusiveness of an intense emotional
state. The metaphor is posited upon " broken intervals ": the
peal of bells, blurred and tonally " spread," represents the
intensity of feeling in the lover who confesses his inability to
grasp the illusory quality of his experience, just as he is unable
to grasp the dissonances leaping from the belfry. Thus he
enters the " broken world " of ringings and cessations, " to
trace the visionary company of love," its voice " an instant in
the wind." Even with the most studied distortion, the tower of
Crane's poem could not be made to fit the Freudian obsession
with phallic representation save at the expense of making it a
grotesque instrument of a comic absurdity, which it clearly is
not. By the same token, the concluding images of Melville's
story may not be read with critical validity as emblems of a
dream of castration. The archetype of the tower should be acknowledged. But the tower itself is fashioned by each artist
according to his particular symbolistic purpose. Crane achieves
a lyric description of intermittent emotion; Melville creates a
symbol of modern man annihilated by his own ingenuity. In
the individual act of each a common artistic significance is
rendered impossible.

Melville's legend of *The Bell-Tower* is one of the most intricately wrought forms of his art. To begin with, we are given a

---

[20] In *Collected Poems*, ed., Frank, pp. 135-36.

landscape which looks more like the familiar " modern " desert of Surrealist painting than any locus from the poetry or fiction of his contemporaries. We are shown a city on a plain, " in the south of Europe." At the edge of the city stands a " black mossed stump," as though it were the base of some " immeasurable pine " fallen in a remote time. Where the pine fell, " its dissolution leaves a mossy ground." Thus Melville establishes the setting: an image of flat land where a solitary track of moss grows upon the tapering length of a rotting tree. " So westward from what seems the stump, one steadfast spear of lichened ruin veins the plain." It is the ruin of a bell-tower, " a stone pine; a metallic aviary in its crown." [21] This broken spear of ruin pointing away from the city into the plain is the master figure. The actors of the legend move against the background of a magic and distorted reality. These ruins of a monument from the city take the form of a primitive tree, as though Melville would remind us again that every state of civilization returns to original nature.

In this city of the plain, made rich by its commerce with the Levant, there lives a renowned builder-architect who resolves with certain of his townsmen to build the noblest bell-tower in Italy. It is agreed that the tower must be a union of both bell and clock towers, commonly built separately.[22] This plan is followed, and as the tower nears completion, Bannadonna, the architect, designs a massive clock bell. Around the sound bow are twelve girl figures, representing the hours. He designs also a mysterious striking mechanism which is kept veiled from the magistrates and the citizenry until the hour when the tower is to be dedicated. Bannadonna announces that on the day of the unveiling, the stroke of the mechanism will fall upon the hand of the first hour, Una, where it clasps the hand of Dua. The chief magistrate, inspecting the clock bell, remarks that the face of Una is unlike that of her sisters: it looks like the face of Deborah, the prophetess.[23] Bannadonna replies that there is a

[21] *The Bell-Tower* in *The Piazza Tales*, p. 253.
[22] *Ibid.*, pp. 254-55.
[23] *Ibid.*, pp. 259-60.

law in art which bars the possibility of duplicates; but the magistrate remains disturbed as he contemplates the mysterious face of Una. On the next day at one o'clock the citizens await the striking of the bell in the tower. No sound is heard.

When a party is sent to the summit of the tower, Bannadonna is found, prostrate and bleeding, at the base of the bell. He lies at the feet of Una, crushed by the striking mechanism. It is discovered that, as the hour approached, Bannadonna had attempted to alter the face of Una; and there he was clubbed to death by the "domino," his intricate automaton advancing to strike the first tone. "It had limbs, and seemed clad in a scaly mail, lustrous as a dragon-beetle's. It was manacled, and its clubbed arms were uplifted, as if, with its manacles once more to smite its already smitten victim. One advanced foot of it was inserted beneath the dead body, as if in the act of spurning it." [24] The body of Bannadonna is lowered from the tower for burial, and the great mechanical monster is dismantled, hauled to sea, and sunk. The state bell is rung at the funeral; but it crashes from the tower and buries itself in the earth. A year later an earthquake occurs, the tower careens from its base, and the masonry falls into the pattern of a stone spear on the plain. Melville relates that it was Bannadonna's aspiration to create Talus, an iron slave for man, "a new serf, more useful than the ox, swifter than the dolphin, stronger than the lion . . . in patience, another ass." [25] Bannadonna, the master architect of the city, thus becomes the representative of all urban culture: "With him, common-sense was theurgy; machinery, miracle; Prometheus, the heroic name for machinist; man, the true God." [26]

The similarity of this theme to the symbolic motif of the dynamo as this has been employed by Henry Adams, and more recently by Eugene O'Neill, is immediately apparent. Modern man is the victim of his own ingenuity. But the intricacy of Melville's symbol of the tower far exceeds the simple moral

[24] *Ibid.*, p. 264.
[25] *Ibid.*, p. 267.
[26] *Ibid.*, p. 268.

significance of the dynamo. What we have here is a master symbol describing cultural failure, in which the tower itself is the embracing form containing the multifarious meanings of the infernal city. Thus in the symbolistic imagination the tower is the monument of the modern city, as in that same imagination the White Whale became the essence of waters and the containment of irreducible polarities existing in God. The builder of the tower is the man of the city, the maker of mechanisms. Una bears the traditional allegorical name of Truth. Her face is seen to reveal the absolute truth of Deborah, the prophetess, who commanded Barak and his armies to the river Kishon, where Sisera would be slain (*Judges*, 4). Bannadonna, as the maker of Una, is yet another absolutist of Christian civilization. Not only does he presume to control Truth; he also creates her. Thus the voice of Truth will be made to sound by a mechanical monster of his own devising. And in that fatal hour when she is to speak through the tone of the bell, this fool of Truth, this man of over-reason who aspired to make an iron slave to serve him, is mangled by his servant upon the chill metal of Truth herself.

There is, of course, no evidence here of the polarity which distinguishes Ishmael's symbols of ideality invoking the Orient. But the tower, containing its own significance as a monument of the city, and the meanings of the mechanical agent of Truth and of the master architect in death, takes its place as one of Melville's supreme symbols. Furthermore, polarity is clearly evident in the symbolic act of " burying " the monster in the sea and in the final shape of the ruined tower as the trunk of the primeval pine, the spear pointing away from the city into the wasteland of a surrounding meaninglessness.

The collapse of Melville's bell-tower symbolizes the collapse of culture as religion. As an archetype, this tower in ruins appears through the same feeling which shapes the avatars of the Orient in primitivism; and it is precisely this archetype which unites Melville and Verhaeren as observers of cultural failure. It is Verhaeren's distinction that in his poetry the tower becomes one of the dominant structures of all recent symbolism.

In the tower, half monument of the city, half spire of the Christian church, are the memorials of the Christian symbolic center, the holy wafer of the Eucharist.

Verhaeren's description of symbolic disintegration in Christianity appears in the chaotic scenes of " La Révolte," published in *Les Flambeaux Noirs* (1890), and later in *Les Villes Tentaculaires*. The clock face, the most familiar of Verhaeren's obsessive images, is united with the disc of the holy wafer. The symbol of the Eucharist is " elevated " to the belfry of the church, which is both clock-tower and bell-tower as in the Italian structure of Melville. We see the Host in the round clock-tower as though its whiteness were displayed in a monstrance. The dial of the clock and the white roundness of the consecrated bread become one, and the spire looms in the darkness as a symbol of destruction. " The ancient dial-plate of a black belfry / Hurls its disc at the center of the evening, / Against a sky of red stars." [27] With this beginning, the theme is extended in the second version, appearing in 1895, with other studies of tentacular cities. Now the signs of the white disc flying into a blackness illuminated by red stars, as though the heavens reflected the chaos of earth's civilization, move into scenes of violence predicted in the initial images. The clock faces of belfries are smashed with stones hurled from the hands of desperate men, " a normal time no longer existing / For the mad and determined hearts / Of these hyperbolic mobs." [28] In the churches the figure of Christ is shattered with blows of fists and blasphemies.

> The Saints standing near the altars are insulted,
> And in the great nave from one end to the other,
> —Such a snowfall—the consecrated wafers are scattered
> To be ground beneath the raging heels.[29]

This is symbolic anarchy. The violent images of the snowfall in the nave project the meaning of the ruined belfry of Christendom, with its white disc of clock face and holy wafer. The

[27] *Poèmes* (Nouvelle Série, Paris, Mercure de France, 1906), p. 150.
[28] *Les Villes Tentaculaires* (Paris, Mercure de France, 1913), p. 176.
[29] *Ibid.*, p. 180.

hyperbolic mobs are incarnations of swirling and eddying tur-
moil in the corporate soul of the city. They are physical representations of spiritual states. In the poet's dream, every symbol
of Christianity is overturned and shattered by men of the city
revolting against the unrealized promise of Christian doctrine
and standing at the threshold of a new era of symbols to be
made from a new culture. The vision is by no means hallucina-
tion. It is the confession of an artist of impassioned feeling who
wrests his symbols of the shattered belfry, the desecrated Christ,
the holy wafers pulverized by trampling feet, from the immediate circumstance of a Western culture in transition. The crisis
is both the poet's and the city's.

From the crisis Verhaeren moves into the serenity of the last
period, the promise of the future expressed in *La Multiple
Splendeur* (1907). Although some students find the poetry of
this volume radiant with a new faith in the destiny of man, I
think it certain that nothing in this later work possesses the
arresting power and the commanding imaginative stature displayed in the symbols of the city in crisis.

Between the black spire under red stars, and the symbols of
the church destroyed appears the terrible vision of " Le Sonneur," published in 1894 in *Les Villages Illusoires.* It is here
that Verhaeren and Melville meet. The bell-tower, as the symbol of a total culture, is destroyed. In Verhaeren's poem it
burns; in Melville's legend it is demolished by an earthquake.
Baudouin has called attention to Verhaeren's use here of his
memory of a burning belfry seen in his childhood.[30] There can
be no question that the power of this autotype exerts a profound influence upon poetic feeling; Melville, on the other
hand, constructs his bell-tower without the direct experience
which we expect to find in the symbols of primitivism.

" Le Sonneur " opens with the alarm of the bell ringer in a
village church. It is night, and flames rise toward the tip of the
spire.

> The tower
> With the brandished cross at its summit,

[30] *Psychoanalysis and Aesthetics*, pp. 64–65.

> Spreads toward the hallucinated horizon
> [A] red mane of fire.
> The whole village is illuminated.
> The faces of appearing mobs
> People the streets of fear and uproar,
> And on the walls suddenly resplendent,
> The black tiles drink blood.[31]

Then the summit crashes.

> In the collapse of the pinnacle, the cross
> Falls into the furnace, which twists and grinds
> Its Christian arms as its prey.

The old bell-ringer, faithful to his post, is killed. A large bell bounds to earth, and " burying itself in the soft ground, / Dug his grave and formed his coffin." [32]

The symbol of bells falling from the towers of civilization has the same significance in the poetry of Verhaeren and the prose legend of Melville. The old bell-ringer is buried beneath the metal of Christian truth; Bannadonna, the master builder of the city, perishes upon the same metal of the same truth, and the bell of his own devising commemorates his death in its falling from the tower. In Verhaeren's poem, the symbol of the cross is consumed in the flames of a transition into the future, whatever that future may be; in Melville's legend the collapse of the tower of Bannadonna's truth leaves a spear of broken stone pointing away from the city into the plain. The archetype of the tower—whether it becomes a black spire under red stars or a pyre of symbols burning in the night, whether it becomes Melville's stone-pine emblem of ruin—is revealed through the same awareness of cultural failure. In these recent years of the city represented in Verhaeren's London of broken spars reaching toward a sky of crucifixion, Western man arrives at another great *transitus* in his existence.

The precocious Rimbaud understood the same crisis in culture. In his dream of the city, presumably inspired by London as he knew it through the abandonment of his days there with

[31] *Poèmes* (3e série, Paris, Mercure de France, n. d.), p. 35.
[32] *Ibid.*, p. 38.

Verlaine, one finds the same tower again brought to symbolic form. The feeling of Rimbaud goes straight to the company of poetic feeling given shape by Melville and Verhaeren. These three meet at the tower (and I leave it to another student to interpret yet other artists who have known that same place of congregation). Rimbaud's bell-tower is a castle of bones. But the material of the builder—bone, burning wood, stone—is unimportant to the sensibility that chose each element of the structure. It stands universally among these men as the perishable material of symbolic meaning in the changing culture of man. The following portion of Rimbaud's prose poem from *Les Illuminations,* " Villes I," describes the infernal city, not in its material indigence, but in the impoverishment of its modern culture as religion. And this, as I understand it, is the city of Melville's mature art.

> These are cities! These are a people for whom these dream Alleghanies and Lebanons have risen up. Chalets of crystal and wood move on invisible rails and pulleys. . . . The sound of love feasts rings out over the canals suspended behind the chalets. The pack of chimes echoes in the gorges. Corporations of gigantic singers come together in garments and banners as shining as the light on mountain tops. On platforms within abysses Rolands blare forth their valor. . . . Groups of bell-towers intone the ideas of the people. Unfamiliar music comes from castles built of bones.

The images involved in Rimbaud's symbol all speak for themselves. I call attention only to " Rolands " as ministers of the church trumpeting the theme of Christian valor. This image gives additional stature to the tower, the cathedral of bones.

You live shamefully, without dream or purpose,
Older, more sterile than the barren land,
Emasculated from the cradle by the assassin century
Of all vigorous and profound passion.

Your brain is as empty as your heart,
And you have defiled this miserable world
With blood so corrupt, with breath so sickly
That death alone springs in this unclean soil.

Men, killers of Gods, the time is near
When, sprawled upon a heap of gold . . .
Having wasted your parent earth to a stony mass

And knowing how to do nothing by day or night,
Lost in the nothingness of supreme ennui,
You will die idiotically in filling your pockets.

Leconte de Lisle
" Aux Modernes "
Poèmes Barbares

XV

The Holy Sepulchre

The assassin century of Leconte de Lisle's address to
modern man is named as the destroyer of " vigorous passion."
Men, the killers of gods, are the unfeeling makers of nothingness, and its victims. Again the city appears as the tomb of men
who die bestially in the evening of a culture. The description
proceeds from the same feeling which is shared by Melville,
Verhaeren, and Rimbaud. But the limitations of Leconte de
Lisle as a symbolist are clearly evident. The man of the culture
of cities is not the killer of gods solely because he is indentured
to materialistic acquisition. The grossness of that process is to
Melville, Verhaeren, and Rimbaud only the outward sign of
decay. As poetic observers, these three possess the greater
authority in their awareness of religious decay as the germinal

soil of a rank materialistic falsehood. Their symbols of ruin are superior to the denunciation of Leconte de Lisle; for each recognizes the modern circumstance of cultural failure, the impoverishment of the symbolic life, which underlies every circumstance of contemporary hedonism. Each understands the materialistic substitutes of modern man as compensations for the loss of cultural meaning.

Thus, when Rimbaud observes that the belfries intone the ideas of the people, he reflects sardonically the recent cultural fact that there are no uniform ideas to be proclaimed. Below the towers of Christendom acquisitive men move through the streets. But the music heard by Rimbaud from these cathedrals of bones is unfamiliar. It is this condition of unfamiliarity that describes the meaning of assassination and of nothingness, the secondary conditions from which Leconte de Lisle presents his soundings of the modern world. In the view of the symbolist it is the loss of *corporateness* which stands as the central fact of a spreading disintegration of religion.

The last of Melville's real voyages which brought his art to the ultimate theological resolutions of *Clarel* is the pilgrimage to Jerusalem and the Holy Sepulchre. At this time of 1856–57 the symbolistic destiny of Ishmael is entirely clear. All that remains as essential to the completion of feeling in symbolic form is the journey to the source of Christian tradition. There Melville revisited traditional Christianity, and there he joined a long procession of itinerant primitivists and near-primitivists who felt the compulsion to see for themselves the place of the supreme Crucifixion. Some came and went away as mendicants. Melville came as the observer, and went away, not as a beggar, but as the voyager confirmed in the ideality of his primitivism. That confirmation made possible the theology of *Clarel* and the eminent sacramentalism of *Billy Budd*. The original Christ, as Melville must have suspected before he sailed, was nowhere known in these holy places; the symbols of Christ's presence upon earth he found to be empty of meaning. Melville traveled alone to the source. But among those who went there before him and after him in search of a restoration of faith, he took

his place in a distinguished procession. The solitary file of
these travelers is, like Ishmael himself, a symbol of symbols.
It is the symbol of primitivism in its backward glance over
tradition, over the religious meaning of Western civilization in
the last century of its Christian history.

1 *The Voyage to Jerusalem*

As Chateaubriand's journey westward to the primitive forests
of North America is unlike the symbolistic descent of Melville
into Typee Valley, as the meaning of conversion to Christianity
in *Atala* disagrees entirely with Melville's symbolic descriptions
of Polynesian ethos, so does Chateaubriand's journey to Jerusalem differ from Melville's later pilgrimage. For literary history, it is an almost felicitous circumstance that he is the first
renowned modern predecessor of Melville at the Holy Sepulchre. What was true of Chateaubriand's journey to the savages
and what was true of *Atala* are alike true of the same traveler in
Jerusalem. The exotic art of this *littérateur* is incapable of any
description save that of exotic effect. The same artistic distance
again separates him from Melville, and almost the same distance
in point of time. Leaving Paris in the summer of 1806 and
returning there in the summer of 1807,[1] he preceded Melville
in Jerusalem by fifty years. One suspects that if he had made his
pilgrimage fifty years later, the literary result, in consideration
of his exotic propensities, would have been exactly the same.

Melville was at least aware that Chateaubriand had preceded
him, although it is improbable that he knew this from French
sources. He mentions the " holy " journeys of both Chateaubriand and Lamartine in *Clarel*.[2] Chateaubriand's *Itinéraire de
Paris à Jérusalem* is the fruit of a crowded year of wandering,
a year which took him to Greece and Turkey, as well, and
then to Tunis and Spain as he turned homeward. (The approach to Jerusalem is, strangely enough, exactly the same as

---

[1] See Pierre-Maurice Masson, " Chateaubriand en Orient," *Revue des Deux Mondes*, vol. 24 (6e période, 1914), p. 96.

[2] *Clarel*, vol. 1, p. 234.

that followed by Melville, who visited Constantinople en route.) It is difficult to evaluate this work unless one can content himself exclusively with autobiography and the idiosyncrasies of the style. As the performance of an artist, it is wholly characterless. This fact is the more striking when it is remembered that the author is the defender of the faith in the *Génie du Christianisme*. The *Itinéraire* is a plodding inventory of physical equipment discovered in certain cities. As a religious document, it is totally devoid of feeling of any sort, unless once excepts such slight touches as Chateaubriand's hearing the *Kyrie eleison* sung by sailors on a Greek ship bound for Rhodes. " The effect [note *effect*] of the Kyrie is extraordinary in its sadness and its majesty: it is without doubt a residue of the ancient chant of the primitive Church." [3]

Pierre-Maurice Masson, in his study of the *Itinéraire*, speaks of Chateaubriand's dryness of soul (*sécheresse d'âme*) [4] revealed in these curious chapters. The phrase is exactly right. Nothing could be more arid than this prose, so entirely lacking in sentience of any sort. Of the subterranean Church of the Nativity he writes as though he might be a building inspector. "The holy grot is irregular because it occupies the irregular site of the stable and the *crèche*. It is thirty-seven and a half feet long, eleven feet three inches wide, and nine feet high. It is carved from rock: the walls of the rock are covered with marble, and the pavement of the grot is also of a precious marble." [5] In Jerusalem he describes the church properly called the Holy Sepulchre as a building in the form of a cross. It is situated in the valley adjacent to the Mount of Calvary. It has sixteen columns of marble, niches and arcades, etc. [6] Ascending Calvary by the Stations of the Cross, he desists momentarily to speak of the story that makes tears flow with its beauty. These saintly places are more impressive than the monuments of ancient Greece! [7] Later, at the arch called Ecce Homo, where Mel-

---

[3] *Oeuvres Complètes de Chateaubriand* (Paris, Librairie Générale de France [1827?]), vol. 7, pp. 189–90.

[4] *Revue des Deux Mondes*, vol. 24, p. 97.

[5] *Oeuvres Complètes* (Paris, [1827?]), vol. 7, p. 216.

[6] *Ibid.*, p. 241.   [7] *Ibid.*, p. 244.

ville's Celio of *Clarel* reflects upon the distortion of the
original Christ by " creeds malign," Chateaubriand turns to the
ruins of a church nearby, once consecrated to Notre Dame des
Douleurs. His " meditation " at this point supplies an account
of Saint Boniface and Saint Anselm as reporters of what the
dead Christ said to the Virgin as she lay speechless and en-
tranced before the body of her son.[8] It would be foolish, probably, to quibble with Chateaubriand's scholarship. It seems as
dispassionate and exact as his inspections of buildings.

What Chateaubriand sought was the conviction of religious
feeling, the feeling of allegiance to the symbols of culture as
religion. The curiously dead pages of the *Itinéraire* tell us at
least one significant truth: Chateaubriand, as the first of recent
pilgrims belonging to the age of Melville, found in the symbols
of Jerusalem no more authority to command feeling than Melville found there. But at the outset of this study the distance
between Chateaubriand and Melville as artists was suggested.
The same distance prevails in Jerusalem: the one evades the
truth for the sake of reputation; the other confronts the demands of religious consciousness and forms the symbols of a
new authority of feeling.

Lamartine, as the second of Melville's predecessors in Jerusalem, requires little notice here, except for his description of
feeling at the Holy Sepulchre. This is the feeling which
Chateaubriand sought; and Lamartine's account is an expression of orthodox faith which may be matched, in our time, by
the orthodoxy of Paul Claudel. Lamartine visited the Church
of the Sepulchre in 1830–31. The intense conviction which he
experienced there was related a year later in the *Voyage en
Orient*. " I entered in my turn, and the last, into the Holy
Sepulchre, my mind besieged by these overwhelming ideas, my
heart moved by such inward emotions as remain mysteries between man and his soul, between the reflecting insect [man]
and the Creator. These emotions cannot be written down; they
exhale amidst the smoke of the consecrated lamps, amidst the
perfume of the censers . . . all the joys and afflictions of which

[8] *Ibid.*, p. 245.

these prayers were the expression. . . . [They] produce . . . that overpowering of the intellect, and that melting of the heart, which find no words." [9] There is no reason to question Lamartine's sincerity. The " overwhelming ideas " and the " overpowering of the intellect " name the conditions of feeling in a sensibility which is dominated by the symbol at hand. This is the capacity for " love " in the sense of Chateaubriand. The individual will is assimilated in the corporateness of a symbolized existence.

The young Englishman A. W. Kinglake, recently of Cambridge, and of Switzerland, where he had been reading Rousseau for some months, arrived in the Holy Land in 1835.[10] The record of the journey in his *Eöthen* (1844) does not belong to the history of authentic primitivism, as a comparison of its impressionistic narrative with the symbolism of Melville's *Clarel*, for instance, immediately reveals. But of all the works of primitivism contemporary with Melville's voyages, this book was not only the most popular of its day, but was also the most familiar to Melville. Kinglake is mentioned twice in Melville's journals, in an entry of 1849 listing him as one of several dinner companions at the Erechtheum Club in London,[11] and again in 1857, as Melville wrote in his notebook an account of his embarkation from Greece in the steamer *Cydnus*.[12] Kinglake's biographer and critic, Tuckwell, notes the absence of history, geography, description, and statistics [cf. Chateaubriand] in *Eöthen*.[13] He finds it a work of pure sensation. This it is. Furthermore, as Tuckwell suggests, Kinglake possesses a curious ambivalence in his devotion to both Greek paganism and Christianity.[14] Paphos and Nazareth were equally stimulating.

[9] Translated by William and Robert Chambers (Edinburgh, 1839), p. 84.

[10] W. Tuckwell, *A. W. Kinglake: A Biographical and Literary Study* (London, 1902), pp. 14, 17–18.

[11] Manuscript Journal of 1849, Part 2, entry of December 23, 1849, Melville Papers, Metcalf Collection, Houghton Library, Harvard.

[12] *Journal up the Straits*, ed. Weaver, pp. 113–15. The entry is dated February 11, [1857]. Melville meets on board the *Cydnus* a Greek interpreter named Mysseri who is recalled in Kinglake's *Eöthen*.

[13] *A. W. Kinglake*, pp. 26–27.

[14] *Ibid.*, p. 15.

The "new" feeling acquired in the Near East is equal in Kinglake's experience to Melville's sense of "liberation" in Typee Valley. Thus, in Constantinople the voyager of *Eöthen* rejoices in his freedom from the "stale civilization" of Europe where men are "pinioned at dinner tables . . . or cruelly planted in pews." [15] And on Cyprus he wants to believe, "to believe for one . . . moment that in the gloomy depths of the grove by the mountain's side there was some leafy pathway that crisped beneath the glowing sandal of Aphrodētie [sic]." [16]

Kinglake at the Holy Sepulchre exchanges the feeling experienced on Cyprus for the feeling of Christian man in search of the god-symbols of his world. His description of the shrine is exactly like the one which Melville was to write in his journal of 1857: "[The priests of the Sepulchre] . . . seemed to be not 'working out' but *transacting* the great business of Salvation." [17] Aphrodite is dead, and so is the god of this mummery in the museum of the Sepulchre. Kinglake's adventure in feeling, if it achieves none of the power shaping the art of primitivism, at least demonstrates a partial understanding of symbolism in relation to culture. In the solitude of the desert near Gaza, he reaches Melville's conclusion that the man born to Christendom is inevitably bound to Christian culture: ". . . wherever man wanders he still remains tethered by the chain that links him to his kind." [18] Like Verhaeren, as though he sensed the crossing from old to new symbols of meaning, he leaves the past for whatever is to succeed it.

Seven years before Melville reached Jerusalem, Gustave Flaubert, who belongs with the company of the exoticists so far as the criteria of primitivism are concerned, wrote of the Sepulchre what Chateaubriand in honesty might have written. On August 11, 1850, three days after his arrival in the holy city, Flaubert concluded that he had found nothing which he had looked for, neither religious enthusiasm nor imaginative stimu-

---

[15] *Eöthen: or Traces of Travel Brought Home from the East*, ed. S. L. Bensusan (London, n. d.), pp. 48–49.

[16] *Ibid.*, p. 101.

[17] *Ibid.*, p. 173.

[18] *Ibid.*, p. 200.

lation, nor even hatred of priests, which would, at least, have been something.

> I feel, before everything I see, as empty as a hollow cask. This morning, in the Holy Sepulchre, a dog would have been more touched than I. Whose fault is this, God of pity? theirs? yours? or mine? Theirs, I believe; mine next; yours finally. Everything is false! every falsehood they tell! everything is whitewashed, veneered, varnished, made for exploitation, propaganda, custom. Jerusalem is a charnel-house surrounded by walls; the first singular thing we have encountered is carnage.[19]

He speaks here of carrion, the refuse of the abattoir thrown into the filthy, narrow streets. But this condition of filth is not, of course, the maker of the "emptiness." It is only the outward sign of the death of holiness. Ruin lies everywhere; Jerusalem breathes of the sepulchre and desolation; the curses of God himself seem to fall upon the city.[20] In the Church of the Sepulchre Flaubert notes sardonically that a portrait of Louis-Philippe decorates the holy place, illuminating with its royal light the tomb of Jesus. The most impressive aspect of the church itself is its division among three sects, Greeks, Latins (Romans), Copts; each sect hates its neighbors above all other men of the world. To this voyager the shrine is a "union of reciprocal curses."[21]

Could not this man, the maker of his mediaeval legend of Saint Julian, Flaubert looking backward even as Chateaubriand in that moment of hearing the *Kyrie* of sailors at sea, could not he perhaps have remembered the devout victory of the Crusaders? On the 15th of July, 1099, having put to death most of the Turkish population in the capture of Jerusalem, these Christian victors marched weeping and singing to the Holy Sepulchre; and the twelfth century, the supreme century of Christian symbolism, the age of the faith of Chartres, began. The whole structure of symbolic faith in that triumphant century depended, like a pyramid inverted to rest upon its apex,

---

[19] *Voyages*, vol. 2, *Voyage en Orient* (Paris, 1948), p. 198.
[20] *Ibid.*, p. 199.
[21] *Ibid.*, p. 203.

on that much-contested Sepulchre with its inexhaustible relics and its endless accretions of symbolic meaning. And now, after eight centuries, the Sepulchre becomes a union of reciprocal human curses in a city cursed by God. Thus the difference between the Christian sensibility of Flaubert and the faith of France that built Chartres.

Melville's revulsion as he stood before these same tokens of Jerusalem in 1857 cannot seem to anyone very different from Flaubert's reaction. The following description of the church and the Sepulchre appears in his journal:

> Labyrinths and terraces of mouldy grottos, tombs, and shrines. Smells like a dead-house. Dingy light . . . continuous troops of pilgrims entering and prostrating themselves before the anointing-stone of Christ, which veined with shreds of mouldy red looks like a butcher's slab,—. . . by the smoky light of old pawn-brokers' lamps of dirty gold, the hole in which the cross was fixed. . . . A sort of plague-stricken splendor reigns in the painted and mildewed walls around. . . . [Of the Holy Sepulchre] It is like entering a lighted coffin. . . . A sickening cheat.[22]

The stench of Jerusalem itself seems to relate oddly to these images of plague and death: Melville says it is at all times full of the smell of burning refuse.[23] Leaving Jerusalem for Beirut, he records an account of the captain of his ship. The captain has told him that the Greek priests in Jerusalem do a thriving business in selling tickets to heaven: " Printed paper with Dove in middle and Father and Son each side." [24] These are the vistas of death which led Melville to the theology of *Clarel*.

Long ago in *Redburn* he had recalled the emotions of a youth on his first journey to England, a youth who had seen nothing of the world and who could believe that it was a " most Christian thing, and a matter most sweet to dwell upon and simmer over in solitude, that any poor sinner may go to church wherever he pleases." But this was a thought (*Redburn*, Ch. XLI) recalled from Wellingborough Redburn's (and Melville's) early

[22] *Journal up the Straits*, ed. Weaver, pp. 84–86.
[23] *Ibid.*, p. 91.
[24] *Ibid.*, p. 108.

unknowingness. *Moby-Dick* announces Ishmael's knowledge of the world; and though it may be in part true that Melville, as Olson believes, was " sealed " by those two weeks in the Holy Land " in a bitterness of disillusion from which he never recovered," [25] I doubt that the journey really amounted to the bitter knowledge which Olson proposes. Melville's mature symbols from *Moby-Dick* onward point to what he was to find. Jerusalem merely confirmed what he had already come to feel of dogmatic and sectarian Christianity. In Jerusalem he interpreted the meaninglessness of Christian civilization as its universal loss of the original Christ.

Thus, Schweitzer is the master spokesman of the twentieth century who illuminates the meaning of Melville's discovery. In his essay of 1931, " The Historical Jesus and the Christianity of Today," Schweitzer observes that the original Son of Man has been obscured by an externalizing, dogmatic Christianity. " In what a condition we find ourselves to-day merely because in the earliest Christian period writings were allowed to appear, bearing quite falsely the names of apostles, in order to give greater authority to the ideas put forth in them! " [26] The apostles, true or false, contemporary or succeeding, of any religion are invariably the interpreters, the elaborators, the embellishers of doctrine, and the originators of divisiveness. Schweitzer's judgment reveals the apostles of Christianity as the obstacles between Western man and the historical, the original Christ. It is the theology devised by the saints, and, on the other side of Christianity, by the Reformationists that obscures Christ.

To the mind of Melville it is also the symbolism of this multiply derived theology that perishes. Two passages from *Clarel* complete all that need be said finally of Melville in this last visit to Christianity. Midway in the poem he thinks of the original Christ and his followers as teachers of the ideal: man's divinity is revealed in the gladness of his earthly existence and in his love of his fellow creatures.

[25] *Call Me Ishmael*, p. 99.
[26] *Out of My Life and Thought*, p. 66.

> But it died;
> Back rolled the world's effacing tide:
> The "*world*"—by Him denounced, defined—
> Him first—set off and countersigned,
> Once and for all, as opposite
> To honest children of the light.
> But worse came—creeds, wars, stakes. Oh, men
> Made earth inhuman; yes, a den
> Worse for Christ's coming, since His love
> (Perverted) did not venom prove.[27]

The character speaking is Rolfe, who, with Billy Budd, is descended from Jack Chase in Melville's ideality of *tayo*. And it is Rolfe who speaks again in answer to Ungar's desperation as the poem approaches its end. Ungar sees the symbolic death of Christianity:

> Now the world cannot save the world;
> And Christ renounces it. His faith,
> Breaking with every mundane path,
> Aims straight at heaven.[28]

Rolfe replies thereafter to Ungar, in words which are spoken unmistakably by Ishmael, the symbol-maker.

> The world has now so old become,
> Historic memory goes so far
> Backward through long defiles of doom;
> Whoso consults it honestly
> That mind grows prescient in degree;
> For man, like God, abides the same
> Always, through all variety
> Of woven garments to the frame.[29]

The woven garment is the culture of man; and this, like the nature of God read again and again through endlessly exchanged theologies, will be exchanged for new. The source of Melville's despair is not, I think, the decline of dogmatic Christian symbolism, or the loss of meaning in Christian emblems. The lament of *Clarel* is concerned rather with the distortion of

---

[27] *Clarel*, vol. 1, p. 254 (Part II, Sec. xxi).
[28] *Ibid.*, vol. 2, p. 243 (Part IV, Sec. xx).
[29] *Ibid.*, vol. 2, p. 248 (Part IV, Sec. xxi).

the original Christ as a man supremely alive, supremely rejoicing in the miracle of existence. In life he was the man of primitive acceptance and the giver of *vital* symbols; after his life on earth he was made the man of over-reason by the dogmas of apostles and sectarians, who achieved finally the destruction of communion in his faith.

2 *Mar Saba*

Into a stony gorge of the barren Judaean mountains the monk Saint Saba came in the fourth century after Christ to live in solitude and to spend his days in prayer; and after him came hundreds of followers to build a monastery in his honor. There the heights of Mar Saba rose; and there they stand today, clinging, as some travelers have observed, like a wasp's nest to the crags. From the autotype of this stony place Melville creates the master symbol of his pilgrimage: the monks of this ancient community become the signs of a last Christian inheritance. They bear to the contemporary condition of Christianity in the church exactly the same relation which the tower bears to the condition of culture as religion in the tentacular modern city. Chateaubriand had preceded Melville at Mar Saba, and his description matches several aspects of Melville's landscape from the third part of *Clarel*. This retreat seemed to Chateaubriand one of the most desolate places of the earth. " It is built in the ravine of the river Kedron, [a gorge] which must be three or four hundred feet deep at that point. The river is dry; it flows only in spring with muddy and reddened water. . . . [T]he buildings of the monastery rise along perpendicular stairs and passages carved from the rock along the flank of the ravine, and succeed [one another] in this fashion to the top of the mountain, where they terminate in two square towers. One of these is outside the convent; it . . . serves as a look-out post for guarding against Arabs." [30] Nearby, in an opening of the mountains, Jerusalem, " the queen of the desert," can be seen rising " as a sudden apparition of desolation." [31]

[30] *Oeuvres Complètes* (Paris, [1827?]), vol. 7, p. 221.
[31] *Ibid.*, p. 222.

There Mark Twain was to follow Chateaubriand, and Melville. The description from Mark Twain's *Innocents Abroad* exceeds Chateaubriand's in detail and is even more useful in its picture of the monks who enter Melville's symbol. There is little difference between the feeling contained in this passage and that which inspired Melville to devote one fourth of *Clarel* to reflection in the shadow of the old monastery.

> Mars [sic] Saba, perched upon a crag, a human nest stuck high up against a perpendicular mountain wall, is a world of grand masonry that rises, terrace upon terrace . . . . The present occupants of Mars Saba, about seventy in number, are all hermits. They wear a coarse robe, an ugly, brimless stovepipe of a hat, and go without shoes. They eat nothing whatever but bread and salt; they drink nothing but water. As long as they live they can never go outside the walls . . . .
> Some of these men have been shut up there for thirty years. . . . They are dead men who walk.[32]

Had Melville never returned through the demands of his art to the spectacle of these living dead, had he never recreated this place of desolation in *Clarel*, we should still justifiably understand his experience on the mount of Saba as another extension of the proof which he took with him from Jerusalem. The original Christ was here unheard of, as much as he was unheard of in the stony gorges of the modern city, and in the Holy Sepulchre. But Melville chose here the material for his one master symbol of the pilgrimage: the monks of Mar Saba become the sign not only of the desolation of Judaea but also of the total apostolic history of a distorted Christianity, terminating finally in man's disavowal of his nature as a human being. Always, in that bleak recollection of *Clarel*, Melville sees them in their endless black files.

> Aloof the monks their aerie keep,
> Down from their hanging cells they peep,
> Like samphire-gatherers o'er the bay
> Faint hearing there the hammering deep
> Of surf that smites the ledges gray.

[32] *The Innocents Abroad* (London, 1899), vol. 2, pp. 379–80.

> But up and down, from grot to shrine,
> Along the gorge, hard by the brink
> File the gowned monks in even line . . . .
> With litany or dirge they wend
> Where nature as in travail dwells . . . .[33]

The use of Shakespeare's image of the samphire-gatherers from
King Lear (IV, vi) leads to reflection upon infinitesimal
human figures on a beach, and invokes a sense of endlessness
in the succeeding lines, as though these monks chanting the
litany to the stones were the supreme emblems of utter meaninglessness. Beyond this gorge of Kedron lies Bethlehem where
the voyage of *Clarel* ends. The monks of Mar Saba seem transposed, in the meaning of the symbol, to the Palm Sunday procession which Clarel watches in the street of the Broken
Fountain.

> But unto Clarel that bright view
> Into a dusk reminder grew:
> He saw the tapers—saw again
> The censers, singers, and the wreath
> And litter of the bride of death
> Pass through the Broken Fountain's lane; . . .
> The men and boys he heard again
> The undetermined contest keep
> About the bier—the bier Armenian.[34]

The "dusk reminder," "the bride of death," and the bier
created by the Armenian rite are the signs of Christian loss.
These are the pale remnants of Christ. Even the succeeding
description of Easter Day speaks only of ritual habit. The
"Alpine freshet" of Easter emotion passes into the "sluggish
stream"; man "bereft" is "unrepaid" by the ancient rite; the
symbols of Easter fall like cherries dropped upon a pall; the
supreme celebration finished, the Easter confluence of nations
disperses; and Bethlehem, the place of the birth of innocence,
is depopulated, and left alone, says Melville in one of his most
compelling American images, like a country church on a week-

---

[33] *Clarel*, vol. 2, p. 43 (Part III, Sec. ix).
[34] *Ibid.*, p. 290 (Part IV, Sec. xxxii).

day, when the empty benches reflect the brown light of November.[35]

The meaning of Mar Saba and Bethlehem in *Clarel* is amplified by the symbols of monks in Verhaeren's early poetry, particularly in *Les Moines* (1885). These figures join the symbolic procession making its way along the stone, whether that of a Judaean monastery or of a European wasteland. Verhaeren introduces the theme in "Aux Moines"; and this is restated and developed throughout the descriptions of its companion pieces, all in poetic feeling remarkably close to the final sections of *Clarel*.

> You alone survive, great, in the dead Christian world;
> Alone, without bending your backs, you carry its burden
> As if it were the body of a king enclosed in a golden coffin.
> Monks—you seekers of sublime chimeras—
> Your dreams pass beyond tombs,
> Your eyes are magnetized by the glimmering of peaks,
> You are the bearers of crosses and of torches
> Around the divine ideal which is being buried.[36]

The burden carried so lightly by these dreamers is, to Verhaeren, the death of Christian culture. These are the last inheritors, and in a second appearance they become also the dwarfs of a world of shrinking faith. The poet recalls a procession of monks moving across country fields, those, undoubtedly, of his native Flanders. Like the Christian symbols perishing in the destruction of the burning tower, these figures are expressions of distortion. In the vision of "Rentrée des Moines" they are the twisted and emaciated descendants of giants.

> The white monks cross the black fields,
> Creating dreams of a time of biblical youth
> When angelic giants were seen wandering
> In long mantles of linen, in the pale gold of the evenings . . . .

---

[35] *Ibid.*, pp. 292–94 (Part IV, Sec. xxxiii). The image of the cherries here, as tokens of the natural man, should be compared with Ahab's memory of cherries as the *Pequod* is sinking.

[36] *Poèmes* (Paris, Mercure de France, 1895), pp. 219–20.

Those whose harsh and pale solitude has rendered
The soul seeing, and whose wan and tight skin
Flings toward God the voice of its bleeding thinness
[Are] those whose black torments have made their bodies
    twisted.[37]

The whole of *Les Moines* is a vast symbol of Christian loss.
Each unit element of this symbol with its own distinctive
imagery reveals the unequaled power of Verhaeren's art in its
masterly variations. The theme of loss, as in *Les Villes Tentaculaires*, appears again and again, each time with new projections of an intense religious feeling. Although Verhaeren's
setting is European, the barrenness of Melville's Mar Saba
and Bethlehem is made even clearer in its topography through
comparison with the scenes of these poems.

3 *After Melville*

The special character of primitivism in the art of Mark
Twain has already been defined. There is no possibility of
equating the ideality of *Huckleberry Finn* with the significance
of Oriental ethos in Melville's art; nor is there any critical
reason for attempting to do so. These artists belong to different
areas of feeling and expression; and the fact that both are
American does not compel them into unity. Yet, to the literary
historian it is at least clear that Mark Twain at the Holy
Sepulchre encounters the same tokens of cultural failure which
had been apparent to Melville. There is a continuity of American feeling here which is interesting: Mark Twain in 1867
repeats the denunciation of Melville in a description which
might have been taken from Melville's journal, so vehement
is its attack upon the same fraudulence, in the same manifestations.

All sects of Christians (except Protestants) have chapels
under the roof of the Church of the Holy Sepulchre, and
each must keep to itself and not venture upon another's
ground. It has been proven conclusively that they cannot

[37] *Ibid.*, pp. 228–29.

worship together around the grave of the Saviour of the World in peace.[38]

The shrines of Jerusalem, he continues, are imaginary holy places created by the monks. The altar of Calvary is adorned with so much bejewelled trapping that he must remind himself constantly: this is Golgotha.[39] Mark Twain withdraws with the feeling expressed by Melville's Clarel: the original Christ has been lost in this Christian era of sectarians. He observes that the Sepulchre, the most sacred spot of earth to men of Christian civilization, is a place of clap-trap sideshows and impostures. Yet beneath this corruption there must lie somewhere the original truth of Christ the teacher: for a god died there.

Mark Twain left to the twentieth century at his death, in 1910, the confession of his disillusionment. The posthumous legend of *The Mysterious Stranger* is one of the most deeply exploring of all modern parables in its theme of irrationality and chaos in a Christian world. I do not attempt to compel opposite religious confessions into proximity when I suggest here that Mark Twain's legend stands nearer to the poetry of contemporary irrationality in Rimbaud's *Les Illuminations* than to any other art form of the recent past. Thus it is not surprising that Rimbaud's journey to Jerusalem (c. 1881) should have discovered the same loss of meaning which Mark Twain found at the Sepulchre.

Marguerite Méléra's study of Rimbaud's pilgrimage is based upon unpublished materials which have not been available for this discussion. Thus I must depend upon her conclusions. Something of Chateaubriand's "dryness of soul" would seem to distinguish the disillusionment of Rimbaud, were it not for the fact that his poetry sets him apart from all the exoticists of his century. Midway in his flight from Europe which was to end in Abyssinia, Rimbaud made his way to Jaffa, and then to Jerusalem, asking directions of camel-drivers as he walked over the desert. But the scenes of the Gospel were empty when he reached the shrine, the legends of the Bible "a collection of

---

[38] *The Innocents Abroad* (London, 1899), vol. 2, pp. 330–31.
[39] *Ibid.*, pp. 345–46.

dried plants." [40] How much he saw in Jerusalem is not known. It is enough to understand that his journey to the source of Christian symbolism identifies him with Melville and Mark Twain, and with his own countrymen who had entered the Sepulchre before him. The bones of cathedrals in London had already become the tokens of this journey. Of all the silences of primitivists, Rimbaud's is the longest and the darkest, since it had no end. But we know enough, probably, to suppose what he might have written had he spoken again through art.

Pierre Loti is the last of Melville's successors, the last primitivist in the perpetuity of Ishmael who requires notice here. Loti reached Jerusalem in 1895. Ten years later he attempted to forget the emptiness of the Sepulchre through his journey to India. He is the only primitivist who extends the quest for religious meaning through an actual progression from Jerusalem onward to the Orient; his pilgrimage to the teachers of Benares is his last expedient toward a restored symbolism. The record of the voyage to Jerusalem brings him again to the company of Melville, where he has earlier stood in his symbols of Polynesian ethos and of the sea. In the confession of *Jérusalem* he expresses the religious meaning of *Clarel*. He stands at the center of Christian man's time and religious strength, feeling himself profane in daring to place at the head of his account of the Holy City the name of a pilgrimage without faith.[41] He speaks for Christian man at the end of a century: ". . . [W]e are people of sombre anguish at this moment, people at the edge of a black pit where all must fall and perish, people who see again, over an immeasurable distance, towering above all . . . human religions, that forgiveness which Jesus announced, that consolation and that celestial reunion. . . . [From] our abyss a vague desolate adoration continues to rise toward . . . the Redeemer." [42]

The barbarisms of modern Christian man become the barbarisms inflicted by ancient societies upon the first Christians;

[40] "Les Voyages d'Arthur Rimbaud," *La Revue·Universelle*, vol. 35 (1928), p. 654.

[41] *Jérusalem* (Paris, Calmann-Lévy, n. d.), p. 1.

[42] *Ibid.*, p. 2.

barbaric faiths replace the Christian faith which, in the Middle Ages, overcame a thousand pagan beliefs in the primitive forests of Europe. In this time of extinction in the modern soul, " it is again toward that human veneration of places and memories that the unbelieving, such as I, are reclaimed through the torturing regret for a lost Saviour." [43]

The despair reflected here alone accounts for Loti's subsequent voyage to India. He went there in search of the corporateness which was lost to Christianity. Specifically, he went to Benares in search of escape from the intolerable state of the ego in its I–You relationship with God (as defined from Jung's theory in the opening chapter of this study). In the communion of the sages of Benares he discovered the discipline of escape from self (whether he learned it or not) : " You can only desire that which is different from yourself, that which you have not; and did you but know that the things you seek are within you, for the Essence of all things is within you, then desire would melt away." [44] There he discovered Brahma, the creator, Brahma beyond the reach of all the theologies of man, " Brahma, the ineffable—he of whom we cannot even think, and of whom no words may ever be spoken, and whose nature may only be expressed by Silence." [45] " Can it be," he asks, " that the delusion from which the desire to be a separate entity springs has already fallen from me? " [46] *India* is an equivalent of Melville's *Clarel* as an exploration of the possibilities for contemporary religious faith.

The *India* of Loti proposes salvation in the Orient. It must be said in conclusion that a contemporary return to the Orient can no longer be expected to uncover the ideality revealed in the symbolism of Melville and, generally, that of primitivism. Schweitzer's dictum, that there are no new lands to tell us anything which we do not already know, probably means that no alien culture exists which will inform a reconstitution of exis-

[43] *Ibid.*, p. 63.
[44] *India*, trans. Inman, p. 276.
[45] *Ibid.*, p. 278.
[46] *Ibid.*, p. 277.

tential meaning in the Western world. The evidence of Western culture abroad at mid-century indicates, if anything, the reverse of any such probability. The imposition of American culture upon Japan during the last ten years is only one case in point. It may be argued that the Japanese assimilate readily enough. The fact remains that several devices of American life which are immediately effective in the further disintegration of our culture as religion are now widely supplied to as much of the Orient as we are still able to reach. They need not be enumerated; every intelligent person knows what they are. The important fact is that we are here successful in imposing the emblems of our culture upon a culture of meaning, however unacceptable this meaning may have been to our politics. In a very real sense, the Orient and the West appear now in precarious balance. Either the culture of the West, itself in religious crisis, will overflow the Orient, making in this event the symbolic confusion noted in one small corner of Polynesia by Segalen, confusion resulting when the symbols of Christianity were mixed with the indigenous symbols of Tahitian existence; or the Orient, to the Western mind at present in a state of chaos and of sporadically irrational existence, will overflow the West.

The alignments of these cultures are already prefigured in the history of the last decade. In this study I have been concerned with the genesis of art in primitivism, only incidentally with the history of societies and politics. But since it is true, in my premise, that the symbols of existential meaning in any culture govern the direction of artistic expression, it must be said that the Orient will probably never again assume the symbolic meaning which it is seen ideally to possess in the symbols of Ishmael. We understand that art will make new symbols; we understand, too, that Yeats expected a new cycle of symbols like no other before seen. The degree of our acceptance of Yeats in this theory depends, of course, upon the degree of Christian orthodoxy in the individual.

If the artist of the Western world looks toward the Orient at all, he will look there with a feeling unequal to that of Melville, for the reason that the contemporary Orient now emerges from the unknown to the known. Presumably Western art cannot longer place in some Orient of feeling the ideality which it does not discover in its own culture. The question of the present becomes the interesting one of genesis for the symbols of feeling that are to be. If these are to be symbols of polarity, as exemplified in Melville's reincarnations from the Orient, they will have to encompass what the German primitivist Hermann Hesse sees as Oriental irrationality, as this appears to the mind of the West. In a masterly discussion of Dostoevsky's Karamazoff, Hesse speaks of Oriental character: " . . . the rejection of every strongly-held Ethic and Moral in favour of a comprehensive Laissez-Faire." [47] Thus, in Hesse's view, Dostoevsky conceives Karamazoff as *russischer Mensch*, including every bearer of the name in the novel. " [He] . . . is assassin and judge, ruffian and tenderest soul, the completest egoist and the most self-sacrificing hero. We shall not get a grasp of him from a European, from a hard and fast moral, ethical, dogmatic standpoint. In this man [i. e., the inclusive Karamazoff] the outward and the inward, Good and Evil, God and Satan are united." [48] Of this " primeval," this Oriental nature of Dostoevsky's great figure Hesse says: " The ideal of the Karamazoff . . . Asiatic and occult, is already beginning to consume the European soul. That is what I mean by the downfall of Europe . . . a turning back to Asia." [49] I present here these judgments of Hesse because they signify the most recent expression of authentic primitivism in its encounter with the Orient. It is at once obvious that the Orient to this man means an irrational equivalence of good and evil. This equivalence, which is chaos to our Western minds, is further emphasized in the doctrine advanced by Hesse's *Siddhartha*:

[A] . . . truth can only be expressed and enveloped in words if it is one-sided. Everything that is thought and expressed in words is one-sided, only half the truth; it all lacks totality,

---

[47] *In Sight of Chaos*, trans. Stephen Hudson (Zurich, 1923), p. 14.
[48] *Ibid.*, pp. 18–19.
[49] *Ibid.*, p. 13.

completeness, unity. When the Illustrious Buddha taught about the world, he had to divide it into Sansara and Nirvana, into illusion and truth, into suffering and salvation. One cannot do otherwise, there is no other method for those who teach. But the world itself, being in and around us, is never one-sided. Never is a man or a deed . . . wholly a saint or a sinner. . . . And if time is not real, then the dividing line that seems to lie between this world and eternity, between suffering and bliss, between good and evil, is also an illusion.[50]

Should Hesse choose to say, beyond this representation of irrationality, that this is the Orient which stands now known, uncovered, learned, experienced by Western man, he may not be challenged by any student who knows less of the Orient than he. His long residence in the East and his longer study of India cannot be dismissed. If it is true that Europe succumbs to the " new psyche " embodied in Karamazoff, then this turning back to Asia is total desertion of Western morality with its distinctions between good and evil. Hesse's conclusion is that we must accept chaos, return to Asia, and find a new way.[51]

Lest it be supposed that these notices of a " new " Orient are extraneous at the close of this discussion of primitivism, it should be finally said that Melville is again involved in each of them. To offer conjecture upon the nature of symbols which Melville might at this moment shape from the feeling of the man of Western civilization can mean nothing. I am concerned rather with the relevance of his symbols to contemporary sensibility. It has been seen that Melville was thoroughly aware of the modern difficulty of Western man in describing truth from one pole without regard for its opposite. He knew profoundly that the world, in Hesse's words, " being in and around us, is never one-sided." From that knowledge comes the dominant principle of his symbolic power, the demonstration of reality by the interillumination radiating between opposite values. He knew again that words, used in their expository functions, express only half-truth. Hesse's judgment would not have astonished him.

[50] Trans. Rosner, p. 144.
[51] *In Sight of Chaos*, pp. 63–64.

Furthermore, Melville had had experience with man whose being is to Christian civilization totally irrational. His symbol of irrational man is Claggart of *Billy Budd*. Melville was fascinated by his studies of this creature of his own making. Claggart is a man of " Natural Depravity." He has " no vulgar alloy of the brute " in him; he is dominated by intellectuality. He is cloaked in the respectability of civilization; he has " certain negative virtues serving as silent auxiliaries "; he is even without vices and small sins; and he has pride which excludes him from the mercenary and the avaricious. " In short, the depravity here meant, partakes nothing of the sordid or sensual. It is serious, but free from acerbity." Melville continues: " But the thing which in eminent instances signalises so exceptional a nature is this: though the man's even temper and discreet bearing would seem to intimate a mind peculiarly subject to the law of reason, not the less in his soul's recesses he would seem to riot in complete exemption from that law, having apparently little to do with reason further than to employ it as an ambidexter implement for effecting the irrational. . . . These men [such as Claggart] are true madmen, and of the most dangerous sort, for their lunacy is not continuous, but occasional." [52] It is in his own full view of this man of Natural Depravity, " God's own scorpion," as he calls him, that Melville holds aloft the sacramental symbol of Billy Budd. Claggart is a Karamazoff; and through Hesse's view of the irrational hero, he is Asiatic. He is a man without a motive for evil, save in his compulsion to render the world irrational in conformity with his own nature. (He transcends even the irrationality of Shakespeare's Iago and Milton's Satan, both of whom had, at least, the initial motive of pride.) Melville understands Claggart as naturally depraved by the God who made him. Here he may *seem* to reach Hesse's dismissal of the dividing line between suffering and bliss. To say that he does so would be to deny every meaning of Melville's symbolism and every process in his making of art as religion.

---

[52] All these judgments of Claggart's depravity are very quietly rendered by Melville in this last examination of innocence and evil. See *Billy Budd and Other Prose Pieces*, pp. 45–46.

For in his acknowledgment of irrationality Melville stops unmistakably with his completion of the symbol of whiteness and the companion symbol of the White Whale. He contends here for the unknowableness of God, and this he takes as the essence of God's truth which in the limited observation of man may be seen only as endlessly contradictory within itself. Melville does not proceed from this symbol to equate man with God. It is Hesse's conclusion that since God is contradictory within the measurable distances of all being, man therefore, in the wisdom of the Orient, reflects a divine irrationality. In contrast, Melville stands in our time as the heroic Christian. His faith depends upon the original Christ whose humanity lies somewhere in the Christian past, behind the dogmas of saints and theologians, of ascetics and masochists, of sectarians and agnostics. The symbols of this faith restore in art the oneness of Christianity which has been lost. The Orient, as the country of his symbolistic ideal, is the dominant realm of an imagination which sought the meaning of humanity in the meaning of all time. Melville's symbolism bespeaks life as the heritage of man, life which was given by a God unknowable, and yet wonderful in his certainty of being. It represents the order and the rationality possible to man if he could destroy in himself the folly of the over-reacher who would equate himself with God. This symbolism is art which fortifies its maker against a threatening meaninglessness of existence. Melville shaped there a new affirmation of life. No man has given more than that; no man will give more to the civilization of the West.

Heracles in the *Alcestis* of Euripides contends: " Mortals should think mortal thoughts. To all solemn and frowning men, life I say is not life, but a disaster." [53] These ancient words from the center of Greek humanism summarize all that the symbols of primitivism in essence represent of man's just moral destiny. Whether the same wisdom can pertain to the symbols of the future celebrated by Verhaeren no one can say.

[53] Trans. and ed., Whitney J. Oates and Eugene O'Neill, Jr., in *Seven Famous Greek Plays* (New York, 1950), p. 271.

The poet's resolution toward the light in " À la Gloire des Cieux " (*La Multiple Splendeur*) is prophetic, but only to a certain point which civilization has recently passed.

> Today, eyes that see, search the heavens
> No more for some ancient God who exiles himself,
> But find him intricate in wondrous problems
> That veil from us his mighty power in its red cradle.[54]

In " La Ferveur " the poet glorifies humanity, " drunken with the world and with ourselves, / The hearts of men new in an old universe." [55] Then we are new men. But we are men also who have seen power in its red cradle. Since August 6, 1954, we have been looking at the ever-young and ever-old cradle where the time of man began. How much of this sight may be encompassed in " mortal thoughts " we do not yet know. We stand, too, in moral positions not at all unprecedented in human history. Dante described them in his view of the tormented Ulysses; so did Marlowe in the tragedy of Faustus who sought to practice more than heavenly power permits.

But in these great symbols of art, man was only hypothetically, metaphorically there, outside the just range of mortal thought. What the difference may be between an imagination which has dreamed a vision of force in its red cradle and the sensibility of men who have actually looked into that seething flame only art can tell us. For the power of man as the symbol-maker comes from the same progenitor who made the beginnings of time in its mighty redness of burning stars. This power of man orders the continuity of his earthly life of spirit. It will wrest meaning from chaos in the abstractions of its art as long as man permits himself to inhabit the planet. These abstractions seem already destined to pass beyond the range of mortal thought, as this limit has been understood through recorded history. So far as civilized man's necessity for describing the meaning of his existence through symbols is concerned, this is the future.

[54] *La Multiple Splendeur* (Paris, 1907), p. 42.
[55] *Ibid.*, p. 157.

INDEX

Index

Adams, Henry: and the archetype of the wise man, 247; and the cathedral of Chartres as life-symbol, 147; compared with Melville, 123, 147; his friendship with Marau Taaroa, Queen of Tahiti, 143; *Mont-Saint-Michel and Chartres*, 142, 146–48; his monument to Mrs. Adams, 142; his relation to primitivism, 142–46; on the primitivity of Cuba, 145; in Fiji, 142; in Japan, 142; at Papeete, Tahiti, 143; in Samoa, 232; his symbol of the dynamo, 70, 398; his symbol of the Virgin of Chartres, 142

Anderson, Charles R.: on Melville's observation of Marquesan religion, 100

Animism: defined by W. H. Hudson, 265; in Melville's attention to archaic stone, 283; in Melville's *The Confidence Man*, 368–69; in Melville's *Moby-Dick*, 330; in Melville's *Pierre*, 286; and Melville's symbolism of trees, 176; and Melville's symbolism of whiteness, 265–66; in the symbolistic imagination, 362. *See also* Symbolism

Anthropomorphism: Melville's rejection of Judaic myth, 319–20

Archetype: *anima* and *animus* (Jung), 65–66; archetype of transformation defined (Jung), 171; and atavistic regression, 52; Benjamin Franklin as archetypal wise man, 247–49; and the cultism of the snake, 202; George Washington as archetypal wise man, 247; nature of archetypes defined,

62; *puer aeternus* as archetype of transformation, 202; in snake-handling of Protestant revivalism, 61–62; as the tower in modern poetry, 54, 394–95; the wise man (the Dansker) in Melville's *Billy Budd*, 249–51; the wise man in Conrad's art, 230. *See also* Jung, Carl

Arnold, Edwin, Sir, 42

Arnold, Matthew: "Dover Beach," 348

Arvin, Newton: on Melville's experience in Typee Valley, 91; on Polynesian sensualism, 287–88; on primitive cultism of the whale, 322

Atavism: and the appearance of archetypes, 52; in the art of W. H. Hudson, 363; defined in relation to cultural failure, 18; and Melville's interest in geology, 172–73; in the poetry of T. S. Eliot, 173; and its source, 19; and Whitman's interest in geology, 172–73. *See also* Symbolism

Auden, W. H.: on the modern city and contemporary art, 388–89; on the symbolism of *Moby-Dick*, 282; and his poetic tribute to Melville, 277 n

Autotype: defined, 18; and sensuous experience, 18; as obsessive image, 96; and the Pacific geography of Melville's imagery, 353. *See also* Symbolism

Avatar: defined, 171; as incarnation of Vishnu, 172

Ayscough, Florence, 46

Barrie, James M., Sir, 141

431

The ornaments used in this book were borrowed from *Tattooing in the Marquesas* (Honolulu, the Bernice P. Bishop Museum, 1922), by Willowdean Chatterson Handy. The symbolic meaning of the tattoos has long been lost to the natives of the Marquesas Islands and, hence, was unknown to Mrs. Handy and the author of this book, James Baird. The tattoos have been used here purely for decoration.